FOR OHIO DOCTORS

Shedding Light on Asset Protection, Tax and Estate Planning

Jason M. O'Dell, CWM • David B. Mandell, JD, MBA
Christopher R. Jarvis, MBA • Ted Gudorf, Esq.
C. Lawrence Huddleston, Esq. • Charles J. Kay, Esq.
Brian C. Layman, Esq. • D. Bowen ("Bo") Loeffler, Esq.
with contributing authors
H. Michael Lewellen, CFP®, R. Paul Wilson,
and Carole C. Foos, CPA.

Guardian
Publishing LLC
2010

FOR OHIO DOCTORS:
SHEDDING LIGHT ON ASSET PROTECTION, TAX AND ESTATE PLANNING
By Jason M. O'Dell, CWM, David B. Mandell, JD, MBA, Christopher R. Jarvis, MBA, Ted Gudorf, Esq., C. Lawrence Huddleston, Esq., Charles J. Kay, Esq., Brian C. Layman, Esq., D. Bowen ("Bo") Loeffler, Esq., with contributing authors H. Michael Lewellen, CFP®, R. Paul Wilson, and Carole C. Foos, CPA.

Tel: (800) 554-7233

Book interior design by Rebecca Krzyzaniak. Sabon and DIN typefaces used throughout.

ISBN: 978-1-890415-12-9

Manufactured in the United States of America.

About The Authors

Jason M. O'Dell, CWM

Jason O'Dell is a Chartered Wealth Manager and one of the principals of the financial consulting firm O'Dell Jarvis Mandell (OJM). Jason is the author of the book *Financial Planning for Physicians*. Jason has experience as an entrepreneur, financial consultant and investment advisor and has been working with clients for over 15 years.

Jason has conducted financial planning, asset protection and wealth management lectures nationally. Jason has been recognized by Medical Economics as "One of the Best Financial Advisers to Physicians" and has been published in over twenty medical periodicals, including *General Surgery News*, *American College of Emergency Physicians*, and *Orthopedic News*.

Jason graduated with a Bachelor of Arts degree in Economics from Ohio State University. Jason is a member of the Financial Planning Association, Cincinnati Estate Planning Council, Cincinnati Chamber of Commerce and the CEO Roundtable Group. Jason is also a member of the Board of Directors of The David Bradley Wick Foundation. Jason lives and works in the Cincinnati area. He can be reached at odell@ojmgroup.com or 877-656-4362.

David B. Mandell, JD, MBA

David B. Mandell, JD, MBA is a principal of OJM. David is an attorney, author, and renowned authority in the fields of risk management, asset protection and financial planning. In addition to his role at OJM, David serves as an attorney in the Law Office of David B. Mandell, P.C.

As a writer, Mr. Mandell has co-authored the book *Wealth Protection: Build & Preserve Your Financial Fortress* and *Wealth Secrets of the Affluent: Keys to Fortune Building and Asset Protection*, both published by John Wiley & Sons, the oldest book publisher in the U.S. and the largest publisher of business books in the world.

For physicians, Mr. Mandell has also written *Wealth Protection, MD*, *The Doctor's Wealth Protection Guide* (endorsed by five state medical societies) and *Risk Management for the Practicing Physician*. His articles regularly appear in over thirty leading national medical publications, including *The American Medical News and Physician's Money Digest*, and he has been quoted extensively in *Medical Economics*. He has been interviewed as an expert in such national media as Bloomberg and FOX-TV.

Mr. Mandell holds a bachelor's degree from Harvard University, from which he graduated with honors. His law degree is from the University of California Los Angeles' School of Law, where he was awarded the American Jurisprudence Award for achievement in legal ethics. While at UCLA, Mr. Mandell also earned a Master's in Business Administration from the Anderson Graduate School of Management. He can be reached at mandell@ojmgroup.com or 877-656-4362.

Christopher R. Jarvis, MBA

Christopher R. Jarvis is a principal of OJM. He is a financial services professional who specializes in working with successful physicians and business owners. Chris has experience as a financial consultant, actuary and entrepreneur. He has helped start insurance companies for Fortune 100 firms and has consulted with high net worth individuals nationwide.

Mr. Jarvis has been quoted in the *Wall Street Journal* and the *Los Angeles Business Journal.* Chris has appeared on Bloomberg Television and been a guest on over 100 radio programs. He has co-authored financial and legal texts for Doctors, business owners, real estate investors and financial planners. Mr. Jarvis has co-authored six books specifically for doctors, including *Wealth Protection MD: The Ultimate Financial Guide for 21st Century Physicians* and *For Doctors Only: A Guide to Working Less and Building More*. He has also coauthored two books for John Wiley & Sons, *Wealth Protection: Build and Preserve Your Financial Fortress* and *Wealth Secrets of the Affluent*.

Chris has addressed over 100 groups, including the International College of Surgeons, American Association of Neurological Surgeons, the Association of Chamber of Commerce Executives, Associated General Contractors, UCLA Law School, American Medical Women's Association and The Anderson School (UCLA's MBA Program). Chris' articles have been featured in over 100 national publications.

Chris holds an honor's degree in applied mathematics from the University of Rhode Island. He earned a Master's of Business Administration from UCLA where he majored in finance and entrepreneurial studies. Chris was awarded the Los Angeles Chapter of the Young President's Organization's (YPO) Ken Kennedy Fellowship for his entrepreneurial achievement. Mr. Jarvis grew up in Providence, Rhode Island and now lives in Austin, Texas. He can be reached at jarvis@ojmgroup.com or 877-656-4362.

Ted Gudorf, J.D.

Ted Gudorf, J.D. is the owner of Gudorf Law Group, LLC, a boutique law firm located in Dayton, Ohio which provides significant tax, asset protection and estate planning expertise to the firm's clients. He is also the owner of Wealth Counselors, LLC, a financial consulting firm.

Mr. Gudorf is one of the first attorneys in Ohio to become certified as a specialist in estate planning, trust and probate law. He is Past President (2006-2008) of the Ohio Forum of Estate Planning Attorneys, Inc. and is a member of WealthCounsel, the nation's leading provider of educational and support services to estate planning attorneys. Ted also serves as an adjunct professor at Wright State University and serves on the advisory board of Children's Medical Center and is a founding Trustee of the Greater Dayton Volunteer Lawyer's Project.

As a writer, Mr. Gudorf has co-authored the book *Estate Planning Strategies: Collective Wisdom, Proven Techniques* published by Wealth Builders Press, LLC in 2009. Specifically, he authored the chapter titled "Estate Planning for Physicians and Other Professionals". He is a frequent lecturer throughout the country on estate planning and asset protection topics.

Mr. Gudorf graduated with honors from Wright State University with a Bachelor of Arts degree. He received his Juris Doctorate from the University of Dayton School of Law where he served as President of the Student Bar Association. In addition, he received the prestigious American Jurisprudence Award for receiving the highest grade in the individual income tax and complex litigation classes. In 2002, he obtained the designation of Advanced Wealth Strategist Planner from the Esperti Peterson Institute. Mr. Gudorf will be awarded his Master of Laws degree (LL.M.) in estate planning and elder law by Western New England College School of Law in May, 2010. He can be reached at tgudorf@GudorfLaw.com or 877-483-6730.

C. Lawrence Huddleston, Esq.

Larry Huddleston is the founding partner of Huddleston Law Group, LPA, a Columbus-Dayton boutique law firm that limits its practice to what is traditionally called "estate planning" but which may more accurately be termed "wealth and health" law.

Admitted to practice in 1977, he was in the first group of Ohio attorneys to become a Certified Specialist in Estate Planning, Trust and Probate Law. He was a founding member of WealthCounsel, the nation's leading provider of educational and support services to estate planning lawyers and has twice chaired the Ohio Forum of Estate Planning Attorneys.

Mr. Huddleston has spoken on various wealth preservation topics at conventions and other meetings in more than 20 states, including national and state meetings of the Arthroscopic Association of North America, American Society for Surgery of the Hand, Ohio Medical Association and the Orthopaedic Research and Education Foundation.

He serves on the Professional Advisory Board of The Columbus Foundation and was one of the first persons ever honored by the Central Ohio Council on Planned Giving with its prestigious "Leave A Legacy" award. He earned Fellowship status in both the Esperti Peterson Institute and the Laureate Circle.

Mr. Huddleston earned his BA from Muskingum College and JD from the Capital University School of Law. He can be reached at 888-488-7878 or by email clh@huddlaw.com.

Charles J. Kay, Esq.

Charles J. Kay has served as a trusted advisor to numerous medical and dental professionals in Northeast Ohio for more than fifteen years. In addition to these professionals, his clients have included physician and dental group practices, a hospital, an ambulatory surgical center, and numerous entities in the health care field. Mr. Kay currently devotes a substantial part of his practice to providing personalized legal counsel to physicians, dentists, business owners and entrepreneurs, as well as their families and professional partners.

His areas of expertise include asset protection and wealth preservation; business formation, planning, and succession; estate planning; trust and probate law; real estate law; and contract law.

Mr. Kay received his undergraduate degree from Brown University in Providence, Rhode Island. He earned his Juris Doctorate degree at Case Western Reserve University School of Law, where he was awarded second place in a national legal research and writing competition sponsored by the University of Oklahoma College of Law. While attending law school, Mr. Kay served as an intern for the Honorable Nathaniel R. Jones, of the U.S. Court of Appeals for the Sixth Circuit, in Cincinnati, Ohio.

He is a member of the Ohio State Bar Association, the Mahoning County Bar Association, the Estate Planning, Trust & Probate Law Section and Real Property Law Section of the Ohio State Bar, the Ohio Forum of Estate Planning Attorneys, WealthCounsel, and the National Academy of Elder Law Attorneys. Mr. Kay is also a member of the Board of Directors of the Mahoning County Mental Health Board and has served as an officer and director of numerous nonprofit and community organizations. He can be reached at ckay@kaylawllc.com or 330-953-1280.

Brian C. Layman, Esq.

As a principal with Layman, D'Atri & Associates, LLC, Brian C. Layman provides significant tax, asset protection and estate planning expertise to the firm's clients. In addition to being admitted to practice law in Ohio and Florida, Mr. Layman maintains his CPA license in the State of Ohio. Mr. Layman has published several articles, is a frequent speaker and is actively involved in professional and civic organizations.

Mr. Layman is certified as a Specialist in Estate Planning, Trust and Probate Law by the Ohio State Bar Association. This certification makes him one of a small group of attorneys in Ohio to have earned this distinction. The Ohio State Bar Association has also appointed him to the Estate Planning, Trust and Probate Law Section Council, which consists of approximately 60 attorneys who study and make recommendations regarding legislation in this area of the law.

Mr. Layman earned his B.S. in Accounting, Master of Taxation and Juris Doctorate (summa cum laude) from the University of Akron. While attending law school, he served on Law Review as the Assistant Editor and as Editor-in-Chief of the *Akron Tax Journal*. Mr. Layman's published article on *Dynasty Trusts* has been cited on multiple occasions by the U.S.

Senate Committee on Finance, Joint Committee of Taxation. He can be reached at brian@laymandatri.com or 330-493-8833.

D. Bowen ("Bo") Loeffler, Esq.

Bo Loeffler is the founding member of The Loeffler Law firm, LLC, located in Port Clinton, Ohio. He knows from first hand experience the estate planning and asset protection concerns that physicians have. His father, uncle, father-in-law and three cousins are all physicians. After a couple of business career stints in Washington, D. C., Bo returned to his hometown to build his legal practice and career. He is a former prosecutor, U.S. Bankruptcy Trustee, commercial litigation attorney and former board member of a community bank. In recent years, he has limited his practice focus with his clients to asset protection, estate planning, medicaid/nursing home planning and business planning. Additionally, in recent years, he has had the opportunity to represent and consult with a number of Ohio Lottery winners. Bo's client base is located throughout Ohio.

Bo is a member of the National Network of Estate Planning Attorneys (NNEPA) and the Medicaid Practice Systems Collaborative (MPS) and has completed their lawyer training programs. He is also a graduate of the Esperti-Petersen Institute for Advanced Estate Planning and is also a member of the InKnow Vision Institute, of Chicago, Illinois, which is one of the leading advanced estate and business planning organizations in the country. Bo has recently authored and presented a number of CE presentations to both local and national organizations: *Ohio Asset Protection: Fundamental Theories and Basic Practice Points* (co-presented with John Sullivan to the Ohio State Bar Association Annual Convention May-2010); *Domestic Asset Protection Trusts (DAPTs): A Survey and Basic Practice Points* (co-presented with Randall Borkus to the National Network of Estate Planning Attorneys (NNEPA), Indianapolis, Indiana, Spring 2010 Collegium); *Asset Protection Tools and Strategies for Ohio Attorneys* (co-presented with Steven J. Oshins to the Ohio State Bar Association-District. 3-Oct. 2009), *The Fundamentals and Opportunities of Asset Protection* (co-presented with John E. Sullivan III to the North Coast Estate Planning Council-July 2009), *Representing and Counseling the Lottery Winner- from Claiming the Prize to Estate Planning* (NNEPA, Indianapolis, Indiana, Spring-2009 Collegium); *An Overview of Asset Protection Tools from the Simple to the Advanced* (Financial Planning Association of Toledo-Fall 2008); *Medicaid Planning Options and Protections in Ohio* (Put-in-Bay/Ottawa County Bar Assn. Summer Seminar Series-2008) and *The Realtor's Guide to Trusts, Powers of Attorney and LLCs*, (Firelands Board of Realtors Spring 2005).

Bo is currently a member of the Ohio State Bar Association and was recently appointed to its Ohio Legacy Trust subcommittee, which is in the process of drafting model legislation which will involve the possible adoption of a domestic asset protection trust statute for the State of Ohio. Bo received his J.D. from the University of Toledo and his B.A. from the College of Wooster.

H. Michael Lewellen, CFP®

Michael Lewellen is the Director of Financial Planning at OJM. Michael has conducted seminars in Cincinnati, Columbus, Lexington, and Louisville that cover the areas of basic financial planning, wealth accumulation, asset protection, and debt management.

Michael is a co-author of the book *Financial Planning for Physicians: Strategies for Saving Money and Securing your Financial Future—From Student Loan Repayment Through Retirement.*

Michael graduated from the University of Kentucky with a Bachelor of Business Administration degree. He is continually striving to increase his knowledge, skill, and value to clients. He is very active in multiple community activities. He can be reached at michael@ojmgroup.com or 877-656-4362.

R. Paul Wilson

Based in Cincinnati, Ohio, R. Paul Wilson is the Regional Manager of Private Client Services for OJM. Paul has been providing comprehensive financial planning solutions to physicians since 1999. He has been recognized in 2008 and 2009 by *Cincinnati Magazine* as one of the areas "5-Star Wealth Managers; Best in Client Satisfaction".

Paul has lived in Cincinnati, Ohio since 1980. He attended the University of Cincinnati, College of Business Administration, and majored in Marketing and Family Business. He maintains life and health insurance licenses, as well as securities Series 7 and Series 63 licenses in several states. He has a personal understanding of the challenges physicians face through numerous family members and close friends, who are all physicians. Paul currently lives in the Kenwood area of Cincinnati with his wife and three children. Paul can be reached at paul@ojmgroup.com or 877-656-4362.

Carole C. Foos, CPA

Carole Foos is a Certified Public Accountant (CPA) offering tax analysis and tax planning services to OJM clients. Carole has over 20 years of experience in public accounting in the field of taxation. She was formerly a manager in the tax department of a Big 4 firm and spent several years in public accounting at local firms. She has been a tax consultant to both individuals and businesses providing compliance and planning services over the course of her career. In addition to her work for OJM, Carole maintains a tax practice in Cincinnati.

Carole received a Bachelor of Science in Business Administration from Xavier University where she majored in accounting. Carole lives and works in the Cincinnati area and can be reached at carole@ojmgroup.com or 877-656-4362.

Table of Contents

Lesson #5: Turn Your Practice into a Financial Fortress and Wealth-Building Engine 99

Lesson #6: Protect Personal Assets from Lawsuits 151

Lesson #7: Legally Reduce Taxes 219

Foreword

As a Doctor in Ohio, you are faced with some of the greatest challenges of any group of doctors in the country. Sure, Ohio is generally considered a great place to raise a family, but it is one of the hardest places to get ahead financially—especially as a doctor. Consider the following factors:

- While medical malpractice claims and insurance premiums have decreased since Tort Reform was enacted in Ohio in 2003 and updated in 2005, these claims and costs are still quite high, as they rose dramatically earlier in the decade.
- Many parts of Ohio have experienced high penetrations of managed care—resulting in lower reimbursement rates than those received by your colleagues in other parts of the country.
- Once you have profits, Ohio has a significant state income tax—with most doctors paying nearly 6% of their income to state income taxes. Remember that your colleagues in Florida, Texas, and other states pay 0%.
- If you are ever sued for any reason, Ohio provides a mixed bag of protection against lawsuit and creditor judgments. It has one of the worst exemptions in America for protection of a primary residence, but a tremendous exemption for cash value life insurance.
- Many of you are choosing to sell or merge your practice into a hospital—which can cost you significantly in terms of tax, benefit, and retirement planning, unless you bring new ideas to the hospital that we can introduce.
- You better not get divorced in Ohio. As an equitable division state, it is very easy to lose family assets to a divorce (even though you do not think the judge's division is equitable).
- When you die, it gets no better for your heirs. Probate costs in Ohio are also some of the highest in the country (between 3% and 5%). Ohio boasts the largest

estate tax burden in the entire country on estates valued at less than $3.5 million (Ohio estates are subject to a 7% tax on estates that exceed a very modest $338,333).

If you have interest in getting the most out of your practice without having to work any harder, sleeping better at night knowing that your personal and practice assets are protected, and learning how to assemble the right team of experts to help you reach your long term goals, this book is ideal for you.

The co-authors have hundreds of years of combined knowledge in the fields of asset protection, tax, estate planning, litigation, financial planning, insurance and investing. They have offices from Port Clinton to Cincinnati to the Youngstown area, and in a number of areas in between. They are well-networked with other professionals in your area and can offer you a level of service you've likely only imagined possible.

The first step for you is to read this book and learn the important lessons every doctor needs to know. Then you can decide how to proceed. You may contact the authors for a consultation or arrange a seminar in your area to learn firsthand how to improve your situation, or arrange a seminar in your area to share this information with your friends. Whatever you decide to do next, we hope we can be of assistance.

Thank you for reading our book. We appreciate your dedication to improving your situation.

IMPORTANT NOTE:
Throughout this book, we will refer to the term "Doctor" or "Physician." Please note that this book is intended for all medical professionals, including physicians, dentists, psychologists, optometrists, pharmacists and chiropractors. The Lessons contained within this book apply equally to all medical professionals.

LESSON 1

Work "On" Your Practice, Not "In" Your Practice

In medicine, patients come to physicians when their bodies are unable to heal themselves. Patients who delay seeking medical treatment are missing out on the power of modern medicine and failing to take advantage of an opportunity to dramatically improve their health. Similarly, the financial and legal ailments impacting your medical practice cannot be healed without professional care. Simply working harder and hoping that your practice's problems will solve themselves is just as foolish as the patient hoping his body will heal itself. In addition, you may not see any "problems" yourself, but you will not be working at maximum efficiency without consulting an expert.

In this Lesson, we will delve further into the concept of working "on" your practice with the assistance of expert advisors. We will examine the concept of Leverage in an attempt to help you shift away from "just seeing more patients" as a cure-all for your practice and personal financial challenges.

We will also discuss the demographics of the Average American, the demographics of the American Doctor, and compare the planning challenges and financial goals of both groups. We will also discuss how Doctors who look for information in magazines and websites can be dangerously misled. We will conclude with a discussion of how the information in this book is unique for Doctors and can be used to help Doctors meet their asset protection and wealth accumulation goals.

1-1

Be Different. Be Rich. Be Worry-Free.

When you were in medical school, residency, and first starting practice, you relied on a number of mentors to "teach" you valuable lessons about medicine. Undoubtedly, this training was critical to your development as a physician. Despite the valuable clinical training you received, you were left inadequately prepared to practice medicine as your profession. While you have learned the "medical" part quite well, do you think you were trained how best to "practice?" In other words, did your education and residency prepare you to build a "practice" into an optimal business?

The successful practice of medicine in the 21st century requires so much more than clinical expertise and a good bedside manner. The days of simply seeing patients and waiting for substantial income to be deposited into your bank account are long gone. Successfully practicing medicine now requires expertise in disciplines that were never even mentioned, let alone taught, in medical school, residency or even in a fellowship. How are Doctors supposed to learn how to protect themselves from billing and coding errors, employee lawsuits, health insurance fraud, HIPAA violations, Medicare fraud, and OSHA issues? Where will Doctors find the time to learn and understand asset protection, business structuring, estate planning, insurance management, investments, benefits structuring, and tax planning? How can you do all this while continuing to stay abreast of important clinical developments and still find time to see patients and earn a living? This is what Doctors MUST know how to do if they want to successfully practice medicine in the 21st century.

Replicating the actions of the physicians who trained you will not replicate their levels of financial success. The environment has changed dramatically. If you do what most Doctors do and focus only on the clinical issues of medicine, you will expose yourself to unnecessary lawsuits and taxes, and will continue to struggle as reimbursements stagnate or decrease while overhead constantly increases. Do you want to follow this path and be the next helpless victim or do you want to learn how to be different?

The only way to achieve financial success and peace of mind is to break away from the pack—to be different and do things differently than your predecessors. Perhaps this seems counterintuitive. While those who trained you no doubt provided priceless guidance in many areas of your practice, today's practices demand new perspectives. Let's look at a practical example.

How Medicine Has Changed

One of the book's authors, David Mandell, comes from a family of physicians. David's brother is a cardiologist. His father is a radiologist close to retirement age, and his grandfather was a general practitioner from the 1930s to the 1970s. The grandfather worked only for cash—except during the Great Depression, when he accepted food from patients who were unable to pay. He made house calls and knew all of his patients by name. Not once did he utter the words "managed care," "malpractice crisis," or "HCFA audit."

David's father, Charlie, spent nearly 30 years in a lucrative radiology practice. He saw reimbursements *increase* for many years and enjoyed an over-funded pension. He took advantage of numerous tax laws (since legislated away) during his career that swelled his after-tax income beyond what he had ever expected to earn when he began his career in the 1960s. The idea of "going bare" (having no medical malpractice insurance) never occurred to him. Premiums were always reasonable and personal liability was never a major concern.

As you well know, the "business of medicine" has changed dramatically through these three generations. The young cardiologist—David's brother Ken—began his career dealing with a medical malpractice crisis (in his state, many Doctors chose to go without medical malpractice coverage because of its outrageous costs), increased time demands for administration and paperwork, shrinking reimbursements, and increasing regulatory concerns. He thinks about terms like "practice buy-in," "malpractice premiums," and "debt repayment." He wonders if he'll ever reap the financial rewards his father did in medicine or if the landscape has just changed too much for him to ever be able to enjoy the fruits of his labor.

Where do you fit within these generations? Perhaps you are between the radiologist and the cardiologist and are in the prime of your career or you are in its second half. If so, the issues on your mind are likely retirement (not only when, but if), asset protection, tax reduction, and even partner buy-out. It is a lot to consider, by any measure.

Treat Your Practice Like A Business

Throughout this book, we will use the term "business of medicine." This is not by accident; rather, it is quite intentional. To use this book as the professionals that helped put it together intended, you must make a paradigmatic shift in your medical career. *You must come to view your practice as a business!*

While we mean no disrespect—medicine is truly a virtuous calling, and your primary motivation to become a physician was likely an altruistic one—the hard reality is that there are a myriad of business issues that affect your practice and personal finances every day of your career. Unfortunately, the vast majority of physicians are completely unprepared for these issues so they suffer from lower incomes, personal legal liability, shorter and less comfortable retirements, acrimonious practice splits, severe financial stress, bankruptcy and sometimes a premature exit from the practice of medicine.

It is no surprise that 99% of physicians do not properly handle the financial and business issues that affect their careers. Why? The short answer is because Doctors have had *absolutely no training* in these business matters. The typical physician may receive over 10 years of clinical training by the time medical school, residency, and fellowship are completed. This is over 3,500 days. How many days of training have you received on topics such as asset protection, compensation arrangements, taxation, investing, and retirement planning? How many days on malpractice insurance options, partner buy-outs, or disability protection? What about employee training, contracts, and practice management?

With this complete lack of non-medical training, it is a wonder that any medical practice survives. Imagine how more economically efficient and less stressful the business of medicine could be if you had been properly trained in all of the above fields. How much better protected would your wealth be from lawsuits? How much more income would you bring home? How much smoother would your practice run? *Imagine.*

While we cannot attempt to change how the American medical establishment trains its physicians (although we have often been asked to speak to medical schools and residency programs), we can make the following urgent recommendation:

Make today the first day of your self-imposed training program by dedicating time to becoming educated about the non-medical issues that affect your business and personal financial situation.

As the subheading of this section states, you must treat your practice like a business, learning the operational and financial issues that are crucial to its success. Otherwise, you will never reach your financial goals. By devoting just a fraction of your time on these practice issues—perhaps one day per quarter or one afternoon per month—you will be working ON your practice. For as long as you toil only as the medical worker, you will suffer from the stress and reduced rewards that come to people who handle matters "half-way." Only when you step back and act like the CEO of your practice—and of your career—can you hope to achieve the financial and lifestyle goals that you certainly deserve and that the business of medicine can still afford you.

Envision Your Ideal Career In Medicine

When you chose to be a physician, you made a decision to rely on your medical practice to provide you with the things you value in life: control over your time, financial security, reduced stress, and a good life for your family, among other things. Think back to before your medical practice, residency, and medical school to your college days. What was your vision of life as a successful physician? What was your vision when you were toiling in medical school or during all-night calls during residency or fellowship? Did you envision your eventual career as a pay-off for all the years of hard work, training and sacrifice?

Now, after considering what the ideal vision of your career looked like to you during different stages of your education and career, take a moment to examine your present practice and personal financial situation. How close are you to your ideal vision? Is there room for improvement? Is it as stress-free, lucrative, and secure as your ideal vision? If not, is it worth devoting a small fraction of your time to working toward this ideal? For the majority of physicians we speak with, the answer is obvious.

In the generation of David's radiologist father, the medical business environment was so easy that physicians could almost totally ignore the business and financial issues described above and achieve their life goals rather easily. Even if Doctors made financial mistakes every day, it did not matter. Doctors simply rode the wave of the financial profitability with minimal regulation. It was truly the "golden age" of medicine for U.S. physicians.

Today's physicians, however, operate in a dramatically different environment. Like David's cardiologist brother, you do not have the luxury to make such financial mistakes. It is still possible to enjoy your own "golden age" of benefits, but to do so you must be as effective and efficient as possible. You must be both a skilled physician and an attentive businessperson or you will suffer the consequences of today's more challenging medical business environment.

Avoid the trap of inertia. Be confident enough to envision your ideal situation and use this book and the advisors who contributed to it to help you achieve your goals. You have worked hard in *medicine* to get to where you are today. Now, work on *the business* of medicine to take you where you want to go.

Be Practical, Not Political

Many physicians reading this book may get riled up enough to march on Washington and Columbus to demand malpractice caps, more effective tort reform, lower tax rates, and greater reimbursements. This emotionally charged effort may or may not have any impact on lawmakers' decisions. Whether any legislative changes will have a significant impact on your specific financial situation is uncertain. Though this is not our area or expertise, we do know that changing laws takes time and you need to change your financial situation today.

We are financial and legal advisors to physicians, not policymakers or politicians. In this book, we will not discuss how the laws regarding non-economic damages in malpractice cases should be limited. We will neither opine on the fiscal policies of the malpractice insurers nor comment on Medicare reform. We will not discuss tax policy or medical education. These elements, and any proposed changes to them, are beyond your control as an individual Doctor. While rallying with your fellow physicians as a political group may be effective over the long term, we will let other voices (like those of your local medical associations) take up that cry.

Our focus here is to show you—in a real and practical way—what you as an individual can do to move your practice and medical career from point A (financially inefficient, high liability exposure, chaotic financial plan) to point B (efficient, asset-protected and organized for maximum financial success). This is the goal of this book, our e-newsletter and our website (www.forohiodoctors.com).

The Diagnosis

Like any worthwhile endeavor, education is just the beginning of a process. For you, this means reading this book and digesting the general ideas before determining which of these strategies will make sense for your practice and personal situation. Reading this book is only the beginning—*education without action is fruitless.*

Like a patient who lets the pills you prescribed sit in the medicine cabinet, a failure to implement the protocols outlined in this book will result in no improvement in your situation. For your planning, the next step after reading this book will be to discuss your situation with one of the authors to put the knowledge you have gained into action. This way, you can ensure that your practice and your life will be as close to your "ideal vision" as possible and that you can enjoy your own "golden age of medicine."

1-2

Work Smarter, Not Harder: Don't Just "See More Patients"

In the last chapter, you read how the business of medicine has changed. The implication for you is that you can't keep repeating the same actions time and again and expect to see the results you may have received just a few years ago. But many of the Doctors who come to this realization still think that the solution is to "see more patients." In this chapter, we will briefly cover the flaws of this strategy and explain the ways in which Doctors can apply the concept of Leverage to address **all** of their financial and legal challenges.

"See More Patients"—A Tragic Flaw

Confronted with any legal, tax, or financial setback, many Doctors follow the business strategy of "seeing more patients." If the practice suffers because of a successful lawsuit, a sudden unforeseen expense, or an unproductive associate, Doctors try to "make up for it" by seeing more patients in hopes of billing more. The same tactic is followed by many Doctors who are behind in their retirement planning, who feel like they are paying too much in taxes, or who are getting divorced. Any financial setback seems to yield the same resulting behavior. Many physicians approach their entire career with the business strategy of working as long and as hard as possible for as long as they can physically endure it. Does this remind you of any of your peers? Do you see someone like this when you look into the mirror?

Certainly, there are many flaws to such a business strategy. Let's examine a few of these flaws so you can understand why other strategies are better:

1. This strategy has diminishing financial returns
Even if you work harder and see more patients, each patient you see will potentially net you fewer dollars. As your marginal expenses for each additional hour of work may be the same and your taxes may increase if you hit new marginal tax levels, your "take home" may actually become less per-dollar as you work harder. Even if this is not the case, the next two flaws certainly apply.

2. This strategy has financial limits

Even if you worked as hard as you possibly could and you could make more on each additional dollar earned, you only have 24 hours per day. Regardless of your specialty or sleep requirements, you cannot work 18 or 20 hours per day over an extended period of time. Thus, you are capped in the total income that you can generate by "just seeing more patients." Chapter 1-4 develops this concept further.

3. This strategy will take a great personal toll on you

Extreme stress, physical ailments, divorce, decreased life expectancy—these are all common symptoms for Doctors who choose "seeing more patients" as their business mantra. Are these extreme personal costs worth it? We think not—especially given #4 below.

4. There is a "better way"

If working as hard as you could was the only alternative available to allow you to meet your financial goals, that would be one thing. However, the truth is that there is a much better concept upon which you can build your practice and personal finances. This concept will be explained below.mailto:chefsuzette@gmail.com

The Concept Of Leverage

Let's consider the following all-too-common scenario. You work a very long day and generate $10,000 of billings. The insurance companies pay your practice $3,000 for your hard work. Your practice overhead is about 50%, so $1,500 of that income is gross profit. However, the $1,500 isn't yours. Of the $1,500 you actually receive, the Federal, state, and local tax authorities will take 40% to 45%, leaving you with only $800 to $900. In other words, less than 10% of the work you do in a given day actually results in money you keep. This means that you have to do $3,000,000 worth of work in order to generate less than $300,000 of money for you to enjoy. Unless you want to continue to work ten times as hard as necessary, you have to learn to work smarter. This is the key to this entire book: **Leverage.**

If you refer to the Merriam-Webster Dictionary and look up the word "Leverage," you will be presented with three definitions:

1. The action of a lever or the mechanical advantage gained by it;
2. POWER, EFFECTIVENESS;
3. The use of credit to enhance one's speculative capacity.

We will offer very simplified interpretations of the three definitions of Leverage stated above. The first definition states that Leverage increases the amount of force exerted. To exemplify this concept, think of Leverage as the act of wedging a stick between two heavy rocks that you could not move with just your hands. In order to efficiently move the rocks, you need to push down on the stick that you wedged between the rocks. In doing so, the rock can be moved. Leverage—the wedging of a stick—allows you to move a rock you would otherwise not be able to move.

The second definition of Leverage simply states that the act of Leverage allows people to be more efficient, effective, and powerful. This can be interpreted to mean that Leverage allows people to get more done in less time. It can also be interpreted to mean that Leverage allows people to get a job done with less effort. In either case, Leverage enables people to be more effective.

The third definition of Leverage applies to credit and loans. In this definition, Leverage allows people to buy things they don't have the money to buy in an effort for them to increase their financial capacity. To illustrate this definition, think of a home loan—the $500,000 home that is purchased by a family with only $100,000 of their own money to use as a down payment. Leverage is the ability to enjoy the use of or participate in the upside potential of an investment you otherwise could not afford.

Quite simply, Leverage is a method by which you can do more with less. Less effort. Less money. Less time. If you are looking for a shortcut to financial success, Leverage is the closest thing to it.

The Importance Of Leverage

Successful physicians know that Leverage is an important tool to increase their wealth. Without Leverage, people would have to do everything themselves, including running their own business, earning money, handling financial affairs, paying for everything with only their own money, micromanaging everything at work and at home, and still finding time to eat and sleep.

If you feel like this is an accurate description of your life, then you are not using Leverage. Leverage makes your life easier. Leverage frees you to do the things that are most important, most profitable, or most enjoyable to you. Leverage is what allows you to achieve greater levels of financial success. No matter what your financial goals, mastering the art of Leverage and incorporating it into your planning will help you reach these goals faster. As we mentioned earlier, Leverage is how physicians can increase the power and effectiveness of their financial planning. You can do the same.

Leverage Limitations

A little Leverage is good. A lot of Leverage is better. Who wouldn't want to get more done with less effort or get more done with less money? Those who understand Leverage have tried to maximize its potential and use for thousands of years.

It may seem like the amount of Leverage one can attain is endless, but there are restrictions on how much Leverage you can achieve. This restriction can be referred to as Capacity. Consider the following:

- You can only exert so much force
- You only have 24 hours in a day
- You only make so much money
- You can only borrow so much money
- You can only manage so many people

The principal goal of Leverage is to maximize efficiency. Efficiency is achieved when Leverage is increased to a point when you have maximized your capacity. When you exceed capacity, problems occur. This causes you to have to address the method of Leverage all over again and possibly repeat certain steps. It is obviously an inefficient process when you have to duplicate any effort. This is why you should be careful not to exceed your capacity and create other, often bigger problems. Examples of problems caused by increasing Leverage beyond your capacity include seeing so many patients that you are: 1.) Making billing and coding errors (Medicare fraud); 2.) Working too fast and making mistakes (medical malpractice cases); 3.) Hiring the wrong employees (employee lawsuits); among others.

You could theoretically increase capacity by working harder, but that is only acceptable if it is the most valuable and profitable use of your time and energy. Leverage is about working smarter, not harder. For this reason, increasing effort is not a viable method of increasing Leverage. The rest of this section will explain ways to increase Leverage and capacity so you can get even more out of your reduced effort. Getting better results from less effort isn't just the subtitle of the book; it is the only way to achieve greater levels of wealth.

The Diagnosis

Leverage makes life easier. Leverage allows you to get more done with less effort or with less money. Once successful investors achieve a measure of Leverage, they use their extra time and money to find better methods of Leverage. This is a never-ending quest to become more efficient and effective in everything they do, so that they can build and maintain their wealth and protect their assets.

The next four chapters will specifically discuss how Leverage applies to financial transactions, effort, employees, and advisors. Lesson #3: Accept Referrals to Specialists is perhaps the most valuable way to increase the capacity of your Leverage. As such, *For Ohio Doctors* is filled with practical strategies that can only be enjoyed if you have a team of advisors to help you achieve greater Leverage.

1-3

Making Your Money Work for You

Now that you understand the basics of Leverage and its importance in allowing you to get things done more efficiently and effectively, this chapter will apply those concepts to financial and legal planning. Subsequent chapters will demonstrate how physicians can apply these lessons to Leverage assets and people to maximize and maintain wealth.

Financial Leverage: The Foundation Of Wealth

For thousands of years, every great construction project required the use of levers to complete the building process. This was true for moving the large stones to build the pyramids of Egypt and lifting the stones for Stonehenge. Levers were used to build all of the great castles, churches, synagogues, and mosques around the world. Financial projects are very similar to construction projects. They both can seem overwhelming at the beginning, a collection of complex tasks that must be executed with skill and precision. The success of both types of projects begins with significant and detailed planning. After the plans are drawn, they must be implemented accordingly. One person alone could never accomplish the implementation of such plans. Instead, the plan requires a team of people working together to accomplish the same goal—for us, that goal is building and maintaining wealth.

Without exception, every high income earner and wealthy family has relied on financial Leverage in one way or another.

Once you grasp the concept of Leverage and the financial applications of Leverage, it becomes impossible to imagine how affluence could possibly be built without it.

Type Of Financial Leverage

Physicians can use different types of financial Leverage to create and build wealth. These include:

Leverage of Effort:

Leverage of effort is a way to get more out of your financial plans and investments. Since the goal of Leverage is to get more done with less effort, all forms of Leverage require that you Leverage your individual effort by including the efforts of others.

Leverage of Assets

Leverage of assets is one way to increase your financial status and get more out of what you currently possess. If you had an unlimited amount of money or land, you wouldn't need to accumulate any more wealth; however, this is not the case for most people. Since we all have limited resources, we want to get the most wealth/asset accumulation and financial protection out of what we have with the least amount of effort and the lowest amount of risk.

Leverage of People

Savvy business owners know that they only have the capacity to do so much and that the Leverage of people is one way to get more than 24 hours out of a day. By leveraging other people's efforts, you can increase the number of tasks you can accomplish in a day. By leveraging people with special skills and expertise you don't possess, you can get things done in much less time than it would take you to do these same tasks, if you could accomplish them at all.

Generally speaking, physicians utilize Leverage to some degree, but they are not thorough in their application. They try to Leverage effort by working hard, we know that. Doctors also may try to Leverage assets in their practice through medical equipment for which they can bill and they may try to Leverage people through technologists, nurses, and physician's assistants, who can generate income to the practice. Still, few physicians apply this concept broadly enough in their practices to result in any real wealth building. Even fewer Doctors effectively Leverage people or assets with respect to their personal finances.

The Diagnosis

Within each of the three categories of Leverage discussed above—Leverage of effort, Leverage of assets, and Leverage of people—there are a number of different applications. In the following chapters, we will review each of these categories, discuss how they can be used to generate wealth and explain which of these types of Leverage are more appropriate for creating wealth and which types of Leverage will best help maintain higher levels of wealth.

1-4

How To Work Less

There is no doubt that hard work is a key to success. However, this character trait is not one we can teach. Some people become harder workers as they mature, but seldom does a zebra change its stripes. There are generally hard workers and not-so-hard workers. The goal of this section on Leverage is to help you get the most out of any level of effort. Whether you fancy yourself hard working or laid-back, Leverage can help you get more out of your desired amount of effort. In this chapter, we will discuss the capacity problems of Leverage, how education can increase your ability to Leverage your effort and then suggest ways physicians can overcome the barriers of capacity.

You Can Leverage Hard Work... But Effort Is A Capacity Problem

The basic and inherent problem with effort is that you only have two hands and two feet, and there are only 24 hours in a day. If we consider the case of two landscapers (Lazy Larry and Manic Mike) with very different work ethics, we can illustrate these physical constraints we all have.

Let's assume that Lazy Larry and Manic Mike earn $50 per house per week. If Lazy Larry works five days per week and landscapes 8 houses per day, he will earn $2,000 per week before paying overhead, staff, equipment, taxes, etc. Manic Mike can work seven days per week and landscape 10 houses per day. This would give him precious little time off for family or personal time, but he would earn $3,500 per week before all of his expenses.

Both of these landscapers might consider themselves successful (depending on their goals and values). But if hard working Manic Mike wants to make more money, there aren't enough hours in the day or days in the week unless he does something that earns him more money per house or he finds a way to Leverage something other than his own effort. The next application of Leverage could help Mike do just that.

Leveraging Education

The idea of leveraging education to create wealth is no secret. In fact, it has become part of the American Dream. For over a century, immigrants have come to America and have taken advantage of the educational system. They have pushed their children to do well in school in hopes that they would get a good job and enjoy a higher standard of living. They have also pushed their children to find careers that pay them more money than a career like Manic Mike chose.

Leveraging education is a key element of building and protecting wealth. To prove this point, consider the following salaries of highly educated professions. When considering the earning potential of these professions, keep in mind that the median U.S. household income for the year 2007 was $48,201, which means that half of all United States households earned less than $48,201 per year. (US Census Bureau's 8/27/07 Current Population Survey (CPS)). According to a USA Today article on 1/18/06, the first year salary plus signing bonus for an MBA (2 years of graduate school) was $106,000.

According to MD Salaries (www.mdsalaries.blogspot.com), the first year salary of a neurosurgeon ranged between $350,000 and $417,000 in each of these cities: Houston, New York, Miami, Los Angeles and Seattle. Neurosurgery requires the completion of four years of medical school, a one-year internship, and a rigorous 5- to 7-year residency. Thus, there is no doubt that leveraging education can help you earn more money per year and increase your wealth faster than if you had a job with a lower level of education. Physicians use this type of Leverage quite well.

Education And Effort Are Not Enough

Would you be surprised to hear that the neurosurgeon mentioned above and Manic Mike have the same problem? While we are not saying that Mike is performing brain surgery, we *are* suggesting that they both have the same fundamental problem—albeit at a different level of income. Mike doesn't have enough hours in the day or days in the week to increase his business. Similarly, a neurosurgeon's income is limited by the number of surgeries he can perform as well as constrained by the number of hours in a day and days in a week. Even if you assume that there is an endless supply of patients who need brain surgery, and there is an endless supply of lawns to be mowed, the surgeon is limited just like Mike. In other words, a landscaper earning $50 per house has the same capacity problem as a neurosurgeon earning $500 per hour because:

1. They are limited in the amount of money they can earn until they figure out how to Leverage what they do, and

2. They only make money when they are actually working.

This is a lesson that savvy business owners and investors figured out long ago. As a result, the most successful business owners:

- Always focus on the Leverage of any business.
- Never consider increasing effort as a legitimate, long term means to increase income.
- Never enter into a business that requires them to constantly "work" to make money.

For these reasons, we prefer to focus our articles, seminars, books, and personal consulting recommendations on strategies that help **Leverage assets** and **Leverage people**.

The Diagnosis

All teenagers have parents, teachers and coaches who tell them to work harder. We prefer to tell you—and show you—how to work smarter without having to work harder (or having to clean your room or take out the trash). The Lesson applies to anyone, no matter how hard working or lazy you may be. If you want to work less and build more, you can do it. Applications of this "smarter working" lifestyle will be the focus of the next two chapters.

1-5

Getting the Most Out of Your Assets

You have undoubtedly heard the phrase, "It takes money to make money." No truer words have ever been spoken. It always takes some investment to generate a return. This chapter will explain how successful investors Leverage assets to create and sustain a high level of wealth. A partial list of assets that can be Leveraged includes:

1. Your own money;
2. Other people's money (sometimes shortened to simply "OPM"); and
3. Intellectual property.

Leveraging Your Own Money

Leveraging your own money is the oldest and most basic form of Leverage. It has been documented all the way back to the ancient times of kings and emperors. These wealthy empires had enough money to fund expeditions to discover new lands and acquire even more wealth. A visit to any of the museums of Rome or other ancient cities will bear witness to this Leverage.

Hundreds of years later, you can witness similar Leverage right here in America. Successful investors make their capital work for them in various ways. To illustrate this point, let's take a look at one of the nation's most flamboyant and public billionaires. If you visit Donald Trump's website, you will see that he has a significant portfolio of real estate which includes properties in New York, New Jersey, Honolulu, Los Angeles, Chicago, Florida, Las Vegas, the Dominican Republic, Seoul, Toronto, Panama, Mexico, and Connecticut. Additionally, he has future plans to develop properties in Soho, Atlanta, New Orleans, and Dubai.

Trump was able to expand his real estate portfolio because he Leveraged his assets. His earnings from real estate generated income for him to support his expansion into golf clubs in six cities, four casino resorts, various television programs and pageants, a university, merchandise, a travel company, restaurants, skating rinks, and other projects. Once Trump started making money from his new ventures, he was able to Leverage those assets into more projects. The profit from those additional projects gave him the capacity to start even more businesses.

You don't have to be a billionaire with a ridiculous haircut to use Leverage. If you have money, you can purchase land or real estate and lease it to others who can't afford to buy the property outright. If you have money you don't need to spend to support your lifestyle, you can invest in long term investments that have higher expected returns than shorter-term investments. These may be investments that otherwise are unavailable to investors who require a short-term return to pay bills. Lastly, when you have money, you can use it as collateral to borrow money and use other's people money to make money, too. This is what Trump and other sophisticated business owners do all the time to maximize wealth. This is the next application of Leverage.

Leveraging Other People's Money

Generally, using other people's money (OPM) is considered to be the "classic" definition of Leverage. Recall from the first chapter in this section that this is the third definition of Leverage in the Miriam-Webster dictionary list. Using other people's money as Leverage certainly relates to credit, but we will broaden its definition to include all types of Leverage involving OPM.

The most common type of OPM is debt. Many wealthy people throughout history have achieved their wealth by borrowing at lower rates and reinvesting the loan proceeds at higher levels of investment return. Donald Trump's empire was built in a similar fashion, typical of most real estate investors. They put down a small percentage of the total costs to build properties and used OPM to fund the remainder of the costs. By borrowing money from the bank at rates that may be as low as 6% to 8%, and developing properties that may have an overall return of 15% per year, the Leverage gives the investor an amazing return on actual dollars invested. Consider the following:

Investor	Amount Invested	Rate	Amount Earned
Total	$10,000,000	15%	$1,150,000
Bank	$8,000,000	8%	$640,000
Trump	$2,000,000	25%	$510,000

Based on this these numbers, Trump can actually get a 25% return on his investment by using OPM Leverage to fund a project he anticipates will yield a 15% total return. This is a classic example of how Leverage works with real estate.

In other situations, like starting a business or making another speculative investment, people were able to take higher levels of risk because they didn't need the money to pay for living expenses. This allowed them to take chances and realize higher investment returns than less risky investments offered.

The other way to Leverage OPM is called equity—that is, taking someone else's money and giving them a piece of a business or investment in return. In this situation, the investor takes more risk, but also gets a higher expected return than the bank would get with debt. Though this kind of deal ultimately costs the investor a higher piece of their total return, it doesn't have monthly or annual payment requirements (like a loan does). This gives the wealthy more short-term freedom with regard to cash flow since no interest or principal payments are due each month. In fact, even if there is a profit, the wealthy may be able to effectively borrow the investor's share simply by not distributing it and reinvesting in the next project.

Equity is best suited for deals that are more speculative and cannot guarantee regular short-term income. Even well established, publicly traded companies (like AT&T, Disney, Oracle, etc.) do this on occasion. Many wealthy Americans have learned a lesson from these companies and have offered equity positions to investors to help fund the growth of their family wealth while offering participation in the upside.

Leveraging Intellectual Property

Since World War II, the most significant wealth accumulation has resulted from leveraging intellectual property. This intellectual property could be an idea, like McDonald's fast food assembly line concept, or a patent on a technology millions of people use, like Microsoft Windows. Other forms of intellectual property include copyrights like the Star Wars films or Harry Potter books. In each of these cases, an individual or a small group of partners comes up with an idea, proves it can work, legally protects the idea, and then attempts to Leverage it in ways where they can make money as a result of other people's efforts. Let's consider three examples.

Bill Gates and Microsoft created the Windows operating system. He (meaning his firm, Microsoft) didn't create a desktop computer or laptop to run his operating system. He just created a system that other people would run on their computers. Every computer that is built that runs Windows results in a license fee to Microsoft. Gates didn't have to drive the increase in the sale of computers. Rather, he found a way to profit from the efforts of all the other companies who were building and selling computers, and from the efforts of all of the software manufacturers who were designing products to make the use of a computer a more enjoyable—not to mention necessary—part of life.

Another example is George Lucas. Lucas created the Star Wars concept. He made a few movies that became classics. But the interest in the characters and story line didn't end with the movies. It expanded to action figures, lunch boxes, video games, and countless other items that were based on his concept. Lucas could have tried the "do it yourself" technique, but that would have only yielded a fraction of the financial profit the Leveraged approach did. Instead, he licensed his intellectual property to other people. Their efforts made Lucas hundreds of millions, if not billions, of dollars.

The last example is the McDonald's restaurant. One successful restaurant might have generated \$100,000—\$250,000 of annual profit. An international chain of restaurants whose focus is on fast, consistent food has served 3 billion customers and is worth billions of dollars. One of the authors of this book has actually had a private tour of one of the three facilities that process and package all of McDonald's food worldwide. It is truly an operation designed to create consistency and maximize Leverage.

In less extreme cases, every city has a restaurant, dry cleaner, or other business that isn't particularly profitable on an individual basis. However, the owner may be able to take the unique approach, branding, experience, or know-how and open additional locations to achieve a higher level of financial success.

The Diagnosis

All three categories of leveraging of assets—leveraging your own money, leveraging other people's money, leveraging intellectual property—can be very valuable. Certainly, many people have achieved significant levels of wealth by doing so. The important lesson is that you need to get the most out of your assets if you want to achieve a higher level of wealth and get the most out of your practice. Now that you know how sophisticated investors Leverage assets, you are ready to learn the most powerful Leverage technique—leveraging people!

1-6

Using Other People to Make You Money

While leveraging assets and capital are fundamental wealth-building techniques, these techniques cannot succeed without also leveraging people. At the end of the day, every deal, investment or transaction needs people to manage or oversee it. No matter how rich you are, you still only have 168 hours per week. To our knowledge, no one has figured out how to be in two or more places at one time. As a result, the single most powerful type of Leverage is the Leverage of people. By properly leveraging people, you can have multiple levers working at once. This is where greater wealth is created.

This chapter is going to explain why—and how—to get the most out of leveraging people. More specifically, we will focus on:

1. Leveraging employees; and
2. Leveraging advisors.

Leveraging Employees

The most common method of leveraging people is by hiring employees. Those with financial means can afford to hire other people to do jobs for them. The employer has successfully Leveraged people if the collective group of employees helps the owner earn more money than the amount it costs the employer in salaries and benefits.

Simple Leverage: Pay Less Than Productivity

The more employees you have, the more potential Leverage opportunities you have. Sometimes you hire staff to support these employees. That is an investment that you hope increases the productivity of the other employees by more than the cost of the administrative help.

To Leverage your employees successfully and yield a profit, a simple rule is to pay people less than the value they provide your firm. Law firms have followed this lesson for years. For example, law firms may bill out attorneys to their clients at $200 per hour and require the attorneys to bill out 2,000 hours per year. Though the firm collects $400,000 for the services of the particular attorney, they may only spend $300,000 for that particular attorney's salary, benefits, and allocated overhead. The firm earns $100,000 per attorney. If they can afford to hire 10, 20 or 100 less-experienced attorneys and can find enough work to keep them busy, the senior partners of the firm can earn a very nice living—10 to 25 times that of Average Americans and 5 to 10 times that of a less experienced attorney. In doing so, law firms are leveraging their employees' productivity. They are training less expensive attorneys to do the work. This, in turn, enables the senior partners to focus on very profitable activities like landing contacts and building relationships for the firm.

Benefits To Leveraging Employees

In many circumstances, it may not be as easy to quantify the financial return on a Leveraged person as it was in the law firm example above. Often, there may be equally important qualitative benefits in addition to the quantitative ones. For example, consider these benefits:

1. By leveraging someone else, you are able to spend your time performing tasks that create greater profits.

This is a quantifiable benefit. Using the example above, by having associates do the work, the law firm partners can also do what they are best at—bringing in new business. This is likely a "highest and best use" of their time. What is your "highest and best use?" You already have someone to sign in patients, take vitals, file charts, do the scheduling, and other valuable tasks. Is it possible to pay someone to do any more of the less profitable tasks you currently perform? If so, you can take advantage of Leverage!

2. By leveraging an employee, you are able to spend your time doing things you WANT to do.

This is a qualitative benefit. If you could have employees perform more of your work, perhaps you could spend time doing something you prefer to do, such as playing golf or spending time with your family. This is not being lazy—it is using Leverage, not for increased profits, but for a better life. What is more important than that?

3. By leveraging experts, you are able to spend time on your own areas of expertise and save money.

As we will see in Lesson #3, leveraging advisors who have more expertise than you have in certain areas is fundamental to long-term success. While it is possible you could learn to become a CPA, money manager, or an attorney, learning these jobs would not be time well spent. This would take you away from things that are a good use of your time.

Leveraging people who have expertise is very economical. You can pay them less to help you in certain areas than what it would cost you (in time, money, and aggravation) to learn these fields yourself and then try and do the work yourself. Bill Gates didn't learn how to build computers and George Lucas didn't learn how to make action figures, yet they both benefited from someone else's expertise in those areas.

Now that you see how important it is to Leverage employees, let's learn the importance of leveraging advisors.

Leveraging Advisors

Leveraging advisors is one application of Leverage that the wealthy believe is integral to their success, yet many Doctors ignore or undervalue it. Look at any wealthy person's inner circle and you will almost always see key business and financial advisors who are involved in most of their decisions. The advisors' charge is to help develop a plan, analyze how every step fits (or doesn't fit) into their plan, and help them avoid numerous pitfalls that could arise from straying from the course.

Simply put, most successful business owners recognize that it makes more sense to hire advisors to help them handle their planning than it does to try to do it themselves. Doing it themselves is not only a bad idea because the client undoubtedly does not have the experience and expertise in all the areas needed in planning, but it also violates the principles of Leverage.

By "doing it themselves," Doctors would be spending their time sub-optimally, instead of in the desired highest and best use of their time. In other words, does it pay for a neurosurgeon to spend three hours of his time researching a disability policy when a disability expert could do it in one hour? Also, consider that those three hours could have been spent seeing patients and making more money than the disability expert will be paid. And do you think the Doctor would enjoy this research more than he would enjoy playing golf or relaxing on the beach? Probably not.

Finally, what is the likelihood that the Doctor will make the right analysis and decision on the policy? Is he an expert? Has he looked at hundreds or thousands of policies in the past? Why would you think he would do any better job performing this task than would the disability expert in performing a neurological exam?

Despite the obvious pitfalls of fighting the principles of Leverage, some Doctors make the mistake of foregoing advisors and attempting to "do it themselves." They are stuck in the mindset of saving a penny and losing a dollar.

This leads us to a very important statement that may seem crazy at first:

Doctors must realize that time is worth more than money.

Instead of looking for ways to save money by doing things themselves, Doctors must look for highly qualified people to handle as many tasks as possible so they can focus on the best possible use of their valuable time.

Since the right advisory team has expertise that physicians don't have, the right advisors can do the job in much less time than the physician or the wrong advisors could. Since a job done poorly will need to be repeated, doing it right the first time, even at a higher hourly rate, can actually save money in the long run. Additionally, when a Doctor can pay someone to do what they do best, this gives the physician more time to do what he does best—which undoubtedly is what will make the most money (seeing patients, running a practice, investing in real estate, etc.).

Complexity Demands Leveraging Advisors

We have found that the greater the wealth of the individual or family, the more important the role of the advisor team. As the client's wealth increases, the more complex the comprehensive financial situation becomes. As the situation grows more complex, the client's need to Leverage the advisors' expertise and experience to save time and maximize total benefit increases exponentially.

To illustrate how complexity grows exponentially, let's consider the following two situations. The first chart below shows the relationship between two people. The second chart shows the six different relationships that exist when you have four people in a group.

Situation 1: Relationship Between Two People

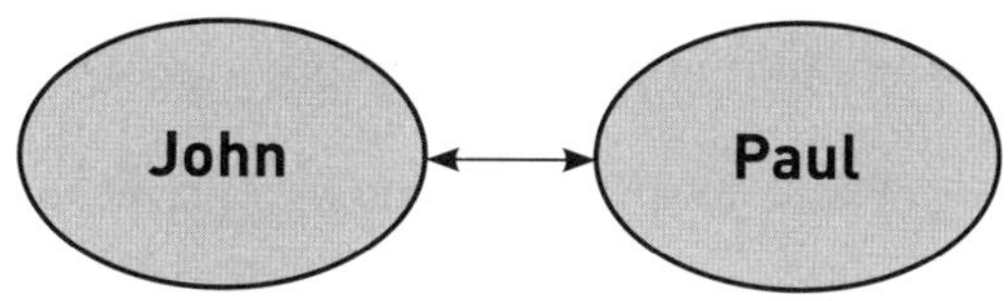

In the chart above, you can see that John and Paul have one relationship. There is only one relationship when you have two people. This seems relatively easy to manage as you have two people and only one relationship. Let us see what happens to the complexity of the interactions when we have four people in a group. This is illustrated in the next chart.

Situation 2: Relationship Between Four People

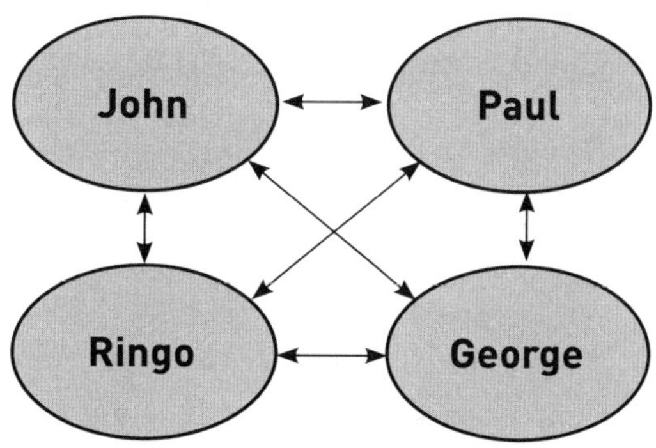

In the chart above, you will see John, Paul, George and Ringo. There are two more people than we saw in the first chart. Doubling the number of people in the group actually increased the unique interactions by 500% from 1 interaction to 6 interactions (John and Paul, John and Ringo, John and George, Paul and Ringo, Paul and George, and George and Ringo). Though it only takes one good relationship for two people to work together, it takes six good relationships for a group of four people to work well together. If one of the six relationships is strained, the entire group may have to be disbanded.

This same analogy can be applied to the elements of your financial plan. All elements of your plan, and all advisors in your plan, must work well together. That means that it is at least 500% more work to manage four businesses or elements of a comprehensive financial plan than it is to manage two businesses or elements of financial plan. If you have eight businesses or elements of a plan, then you have 56 different interactions to monitor. You can see how the complexity of the situation increases quickly!

To see how this general theory of complexity can be practically applied to planning for physicians, we need to understand the physician's concerns. Below is a partial list of common financial planning concerns among physicians:

- Managing growth of the assets
- Managing lawsuit risks from employees, patients, and competitors
- Protecting assets from eventual lawsuits
- Managing the investment risk while attempting to grow assets
- Managing tax liabilities to maximize after-tax growth
- Managing business succession and estate planning concerns
- Protecting family members against a premature death or disability
- Protecting family's inheritance against lawsuits, taxes, and divorce

Surprisingly, physicians worry about all of the aforementioned items while continuing to do *everything* they did to help them reach their current level of success. If you think this is impossible, you are correct. It is impossible to do all of these things as a "one man show." Leveraging advisors is essential—it is a fundamental precursor of long-term success.

The Diagnosis

This section explained why Leverage is such an important key to working less and building more. You learned how successful people—whether they are physicians with "medical businesses" or other business owners or investors—Leverage their own assets, other people's money and people. You learned that the biggest limitation to Leverage is one's capacity. This can be limited time or limited money. In either case, the best way to increase your capacity is to build a team of experts to help you efficiently maximize Leverage and increase your capacity for Leverage. This is the focus of Lesson #3: Accept Referrals to Specialists, which could also be titled *Building the Right Team of Advisors*.

LESSON 2

Don't Try to "Fit In" With the Crowd

When it comes to financial and legal planning, the idea that everyone is created equally couldn't be further from the truth. As a Doctor, you are very different. You went to college, then medical school, then residency, then possibly a fellowship. You have much more education and training than the Average American. Though a society needs people to play various roles, you deal with issues of life and death. As a result of your educational and functional differences, you are in a different situation and have very different concerns.

You have a more complicated and demanding profession. You earn more money. You pay more taxes. You have more liability. As a result, you need better advice that is tailored to your unique needs.

Before you can understand what advice is right for you, you need to know what advice is wrong for you. To know why most advice is wrong for Doctors, you need to understand the quantitative and qualitative differences between physicians and Average Americans. Then, you need to understand how the popular media works and how that information can be very detrimental to a Doctor's planning. These are the issues that are discussed in this Lesson. Once you understand and embrace your differences, you will be ready to take advantage of the practical lessons offered in *For Ohio Doctors*.

2-1

Understanding the Average American

Before you can understand the unique challenge facing Doctors and what the more successful ones do to achieve and maintain their wealth, you must first understand the demographics of the Average American. This is crucial because, in order to learn how to act differently in your wealth planning decision-making, you have to compare your financial circumstances to the circumstances of the "norm." It is only through these comparisons that you can truly appreciate the different wealth challenges you have and how you can effectively deal with these challenges.

In this chapter, we will examine the Average American in terms of income level, federal income taxes paid, source of income, retirement needs, asset protection concerns and estate planning challenges.

IMPORTANT NOTE: Throughout this book, we will refer to the term "Average Americans." We recognize that, to some, this term may at first seem demeaning or condescending, or imply some sort of value judgment. We do not intend it that way. It is simply a demographic term to describe a particular group defined by income, tax rate and financial circumstances.

Average American Income

The first, and perhaps most important, defining characteristic of the Average American is his or her income level. According to recent US Census Bureau's August 28, 2007 Current Population Survey (CPS), the Average American household earns $48,201. Additional Census data shows that, as of 2005:

20% of American households* earned less than $25,616;

40% of American households* earned less than $45,021;

60% of American households* earned less than $68,304;

80% of American households* earned less than $103,100.

** Households may include more than one or two earners.*

Another way the Census Bureau analyzes income numbers for households in America is to break down the population into fifths and look at the average income within each grouping (or "quintile"). Consider the following:

Segment of the Population	Average Annual Income
The lowest earning fifth (1/5) of population	$14,767
The second fifth of the population	$35,137
The third fifth of the population	$56,227
The fourth fifth of the population	$84,095
The highest earning fifth of the population	$176,292

If you consider that physician families typically earn well in excess of $250,000 of annual income, then you can see that Doctors earn more than a considerable majority of Americans (who earn less than $176,292). It is likely that many physicians earn more than 95% to 99% of American households.

The significance of the income analysis is fairly simple. Average Americans, as a rule, are earning just enough to pay the bills on a periodic basis, if at all. In many areas of the country, where expenses are relatively high, there may not even be enough income to cover the bills. Long-term uses of funds, such as retirement accounts, insurance and college savings accounts are often luxuries they cannot enjoy.

Federal Income Tax Rates

As you will learn later in the book, Doctors should consider taxes in nearly everything they do because their tax rates can be very high. Contrast that to the situation of Average Americans here.

If you combine the demographics above with the 2009 federal tax rate schedule below for married couples filing jointly, you can make some interesting conclusions.

2009 Federal Income Tax Table—Married Couples Filing Jointly

If taxable income is over	But not over	The tax is:
$0	$16,700	10% of the amount over $0
$16,700	$67,900	$1,670.00 plus 15% of the amount over $16,700
$67,900	$137,050	$9,350.00 plus 25% of the amount over $67,900
$137,050	$208,850	$26,637.50 plus 28% of the amount over $137,050
$208,850	$372,950	$46,741.50 plus 33% of the amount over $208,850
$372,950	No limit	$100,894.50 plus 35% of the amount over $372,950

After examining this table, you can conclude that about 20% of the population will pay less than 10% of their income to the government in federal income taxes (since the average income for the lowest fifth of the population is less than $16,700).

Further, almost 40% more of the population will pay 10%-15% of their income in federal income taxes. Another 20% of the population will pay less than 18% of their income (average income for the fourth quintile of the population is about $103,000). Only about 5% of the population will earn enough to be subject to the highest marginal federal income tax bracket of 35%.

In other words, Average Americans pay relatively few dollars in income taxes as a percentage of their income. Due to the lower tax rates and the sources of income described below, income tax planning is not a significant concern for the Average American.

Average American Source Of Income

The Average American is almost always an employee who works for someone else. He gets paid as a W-2 employee and may or may not have a modest benefits package. As a taxable employee, taxes are typically withheld from the paycheck each payday and the after tax proceeds are then distributed. Many call this the take home amount. While this eliminates the headaches of calculating and preparing complex quarterly estimated tax payments and saving for these large payments, it also means there is little opportunity for significant tax planning.

The Average American rarely owns his own business. This means that the Average American does not have to manage the complications of a growing or complicated business that may have multiple locations, many employees, and regulatory reporting requirements. This also means that the Average American's income will be determined by someone else. The owner of the company or the management team determines when and if there will be any raises or promotions for the employees. Employees can work hard, but the financial rewards from such efforts are at the discretion of someone else. Because the cost of living increases every year, modest raises may provide relatively modest increased spending and saving potential over a lifetime.

Millions of Americans have made the decision to buy or build a small business. There are countless motivations that drive someone to leave the world of the employed and start or run a business. There are pros and cons of being a W-2 employee instead of running your own business. Let's consider some of the pros and cons of being an employee:

Pros	Cons
Simplified tax reporting	Little opportunity for tax planning
Fixed or predictable income	Little opportunity for significant increases in income
Benefits managed by employer	No control over benefits offered
Job stability	Job stability controlled by employer
Employer Leverages your work	No direct benefit from Leverage
Little lawsuit risk as compared to the employer	
No business succession risk	

There is no doubt that running a business is hard work. The business owner has a lot of responsibility. Owning a business is certainly not for everyone. In fact, most small businesses fail. The point we are trying to make is that there is a trade-off for letting someone else handle all the responsibility and headaches of running a business. Employees have little say in the planning for the business. This is neither good nor bad. It is just the nature of the situation. This is one of the ways that Average Americans who are employees differ from business owners.

Average American Retirement Planning

For almost a century, a major goal of employment for Average Americans has been to work hard and save enough money to retire. Most Americans would rather be doing something other than working and many look forward to the financial freedom of retirement.

In terms of retirement planning, most Average Americans invest in some type of retirement plan offered through their place of employment, typically a 401(k) plan. Most Average Americans also have a checking and savings account and possibly an IRA or small investment account. However, they do not have substantial or sufficient savings in such accounts. This is the result of a combination of factors, such as:

- People are living longer and have greater financial needs in retirement.

- Employers are focused on quarterly earnings and are forced to cut back on employee benefits, including retirement funding.
- Reduced fringe benefits from employers cause increased spending by the employees' families.
- Average Americans are spending more on consumer purchases than on retirement plans simply because their income doesn't afford them the opportunity to do both.

When companies give less to their employees and employees have to spend more just to pay the bills, the employees simply do not have the discretionary funds after bills are paid to save enough for their desired level of retirement and consequently do not put enough money in these plans. Perhaps, many Americans are relying on Social Security to provide a large portion of their retirement income. You need only read a week's worth of articles in the newspapers listed later in this chapter to get a clear understanding that relying on Social Security is not a wise planning decision. Therefore, most Average Americans do not have many retirement alternatives.

Average American Asset Protection

Next to estate tax planning, this is the area of financial planning where the needs and concerns between Average Americans and Affluent Americans (which obviously includes Doctors) differ most. Asset protection—the practice of shielding wealth from potential lawsuits, creditors or other claims—is plainly not of interest to Average Americans for two reasons:

1. They do not have significant assets to protect, and
2. They do not face significant liability through their work or investments.

Later in this Lesson, you will see that Doctor's asset protection situations are polar opposites of those of Average Americans. As a result, asset protection becomes a critical factor in planning for Doctors. In fact, this issue is so important that the authors have written four other books on this topic and have dedicated an entire section of this book to it.

Average American Estate Tax Planning

Under today's laws, an individual's heirs will only be subject to federal estate taxes if he or she has an estate worth greater than $3.5 million. By utilizing one particular estate planning document (you will learn which one in Lesson #9), a family with two living parents can utilize both exemptions and save the heirs from paying federal estate taxes on estates worth less than $7 million. It is true that, unless Congress acts to change current law, the exempt amount (for estate tax purposes) will drop to $1 million per person ($2 million per couple) in 2011. The federal estate tax phase-out schedule is offered below:

Calendar year	Exemption per person	Highest rate
2002	$1 million	50%
2003	$1 million	49%
2004	$1.5 million	48%
2005	$1.5 million	47%
2006	$2 million	46%
2007	$2 million	45%
2008	$2 million	45%
2009	$3.5 million	45%
2010	Repealed	0%
2011	$1 million	55%

With pretax income below $150,000 per year, it is unlikely that even Average American families will be able to pay their living expenses, raise children, pay educational costs for children, secure a retirement, handle the unforeseen financial burdens we all encounter during our lifetimes, and still have over $3.5 million left at the time of death to leave to children as an inheritance. As a result, estate tax planning (focused on reducing estate tax liabilities) is not likely to be a major concern of the Average American family.

The Diagnosis

Average Americans do not have as many opportunities as Doctors to enhance their financial situation as Doctors do. Average Americans spend most of their income on taxes (albeit at a low rate) and on their living expenses. As an employee, they have neither the opportunity to use many tax saving vehicles nor the flexibility to create their own benefits programs. The Average American family has precious few retirement assets and minimal risk of losing assets to judgment creditors. Upon death, almost all American families can easily pass their family assets to children with little or no estate tax. Average Americans spend the majority of their time trying to manage their financial affairs for the week, month, or year. Few have the time or luxury of preparing for long term needs. Because their needs are so different from those of Doctors and because physicians make up such a small percentage of the population, the popular press has focused on delivering information that applies to the Average American. The illustration of this point and the implication this has on physicians is offered in the next chapter.

2-2

The Popular Press Hurts Doctors

Most people believe that there is more financial information available on television, in newspapers and magazines, and on websites than one person could possibly review in a lifetime. They may be right!

Our Google search for "Financial Advice" on November 15, 2009 yielded 112 million results. A search for "investing" yielded 79 million results. We then narrowed our search for sites that had all of the following tags: "investing," "high income," and "financial planning." This narrowed the results down to 27 million.

Obviously, we agree with the sentiment that there are an almost infinite number of places one can look for financial advice. However, to whom is this advice directed? Consider this statement:

Most financial information available in newspapers or magazines, on television, or within websites is inappropriate and often detrimental to a Doctor's planning.

How can there be so many places to find financial information and so few reliable sources for Doctors? To answer this question, let's start by looking at a list of television stations, newspapers, magazines, and websites. Which of these outlets would you consider to be for Doctors and which would you consider to be directed at Average Americans?

Television: Fox News, MSNBC
Newspapers: *New York Times, USA Today, Wall Street Journal*
Websites: FoxNews.com, CNN.com, CNNMoney.com, USAToday.com, WSJ.com (Wall St. Journal), Forbes.com
Magazines: *Smart Money, Money, Business Week, Fortune, Fortune Small Business*

If you are like all of the colleagues and clients we asked informally, you would say that almost all of the aforementioned media would deliver information which would target wealthier Americans, such as Doctors.

To actually compare these media against each other, we went to each of their media kits and compiled a table for you to view. We cannot verify any of the data, but can verify that all of this information was taken from each firm's online media kit as of August 2007. We use the abbreviation HHI to represent household income. If you would like to find out if these numbers have changed dramatically in the last few years, feel free to contact the authors.

Media	**Type**	**Income Demographic**
Fox News	Television	$70,929 median HHI
MSNBC	Television	$75,588 median HHI (adults 25-54)
New York Times	Newspaper	$67,137 median HHI
USA Today	Newspaper	$76,929 median HHI, 34% HHI >$70k
The Wall Street Journal	Newspaper	$253,100 avg. HHI, $2.5 MM net worth
FoxNews.com	Website	$73,000 median HHI
CNN.com	Website	$76,419 median HHI
CNNMoney.com	Website	$83,431 median HHI, 37% HHI >$100k
USAToday.com	Website	$89,263 median HHI, 42% HHI >$70k
The Wall Street Journal*	Website	$111,250 mean HHI, mean investor assets $276,373
Forbes.com*	Website	$146,263 mean HHI, 17.8% HHI >$150k
Smart Money	Magazine	$81,742 median HHI
Money	Magazine	$85,336 median HHI
Business Week	Magazine	$93,811 median HHI, 18% HHI >$150k
Fortune Small Biz	Magazine	$119,986 median HHI
Fortune	Magazine	$137,000 median HHI

** By using a mean and not a median to represent that "Average" media consumer, the numbers can be skewed as a result of readers with very high incomes. The mean is a simple average. The median is the HHI associated with the middle person (after all respondents' data are ranked in order). As an example, if three people with HHIs of $50,000, $80,000 and $320,000, the mean HHI would be $150,000 but the median HHI would be $80,000. When analyzing HHI and net worth numbers, you will find that the mean is almost always much higher than the median. In the case of* Forbes.com, *for example, only 17.8% of visitors have HHI over $150k yet the mean is $146,263. This means that the total combined household income of the 17.8% of its visitors is approximately equal to the total HHI of the other 82.2% of its readers. We are not saying that the average reader doesn't earn $146k, but we are pointing out that fewer than 1 in 5 of the visitors to the site actually earn $150,000. The savvy advertisers understand what this data really means and the content must be focused at the majority of its visitors.*

While you might be surprised to see how the media outlets above focused almost exclusively on non-affluent audiences, take a moment to review the popular outlets below. These have an even less-affluent audience.

Media	**Type**	**Income Demographic**
ESPN (NFL games)	Television	$62,200 median HHI
Los Angeles Times	Newspaper	$55,698 median HHI
ESPN.com	Website	$77,000 average HHI
Oprah.com	Website	$80,000 median HHI
ESPN	Magazine	$62,132 median HHI
People	Magazine	$63,599 median HHI
Sports Illustrated	Magazine	$63,643 median HHI
GQ	Magazine	$67,141 median HHI
Newsweek	Magazine	$70,995 median HHI

The important point we are trying to illustrate with this data is that almost all of the high-end magazines and websites in the first list have an average audience household income of less than $100,000. Every single one mentioned on that list, except *The Wall Street Journal* (*TWSJ*), has an audience with an average household income of less than $150,000.

For the purpose of our next statement, we would like to exclude *TWSJ*. Though *TWSJ* focuses on business and financial markets, its primary goal is to report the news. It does not take a position of encouraging or promoting any particular products, strategies or financial philosophies. Given this caveat, our conclusion from the aforementioned data is:

Even the highest level media outlets in the United States are not targeting and delivering appropriate content to an audience with an average income above $150,000.

Why is this information important to our discussion of financial planning for Doctors? Let us explain what we learned from the publishing of our last book, *Wealth Protection: Build & Preserve Your Financial Fortress* for John Wiley & Sons.

The Media Business: "Get The Eyeballs"

If you are in the media business, it doesn't matter if you are publishing magazines or websites, or producing television or radio programs. The goal is always the same if there is advertising involved—provide content that will attract a large enough audience to generate ad revenue. You generate ad revenue by proving that you can deliver a significant audience and that you can accurately track the demographics of the audience. All of the sites, magazines and newspapers mentioned earlier are in business to make money. If they don't generate content that maintains an audience large enough to support the necessary ad revenue, the company will go out of business. They must "get the eyeballs." Their business model is really that simple.

To attract a large audience, these outlets have to deliver content that appeals to a large audience. After writing our last book for John Wiley, we appeared on over 120 radio and television programs. Though the book *Wealth Protection* had interesting philosophical lessons and over 62 practical lessons on advanced financial, legal, and tax-saving techniques, almost every producer and interviewer wanted us to discuss topics in the book we thought were the most basic. What we were told by one host was that his goal was to keep as many people as possible interested in the interview. He didn't care if the information was fresh and exciting. He wanted to make sure that "Joe Lunch-Bucket" (his words) wouldn't be put off by the topic. He told us that talking about ways to save $100,000 in taxes or ways to efficiently buy rental properties would alienate most listeners—which, in turn, would cause the show to lose "eyeballs" (or "ears," as is the case in radio). He was not going to allow that to happen.

Until John Wiley asked us to write a book about Affluent Americans (*Wealth Secrets of the Affluent*—published April, 2008), we had received very little interest from the popular press in regard to the education we have regularly offered to high-income clients for the last twelve years.

Consider the following:

- Every information/publishing company is in business to make money.
- The money almost always comes from advertisers.
- Advertisers pay more if the audience is larger.
- A publisher must continuously offer appropriate content to the masses to maintain and grow an audience and attract advertisers.
- Even the high-end distribution channels don't target consumers earning over $100,000.

If you consider these five statements you can clearly conclude that:

It is almost IMPOSSIBLE for Doctors to find useful and appropriate financial information from popular newspapers, magazines, websites, or television programs.

This is why most of the information contained in this book may seem foreign to many readers. The tips, tools, and strategies offered here are not the kinds of things that most information outlets would ever deliver because, quite frankly, there is no business reason for doing so. Fewer than 10% of Americans would find much of the information in this book applicable or beneficial. If it is important to "fit in" and do what everyone else does—even if it is not the best course of action—this book is not for you.

2-3

Smart Doctors Don't Want to "Fit In"

We hope that you now understand that there are significant differences between Doctors and Average Americans—at least in terms of basic demographic data. This book will hopefully teach you how you should act when faced with the more complex financial and legal issues that effect Doctors. These very different attitudes and methods of approaching wealth planning are integral to your success.

We also hope that you have gained some insight into why nearly every newspaper, financial website and financial magazine is forced to focus its content on a group of subscribers or readers that have a very different set of concerns than Doctors. These media outlets need to provide "common sense" advice to the general public (i.e. Average Americans) to fit their business model of attracting the most eyeballs. There are simply far more Average American "eyeballs" than there are wealthy, or more specifically Doctor, "eyeballs."

It stands to reason that, if financial "common sense" has been developed for (and should generally be used by) Average Americans, this common sense will not apply to physicians. In fact, the only way Doctors can achieve desired levels of wealth and have peace of mind is to follow advice that doesn't make "common sense."

Going against "common sense" is not easy. There are many deeply rooted psychological factors that push someone to go with the crowd, rather than against it. This is certainly true in the financial planning context. As an example, consider this proposition:

It is a bad financial idea for a Doctor to pay off a mortgage and own a home outright.

For many of you reading this now, this may be difficult, if not impossible, to believe. It is exactly the opposite of what your parents told you (and they are the smart people who taught you so many life lessons). It is the polar opposite of what Suze Orman and hundreds of websites, magazine articles, and television programs suggest. Further, it just may not "feel" right, because it goes against what all of your friends are doing. Keep those feelings and thoughts in mind when you read the other Lessons in the book.

Why Ignoring "Common Sense" Is So Difficult

Most children and adolescents try desperately to "fit in." As we get older, we try to find the right groups in college. In our first jobs, we want to toe the company line. All states have laws that govern our behavior. Most religions have commandments, rules, or other codices of condoned and forbidden activities.

Most people avoid actions they fear their friends and relatives would criticize—or at the very least, they refrain from sharing details of their potentially critical activities with their family and friends. We are not implying that Americans are sheep. Rather, we are saying that society typically rewards those who are similar and creates more challenges for those who are not.

This is not a particularly astute observation. It is merely support for the significance of the #1 challenge that must be overcome if you are to truly work less and build more. To do so, you not only have to admit to being different from Average Americans, but you also have to EMBRACE the fact that you are different.

Embrace Affluence And Your Differences: A Key Lesson

If you want to successfully achieve or maintain wealth, you must be comfortable with your unique circumstances and be comfortable doing things differently than your friends. If your only comfort comes from doing something and knowing that "everyone else is doing it," then you are destined to achieve and maintain mediocrity. Wealthy Americans became affluent by being different or by doing something different. If they did what everyone else did, they would be like 80% of Americans who earn less than $80,000 per year and they wouldn't have achieved the wealth they now have.

Savvy physicians don't want to "fit in." They understand that Average Americans work very hard to pay their bills while scratching to save for retirement, occasional vacations, and precious luxury items. Savvy Doctors understand that the two groups have very different financial challenges that require different types of advisors and strategies.

These physicians don't need the financial and legal advisors and firms that cater to 150,000,000 Average Americans. Doctors don't need techniques, strategies, or products that are adequate for the needs of the many. Doctors don't need free checking, higher money market rates, lower online trading costs, do-it-yourself legal documents, or the advisor with the lowest hourly rate. Doctors don't need advisors to tell them how nice their shoes are or how wonderfully decorated their home or office is. They know these things are nice—they bought them. Doctors don't need to be surrounded with "yes" men or women who agree with all of their suggestions. They need advisors to question them, challenge them, and help them consider all alternatives before taking action. Smart physicians shouldn't put much stock in advisors who send calendars, fruit baskets, or sports tickets, or seek out advisors who will take them golfing or out to dinner. You can pay for all of those things yourself.

Doctors need to understand that there are millions of attorneys, accountants, investment advisors, and financial planners who would all like their business. You should know that many of these advisors and their firms regularly give away "special perks" to try to convince people to become new clients or to guilt them into staying with the firm. You should understand that an advisor referred by a friend is a good start, but a referred advisor from a friend who is in a different financial situation is likely not appropriate for you. There is an entire section on how to build your advisory team in Lesson #3: Accept Referrals to Specialists. The third lesson is a must read for anyone who picks up this book.

Doctors have family and friends just like Average Americans do. You want to spend your valuable and limited free time with your friends (and some of it with family—just like Average Americans). When you spend time with your advisors, you need to make the most of the time by focusing on the important issues you are paying the advisors to help you manage. You should want your advisors to generate a significant return (on the fees you pay them) in value for your family and practice.

Like Average Americans, Doctors can't help but talk business and finance with friends. A common characteristic of successful physicians is that they don't need to brag about their planning or convince their friends to work with the same advisors to generate peace of mind. You need to cherish the novelty of being different. Practically, you should put more effort into choosing your team than you do in the criticism of the solutions and strategies the team recommends and implements. You should not ask friends or other unqualified outsiders for approval of your planning. This would be like one of your patients asking his barber for advice on how you should do your medical procedure. This isn't to say that Doctors shouldn't review and challenge the advisors suggestions and bring in other experts for second opinions. This is a significant and very important part of building and maintaining wealth (Lesson #10).

Average Americans look for bits of cheap advice on websites, in magazines and newspapers, and on television and radio. The Average American relies on mutual fund recommendations that come in a $5 magazine or on a free website that could possibly reach millions of different people per day. Smart Doctors never give a second thought to any financial or legal suggestion that isn't offered by someone who is intimately familiar with their situation and goals. Doctors don't want to spend the time and money for customized planning—they **MUST** spend the time and money on a specially trained and experienced team of advisors to customize a plan that will help them most efficiently and effectively reach their specific, personal goals.

The Diagnosis

Whether you are a young Doctor trying to pay off student loans and save for retirement or a successful physician trying to protect what you've earned from taxes, lawsuits, or a divorce, you have important challenges in your financial life. As we hope you have gleaned from our discussions above, there is an abundance of financial information and advice to be found. However, if you are a physician who wants to learn the lessons that will help you build and protect wealth, this book is for you. Much of the information presented in the 10 Lessons may be financial lessons and advice that you literally cannot get anywhere else. This book contains only some of the important lessons that you can learn when you accept referrals to specialists who are experts at helping Doctors with their unique challenges. To learn more about how these specialists can help you and why you need them, you should read the next section, Lesson #3: Accept Referrals to Specialists.

LESSON 3

Accept Referrals to Specialists

In Lesson #1, you learned that the only real way to build and maintain wealth is by leveraging effort, assets, and people. You learned that leveraging people is the most powerful method of Leverage and that leveraging advisors is the most powerful way to Leverage people. It wouldn't be a stretch to say that once you figure out how to use Leverage to achieve even a modest level of wealth, learning how to Leverage advisors is the single most important thing you can do if you want to save time and money and get the most out of your medical career.

To help you better understand this lesson, you need only look at the practice of medicine. A primary care physician is generally the first line of contact for a patient. Though the Doctor has a very wide range of general knowledge, he or she will have to refer patients to a number of specialists. In some instances, the Doctor may request the help of radiologists to review tests. In other instances, there may be a referral to surgeons who will undoubtedly need to work with anesthesiologists. The Doctor will encounter cases in which patients will need referrals to obstetricians, gynecologists, urologists, cardiologists, orthopedists, oncologists, and other specialists. The situation with respect to your finances is very similar.

In this Lesson—Accept Referrals to Specialists—we will examine the types of advisors who can help you Leverage your time and money, review the benefits and limitations of each specialist, point out some common pitfalls, and ultimately recommend how to assemble the right team of advisors.

3-1

The Value of Financial Specialists

The best way to maximize your benefit from leveraging people is to work with experts in many financial and legal fields. As you learned in Lesson #2, you have very different needs than Average Americans do. As a result, the right specialists for most people are not likely to be the right advisors to help you.

As you become more successful, your need for quality advisors will also increase. The leverage created by adding employees, making additional investments, purchasing equipment and real estate, and creating new businesses add complexity to your plan. This increased Leverage exponentially increases the complexity of an appropriately comprehensive financial plan. This complexity necessitates the need for a team of advisors who can handle such complexity. Without a very strong team, you will struggle to find the time to focus on the important things that make you money, let alone enjoy any free time. To illustrate the value of advisors, refer to the equation below:

Wealth can only be achieved through Leverage

+

Leverage can only be managed with a team of Advisors

=

Wealth can only be achieved with a team of advisors managing the Leverage

In this chapter, we will discuss the reason *why* Doctors need a team of knowledgeable advisors with diverse areas of expertise. Then we will discuss *how* to maximize the value of your advisors and suggest tips for working with your team.

Managing Complexity: The Need For Advisors

Most people realize that wealth creates complexity. What Doctors need to realize is that the management of complexity and Leverage is not the job of a traffic cop. As wealth grows, the number of complicated, technical risks that the Doctor faces also grows exponentially.

As an example, the transition from running a sole proprietorship to having a single employee may not seem to be major, but that couldn't be further from the truth. The addition of just one employee creates a need for:

- Payroll creation, funding, and payments
- Regular payroll tax payments (or you can go to jail)
- Withholding tax filings and payments
- Workers compensation insurance or fund payments
- Occupation Safety Hazard Association (OSHA) compliance
- Separate retirement plan (ERISA) regulations and contribution requirements
- A host of other state and federal reporting requirements

In addition to all of the aforementioned specific issues, the Leverage of assets also increases the need for more general categories of planning, like asset protection, banking (private and commercial), business planning, financial planning, healthcare law, HIPAA, Medicare, income tax management, investing, life insurance analysis, disability insurance analysis, property and casualty insurance analysis, long-term care insurance analysis, educational funding, retirement planning, family law, gift and estate tax planning, charitable planning, Medicaid planning, and a host of other areas.

Each category of planning has its own technical areas that can be competently handled by an advisor who has expertise in that area. Although it is common to find an advisor who has expertise in several areas, there are categories in which the input of two advisors may be necessary. For example, tax issues are typically handled by a both a tax attorney and a CPA. As a result, there is no way that a small team of two or three advisors could possibly handle the needs of a Doctor. This means that, over a career, a Doctor may need to leverage the services of six or more advisors.

While the concept of such a large team may seem overwhelming, consider your profession of medicine. Adult patients do not continue to see the obstetrician who delivered them or the pediatrician who treated them in childhood. Patients need to see a number of specialists as they mature and as their needs change, often consulting with a number of Doctors at once.

If you are like your patients, you may want to be able to keep the same financial "primary care" advisors for as long as possible. Having someone you know and trust as your primary contact is very comforting. This "primary advisor" can help explain situations to you, find the right specialists if a need for one arises, and help communicate with you as complicated procedures take place. Keep this in mind. In Lesson #10 there will be discussion of your team of advisors. One of your advisors on this team is going to be the primary contact to help you through it all.

Working With Your Team

Having the right team of advisors is another step in the right direction, but there is still more to do. Having a team that is run poorly is like having an alarm installed in your house but never turning it on. You have to "work" with the team for the team to provide any value. In our discussion with the partners of The Founders Group in San Diego, we learned some valuable lessons about successful business owners (and Doctors need to consider themselves business owners). The Founders Group only deals with families with businesses or net worth above $25,000,000. They have found that the most successful clients and families arranged annual or semi-annual all-day or multi-day meetings with all of their advisors, business partners, and key family members. Sometimes, the costs of flying in advisors to perform these meetings and paying them their hourly wages can cost thousands of dollars per year.

According to Joe Strazzeri of The Founders Group:

> **"Professionals and business owners who make the effort to spend time with the experts on their team generally see these meetings as the most productive use of time and money."**

Tips For Working Within A Team

As with any collaborative endeavor, just having a collection of people is not enough to ensure success. You need a coordinated team. Every conference call and meeting must have an agenda and someone to manage the meeting to make sure that all-important items are handled within the allotted time. It is common to put one of the advisors in charge of organizing and facilitating information between the other advisors. This is usually a financial planner and not an accountant or attorney—though the "quarterback" could be any one of the advisors on the team. Within the group, you need to identify roles and responsibilities and make one person accountable for the completion of each task.

When considering different options, it is wonderful when there is a unanimous decision on whether to go in a particular direction. However, many decisions will not be unanimous. You need to set the rules on how decisions are to be made within the group and share them with the group. If they know how you are going to make decisions, it will make it easier for them to participate in the group and allow them to continue to participate even when the rest of the group disagrees with a particular decision.

The Diagnosis

You can't possibly expect to achieve and protect wealth while holding on to your sanity unless you assemble the right team of advisors. Trying to achieve financial success without a team of advisors is like a patient trying to get 100% of his or her healthcare from one Doctor. Without the help of orthopedists, dermatologists, neurologists, obstetricians, oncologists, and dozens of other specialists, patients' life expectancies would certainly suffer. Society has benefited from the development of expertise in specialized medicine. Similarly, Doctors need to look to specialized legal and financial advisors to provide the greatest financial benefits.

You must realize that the process of building and maintaining wealth in today's world brings with it potential challenges from all areas of law, accounting, finance, insurance, and business. When you accept this reality and embrace the need to Leverage the expertise of advisors in all of the areas mentioned above, you will be one step closer to reaching your goals.

What types of advisors do Doctors need? How do you divide the responsibilities within the team? How do you choose the actual advisors? In the next two chapters, we will answer all of these questions.

3-2

The Specialists Doctors Need

Before you can choose your advisors, delegate responsibilities to team members or begin to benefit from the Leverage of advisors, you need to understand the types of advisors you need. In this chapter, we provide a list that covers the team members that 90% of situations require. Some advisors, like mortgage brokers, are not discussed because they typically play a transactional role at different points in the client's lifetime. The other advisors may review mortgages, but the mortgage broker typically is looking for the lowest price and isn't changing loan offers based on the other pieces of the comprehensive financial plan. In addition, unique circumstances may call for some teams to require additional advisors with very unique skills. Below is the list of the most common advisors:

- Accountants
- Asset Protection Attorneys
- Estate Planning Attorneys
- Tax Attorneys
- Insurance Professionals
- Investment Advisors
- Financial Planners

Accountants

The term *accountant* will be used to generically describe an accountant, Certified Public Accountant (CPA), or Enrolled Agent (EA).

What They Do: Accountants (and CPAs and EAs) are trained and licensed to prepare tax returns for submission to the Internal Revenue Service. Each state has its own licensing and accreditation procedures for accountants and CPAs. Ohio is no exception. The CPA has a multi-part exam plus an experience requirement that is necessary to earn the CPA accreditation. Enrolled Agents complete a federal licensing process. In all situations, these advisors primarily prepare tax returns. In the most desirable client-advisor relationship, the accountants also provide clients with advice on tax matters.

Limitations of an Accountant:

1. The U.S. tax law is potentially the most complex set of rules created by humankind, and significant changes are made to these rules every year. Therefore, **it is impossible for any accountant to be well versed in all areas of tax policy**. More likely, the accountant may only know intimately one or two areas (of 20 or more potential areas that affect your planning). Tax planning is like medicine—each area has become so complex that one can't possibly expect to become an expert in many disciplines. In the medical arena, most patients and physicians realize that one Doctor can't do everything. They both readily accept being referred to, or referring patients to, other physicians. A gastroenterologist would no sooner make diagnoses for skin conditions than a dermatologist would try and diagnose and treat an intestinal issue. Unfortunately, this happens all the time in the tax arena.

2. **Some accountants are comfortable acknowledging what they know and don't know.** Some accountants feel responsible for answering all tax questions and resist referring clients to other accountants for specific needs for fear of losing the client altogether. This is more of a limitation of an individual than it is a limitation of the profession as a whole, but it must be recognized.

3. **Conflicts of interest may arise.** Many accountants are beginning to look for additional revenue opportunities by getting licensed in life insurance and securities. They will then recommend their clients particular investment and insurance products. This can create significant conflicts of interest with clients who are looking for tax advice, but who are getting financial suggestions. Clients should be concerned how accountants who deal with very complex tax issues find time to become experts in insurance and investments. In revisiting our Doctor analogy—how could a practicing dermatologist find the time to learn oncology on the side and offer high-quality consultation to the dermatology clients who develop cancer? Savvy patients would prefer a full-time oncologist in that situation. Despite the conflict and impracticality, many CPAs with years of accounting experience are now trying to increase revenue by advising clients on investments and insurance, despite having little or no practical experience in these areas.

Asset Protection Attorneys

The term *asset protection attorney* describes an attorney who has a strong working knowledge of and experience in the area of creditor protection. There is no state-specific accreditation for asset protection. All attorneys must be admitted to the Bar Association in the state(s) in which they wish to practice. To see if an attorney is licensed and in good standing in Ohio, you can go to www.forohiodoctors.com where we provide a link to the Ohio Supreme Court website.

What They Do: Asset protection attorneys specialize in the areas of law that help clients arrange their personal and business affairs in a manner that protects their wealth from potential future lawsuits and other creditor risks. Because many of the tools used in asset protection are the same tools used in estate planning and business planning, it is common for asset protection attorneys to also have a strong working knowledge in those areas as well.

Limitations of Asset Protection Attorneys:

1. Because asset protection is a relatively new field of law and most attorneys are overwhelmed in their primary fields of interest (litigation, business law, estate planning, etc.), **few attorneys have found the time or had the interest to study this important field of law.** As a result, there are very few attorneys who are experts in this area.

2. **Asset protection attorneys are NOT estate planning or tax attorneys—or any other type of attorney, for that matter.** Do not expect that you will get estate planning or tax advice from these attorneys unless they also have specific training in these areas. However, your asset protection attorney should be willing to interact with attorneys from the other fields who will be necessary to help you complete your planning.

Estate Planning Attorneys

The term *estate planning attorney* describes an attorney who has a strong working knowledge of and experience in the area of trusts, probate, and estate planning. Most are also knowledgeable in issues of aging, declining capacity, guardianships, special needs and estate administration. All attorneys must be admitted to the Bar Association in the state(s) they wish to practice. Ohio attorneys who focus primarily on this area of the law are board-certified by the Ohio State Bar Association as specialists because they have been peer reviewed, have passed a rigorous exam, have met specific experience requirements and devote a significant amount of their practice to estate planning, trust and probate law.

What they do: Estate planning attorneys focus on helping families address the financial needs that arise throughout a client's lifetime, including disability and death. Estate planning attorneys are required to draft estate planning documents such as wills, limited partnerships, and various types of trusts. They should have a strong working knowledge of gift, estate, and generation-skipping tax issues. Though many estate planning issues are federal issues, there are some state-specific issues that require an Ohio attorney. For very complex issues, the most savvy affluent families will often use the best estate planning attorney they can find (anywhere in the US) and have a local attorney co-counsel the case to address specific Ohio issues.

Limitations:

1. **We have seen many estate planning attorneys who almost exclusively create estate plans using only the legal tools they can be paid to create.** They have little experience or knowledge of important financial vehicles that can play a significant role in the estate planning of wealthy families. By excluding entire categories of planning tools (most often cash value life insurance), these attorneys often fail to help their clients create the liquidity necessary to handle the financial obligations that arise at death. Sometimes attorneys shy away from recommending financial and insurance tools because they do not understand these tools and they fear the potential liability of recommending things they don't understand. The proper solution to this limitation is to do what the savvy affluent do—make sure there are attorneys and insurance experts on the financial planning team, so that the clients can get the best combination of planning tools to most efficiently meet their needs.

2. **Estate planning attorneys often are not asset protection or (income) tax attorneys either.** While attorneys in these different fields may use similar legal tools from time to time, that is not enough. A scalpel in the hands of a surgeon can be an important tool to help save a life. A scalpel in the hands of a mugger is a knife that can kill someone. We are not suggesting that one type of attorney is an angel and one is a devil (readers are encouraged to insert their own jokes here). We are merely saying that tools used differently can have very different outcomes and can offer varying benefits. For this reason, it is best to involve specialists in asset protection and income tax to work with the estate planning attorney, if needed.

Tax Attorneys

The term *tax attorney* describes an attorney who has a strong working knowledge of and experience in the area of income tax and possibly estate tax. There is a state-specific accreditation for tax attorneys in many states. Most tax attorneys have added another year of education beyond law school to earn a degree in taxation, called an LLM (short for Master of Laws). All attorneys must be admitted to the Bar Association in the state(s) in which they wish to practice

What they do: Tax planning attorneys are required to give advice on the tax ramifications of certain transactions (i.e., selling an appreciated asset) or strategies, and to assist with the creation of the legal documents used in these transactions. These specialized attorneys have a strong working knowledge of income and capital gains tax issues, as well as taxation of corporations, partnerships, and other entities. All attorneys must be admitted to the Bar Association in the state(s) in which they wish to practice. Since most states' tax laws are built upon federal tax code, many national tax attorneys can handle all of a client's income tax issues.

Limitations:

1. **Tax attorneys do not generally prepare tax returns.** Though they have a very strong working knowledge of tax, the preparation is a specialty that is generally left to the accountant (as mentioned earlier).

2. **Though some of these attorneys are also experts in estate planning, most do not work in this area regularly.** This results in two limitations:

    a. Tax attorneys may not be as aware of potential estate planning solutions that are more appropriate for very affluent clients

    b. They are likely to have very limited knowledge of financial and insurance vehicles and their place within an estate plan, because they are tax attorneys first and estate planning attorneys second. If full-time estate planning attorneys don't have time to fully understand financial vehicles, how could you expect part-time estate planning attorneys with another full-time focus to have time?

3. In addition, **tax planning attorneys generally are not asset protection attorneys.** While they may know a bit about this area, the same comparison of the surgeon and the mugger needs to be revisited here—a little knowledge can be dangerous. It is best to involve specialists in asset protection and estate planning to work with the tax planning attorney.

Insurance Professionals

Insurance Professional is a term used to describe life and health (life) or property and casualty (P&C) insurance agents or brokers. Life and P&C agents must have a resident agent license in the state in which they reside. In states like Ohio, a weeklong course and a state-sponsored exam are generally required to earn a license. They can apply for non-resident licenses in the other states to provide insurance to clients in those states as well. Certified Financial Planners, accountants, investment advisors and attorneys can all secure life insurance licenses. Many of their regulatory agencies require those advisors to disclose the potential conflict of interest to clients in instances where the advisor could benefit from multiple income sources (e.g., professional fees and insurance commissions).

What They Do: At the most basic level, insurance professionals provide various types of insurance policies to clients. Some insurance professionals also offer financial planning or investment solutions. The life insurance professional works closely with the estate planning attorney to help clients meet their estate planning needs. If you are interested in purchasing any type of insurance, it is imperative that you consult with a licensed insurance professional experienced in the insurance area at issue. Typically, one person can only be an expert in one area of insurance. If you look at the list of types of insurance below, you can see why it is so important to work with a financial firm like O'Dell Jarvis Mandell (www.ojmgroup.com)—that has a number of insurance and investment experts on staff to help clients with their various insurance and investment needs. Despite their wide range of insurance expertise, OJM still needs the assistance of great attorneys like their co-authors to develop a comprehensive book for Ohio Doctors and to bring the proper services to doctors in Ohio.

Life Insurance

In Lesson #8, you will learn why cash value life insurance is a fundamental building block of wealth planning for Doctors. By offering tax benefits, wealth accumulation, liquidity, and protection against financial disasters, life insurance should play a role in every Doctor's financial plan.

Disability Income Insurance

In Lesson #4, you will learn how to protect your family and practice from financial disasters. For Doctors, the single greatest asset may be your earning potential. Disability income insurance is required for every Doctor whose income is needed for the family to pay bills or meet other financial needs. Disability income insurance should be handled by a life and health insurance agent who specializes in disability insurance.

Long-Term Care Insurance

Also in Lesson #4, you will learn that long-term care insurance (LTCI) is an important tool for Doctors who want to avoid losing their hard-earned wealth to a Medicaid spend-down to pay for nursing home, home care, hospice, and a host of other services most of us will need in our final years. Long-term care insurance covers health related expenses that will not be covered by social or private insurance in retirement. In addition, some families use long-term care insurance to protect retirement savings for their heirs (as an inheritance). LTCI can be handled by life insurance agents who have completed the additional LTCI-specific training (that most states—Ohio included—require).

Property and Casualty Insurance

Property and Casualty (P&C) insurance is a separate set of insurances that require a different training course and license than the license needed for the aforementioned types of insurance. P&C insurances are quite common, even though you may not have previously run across the acronym "P&C." This coverage includes homeowners, personal auto, commercial auto, professional liability insurance, worker's compensation, umbrella, premises, product liability, flood, hurricane, and many other policies. To protect wealth, Doctors need to address P&C concerns by adding an insurance agent who is an expert in these areas.

Limitations of Insurance Professionals:

1. **Some are working for the insurance company or themselves, rather than working for you.** Some insurance agents have "**career agent**" contracts with certain insurance companies. These agents are highly motivated to sell a specific company's products, because they must hit their sales goals or risk losing their health and financial benefits.

   Other insurance companies, like Northwestern Mutual, have "**captive**" agents who, due to contract terms, can usually only offer you products from a single company. Many captive agents find it difficult or impossible to shop for the best policy among all the insurance companies, and therefore can't realistically provide unbiased information and advice.

   Doctors should always work with independent insurance professionals who have a range of options they can offer and can display a track record of using different companies for their clients' best interest. Doctors should also look for agents of the highest moral character, who are experienced and successful enough not to be influenced by slightly higher commissions or other incentives that competing insurance companies may offer. One client said about his choice of an agent, "I wanted an agent who wanted my business, but not one who needed my business." Another client said, "I feel comfortable knowing that my agent is interested in a long term relationship and doesn't need to sell me anything to pay the bills."

2. **Many agents work only for commissions.** Doctors should realize that insurance professionals, like all of us, need to make a living. They do not begrudge the insurance professional for earning a commission that is inherent in the insurance product (or the real estate agent or any other commission-compensated person). However, when asking for advice and recommendations on how to address a financial need, you have to expect a commission-based advisor to suggest only commission-based products. You may get the best commission-based solution, but are not likely to receive a recommendation of the best possible solution if that solution doesn't involve a commission. This is the converse limitation to the estate planning attorney that only recommends legal solutions. Doctors should want independence. This is much more important for certain products like life insurance, than for less expensive products such as homeowner's, or even disability, insurance.

Unfortunately, it is true that many advisors in the financial planning and insurance industries allow commissions to bias their view of insurance products. The authors insist that they be compensated on a fee basis for any advising, planning or product consultation that they provide. If an insurance professional works like this, he or she is much less likely to be biased towards lucrative commissions or to "sell" a product at all. Insurance agents who are "commission only" need the sale or commission to stay in business and their business model is shaped accordingly. Therefore, Doctors should work with fee-based advisors when evaluating insurance products and wealth planning involving insurance.

3. **Few have significant training in other areas.** To obtain a license in most states for any of these types of insurance, an individual typically only needs to attend a weeklong class and then pass an exam. Contrast this to earning an MBA (2 years), law license (3 years law school, plus bar exam), or medical license (4 years medical school, 4-8 years internship/residency, plus board exams).

   Because of this limited training, many insurance "professionals" are simply salespeople without the sophistication or training to do more than sell. Doctors would be wise to look for more from their insurance advisors. This "more" they seek should be education, training, years of experience and the professional's "team." Again, as an example, O'Dell Jarvis Mandell (OJM) has 3 MBAs, 2 attorneys, and a CPA among its team's designations. OJM is certainly not the only firm with very highly qualified professionals. We just believe it is a good example of what you should seek out in a firm if you are looking for well-educated professionals who can help you with many facets of your planning.

Investment Advisors

We use the term *investment advisor* to include money managers and stockbrokers. These advisors have to study and pass a 3-hour securities exam and a 90-minute ethics exam or file as an independent Registered Investment Advisor directly with the SEC.

What They Do: Investment advisors essentially handle investments for clients. They typically charge a fee based on the amount of assets they manage. Stockbrokers may also be paid based on the number and size of the trades they make.

Limitations:

1. **Most fail to adequately manage taxes.** The overwhelming majority of money managers primarily handle pension or corporate (institutional) assets, which are not as sensitive to taxes as are the non-pension assets of Doctors. As a result, these advisors focus on their gross, pre-tax investment returns. This gross number is what they publish in their marketing material, how they are measured

against their peers and how they are compensated. This is obviously what they care about most. This is understandable, except that this is exactly what Doctors should be trying to avoid. Doctors should be interested in the post-tax return of the investment. We will discuss this in greater detail in Lessons #7 and #8.

2. **Most have very little knowledge or interest in any kind of "planning."** Like most specialists, investment managers have to focus on their craft. Since the world markets are now integrated, investment management is practically a 24-hour per day job. When Japan is closing, London is opening. When London is winding down, New York is ramping up. It isn't easy for investment advisors to be well versed in other planning areas and it is basically impossible for these advisors to act as the team's quarterback because of their limited knowledge of the areas outside of the markets.

Financial Planners

We use the term *financial planner* to describe someone who charges a fee to create a financial plan for a client. Sometimes, this is a Certified Financial Planner who has taken six courses and passed an exam. Other times, this person is an accountant who has financial training and may have passed an exam in addition to the training as an accountant and possibly passing the CPA exam. Still other times, this could be someone with an MBA, with a concentration in Finance, who has professional experience and has spent two years learning about business, business law, economics and finance.

What They Do: Ideally, a financial planner is someone who uses a planning process to help the client Leverage the other planning areas above. The planner integrates all of the focused planning efforts of the other advisors into one comprehensive plan to help the client's family meet its objectives. They should have a strong working knowledge of many of the disciplines. Their level of proficiency should be enough to allow them to interact at a high level with the various specialists and add some value in each area from time to time. More often than not, this advisor will also act as the "coordinator" or "quarterback" for all of the specialists (like the primary care Doctor analogy used earlier). The financial planner provides motivation, understanding and a disciplined periodic review to make sure all of the various planning areas stay "on track." We will develop the discussion of a quarterback for your financial plan at the end of this Lesson and in Lesson #10.

Limitations:

1. **Can be a Disguised Salesperson.** It can hard to decipher between the true planner and the disguised salesperson that is, in actuality, focused on selling something. It is okay for a planner to be used in the implementation of a plan, but you must focus on the plan itself first. Be wary of financial plans offered for free.

You should know that anything you get for free is not worth much. Further, the business model of such a "planner" is simply to use the "plan" just to sell you something—how else could they recoup whatever little time they spent on creating such a plan?

2. **Weak Knowledge of Other Disciplines.** This could be the biggest potential problem. If your financial planner is supposed to be acting as the quarterback of your planning team, they have to understand what the other advisors can and will do and be able to spot important issues within each of the disciplines. In working with hundreds of insurance agents and financial planners, we have only encountered a handful that have a strong working knowledge of asset protection and tax planning. Bringing only insurance and investment knowledge (the products that they typically sell) is insufficient to make a good financial planner. The top four planners at O'Dell Jarvis Mandell have 3 MBAs, a law degree, and a CPA between them.

Other Advisors

In addition to the list of advisors already provided, there are other advisors who may be valuable to help increase your Leverage. These include business or corporate attorneys, real estate attorneys, private bankers, charitable planners, Medicaid attorneys, and family law attorneys. Each of these experts may have a specific role to play in your planning at some point.

The Diagnosis

You now have an understanding of what types of advisors you could add to your financial planning team. You may even foresee some of the benefits you and your family may achieve from working with the specialists on your team. Before you jump into hiring team members, it is important to learn from the mistakes of thousands of people who have preceded you. Read the next chapter on the seven mistakes to avoid when building and working with your team. Avoiding these mistakes can save you an inordinate amount of time, money and aggravation

3-3

Seven Outdated Procedures to Avoid

In our many years as financial planning professionals, we have seen many clients make mistakes when selecting and working with their advisors. These mistakes are common among Doctors and non-Doctors alike. However, these mistakes can all be avoided. We know this because many of our clients have effectively built their fortune and protected their assets by building the right team of advisors. There are seven pitfalls to be avoided when choosing and working with advisors on your financial plans. The seven pitfalls to avoid are:

1. Friends or Family as Advisors
2. Choosing Only Local Team Members
3. "If It Ain't Broke, Don't Fix It"
4. Never Getting a Second Opinion
5. Hiring Yes Men and Women
6. Not Accepting that Complexity Requires Outside Experts
7. Failing to Insist on Advisor Coordination

In this chapter, we will examine these seven pitfalls and explain how each can be avoided.

Pitfall #1: Friends Or Family As Advisors

One of the biggest mistakes we see is the inclusion of friends and family in the planning team. We can't fault people for thinking that trust is important when choosing people to help manage money. Trust is very important. However, unless you are willing to lose the friendship to achieve the financial goals, this should probably be avoided. It is perfectly acceptable to become friendly with your advisors. This is appropriate because the friendship will have grown out of a business relationship. However, when the relationship instead begins as a friendship, problems may later arise when you disagree on a course of action or when the advisor makes a mistake.

Pitfall #2: Choosing Only Local Team Members

The best available team members need not be the best available advisors in your neighborhood. We have helped clients who built their team with advisors from all four corners of the country. In today's age of technology, information is easily shared through email, fax, and, more recently, online data sharing applications. Unlike the surgeon who needs to be in the room to do surgery, a financial or legal professional doesn't need to be in the room to do what he or she does well. Don't be afraid to enlist the best advisors you can find—even if they are not in your backyard.

Pitfall #3: "If It Ain't Broke, Don't Fix It"

Having worked with someone for 10 or 20 years is not a reason to continue with the same advisor. If you applied that logic to medicine, patients would still be seeing their pediatricians long after turning 18 years old. There is a high likelihood that, as you accumulated wealth, your financial needs changed. Though your advisor may have been adequate when you had simpler needs, you are not required to stay with that advisor if you have outgrown the advisor's, or firm's, capabilities and expertise.

The first mistake that the overwhelming majority of Doctors make in the financial, legal or tax aspects of their careers is the method they use to initially to choose their professional advisors. Whether it was their CPA, investment professional or attorney, many business owners made a poor choices because their method of evaluating the potential advisors was flawed.

When you consider the typical pattern, this is not surprising. Most Doctors chose their advisors when they were starting out in residency or fellowship. They may have needed some life or disability insurance, a Will and someone to prepare and file tax returns. Working long hours, and without the means to evaluate an advisor, young Doctors typically do what other busy people do and take the path of least resistance. They use the same advisor used by their parents or friends, or family member.

Though this un-scientific approach is obviously flawed, it may serve its purpose when there are bigger challenges at hand (like 20-hour work days). Your life was so hectic that you just needed to "get it done fast." The advisor you chose at that point simply had to be competent and inexpensive—and that was good enough. Like a triage nurse in an emergency room, the advisors do not have to be top-trained specialist when all you need are some basic stitches. This approach is quite understandable.

What is so alarming to us is not this initial choice of advisor, but the fact that *so many Doctors stay for the rest of their careers with the same advisors who handled their "triage planning" for the rest of their careers*! The justification for this is rarely anything concrete or, in our opinion, sufficient to explain or justify why the Doctor would choose an advisor over his or her own financial security. Answers like "we've been together so long, I'd hate to change now," or "if it ain't broke, don't fix it" are unpersuasive. Further, this begs the question: "How do you know 'it ain't broke' if you don't get a second opinion?"

Most alarming to us—despite the fact that we see it every day—is when a physician stays with an advisor when the Doctor has clearly outgrown the expertise of the advisor. Consider the case study of Ned the Neurosurgeon:

Case Study: Ned the Neurosurgeon

Ned, a neurosurgeon in Florida, contacted our firm after reading our last book. While his income was over $1 million per year and he was part of an extremely successful practice, he used the same local lawyer who created his wills 20 years ago when he was just starting out. When we were in Florida, we had a meeting with this attorney.

Not only was this attorney not a tax specialist (despite the fact that he was advising on tax issues), but he also continued to advise the Doctor in other areas that were clearly beyond his expertise. While he was certainly a nice gentleman, and perhaps was competent at doing basic planning for someone with minimal tax or estate planning concerns, he had no understanding of the advanced techniques that a Doctor making over $1 million per year should be considering. He had no knowledge of asset protection planning or other fairly routine planning that we implement for high-income Doctors. While this gentleman may have been an acceptable choice for the Doctor when he was starting out, continuing to use this attorney as his primary advisor was a total disservice to this client.

Self Test: How did you choose the professional advisors you work with today? How many other professionals did you interview prior to choosing one? Have you periodically interviewed others as your needs have changed?

Pitfall #4: Never Getting A Second Opinion

A good way to grade your existing advisors and test the competencies of potential team members is to get a second opinion. Good advisors are busy helping clients like you. They are professionals and will expect to be paid for the analysis. Sure, there are plenty of advisors who will analyze your situation for free, hoping to dazzle you with their recommendations to earn your investment, insurance or legal business. However, the goal of these people is to sell you something. As mentioned previously, your planning team should consist of talented advisors who want your business—but don't *need* your business. Treat them fairly by paying them for their time and advice. Stepping through this short-term engagement exercise will provide insight into how organized their firm is and how well they communicate.

Of the flaws discussed here, never getting a second opinion is the most damaging. Unfortunately, it is also the most common. It is most damaging because a second opinion is the primary way of identifying planning mistakes or noticeable omissions from your planning.

Just as good physicians encourage patients to get a second opinion, good advisors should encourage their clients to do the same. This is the only way for you to adequately judge an advisor's performance. You are no more qualified to look at a trust document or tax return and see flaws as we are to examine a report on a chest CT and see a misdiagnosis! With your entire financial future banking on the success of your professional advisors, it amazes us how few of you have paid another professional to review your existing advisor's work. If your life were in jeopardy, wouldn't you get a second opinion? Isn't your financial life important as well?

Case Study: The Value of a Second Opinion

In 2000, co-author David Mandell's prior law firm was retained to perform a self-audit by a long-term client. The client, an extremely successful businessman, was concerned that he might become an IRS target. He hired the firm to do an audit of his personal and various businesses' income tax returns for the prior five years. What the firm found was shocking.

Even though this client had used four different accounting firms for his various returns (including a well-known 500-plus person firm), the taxes he had paid were far from what he owed. Luckily for him, it was an *overpayment*—in millions of dollars.

That is a true story. Because of the self-imposed audit that David's firm oversaw, the client was able to file for a huge refund from the IRS and state tax agency. Luckily for him, he was concerned about poor tax advice and spent the money to hire the firm to perform the audit.

Self Test: Have you ever paid an outside advisor to review your attorney's work? Your CPA's work? Your investment advisor's work? If not, why not?

Pitfall #5: Hiring "Yes" Men And Women

When we asked numerous successful clients what advice they would give, we received many suggestions. The suggestions included: "find experts," "don't look for 'Yes Men'," and "hire people smarter than you are." We put them all in the same category because the end result is the same. The wealthy have wealth because they did something very well. The very successful realize that they can't be experts at everything. Some rightfully believe that they are just as smart or smarter than many advisors, and if they could focus on finance or law they would become at least as capable as their advisors. They also realize that it would take many years to reach an adequate level of expertise. To Leverage their time, they instead choose to hire experts in different disciplines to work for them. The wealthy are likely paying someone less per hour than they could earn running their businesses. An additional benefit is that the advisors are getting the work done in *less time* than it would take the Doctors to do it themselves.

Our most successful clients have told us that they have enough "Yes Men" in their lives. Interestingly, they cherish the moments when advisors stand up to them to challenge their positions or question their decisions. They see this as an opportunity to improve their position. Some even enjoy the challenge.

Pitfall #6: Not Accepting That Complexity Requires Outside Experts

If your medical condition necessitated a stent, you would not go to a general practitioner to have it done. Moreover, you would not consult with any specialists outside of cardiology. In fact, you would not be satisfied with just any cardiologist. You would seek an interventional cardiologist to handle this procedure. The point is that medicine is highly specialized. If you have a specific issue, you want a physician properly trained and experienced with this particular issue.

The notion of seeking out a specialist to help you with your health concerns may be obvious. However, we can attest that in the areas of law, taxation and finance, Doctors fail to see the parallels to the world of medicine. To illustrate this, we should consider the area of taxation. The ever-changing United States tax law is perhaps the most complex set of rules ever created by one society. The lengthy and confusing Internal Revenue Code is only the beginning. It is supplemented by IRS revenue rulings, private letter rulings, tax memoranda, announcements, circulars, and tax court and federal court cases that add additional, bewildering complexity. If you step foot into any law library, you are likely to see an entire floor dedicated to tax law, tax rules and tax cases. Suffice to say, no single person can possibly be an expert in all areas of tax law.

Nevertheless, a physician will typically rely on one CPA to serve as a "tax advisor" in all areas of tax. The taxation issues that require guidance typically include retirement planning, income structuring (salary vs. bonus), payroll tax, whether to be an "S" or "C" corporation, whether to implement a deferred compensation plan, estate tax planning, taxation on sales of real estate, individual tax returns, corporate tax returns and buying or selling a practice. All of these areas are actually particular sub-specialties that require a unique knowledge base. As if this wasn't bad enough, we have seen many Doctors ask their tax advisor to guide them in areas that are far outside of tax planning altogether—such as asset protection or investing.

We cannot tell you how many times we have attempted to work with a Doctor's CPA or attorney to implement a particular strategy and run into the same problem. It was obvious that this advisor had little experience in the Doctor's area of concern. Even some accountants who have many Doctor clients are unaware of the opportunities available to help the Doctors save money. When this situation occurs, the client suffers needlessly.

Because the primary advisor is so fearful of bringing in a specialized advisor who may "steal" the client—even if there is a suitable specialist in the same firm—the attorney or CPA will take an over-protective stance, failing to admit his or her shortcomings to the Doctor and recommend another specialist. One reasonable alternative would be for the advisor to admit his or her lack of experience in the area and agree to review the area in question, and then charge the client for the time needed to "get up to speed." Most advisors are afraid to do this. Possibly, they are afraid that the client will see them as "inadequate." Instead, the advisor will tell the client the idea "doesn't work" without giving any substantial reason (see the "warning signs" below). In the end, the Doctor is clueless as to what is really going on—and the problem is not solved.

Self Test: Ask your CPA or attorney which tax areas noted above are his or her **expertise**. Ask the advisor how he or she would handle an issue for you that occurred outside of this area.

Self Test: Ask your tax advisor if he or she does **asset protection planning**. If the answer is yes, ask a follow up question: "Have you ever created a domestic asset protection trust or self-settled foreign asset protection trust?"

Pitfall #7: Failing To Insist On Advisor Coordination

Even if you have a team of highly-experienced advisors in the fields of tax, law, insurance and investments working for you, your plan can still be in complete disarray. If the advisors are not collaborating to utilize their collective expertise to implement a comprehensive, multi-disciplinary plan for your benefit, your planning will suffer significantly.

All too often, we see the symptoms of such a lack of coordination. Clients who come to our offices often have paid a technically capable attorney to create a very comprehensive living trust, but the family's assets have not yet been titled to the trust (potentially making the document useless). We frequently see life insurance policies and life insurance trusts that, because the proper steps were not taken to combine the two vehicles, do not work as they should. As a result the death benefit of the insurance may be unnecessarily taxed at rates as high as 50%. We notice investment accounts that are managed like they are in a pension, with no regard for taxation—and the end result is often a 24% to 45% reduction in the gain of the investments. Conflicting advice from professionals in different areas OR a lack of respect for work done by other professionals often leads to planning inertia or just plain bad planning.

Like the radiologist, surgeon, and anesthesiologist who must work together to make sure a patient has a successful surgery, your CPA, attorney and financial advisors MUST work together to help you successfully achieve your financial goals. If the surgeon never saw the films or charts, or the anesthesiologist and surgeon didn't speak, it would be difficult to obtain optimal results for a surgical patient.

Self Test: How often do your CPA, attorney, financial and insurance advisors sit down to discuss and coordinate your planning? Once per quarter? Once per year? Ever?

Warning Signs That You Are Ill-Advised

Do any of these "warning signs" that you are ill-advised seem familiar? If so, you are likely suffering from flawed professional advisory relationships:

- You have had the same advisors for years—and never interviewed prospective competitors
- Your advisors don't bring you detailed analyses of your practice and personal situation, complete with helpful suggestions, annually
- You have no idea of the true professional sub-specialties of your advisors
- Your present advisors reject ideas you bring to them without providing detailed written explanations of why they don't make sense for you
- Your present advisors have never told you that a certain idea required further research for which they would need to charge you
- You rarely, if ever, have paid for second opinions from other professionals
- You have trusts, partnerships or other legal entities which may not be funded
- Your CPA, attorney, and financial advisors do not meet periodically to coordinate your planning
- You stay with your present advisor(s) out of lethargy, guilt, or an "if it ain't broke, don't fix it" mentality

The Diagnosis

In the first three Lessons, you have learned very valuable philosophical lessons. The misunderstanding and misuse of these lessons have been the major roadblocks to financial success for most people. Now that you are in the proper frame of mind—keeping an open-mind, recognizing the importance of Leverage, and understanding why you need advisors to help you—you are ready to learn the practical lessons and applications that *For Ohio Doctors* offers.

The next seven Lessons on working less and building more are valuable guides that are built upon the experiences we have had in working with our most successful clients. Inside each Lesson are many chapters with specific suggestions, strategies or tools that may or may not be applicable to helping you achieve your goals. A mentioned strategy might be perfect for one family but detrimental to another. Only by collaborating with your team of advisors can you properly determine the techniques and tools appropriate for your needs. Together, you can identify your needs, analyze all available options, make decisions and implement chosen strategies.

You are now ready to continue. It is illogical to focus on accumulating more wealth only to lose it to inadequate, uncoordinated planning. This is why we want to start by teaching you how to protect your existing and future wealth. The next part—Lesson #4—will teach you how to avoid financial catastrophes. Once you know how to avoid mistakes, you can work on implementing strategies to help build and protect wealth, described in Lessons 5 through 10.

LESSON 4

First, Do No Harm

Many people believe the roadmap to financial success includes focusing on a goal, putting your head down and relentlessly pushing ahead until you reach it. Though hard work and perseverance are common personality traits of most physicians, another key ingredient to long-term financial success exists among all of our most successful Doctor clients. Every single successful medical family we've encountered was able to avoid, or at least mitigate, catastrophic financial losses through a combination of luck and risk management planning. Since we do not espouse luck as a prudent strategy, we will focus on managing financial risk by planning to protect your family from financial disasters.

One common financial disaster that can result in a significant loss of assets is a civil lawsuit. Lessons #5 and #6 will offer almost two dozen specific solutions to help mitigate litigation risks. Though malpractice lawsuits are a significant risk for physicians in today's society, they do not pose the most significant risk to one's wealth if proper professional negligence insurance is in place.

This Lesson will explore those additional—and more devastating—financial disasters that must be addressed if you wish to achieve and maintain wealth. These risks include both health-related and financial events. More specifically, this section of the book will teach you how to:

- Protect your family from an unexpected death
- Keep paying your bills even if you can't work due to disability

- Handle long-term care expenses before they arise
- Make sure you don't run out of money in retirement
- Avoid healthcare and insurance threats
- Avoid employment threats
- Obtain insurance to protect against business and personal risks

4-1

Protecting Your Family from an Unexpected Death

The emotional distress caused by the premature death of a loved one cannot be exaggerated. Long before the psychological scars begin to heal, financial devastation for surviving family members may begin. If proper planning is not undertaken, the value of the medical practice, which could be a saleable asset to help the family, may be lost.

There are various obstacles to successful financial planning in the case of unforeseen death simply because none of us knows when our time will come. The 2003 National Safety Council's study on deaths (http://www.nsc.org/lrs/statinfo/odds.htm) and the 1999 US Census Bureau's Statistical Abstract of the United States, which surveyed the year 1997, reported the following statistics in regard to unforeseen death types:

- There is a 1 in 24 chance (4.17%) that you will ultimately die from a stroke
- There is a 4% chance you will die from an accident or the adverse effects of one

When you add these two risks together, you can see that approximately 1 in 12 people will die from an unforeseen cause. In addition, a number of people will find out they are terminally ill and their families will not be able to purchase personal life insurance to help them manage the financial burden created when they pass away.

Another obstacle to successful financial planning in the case of unforeseen death is that most people don't enjoy contemplating, let alone discussing, the death of a family member. As a result, few families are financially or emotionally prepared for this traumatic event.

In this chapter, we will discuss two financial losses that can occur at the time of death:

- Loss of income
- Loss of an estate (via estate taxes and probate costs)

Physicians and their families can use particular insurance planning strategies to efficiently manage the risks that often result from the premature death of a family member. In addition, proper legal documentation must be created to allow for efficient handling of financial matters at death, including offering the executor of the estate the legal power to effectuate a transfer without having to obtain court approval. If there are unnecessary delays in this process, the patients will seek another practitioner, thus diminishing the value of the practice further. This chapter aims to teach you how to protect wealth from the death of a patriarch or matriarch. Let's explore how this can be done.

Income Protection

One key to successful planning is the ability to put one's fear of death aside and focus on the financial impact a death may have on a family. The first financial impact of death, especially for younger families, is lost income. Once a father or mother has passed away, he or she obviously will not earn any more income. If the family hasn't met all of its saving goals (most don't until they are well into their fifties), there will be a significant financial strain from the death. The key to maintaining wealth is ensuring the family will not be wiped out financially by the death of the income-producing Doctor. To show you how significant this loss of income can be, consider the following.

The present value of twenty years of lost income for the Average American family (with $45,000 of annual income) is approximately $636,000. That means that, at the time of death, the family would be in the same financial situation if they had 20 years of income OR had a lump sum of $636,000.

For the family of a physician who earns $300,000 per year, the present value of twenty years of lost income is over $4,200,000. For the family of a very successful specialist who earns $1,000,000 per year, the present value of 20 years of lost income is $14 million. The simple estimate implies that a family needs approximately 14 times the annual income of the breadwinner to replace twenty years of lost income. If you have a younger breadwinner or a breadwinner who just intends to work 30 more years, the multiple used to approximate the present value of future income is 18 times one year's income.

What these examples illustrate is that a family needs life insurance in the amount of at least 14 times the annual income of each wage earner just to keep them on track to meet their financial goals (assuming that their current earnings were keeping them on track before the death). Also, this estimate assumes no adjustment for inflation. Over twenty to twenty five years, the value of a dollar is reduced by 50%. For that reason, you could estimate that a family needs between 14 and 28 times one year's after-tax salary to replace twenty years of income. Do you have enough life insurance to protect your family and leave them in a position to meet their goals if you were to die?

In addition to lost income, the value of the practice itself—often an asset of significant value—will be lost if proper estate planning doesn't establish a trustee with a power of sale. This is the best possible option since a power of attorney expires upon death in Ohio and the agent or executor would have no authority to sell after death. The asset value of the practice will be significantly diminished or lost altogether if the sale needs approval from the court. Proper estate planning and a well-crafted and documented exit strategy (like a buy-sell agreement, see Chapter 5-5) to sell the medical practice are key elements to have in place long before an unexpected death occurs.

Estate Preservation

Although Lesson #9 focuses on the most common estate planning tools Doctors should utilize, it is important for us to mention in this chapter the impact an unforeseen death can have on an estate. In particular, the second most significant financial disaster that may occur after a premature death can be the decimation of the estate through taxes and fees.

For example, if the sudden death involves the loss of a husband and a wife (or the second of the two of them passes on), there could be significant estate tax liabilities. Estate taxes and unnecessary probate costs can throw a wrench into a family business or real estate portfolio. If there is valuable family real estate or a family business, these assets may have to be sold to generate liquidity to pay the tax bill. The most financially astute Doctors never let taxes or laws dictate when they sell their assets. They make sure that they have adequate liquidity so they can wait out poor sellers' markets and never are forced to have a fire sale. This is a philosophy you must adopt as well if you want to fully protect your family.

There is on the horizon a new threat to family wealth transfer. As this volume goes to press, there are several bills in Congress that seek to impose new taxes. One of those would eliminate a tax that affects any taxpayer—regardless of wealth—that owns real estate, stocks or other capital assets that appreciate in value. Under federal tax law for all but 3 years of recent history, capital assets enjoy a "stepped up" tax basis at death. That means that if your family inherits appreciated stocks or real estate from you and wish to sell them, there would be no capital gains tax, because, while they may inherit the asset, they don't inherit your basis. The basis gets "stepped up" to the date of death value. Congress eliminated stepped up basis in the mid-1980s, but in so doing created such problems for taxpayers and the IRS that they repealed the elimination, retroactively, 3 years later. Our Congress appears to have no institutional memory of this mistake, because almost every Bill before Congress as this book goes to press seeks to do away with this useful tax and recordkeeping benefit. A loss of "stepped up" basis would further reduce the value of virtually every Doctor's estate as it passes to loved ones.

Many clients use life insurance to preserve their estates. The intelligent use of life insurance has helped astute families avoid financial disasters and maintain their level of affluence from generation to generation. Conversely, many Average Americans with less savvy financial planning strategies have lost valuable assets through the combination of poor planning, unlucky timing of deaths, and unexpected taxes. Because we don't know when we are going to die, and certainly don't know whether it will be a good time to sell assets when we do die, we have to rely on insurance policies to give our families the financial flexibility to withstand poor markets that may exist if we die unexpectedly. This, and many other points, will be discussed in greater detail in Lesson #9.

The Diagnosis

Since our surviving family members are likely unable (or possibly unwilling) to support themselves in the event of our premature deaths, we have to consider ways to protect our families. The easier way to do this is by purchasing the correct life insurance policy or policies. Since life insurance is cheaper when the applicant is younger and healthier, and is often unavailable once the applicant develops serious health issues, we strongly suggest you secure life insurance at as early an age as possible. Before you get upset at the idea of purchasing life insurance, you need to understand how this can benefit you and your family.

You will learn in Lesson #5 that many states offer complete asset protection of the cash values of life insurance policies. Even Ohio, which generally has creditor-friendly laws, offers complete protection to the cash value of life insurance policies, provided these policies meet certain requirements. You will learn in Lesson #9 how life insurance is an important piece of the estate planning puzzle. In Lesson # 8, you will learn why the wealthiest Americans invest as much as they can into life insurance policies and how this strategy increases their after-tax investment returns significantly over those returns of mutual funds or most managed investment accounts. From this chapter, you need only understand that life insurance is the only way to protect your family from the financial disaster of a premature death. For those of you who have partners in your medical practice or outside businesses, the next Lesson will explain how devastating a death can be to a business, the partners, and the partners' families. We provide you efficient strategies for addressing this risk.

4-2

Paying Bills Even if You Can't Work

If you are like most of our other clients with high incomes, the single greatest asset your family has is your earning power. This reality motivates people to buy life insurance as protection against a premature death. For most people, purchasing life insurance is "common sense." While the majority of people with whom we speak are underinsured, they do have at least some protection against a premature death. However, Average American professionals, entrepreneurs, business owners, and executives often overlook a more dangerous threat to their long-term financial stability—their own disability. What is the risk that the average individual will suffer a disability? According to marketing materials of more than one life insurance company:

> **"Probability of at least one long-term disability (90 days or longer) occurring before age 65 is: 50% for someone age 25; 45% for someone age 35; 38% for someone age 45; and 26% for someone age 55."**

Inadequate disability income insurance coverage can be more costly than death, divorce, or a lawsuit. Responsible financial planning includes *planning for the best possible future while protecting against the worst possible events*. No one ever plans on becoming disabled—though **half** of those aged 25 will have a disability of three months or longer at least once. This chapter explains not only why you need disability insurance, but also what to look for in a disability policy.

The Need For Disability Insurance

In our opinion, the disability of the family breadwinner can be more financially devastating to a family than premature death. In both cases, the breadwinner will be unable to provide any income for the family; however, in the case of death, the deceased earner is no longer an expense to the family. Yet, if the breadwinner suddenly becomes disabled, he or she still needs to be fed, clothed, and cared for by medical professionals or family members. In many cases, the medical care alone can cost hundreds of dollars per day. Thus, with a disability, income is reduced or eliminated *and* expenses increase. This can be a devastating turn of events and can lead to creditor problems and even bankruptcy.

If you are older (near retirement) and have saved a large enough sum of money to immediately fund a comfortable retirement, then you probably don't need disability income protection. Of course, you may have some long-term care concerns, which is covered in the next chapter. On the other hand, if you are under 50 years old, or if you are older than 50 and have several pre-college age children, you should consider *the right* disability insurance a necessity. The challenge is determining what type of disability income policy is "right" for you.

Employer Provided Coverage Often Inadequate

If you are an employee of a university, HMO, or other large corporation, your employer may provide long-term disability coverage. The premiums are probably discounted from what you would pay for a private policy. We advise you take a good look at what the employer-offered policy covers, and buy a private policy if you and the insurance professional on your advisory team decide you need it. For many people, this makes a lot of sense because employer-provided group policies are often inadequate. They may limit either the term of the coverage or the amount of benefits paid. For instance, benefits may last only a few years or benefit payments may represent only a small part of your annual compensation. Since this is most commonly an employer-paid benefit, the money received during your disability will be taxed as income to you. For most, this arrangement would result in your taking home less than half of the original amount in your paycheck after taxes are paid!

Give Yourself A Check-Up

Most people with employer-provided disability insurance coverage will find the benefits inadequate. To help you determine where your existing coverage may be lacking, we have provided some questions for you to ask when you are giving yourself an insurance check-up. When you are ultimately working with the insurance professional on your advisory team, you should keep some of these questions in mind as well. They will help you better compare coverage options from different companies so that you can find the best policy for your specific circumstances and goals. Below is a list of some questions you should ask yourself as well as short explanations of the appropriate answers:

- How long does the disability coverage last?
- How much is the benefit? (Some plans may cap the benefits at $5,000 per month.)
- What percentage of your income is covered? (Generally, you cannot receive more than 60% of income and the benefit is capped at $7,500 or $10,000, depending

on your age.) Though most group LTD plans are good for the purpose that they serve, they are only a partial cure. Because of the limitations or 'cap,' they have a built–in discrimination against higher income employees—like you!

- Who pays the premiums? (TIP: If you pay the premiums yourself, and not as a deductible expense through your business or practice, your benefits will be tax-free.) You may be seduced by the income tax deduction of the premiums, but the extra tax burden today is much easier to swallow than the tax burden will be if you suffer a disability and have a significantly reduced income *and* increased expenses. When you and your family need the money the most, you will have more.
- Is the policy portable, or convertible, to an individual policy if you leave the group? If so, do you maintain your reduced group rate?
- If your business distributes all earnings from the corporation at year-end in the way of bonuses to all owners/partners (typical of C-corps as a way to avoid double taxation), you should see whether these amounts are covered by the group policy. If not, and if bonuses or commissions make up a substantial part of your income (which we have seen to be the case with many people), you'll probably need supplemental coverage.
- What is the definition of disability in the group policy? Own-occupation, any occupation, or income-replacement? (Please see the discussion of these three terms below.)
- Are your overhead expenses covered if you are disabled? If you can't perform your duties at work, will the business keep paying you? If you can't generate income for the business, many of your expenses will keep on piling up, won't they? For professionals, a business overhead expense policy also covers hiring an outside professional to replace the insured during disability for up to two years.

Getting The Best Insurance Coverage For The Money

Now that you have given yourself a check-up and realize that you may need a new or supplemental insurance policy, you need to know what to look for in order to get the best coverage available at a reasonable rate. The following questions are important for you to ask when considering a disability policy.

What is the benefit amount? Most policies are capped at a benefit amount that equals 60% of income. Some states and insurance companies have monthly maximums as well. You have to ask yourself how much money your family would need if you were to become disabled. Generally, you want to find companies that offer at least 60% of pre-disability after-tax income with maximums of at least $7,500 or $10,000 monthly. There are additional monthly benefits of $5,000 to $25,000 per month available through more specialized channels for those high earners who want more monthly income than the traditional limits.

What is the waiting period? This is the period of time that you must be disabled before the insurance company will pay you disability benefits. The longer the waiting period before benefits kick in, the less your premium will be. Essentially, the waiting period serves as a deductible relative to time—you cover your expenses for the waiting period, then the insurance company steps in from that point forward. This is not unlike the deductible you have on your car, except that auto insurance deductibles are in the form of amounts paid ($100, $250, $500, etc.), not relative to a period of time. If you have adequate sick leave, short-term disability, and an emergency fund, and can support a longer waiting period, choose a policy with a longer waiting period to save money. Though waiting periods can last as long as 730 days, a 90-day waiting period may give you the best coverage for your money.

How long will coverage last? It's a good idea to get a benefit period of coverage that lasts until age 65, at which point Social Security payments will begin. Be aware that many policies cover you for only two to five years. Unless you are 62 to 65 years old, this would be an inadequate period because most people want coverage that pays them until age 65. Unless you are so young that you haven't yet had time to qualify for Social Security, a policy that provides lifetime benefits, at costly premiums, is generally not worth the added expense.

What is the definition of disability in your policy? Definitions vary from insurance company to insurance company, and even from policy to policy within the same company. The definition of disability used for a particular policy is of the utmost importance. The main categories are Own-occupation, Any-occupation, and Loss of Income. The Own-occupation policies, which pay a benefit if you can't continue your own occupation (even if you can and do work another occupation after the disability), are the most comprehensive and, of course, the most expensive. Two important elements to look for in an Own-occupation policy are:

1. Are you forced to go back to work in another occupation?
2. Will you receive a partial benefit if you go back to work slowly after the disability and still make less than you did before the disability?

Does the policy offer partial benefits? If you are able to work only part-time instead of your previous full-time hours, will you receive benefits? Unless your policy states that you are entitled to partial benefits, you won't receive anything unless you are totally unable to work. Also, are Extended Partial Benefits paid if you go back to work and suffer a reduction in income because you cannot keep up the same rigorous schedule you had before you became disabled? For example, this would be an important benefit for anesthesiologists, as they often work excessive hours in their younger years and most likely will work less after any disability.

Important Note: Partial benefits may be added on as a rider in some policies and should be seriously considered, as only 3% of all disabilities are total disabilities. Some policies even have a recovery benefit that, in the event that a business has lost clients during the disability due to the insured not being able to service them and the insured has suffered a loss of income because of this, there may be a benefit payable. The insured does not have to be disabled at all—there can be just loss of income due to disability-related attrition.

Is business overhead expense (BOE) covered? When you go out on your own, the last thing you think about is how you *won't* be able to pay your bills. Whether you have $10,000 or $20,000 of monthly disability benefit, you likely don't have enough to cover your lost income PLUS the costs of running the business. Though most companies have limited how much an individual can get in monthly benefit (often 60% of after-tax monthly income—capped at $10,000 per month), many carriers still offer up to $25,000 or more per month to cover business overhead expense. Many business owners who contact us have failed to implement this important defensive policy.

Is it non-cancelable or guaranteed renewable? The difference between these two terms—non-cancelable and guaranteed renewable—is very important. If a policy is "non-cancelable," you will pay a fixed premium throughout the contract term. Your premium will not go up for the term of the contract. If it is "guaranteed renewable," it means you cannot be cancelled, but your premiums could go up. As long as non-cancelable is in the description of the policy, you are in good shape.

How financially stable is the insurance company? Before buying a policy, check the financial soundness of your insurer. If your insurer goes bankrupt, you may have to shop for a policy later in life, when premiums are more expensive. Standard & Poor's top rating for financial stability is AAA. A.M. Best Co. uses A++ as its top rating for financial strength. Duff and Phelps rates companies on their ability to pay claims and uses AAA as its highest rating. Moody's uses Aa1 to rate excellent companies. There are no guarantees in life, but buying a policy from a highly rated company is the safest bet you can make and we would not recommend gambling on your disability insurance to save a few dollars.

Other issues to consider when determining if you are getting the best disability insurance coverage for your money so that you can avoid financial disasters caused by the disability of the breadwinner in your family include:

- Increased Coverage
- Cost-of-Living Increases
- Waiver-of-Premium
- Return-of-Premium Waiver
- Unisex Pricing
- HIV Rider
- Multi-Life Pricing Discounts
- Protection of Future Pension Contributions

Disability Of A Business Partner

The disability of a business partner has the potential to be just as financially crippling as the disability of the family breadwinner. There is a strong financial tie between business partners. The financial dependence between business partners can be even stronger than that between spouses. When a partner becomes disabled, the business will undoubtedly lose significant revenue, while possibly facing increased costs in an attempt to replace the disabled partner. This will put a significant strain on the remaining partner who now needs to run the business without the help of the deceased partner and replace the income of the disabled partner. Absent a buy-sell agreement tied to disability income insurance with a lump sum payout to generate funds to buy out the disabled partner and have sufficient funds to pay for a replacement physician, the end result could be financial devastation for the remaining partner and the business.

The Diagnosis

The likelihood of a disability is greater than the probabilities of a premature death, a lawsuit, and a bankruptcy combined. Doctors see patients every day who are hurt and can't go back to work. Most Doctors know this is a risk, but fail to adequately address it in their own planning. A disability income insurance policy is the best way to protect your future income. We cannot overstate the importance of having a comprehensive disability policy as part of any personal financial plan and a policy as a funding mechanism for a buy-sell agreement in the case of the disability of a business partner. This is handled in Lesson #5, where you will learn how to turn your practice into a Financial Fortress. For now, let's move on to the next chapter, where we will show you how to manage health risks that may arise after you retire.

4-3

Handling Long-Term Care Needs Before They Arise

Some people are lucky to accumulate wealth because they are in the right place at the right time. Others are unfortunate and lose assets because they are in the wrong place at the wrong time. Doctors obviously don't believe in relying on luck to build wealth. If they did, they wouldn't spend so many years in training. Would it surprise you to learn that, after all that hard work to build careers in medicine, most Doctors ultimately leave their wealth accumulation and asset protection to chance?

We are not saying that Doctors don't work hard after they get into practice. To the contrary, the opposite is true. Doctors work too hard when they need to be working smarter. This chapter explains how Doctors can efficiently protect themselves from long-term care risks, get a valuable tax deduction, and preserve their valuable retirement assets. This is a key to working less, as it allows a retiring Doctor to quit practice with a smaller, yet more effective, safety net!

Before we discuss long-term care insurance and how to most efficiently purchase the right policy for you, we need to first see how big a risk the expenses associated with long-term care really are.

Why Is Long-Term Care A Big Risk?

According to the AARP Research Report on Long-Term Care (Ari N. Houser, AARP Public Policy Institute, October 2007—http://www.aarp.org/research/longtermcare/ternds/fs27r_ltc.html), on average, two-thirds (69%) of people over age 65 today will need some long-term care. The average duration of need, over a lifetime, is about three years. Women live longer and have higher rates of disability than men, so older women are more likely to need care (79% v. 58%), and, on average, need care for longer periods (3.7 years v. 2.2 years).

In the U.S., the average stay in a nursing home is between two and three years. In some areas of the country, the cost of nursing home care or quality around-the-clock in-home care may be $200-$300 per day. This means that the average home healthcare stay costs between $150,000 and $320,000. Additionally, the U.S. Health Care Administration reports that costs are increasing 5.8% per year and are expected to more than triple in the next 20 years. At these projected rates, the costs may be between $500,000 and $1,000,000 by the time you or your spouse need long-term care. Are you sure that you, your parents, and your in-laws all have hundreds of thousands of dollars in "extra" funds within your retirement and estate plans to cover this highly plausible expense?

Long-Term Care Insurance (LTCI) covers health insurance costs for those people who cannot take care of themselves. These costs may include nursing home care, in-home care, and many other expenses. This chapter will explain why and how the most financially astute Doctors make long-term care planning a high priority in their planning. More specifically, this chapter will discuss the need for LTCI, why it is often overlooked, why the government won't help you, what types of coverage exist, and how those different types of coverage can help you.

The Need For Long-Term Care Insurance (LTCI)

There are two basic reasons why many Americans may need to obtain long-term care insurance. First, modern advancements in medicine, science, and technology have helped increase the average life expectancy of people. Predictably, with this increased life expectancy, there is a greater chance that people may suffer a debilitating illness that will require them to seek significant long-term care. There are incurable diseases that don't kill you, but will leave you requiring assistance. Neurological disorders like Alzheimer's are perfect examples. An Alzheimer's patient could need significant care for 15 or 20 years before dying. The advances in medicine that promote longevity often come with a hefty price tag for some families.

With the increasing life expectancies and increasing costs of medical expenses, long-term care will impact an increasing percentage of the population and can be very expensive. Doctors are aware of increased life expectancies and rising medical costs, but need to be consciously aware that long-term care costs can easily wipe out retirement savings and eliminate any inheritance you would have otherwise left for children or grandchildren (or would have received from your parents or in-laws). When armed with the right information, Doctors can make the decision to include LTCI in their comprehensive plans and work with their advisors to do so as cheaply and efficiently as possible.

In addition, having a plan for long-term care demonstrates a desire to have quality care in the event it is needed and represents a financial prioritization of that desire. Having a system in place will make it more likely that necessary care and assistance is provided *earlier*. Children of aging parents often delay getting help because they are concerned about how it will be afforded. According to the National Census Bureau (2006), the average national income is $48,201 and adult children may be ill-prepared to spend from their own income for supplemental care and reluctant to spend from their parents' funds to obtain the needed help.

An AARP Study, *Valuing the Invaluable: A New Look at the Economic Value of Family Caregiving* (June 2007), found that the contributions of family caregivers often go unnoticed, but in fact their contributions are the backbone of the nation's long-term care system with an estimated economic value of **$350 billion** in 2006. The study concludes that, "the unpaid services family caregivers provide are not without costs to the caregivers and society. Lost time at work, lost benefits and declining health can add to the emotional and physical strain of actually caring for a loved one. The study underscores the need to better support family caregivers through programs that provide respite (a break from caring), tax credits, information and other supports." Having a plan in place makes it easier to get needed care earlier, while minimizing stress and financial strain on family members or other loved ones.

Why Most People Fail To Secure LTCI

Before we discuss the various types of LTCI policies, it is important that we address some reasons that LTCI is not often a part of people's financial plans. In this section, we will answer the following questions:

- Why won't the government cover these long-term care costs?
- Why don't most people have LTCI?

Why Won't The Government Cover These Long-Term Care Costs?

To many people's surprise, the government will not cover long-term care costs the way people would like them to. Did you know that in Ohio, an individual does not qualify for government provided LTCI coverage (Medicaid) unless his or her net worth is LESS THAN $1,500? In addition, once that individual begins receiving Medicaid benefits, the state takes all but $40 per week of income from the patient. Many Average Americans and all Doctors would have to spend every last dollar of their savings before they could receive any health care help. Even if you may have more than enough saved to pay for these types of expenses, your potential health problem could wipe out your entire inheritance, which you had hoped would go to your children or grandchildren.

Incidentally, many of our clients buy LTCI policies on their parents, because they know they will have to take care of their parents if the need arises and they want to make sure that it does not affect their financial status. After all, such unplanned expenses could result in a major financial disaster and emotional problem. Imagine if you are getting ready to retire and suddenly one of your parents or in-laws gets sick and needs $75,000 to $150,000 per year of medical care. Unfortunately, this will most likely be paid with after-tax dollars if you do not plan accordingly and have LTCI.

Why Don't Most People Have LTCI?

You may be surprised to learn that many people do not have LTCI. However, many people do not want to bear the risk of self-insuring their long-term care costs. So why haven't more people purchased LTCI? In one word: ignorance. We see clients insure their lives, homes, cars, and income, but not events (like long-term care and disability) that have the next highest probability of occurring in one's lifetime (behind only death). Why? It could be an "it's not going to happen to me" mentality. It could be a false sense of security that Social Security will take care of things. It could also be frugality—that is, some Average Americans may not want to pay LTCI premiums for the next 20 to 40 years with only a 50% chance of getting a benefit from the insurance.

LTCI on Sale In Ohio.

The Ohio Long Term Care Partnership Plan went into effect in September, 2007. It creates a new partnership between the public sector (Ohio government) and the private sector (Insurance companies) to fund long term care.

The purpose of the Ohio partnership program is to increase the number of people covered by private LTCI and thereby reduce the number who end up relying on Medicaid. So Ohio modified its Medicaid eligibility rules to give a financial incentive for the purchase of LTCI policies.

If a person buys an LTCI policy meeting the program requirements and if they need long term care, their LTCI benefits will help pay for it, and Medicaid does not have to cover the cost. However, if the LTCI benefits run out, the individual can apply for Medicaid and NOT have to spend down all their assets. The individual will be able to keep assets equal to the LTCI benefits he received in addition to any other exempt assets. These assets are also exempt from Medicaid estate recovery.

Types of LTCI Policies

Now that you know why you need an LTCI policy, you need to know what you should look for in such a policy. Common types of policies include:

Traditional LTCI Policies: Traditional LTCI policies feature benefits, options, and riders that vary in availability and scope among carriers. These traditional policies do not have cash value, nor do they have a death benefit. Once a person becomes eligible for LTCI benefits, (inability to perform two of six Activities of Daily Living), the traditional policy pays a daily reimbursement for approved expenses up to the maximum daily benefit chosen by the insured. Upper and lower limits vary among carriers but are in the $20-$300 per day range. Benefits can be received for life or for a period of time, as determined by a total insurance dollar value of the policy, often referred to as "the pool of benefits." "Facility-only" or "facility and in-home care policies" are also available. Elimination periods (deductibles) apply and can range from 0 to 90 days.

Other features, options and riders that vary among carriers are inflation protection, bed reservations, alternative plan of care, restoration of benefits, personal care advisor, respite care, joint policy discounts, premium waiver, rate classes, nonforfeiture benefits, indemnity benefits, caregiver indemnity benefits, and 10 year paid-up, 20 year paid-up, and non-level payment options.

A major resistance to purchasing traditional LTCI is the possibility of paying long-lasting premiums, in conjunction with the fact that a person may never actually use the policy's benefits. If this is the reason you do not have LTCI, one should seek a carrier that offers paid-up policies and/or non-forfeiture riders. Paid-up policies will require yearly premiums for a specified number of years, usually 10 years or 20 years. After this time, premium payments stop and the insured owns the policy for life. Nonforfeiture riders allow the policy owner to name a beneficiary and, upon death, all premiums that have been paid are then paid to the named beneficiary, even if benefits have been received. However, the policy must be in force at the time of death for the beneficiary to receive the paid premiums.

Universal Life Insurance Policies: A different method of addressing long-term care needs is to purchase a Universal Life Insurance policy with an attached rider that can accelerate all or a portion of the death benefit to be used for approved long-term care costs should the need arise. Benefits are received in much the same way as a traditional long-term care policy. This requires a single premium payment and purchase of a paid up policy. In most cases, an existing cash value policy can be exchanged with no tax consequence (consult your tax professional regarding your particular situation). The larger the single premium paid, the larger the death benefit that can be converted to daily benefit maximums for approved long-term care costs divided over a two-year, four-year or lifetime period at a decreasing daily maximum amount. The policy can be purchased to provide benefits for an individual or couple. ***These policies are especially attractive in Ohio because Ohio's 7% estate tax is not assessed against life insurance death benefits.***

Asset-based LTCI Policies: Some companies offer LTCI policies that allow people with assets to invest those assets and secure leveraged LTC coverage (about 4:1). These policies are unique in that they pay regardless of outcome: If you need coverage, it's there; if you cancel your coverage, you get your assets back; if you never make a claim and pass away without needing the policy, your children will inherit the assets you invested. When wealthier individuals have the funds to invest in this sort of policy, it can be a no-lose proposition.

Overall, the most important feature of a good LTCI policy is a financially sound insurance carrier. Do not consider purchasing the cheapest LTCI policy that you can find. LTCI carriers must have the financial strength to sustain their ability to pay claims well into the future, when the millions of baby boomers will begin needing LTC benefits. In a nutshell, don't be pennywise and pound foolish.

Using LTCI To Protect Your Retirement Income

Would you consider paying for your LTCI premiums if you could do so in a tax-deductible manner and do so over a finite period, like five or ten years? Would you consider paying for LTCI if you knew your heirs would receive every dollar of that premium at a later date?

Most baby boomers are saddled with the problem of having to take care of their children, themselves, and possibly their parents. The biggest financial disaster that can effect your retirement is that you, your spouse, your parents, or your in-laws suffer significant health problems and do not have a sound financial plan. The omission of a LTCI policy for family members would certainly destroy your retirement and any inheritances that might exist before the illness arose.

As established earlier in this chapter, the cost of long-term care for one person can be hundreds of dollars per day. For this reason, many physician clients don't just purchase long-term care insurance on themselves and their spouses, but they also buy long-term care insurance on their parents and in-laws. This is a growing trend we are noticing with our younger clients. They are buying LTCI policies on their parents and in-laws as a way to take care of their parents and protect their own retirements. There are many different bells and whistles to consider and a variety of LTCI payment options, which range from single payment to 10-payment, 20-payment and life-pay programs. Regardless of the payment option you choose, remember it is essential that you have LTCI to help you avoid financial disaster and protect you and your family's assets and retirement income.

The Diagnosis

Increasing medical costs and increasing life expectancies have led to ballooning spending on medical-related expenses. The reduced benefits of social insurance leave this increased burden to individuals and families. The impact of this expense can be devastating. Hundreds of thousands of dollars per year can be spent on long-term care. With a mental illness that could last ten or more years, the cost to a family could be millions of dollars. For retirees on a fixed budget, this could bankrupt them. For physician families, long-term care expenses could unnecessarily decimate the bulk of an estate. Luckily, LTCI is available and can be purchased through a corporation to make it more tax efficient. To learn another way to make sure that you, your parents, and your in-laws don't run out of money in retirement, read the next chapter.

4-4

Making Sure You Don't Run Out of Money in Retirement

The last, and one of the most important, financial disasters that we will discuss in this Lesson is the threat of running out of money during retirement. In this chapter, we will focus on the type of investments you can make to ensure that you don't run out of retirement savings.

This may sound odd, but the reason this chapter is so important is because we don't know when we will die. Because you cannot predict that day you will die, you can't possibly know how much in retirement savings you need or know how much retirement income you can afford to take out each year. Many retirees operate in such fear of running out of assets that they make the mistake of never touching their principal. This leads to a lower quality of life in retirement and to unnecessary estate taxes at death.

One of two things will certainly happen. You will be like many retirees and either die with money leftover for your heirs (and for the government via estate taxes) or live longer than expected (or spend too much) and run out of money in retirement. If you die with money leftover, we assume you would rather leave it to your heirs than to the federal government (this is where this chapter overlaps with the estate planning topics discussed in Lesson #9). We also assume that you don't want to have to rely on your children, your children's spouses, or your grandchildren to support you.

In this chapter, we will explain how certain Doctors get the most out of their retirement plan assets without risking running out of money in retirement. These savvy physicians get the most out of all of their assets. They also make sure that they don't have to experience financial and emotional disasters like running out of money in retirement and having to ask children or grandchildren to support them. A very valuable tool to help avoid this financial catastrophe is the Life Annuity.

Life Annuities

Retirement is a time for you to worry less, not more. You have already worked for thirty or more years, raised children, dealt with weddings (and maybe divorces), and handled thousands of day-to-day crises with your kids, among many other challenges. The last thing you want to do in retirement is worry about how you're going to support yourself and still leave something for your children, grandchildren, or your favorite charity. The Annuity and Insurance strategy eliminates the risk, "guarantees" you an adequate income in retirement, and optimizes the amount of money you can leave to your heirs and/or charities. In our best-case scenario, we can do all of this while reducing, if not eliminating, income and estate taxes in the process. The first part of that strategy mentioned above includes a life annuity.

The life annuity (not to be confused with the variable annuity) is designed by actuaries to pay interest and principal back to you over your lifetime. The amount the insurance company pays you is "fixed" and will not decrease if the stock market crashes or if interest rates fall. Moreover, if you outlive your life expectancy, the insurance company continues to pay you or your spouse for as long as you are alive. This is a good way to remove the investment risk of your retirement plan assets and "lock in" a fixed income in retirement.

You may be wondering how much income one can expect from a life annuity. To answer this question, simply look at the table below, which shows some numbers for clients of ours (some individuals, some couples) at varying ages. Of course, these numbers are only examples and may differ based on a variety of economic and medical factors. However, once a life annuity is purchased, the monthly or annual income amount cannot change (unless you purchase a cost of living rider that can increase the annual payout 1% to 3% annually).

If you are afraid of running out of money or are just uncomfortable with investment risk and how it may impact your retirement, you may want to consider what sophisticated clients have utilized for years—Life Annuities. Your multidisciplinary planning team can help you integrate life annuities into your planning to minimize risk, maximize after-tax retirement income, and maximize your estate. How life annuities can be part of an estate plan will be discussed next.

Client's Income from Life Annuity*

Client	Cost of Life Annuity	Monthly Income for Life
Dr. B—age 82	$433,000	$6,243
Dr. F—age 65	$1,000,000	$7,900
Dr. and Mrs. G—ages 67 & 63	$1,500,000	$9,200*

**Pays this amount as long as either Dr. or Mrs. G is alive.*

Using A Life Annuity To Leave Money For Heirs

Life Annuities also are valuable tools in helping you give funds to your children and grandchildren, when combined with life insurance and irrevocable trusts. In the case where the life annuity pays you more than you need to cover your cost of living, or where you have additional funds, we may recommend that you gift some of the "excess" to an irrevocable life insurance trust (more in Lesson #9, which focuses on estate planning) and buy life insurance to replace the value of the pension assets. Because pension may be worth as little as 25 cents on the dollar to your heirs after income and estate taxes (also discussed in the estate planning Lesson), this solution almost always gives more to the heirs, reduces income taxes paid on withdrawals, AND provides a fixed income stream in retirement. If you're not sure how this solution would work in your situation, please feel free to call us and we will run an illustration for you.

The Exclusion Ratio Can Save Taxes

Interestingly, there is a way to get tax-free income with a life annuity. If you purchase a life annuity with non-retirement plan assets, you will receive a significant tax benefit. Savvy Doctors know this and consequently implement a life annuity policy into their financial plans so that they can save even more in retirement and avoid financial disasters.

Each life annuity of this type has what is called an "exclusion ratio." This is the amount of the monthly or annual payment that is NOT income taxable. The older you are, the greater the tax-free percentage of the life annuity payment. For an 80-year old retiree, 70% of the annuity payment may be tax-free. As an example, if you received annual annuity payments of $100,000 that were 70% tax-free, you would pay tax on only $30,000 of that payment per year. Assuming a cumulative tax rate of 25%, you would pay only $7,500 in taxes on $100,000 of income. For this reason, many retirees like to purchase life annuities rather than live off of the interest of their savings and subject themselves to the risk of outliving their funds.

In the context of retirement plans, should you decide against utilizing the life annuity and take your chances with the stock market, it is possible that you could end up with a sizeable retirement plan balance at the time of your death. While you think this is desirable because it will benefit your children or grandchildren, you would be gravely mistaken. Many of your retirement plans will be subject to taxes of 80% when you die. Avoiding this hidden tax trap is a concern that warrants its own chapter within Lesson #9.

The Diagnosis

One of the biggest fears most Americans share is running out of money in retirement. Not only would this create a financial challenge, but it would also bring about a number of emotional issues. Most Doctors are "independent," responsible people who don't want to have to ask children for money or be forced into a nursing home. By seeking the assistance of your advisory team in addressing protection of your income in retirement, you can avoid this important financial challenge that is becoming more serious as people live longer while relying on retirement vehicles that were designed when life expectancies were twenty years less than they are today.

Before we proceed to strategies for structuring your practice, there are two more specific issues that every Doctor must understand—Healthcare/Insurance issues and Employment issues. These are growing risks that threaten Doctors' livelihoods more than medical malpractice and cannot be ignored.

4-5

Avoiding Healthcare & Insurance Issues

Before we can show you how to turn your practice into a Fortress and an Engine in the next Lesson, we have to show you what to avoid in your practice so that you don't cause any insurmountable financial damage to yourself or your practice. In addition to personal lawsuits, Doctors need to worry about business issues as well. This is consistent with our previous discussions about the "business of medicine."

Many physicians have a false sense of security and believe that malpractice insurance will protect them from lawsuits. We agree with you that a medical malpractice claim is not "likely" to result in a significant depletion of your estate. However, if you go to trial and lose, you could be in serious financial trouble. According to *Current Award Trends in Personal Injury* (Copyright 2007), half of all jury awards for medical malpractice claims in 2005 exceeded $1,184,000. The average medical malpractice jury award in 2005 was $3,830,000. If you consider that most doctors carry $1 million per occurrence medical malpractice liability insurance, half the doctors who lose a judgment will be out at least $200,000 and the average personal loss from a malpractice lawsuit judgment will exceed $2.8 million of the doctor's own money (after insurance has paid its limits).

In addition to medical malpractice threats, there are unexpected risks that carry an even higher likelihood of causing asset depletion. As a Doctor, business issues include liability for your business as well as liability that may result from regulatory issues and administrative investigations (i.e., OPMC, HCFA, Stark, HIPAA, OIG, etc.) and contract issues (i.e., Medicare/Medicaid Fraud investigations, over-billing claims, and refund audits from insurance companies). These types of claims are increasingly overshadowing the threat of medical malpractice because, unlike malpractice risks, they are usually not covered by insurance, leaving the physician to privately fund the defense costs out of pocket. In addition, mistakes in regulatory issues can even land a Doctor in jail. No other risks in this book carry such a serious threat.

In this chapter, we will discuss some of the specific healthcare and insurance-related risks, explain how they can be avoided, and offer suggestions on how to protect yourself from mistakes that may occur even when you do your best to avoid them.

HIPAA

The Health Insurance Portability and Accountability Act (HIPAA) of 1996 was originally enacted to enhance (not guarantee) certain health care insurance coverage for Americans. HIPAA also creates standardized national rules for maintaining (security) and protecting (confidential) patient medical information known as PHI (Protected Health Information). The failure to institute a good faith and reasonable office compliance program, to provide privacy notice to patients concerning their rights, to protect against the unauthorized release of confidential records and implement security safeguards for data in transit and maintained in the office could potentially place physician owners, their employees (including administrative office staff) and even business associates at grave risk for monetary fines and even criminal penalties for the unauthorized disclosure of PHI which is enforced by the OCR. Such penalties and sanctions could include civil penalties and fines for each violation ($100 per violation with a maximum penalty of $25,000/year for identical penalties) and for intentional violations of the law could even include criminal penalties (i.e. fines between $50,000—$250,000 and imprisonment terms from 1 to 10 years).

Over-Billing Issues

A key operational element in the business of medicine is the process of billing, coding and collecting professional fees from insurance companies. In some cases the payers are insurance companies and in other cases, the payers may be Medicare or Medicaid. Aside from the United States tax code (which in Lesson 7 we call the most complex system of rules in the history of mankind), the Medicare coding system may be the most complex system of rules ever created.

Despite best efforts to train administrative staff, medical offices are regularly audited by insurance companies, Medicare, and Medicaid. These audits routinely result in claims of over-billing. Many Doctors fight a losing battle against the large insurance companies (and their teams of attorneys) and ultimately have to surrender funds they previously collected for services rendered. Unfortunately, when the audit comes from Medicare or Medicaid, Doctors have more to lose than just money. A Doctor found guilty of Medicare fraud can actually go to jail. Because of the significant costs resulting from both Medicare fraud and commercial insurance carrier audits, we will examine them separately.

Medicare Fraud

Anyone who provides, or receives, healthcare services, could commit Medicare fraud. Fraud is defined as an intentional deception or misrepresentation that someone makes, knowing it is false, that could result in the payment of some unauthorized benefit. Abuse, on the other hand, involves actions that are inconsistent with sound medical, business, or fiscal practices. Abuse directly or indirectly results in higher costs to the Medicare program through improper payments that are not medically necessary. In the eyes of investigators, fraud and abuse both have the same effect. They steal valuable resources from the Medicare Trust Fund that would otherwise be used to provide benefits to Medicare recipients.

Fraud Investigations

The federal law enforcement agency responsible for investigating Medicare fraud is the Department of Health and Human Services, Office of Inspector General (HHS-OIG). In some cases, HHS-OIG may involve other agencies, such as the Federal Bureau of Investigation (FBI), the Internal Revenue Service (IRS), or the Postal Inspection Service.

Many complaints are simply misunderstandings or billing errors and can be resolved fairly easily. Some complaints help identify abusive billing practices. The Medicare contractor will educate the health care provider, collect any overpayment, and then follow up to make sure the provider does not make the same mistake again. Other complaints involve Medicare fraud. These cases often require long, complex investigations by federal law enforcement agencies.

Penalties

The U.S. Attorney General's office targets health care providers for civil and/or criminal prosecution. Some of the penalties for someone convicted of Medicare fraud are listed below.

- The False Claims Act provides fines up to $10,000, treble damages, and up to five years in prison.
- The Anti-Kickback provisions of the Social Security Act provide for fines of up to $25,000, and up to five years in prison.
- Civil monetary penalties provide for fines up to $50,000 and treble damages.
- RICO—the Racketeering Influenced and Corrupt Organization Act—has recently been used in Medicare fraud cases. Those convicted criminally can get prison terms of up to 20 years. Civil conviction under RICO provides for asset forfeiture.
- The Health Insurance Portability and Accountability Act, often called Kassebaum-Kennedy, created a new crime called Health Care Fraud. This crime allows up to 10 years in prison, or up to 20 years if serious bodily injury results, and even life in prison if death occurs.
- In addition to these penalties, the Department of Health Services can also exclude a health care provider from the Medicare system.

Commercial Carrier Audits

The practice of medicine has undergone a transformation with the advent of managed care healthcare delivery. Physicians need to be cognizant of the coding and billing requirements set forth by third party insurers for services rendered to ensure that their documentation satisfies the level of services provided. Managed Care organizations have recouped millions of dollars in refunds from providers who are unable to justify the level of services provided.

What physicians should realize is that a health insurer's fundamental existence and financial success require detailed analyses of each provider's practice patterns using information management systems that cost millions of dollars. Insurance companies make huge financial and personnel commitments to information technology over-utilization within the medical services industry.

As a result, carriers have extensive data banks that report the frequency with which each participating physician bills a particular CPT code and how that compares on a percentage basis with CPT codes billed by providers serving a similar patient population. The third party payers generate practice profiles by gathering data indicating how often a physician performs specific procedures (e.g., colonoscopy), where the physician those procedures (e.g., in or out of a hospital setting), and what CPT code the physician assigns to that procedure.

All the while, insurers are comparing each physician's practice profile to other providers. Additionally, insurers maintain data banks that compare how often a provider orders laboratory tests and which tests they order and, similarly, generate provider profiles based on this information.

Once the insurer determines that a physician or a group of physicians has billing/coding patterns that deviate from a calculated norm, the insurer will, in all likelihood, commence an expanded investigation. Unfortunately, physicians usually are unaware that their billing patterns deviate from such a norm until the insurer initiates an expanded investigation. As a result, physicians have little opportunity to amend their coding and billing practices and often are completely surprised when learning they are the subject of an insurance audit.

Licensure Investigations

Each state has set up, through its Department of Health, a licensure division that has jurisdiction to investigate and prosecute matters that are perceived to be indicative of professional misconduct. This prosecution can result in sanctions against a professional's medical license. Unlike a civil proceeding where a physician can be sued for monetary damages and would be normally insured to cover damages and defense costs, most physicians don't have insurance to protect against the cost of this potentially costly administrative proceeding.

Investigators have a number of tools at their disposal to obtain information after a complaint is received. These include obtaining medical records, obtaining other documents pursuant to subpoena issued by the Board (such as hospital quality assurance or personnel files of the physician under investigation), interviewing witnesses, colleagues, and the physician under investigation (if he/she consents), reviewing a database of the malpractice history of the physician under investigation, and occasionally even personal surveillance.

When clinical issues are the basis of the complaint, the physician's office records and hospital records will be reviewed to determine whether there is any basis to conclude that professional misconduct has occurred. Investigators will routinely review a physician's hospital quality assurance files to determine whether the physician under investigation has other cases that might create a pattern of deficient conduct.

Stark, Stark II and Stark III

On March 26, 2004, the government released the latest version of that hydra-headed monster known as Stark II in an effort to clarify the original vaguely worded language. But the new, more precisely worded language may be more troubling for Doctors who now find it harder to meet the tougher updated standards. In addition, most states, including Ohio, have laws prohibiting self-referral. Typically, these laws apply to Medicaid, state health and workers' compensation plans, and to private health plans.

For something as complex and sprawling as Stark, its basic message is fairly simple: You can't refer Medicare or Medicaid patients for certain services to which you—or an immediate family member—has a financial relationship, unless an exception applies. If you ignore the basic Stark prohibition, and then bill CMS for those designated health services, you may be subject to civil monetary penalties of up to $15,000 for each service plus twice the reimbursement claimed, and may be excluded from participating in Medicare and Medicaid.

Protecting Yourself

As a professional, you certainly want to do everything possible to avoid these various threats. This will require you to become more educated on the issues at hand, consult an expert, and possibly change your behavior to reduce risk. Even after taking all of those steps, you will still need to prepare for inevitable mistakes. We will examine each of these steps now.

Step 1: Educate Yourself

More often than not, mistakes are unintentional. Doctors often make mistakes because they were unaware of the issues and how to manage them. It is important for you to continue to read your professional journals, attend the seminars offered by your association, and send your administrative staff to the appropriate programs. In addition, you should consider reading our other recent book for physicians.

Risk Management for the Practicing Physician©, from Guardian Publishing, is accredited for four hours of Category I CME Credit in Risk Management for all specialties in all 50 states. Co-written by a practicing physician, an attorney and a financial advisor, this 99-page monograph includes chapters on: providing care in today's malpractice environment, liability and the doctor-patient relationship, managing diagnosis-related liability, minimizing risks of miscommunication, managing high risk communication areas, managing the dangers of drug therapy, non-medical liability risks for the practicing physician, and liability in the new health care delivery system.

You can purchase this book by using the tear-away discounted order form in the Appendix of this book or you can go to www.forohiodoctors.com and order the book online.

Step 2: Find An Expert To Help You

No matter how much effort you make to understand the rules, it is unlikely you will be able to stay abreast of all of the developments and changes while trying to practice medicine and run a busy practice. There are law firms who have teams of people studying the latest legislative changes. In some cases, these firms are involved in lobbying for and drafting legislation. It is in every Doctor's best interest to have a healthcare attorney on retainer. When you understand that any mistake you may make could result in civil and/or criminal penalties, you will recognize the importance of having an expert on your team to give you advice on every element of your practice's operations.

Step 3: Change Your Behavior

After reading ***Risk Management for the Practicing Physician©***, attending all of the appropriate seminars, and consulting with your healthcare attorney, you are likely to identify a number of areas where you should make changes to reduce your risk. These changes may include creating an effective confidentiality and security compliance program to help avoid the HIPAA penalties and sanctions that apply for noncompliant programs. You may need to change your referral process to comply with Stark. You may have to hire additional staff or a specialty consulting firm to make sure you are properly billing and coding so that you avoid claims of over-billing. This may help protect you from having to pay to defend yourself in Medicare fraud or insurance company audits.

Step 4: Prepare For Inevitable Mistakes

Once you have made all the changes to your operations that were suggested by ***Risk Management for the Practicing Physician©***, your healthcare attorney, and your practice consultants, you will be much less likely to be sued. However, accidents and mistakes happen. When they do, you need to be protected.

The first step to protecting assets is structuring your practice properly. If your practice is not structured properly, mistakes by you or anyone working at your practice could lead to losses of personal and practice assets. Lesson #5 will explain the core strategies that you should adopt at the practice level.

The second step is to employ all of the personal asset protection techniques offered in Lesson #6. In many healthcare law claims, the Doctors can be found personally liable for judgments even if they have a corporation. For this reason, you need to protect personal assets—most effectively by using exempt assets (see Chapter 5-6).

The third step to protect assets from healthcare lawsuits is to consult with a healthcare attorney. Any significant change to the structure or operation of your practice—like creating an agreement between Doctors, opening a new practice location, or making structural changes to your business—should begin by consulting a healthcare attorney. It is also a wise strategy to execute a practice audit every 12 to 24 months. This review will help save you unnecessary fines and fees and keep you out of jail. Can you think of any more important goals?

The Diagnosis

In medical school, you learned about anatomy and about the clinical practice of medicine. When you entered private practice, you had to figure out that you were also a business owner and how to negotiate a dangerous business landscape. As a successful Doctor, you have all of the clinical risks of being a Doctor, all of the risks of being an employer AND the specific risks of Healthcare law that only apply to medical practices. Compounded and navigated without proper consultation, these risks can cost you a great deal of money or even time served in jail.

Unless you don't care about money and don't mind going to jail, you must take these risks very seriously. By educating yourself and by hiring specialists (see Lesson #3) to assist you, you can effectively manage these risks so that you can worry less and enjoy your practice more. In the next Chapter, we will discuss other employer issues that weren't taught to you in medical school or residency.

4-6

Avoiding Employment Threats

After over a decade of educating Doctors on the importance of asset protection, we are seeing a noticeable increase in awareness. Unfortunately, the majority of Doctors who fail to employ asset protection planning give the same excuse: "Doctors never lose malpractice lawsuits with awards in excess of coverage limits." This is wrong for two reasons. First, half of jury awards against physicians are over $1,000,000. Second, malpractice suits are only a small percentage of the awards against Doctors. A less visible but arguably larger concern is that an employee will file a suit against the Doctor. In this Chapter, we will discuss the challenges of employment liability, which may result in very expensive defense costs—even in the event of fraudulent cases that you win. We will give some examples of cases that may be of interest, explain increased risks in the information age, and offer some solutions.

The Risk Of Employment Lawsuits

Over the past 20 years, there have been monumental changes in the employment arena. There are a host of Federal Laws that protect employees' rights and open the possibility of lawsuits against employers. Many argue that these laws are appropriate to protect the rights of workers while employers often argue that these laws place undue restrictions on their ability to manage their firms.

Regardless of which side of the issue you take, the reality is that there are numerous "Laws of the Land" which employers must follow. Inclusive of these are the FLSA [Fair Labor Standards Act]; the ADA [Americans with Disabilities Act]; FMLA [Family Medical Leave Act]; Title VII of the Civil Rights Act of 1964; The Civil Rights Act of 1991; and many more. In addition to the federal law, Ohio laws add another layer to these regulations. So what does it all mean? It means that you have to learn how to protect yourself against one of the fastest growing areas of business and employer liability. The more rules there are, the easier it is to violate one.

What many employers—including Doctors—face today is the challenge of working in an increasingly complex world of employment regulations and guidelines. Most small business owners may have few resources with which to address human resources concerns and little or no training. This can result in owners being held financially responsible for any mistakes they make. It means that age-old established practices may plot a course for a company to end up in ruin. It means that business owners—including Doctors—must pay greater attention to how they hire employees; how they supervise them; and how they terminate them.

This environment has fueled the growth of Human Resources ("HR") outsourcing. Many firms have established themselves as specialized providers of these functions for businesses, with the intent of alleviating the business owner's HR headaches. While these firms do provide reliable HR services, they typically do not provide liability coverage for the companies they serve, especially in the realm of employee suits claiming sexual harassment, unlawful termination or discrimination. So, while business owners may benefit from outsourcing some HR tasks, they cannot outsource the risk and their companies are still responsible for their own actions. Insurance policies that address these risks are available to protect against catastrophic liability—one example is EPLI [Employment Practices Liability Insurance], also known as HIRE insurance (see www.hireins.com for more information). If the risk is real, and protective insurance is available, why are the vast majority of small business owners, including Doctors, operating without such coverage?

To small business owners, this type of coverage has historically been out of reach due to cost restrictions. Thankfully, this is now beginning the change. More affordable coverage solutions are making their way into the market. In fact, low deductible policies with coverage amounts as high as one million dollars can now be found. These more accessible policies, coupled with employment risk management services, provide a shield that can protect small business owners—including Doctors—from these potentially devastating claims.

Examples Of Employee Lawsuits

In June, 2007, the 1st U.S. Circuit Court of Appeals ruled that a hotel president was personally liable for multiple wage-hour violations. The court found that he "was not just any employee with some supervisory control," but that he "had ultimate control over the business's day-to-day operations," and was "instrumental in 'causing' the corporation to violate the FSLA [Fair Standards and Labor Act]." Chao v. Hotel Oasis Inc., 493 F.3d 26 (1st Cir. 2007).

In September, 2006, the 5th Circuit established a new law by holding that a public supervisor can be held personally liable for retaliation against an employee. This Texas case involved a woman who claimed that her boss retaliated against her, refused to grant her leave under the Family Medical Leave Act and fired her. Modica v. Taylor, 465 F.3d 174 (5th Cir. 2006).

And, in 2006, a federal judge allowed a suit to proceed against ex-Environmental Protection Agency chief Christine Todd Whitman personally for allegedly misleading New York residents and workers by stating that the air quality was safe enough for people to return after the attacks of Sept. 11, 2001. The case is presently on appeal. Benzman v. Whitman, No. 04-CV-1888 (S.D.N.Y.).

Protecting Your Practice

There are two ways to protect your practice assets from risks. First, you can insure against the risk, effectively sharing the risk and passing it along to someone else. Second, you can assume the risk yourself and use asset protection and risk management strategies to protect assets from the threats. The second strategy is covered in Lesson 6. Here we will focus on passing off risk to other people through insurance.

Fewer than 5% of small businesses (and, we imagine, even fewer medical practices) have any insurance coverage providing protection from employment-related lawsuit risks. This is despite government statistics clearly indicating that this threat is a growing problem. Additionally, recent federal court rulings have begun finding owners and management "personally liable." This means that just incorporating a business will NOT, by itself, protect a business owner from being found personally and financially liable in employment-related suits. Thus, insurance coverage is key to protecting a business owner's interests. **For more information on employment-related risks, please contact the authors at 877-656-4362.**

Risks In The Information Age

Information is currency in Twenty-first century commerce. The role of the Internet—and its ability to locate and distribute information—has exploded in recent years. It has become so much the source of much of our information—our *de facto* provider of answers—that the first thing a person will do when faced with a potentially life-changing issue is often to "Google" it.

What else, then, would you expect of an employees who feel they have been treated unfairly? Most likely, they will explore the information available online and learn their options. In the past, individuals seeking to file a complaint would have to first take the step of consulting an attorney. But in today's "instant information" culture, the EEOC's website now features a simple form for initiating a federal claim without requiring any legal consultation.

The wealth of information and ease with which claims can be filed may partly explain why the number of claims filed with the EEOC jumped from 77,990 in 1997 to over 84,400 in 2003, following a period of decline from 1995, when the number had exceeded 91,000. Coincidentally, this appears to correlate to the number of Americans that consider themselves "web-centric," which has consistently grown since the late 1990s.

Federal courts are also getting into the act and ruling more consistently to hold the individual business owner liable in employment cases.

The Diagnosis

The solution for small business owners today is to be educated about the risks and take reasonable steps to lower their overall risk of employee complaints. However there is no substitute for obtaining proper insurance coverage to protect one's business and personal assets. This can be accomplished by instituting a Risk Management course and appropriate EPLI coverage. When a small business owner can get both at the same time in a cost effective manner, he or she is truly protected.

The bottom line is that the potential exposure to small business owners, including Doctors, is increasing and the federal courts are more consistently holding owners personally liable. Therefore, it is more important than ever for small business owners to protect their assets and get serious about the HR world like their big business counterparts.

Life insurance can protect a family from the financial disaster of a premature death. Disability income insurance can protect a family from an injury that reduces a breadwinner's ability to earn a living. Long-term care insurance can protect a retiree from losing retirement funds and can help protect a family's estate. Various annuities can help protect a retiree from running out of money. If you want to avoid the financial disasters that have stopped many families from achieving their desired levels of wealth, you and your advisory team must consider all these tools in your planning. Once you have protected your family so you can "do no financial harm," you will be ready to learn more advanced lessons in asset protection and wealth accumulation.

The next Lesson discusses how to turn your practice into a financial Fortress and wealth-building Engine. Since a Doctor's income and liability almost always start at the practice level, this is a lesson you need to understand and embrace before you begin protecting personal assets or learning how to build greater wealth.

LESSON 5

Turn Your Practice into a Financial Fortress and Wealth-Building Engine

Do you run your own practice or hope to run your own practice in the near future? If your answer is "yes," then you will want to pay close attention to the information within this Lesson. The purpose of this section of the book is to help you get the most—financially speaking—out of your practice. You will have to do more than the typical cookie-cutter planning that many CPAs and attorneys will suggest. As you learned in Lesson #3, an advisor who doesn't specialize in the unique issues Doctors face is likely to miss a number of key elements in their planning.

If your goal is to efficiently get the most out of your practice, you may find this Lesson to be the most valuable in this book. While intelligent planning can improve all aspects of your life, the impact on your practice can be the most significant. You need to begin thinking about your practice not only as a treatment facility for patients, but also as a financial Fortress and a wealth-building Engine for you.

The Fortress analogy is important because we want to make sure your practice is fortified. As the vehicle through which you will make most of your career earnings, the practice needs to be protected against all financial and legal threats. As you learned in the previous sections of the book, these threats are not just medical malpractice lawsuits. They include healthcare issues, employment risks, and other financial threats that can impact your ability to work and make money.

The Engine analogy is crucial because we want your practice to be an engine for wealth accumulation. You will want to apply the important concepts explained earlier in this book (e.g., Leverage and Efficiency) to your practice structure and operations. By doing so, you will finally be able to derive as much financial benefit as possible out of your practice—both during your working years and through your retirement.

In this Lesson, we will discuss ways to structure and operate your practice so it will act both as a Fortress and an Engine. Specific chapters will cover other risks to the practice not yet discussed, including the premature death or disability of a partner. This Lesson will explain how to turn the practice into a Fortress by protecting your accounts receivable, real estate, and equipment. You will also be introduced to tools that can be used to transform your practice into a smooth-running Engine—including the use of qualified and nonqualified plans, friendly lease-back arrangements, and captive insurance companies. Finally, we will explain the ultimate wealth-building Engine—the million-dollar retirement buy-out.

NOTE: The manner in which you choose to practice—your choice of "entity"—affects both taxes and asset protection. Periodically in this Lesson you will note parenthetical numbers, such as (+5) or (-2). These are references to the "sliding scale of asset protection" and represent choices you can make that are good for asset protection purposes (+1 to +5) or bad for asset protection purposes (-1 to -5). The sliding scale of asset protection is described more specifically in the following Lesson 6.

5-1

How NOT to Structure Your Practice

Every year, we meet many Doctors who are practicing within a structure that offers very little, if any, protection for the assets of the practice. Even worse, we encounter Doctors who have put absolutely no barrier between the potential risks of their practice and all of their personal assets. In some cases, this is due to ignorance on the part of the Doctor. Other times, this is the result of poor advice. Many accountants have suggested that Doctors might not see enough benefit from incorporation to warrant the added time and expense corporations require. Other advisors still recommend general partnerships, although this practice form is all but extinct. In this chapter, we will discuss the pitfalls to avoid when structuring your medical practice.

It may be difficult to believe, but most Doctors who call us have practices that are structured with two potential outcomes in common:

- Maximum lawsuit exposure
- Minimum tax-saving potential

In this chapter, we will discuss the common medical practice structural and operational mistakes that can cause these two highly undesirable outcomes. After you learn how *not* to structure your practice, you can continue reading the rest of this Lesson and learn how you can structure your practice for maximum flexibility and efficiency, enabling you to create the Fortress and Engine you desire.

The Worst Way To Structure A Practice: As A General Partnership

Fortunately, it is far less common for Doctors and their advisors to structure new medical practices as general partnerships today. Though new practices are rarely configured as general partnerships, we still come across dozens of mature (and profitable) practices every year that continue to be operated as general partnerships. There are rarely absolutes in medicine, finance, or the law. However, here is one simple rule: *You should never operate any medical practice or other business as a general partnership*. Why do we say this? The general (pun intended) reason is because a general partnership is a creditor's or plaintiff attorney's dream and a partner's liability nightmare. More specifically, let's consider the three hidden dangers of a general partnership:

1. Partners Have Unlimited Liability for Partnership Debts

This tragic fact goes unrealized by many Doctors who are involved in general partnerships. Without signing a personal guarantee on every debt, each Doctor involved in a general partnership is, by default, personally guaranteeing every partnership debt and personally assuming the risk for malpractice, accidents, and other liability sources of the entire partnership. These Doctors fail to consider that their liability as a partner is joint and several with all other partners. A plaintiff who successfully sues the partnership can collect the full judgment from any one partner. Let's look at an example to see how dangerous this arrangement can be:

Case Study: Jane and Ted's Real Estate Venture

Jane and Ted were physician colleagues who wanted to increase their income by buying "fixer upper" houses, renovating them and then selling them. Events went well for a while, but the real estate market went sour and they defaulted on a $650,000 loan to the bank. Jane was much wealthier than Ted, so the bank pursued Jane for the full amount, ignoring Ted, under the theory of joint and several liability. To collect Ted's share of the liability, Jane had to file suit against him, thereby destroying a long-term friendship.

---

2. Partners Have Unlimited Liability for Their Partners' Acts

When your business is structured as a general partnership, you assume all risks that any partner in the partnership could cause. When a lawsuit arises from one partner's acts or omissions in the ordinary course of practice, every other partner is personally liable. This is where the dreaded joint and several liability applies. This means that each partner can be 100% liable for the actions of any of the other partners. If you operate within a general partnership and one of your partners gets into trouble, you can be personally liable for the entire amount, even if you were neither involved in the alleged incident or even aware of it.

Think of the many ways a partner could get you into trouble: He commits (or is convicted of) malpractice, gets into a car accident while on partnership business/time, defrauds someone through the practice, sexually harasses an employee, wrongfully fires an employee, directs an employee to improperly bill an insurance company or Medicare, etc. Multiply this risk times the number of partners in your partnership. You have a lawsuit liability nightmare! Here is a real-world example that should help illustrate the point further:

Case Study: Michael Gets Burned By His Partner

Michael was the founding partner in a successful three-owner surgery center. One of the firm's employees sued the firm for sexual harassment. Settlement negotiations were unsuccessful and the trial jury awarded an extremely large verdict against the partnership. Of course, this was not covered by any malpractice policy. Since Michael was the wealthiest of the partners and his assets were unprotected, the plaintiff's lawyer pursued him first. This was the plaintiff's quickest way to receive cash. Michael was forced to pay the entire $250,000 judgment from his personal savings. Although Michael had much less contact with this employee than his partners, he was stuck with the bill. Now, Michael has to begin his own costly legal battle against his partners to prove that they owe more than he does because they were more involved with this former employee. This is a no-win situation for Michael—who now understands the risks of a general partnership.

3. You May be an "Unaware" General Partner

A general partnership does not require a formal written agreement like a limited partnership does. You can verbally agree to start a venture with another person which, by default under the law, creates a general partnership, with all of its liability problems. Think about this whenever you start a new practice (or any other business) venture with someone.

Even if you make no agreement to partner with another person, the law may impose general partnership liability on you if the general public reasonably perceives the two of you as partners. You may already be part of a liability-ridden general partnership and not even know it.

Case Study: Roger Inadvertently Has Partners

Roger was one of four physicians who used a common office arrangement. They each had their own patients, which they did not share. They did, however, share a common waiting area, some support staff, and used the same in-house bookkeeper/accountant to help them manage the costs of their practices. Each professional had his own practice methods, set his own hours, and was not otherwise accountable to the other Doctors.

When one of the Doctors was sued by a patient for professional misconduct, Roger and the two others had a rude awakening. Although only the patient's physician was negligent, all four were defendants in the lawsuit. The court found that the patient could reasonably conclude the four professionals were partners together because of their office set-up and common support staff. Therefore, the court allowed the plaintiff to proceed with the suit against all four as a general partnership, with each jointly and severally liable for the plaintiff's losses.

If your practice still operates as a general partnership or may be considered one as above, you should review your situation and the alternative structures with experienced counsel as soon as possible.

The Second Worst Way To Structure A Practice: As A Sole Proprietorship

While relatively few general partnership medical practices exist these days, we cannot say the same thing about practices that operate as sole proprietorships. Every week or two we speak to Doctors who have been operating their practice as a sole proprietorship. In other words, these practices have no legal entity and all income and expenses are recorded on the Doctor's Schedule C of the personal tax return. These Doctors simply operate the practice in their own name, with their own social security numbers, often with a "DBA" in the name of a medical practice (i.e., "Smith Medical Practice"). At its most basic level, the flaw of a sole proprietorship is that it provides absolutely no barrier between the Doctor's professional and personal life. As a result, any risks and liability from the medical practice threatens all of the Doctor's personal assets and any personal lawsuit against the Doctor or the Doctor's family (including teenage children) threatens the assets of the medical practice (including accounts receivable, real estate and equipment). Let's examine these problems more closely.

Drawbacks of Sole Proprietorships

The two significant drawbacks of sole proprietorships are the following:

1. There is no shield between practice liability and all of the Doctor's personal assets. This is a crucial asset protection failure. Because there is no legal entity, there is no Fortress at all. While no legal entity will protect the Doctor from personal liability for professional malpractice, medical malpractice is not the only risk from the practice. As you read earlier in this Lesson, employment liability can be significant. Healthcare-related lawsuits are increasingly common and judgments can be huge. Add to these premises liability and other non-medical claims and one would wonder why any Doctor would choose to expose all of his or her personal wealth to such risks!

2. Without a legal entity, the practice's options for tax reduction are limited. In addition to the asset protection drawbacks above, using a sole proprietorship also limits a Doctor's tax planning options in the practice. A number of benefits plans and tax planning options are available to corporations and not available to sole proprietorships. Every Doctor with whom we have spoken over the years wants to get more retirement dollars out of their practice and wants to legally reduce income taxes. Since you can't accomplish these goals as efficiently with a sole proprietorship as you can with a corporation, you have to wonder why Doctors would ever continue to operate as sole proprietorships once they learn of these opportunities.

Why Doctors Get Stuck in Sole Proprietorships

Given the significant drawbacks of using a proprietorship to operate a medical practice, it does seem strange that thousands of Doctors would do so. In our combined experience, this cannot typically be blamed on the Doctor. ***In fact, what we have seen over the years is that Doctors who use proprietorships almost always have been told to do so by an accountant.***

Unfortunately for their Doctor clients, there are a large number of accountants across the U.S. whose view of this issue is extremely limited. For these accountants, the costs and headaches of using any kind of legal entity for a single Doctor medical practice is not "worth the trouble." Thus, they advise their client to simply operate the medical practice as a proprietorship. Let's examine their logic.

If the simple alternative to a proprietorship is to use a professional corporation (PC), a savvy businessperson would look at the costs and benefits of each strategy, weigh them, and make a choice. To do so here, you need to first understand the costs and headaches of such an entity (we will use PC throughout this chapter to also mean Professional Association or Professional Limited Liability Company).

You can expect the one-time legal fees (drafting Articles of Incorporation if a corporation or Articles of Organization if an LLC, Bylaws if a corporation or Operating Agreement if an LLC, and Organizational Minutes for either) and filing costs (Name Reservation for either a corporation or LLC, Articles of Incorporation or Organization and Filing Fees for either) of creating a PC to be between $3,000 and $5,000, and annual State of Ohio fees and legal and accounting costs to be roughly another $2,000 to $3,000.

If you pay such costs to a competent advisor, the only "headache" should be signing a few documents and making sure you use business checks for business expenses and personal checks and debit cards for personal expenses. Thus, the question becomes: Are the significant asset protection and tax benefits provided by a PC worth about $2,000 per year, especially when those dollars are tax-deductible?

The key factor that many accountants seem to miss when advising Doctor clients about business entity formation is the asset protection concern. Accountants typically focus on the fact that a PC cannot protect a Doctor from his or her own malpractice. While this is true, the PC can protect that Doctor from the following: patients or vendors who may slip and fall when they visit the practice, claims from acts of employees and many other risks we referenced in the first two chapters of this Lesson. Attorneys know about these tradeoffs and have a very similar issue. How many attorneys forego the "cost" and "hassle" of a PC and run their law practices as proprietorships? We rarely see one. If knowledgeable attorneys who understand legal risks never use proprietorships, why should Doctors be any different? It is unfortunate that some accountants have not learned the same lesson and continue to give bad advice to Doctors who are relying on them. Sadly, those accountants fail to consider the normal business risks faced by all Doctors who operate their own practices.

If your practice still operates as a proprietorship, you should engage experienced counsel to remedy this as soon as possible!

The Protections Of Professional Corporations

If you are not in the minority of Doctors who are stuck in a general partnership or proprietorship, you are using some form of professional entity. This could be a professional corporation (PC), professional association (PA), or professional limited liability companies (PLLC). For simplicity, we will use "PC" for all of these. The most important benefits of a PC are.

- **PCs can protect the Doctor from the acts or omissions of subordinates and associates.** For instance, a Doctor can protect him or herself from the acts or omissions of nurses or other Doctors, if the Doctor at issue was not involved in the act of liability.
- **PCs may protect Doctors from non-malpractice lawsuits.** As we outlined earlier in this Lesson, there are many non-medical malpractice liability risks facing Doctors today. The PC may provide a shield for the Doctor's personal assets in many situations.
- **The PC may allow the Doctor to take advantage of certain tax-saving options not available for proprietorships.** Deducting long-term care insurance premiums, plans authorized under Section 79 of the tax code, non-qualified deferred compensation plans—all of these options, as well as several others, are only available to practices that operate as PCs.

The Bare Minimum Way to Structure a Practice: Lone PC

You may be surprised, given the discussion above, that we would call the use of a PC as a "bare minimum" technique. Certainly, when compared to a general partnership or a proprietorship, the PC is much better. However, it is still far from ideal. The following diagram illustrates how nearly all medical practices are arranged in the United States. Perhaps yours is organized this way.

In this arrangement, there is one legal entity that operates the practice and hires all the employees. This same entity also owns all of the key assets of the practice—the accounts receivable (AR), the real estate (RE), and any valuable equipment. In addition, this same entity is the one that bills insurance companies, Medicare, and patients. Finally, this same entity offers the benefit plans to the Doctors and other employees. What is wrong with this picture below?

“All Eggs in One Basket” Practice Structure

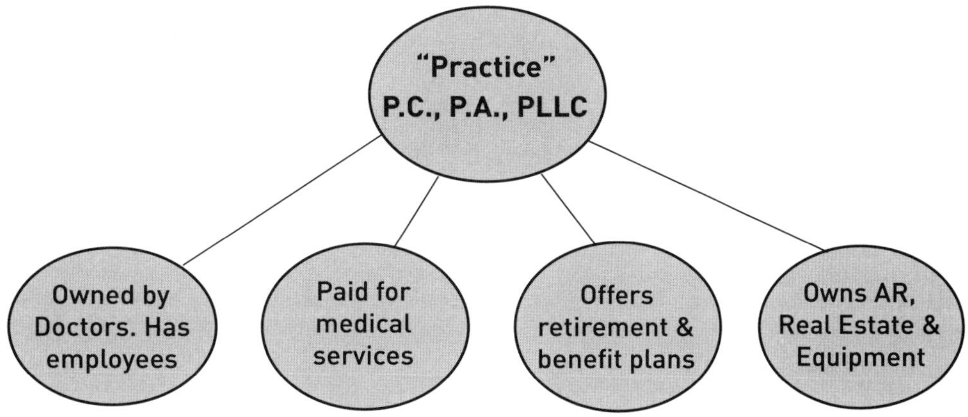

The problem with this diagram, and the legal structure it represents, is fairly simple—all of the practice's “eggs” are in one basket. In fact, not only are the “eggs” (assets) in the one basket, but so are all of the threats to those assets. Employees, partners, and all of the services provided by the practice are within the entity. As you will learn in Lesson #6 (personal asset protection), *it is never a good idea to mix assets with liabilities*. The crux of the problem is that all of the assets are exposed to the myriad of liability threats of the one legal entity. This means that one mistake from any of the risks could threaten all of the assets of the practice. This is obviously not a desirable condition. Also, with only one corporation, you only get the tax benefits of one type of taxed entity. With multiple entities, you might be able to benefit from two types of tax environments. In the next 2 chapters, we will examine ways to solve this problem.

The Diagnosis

In this chapter, we pointed out that many Doctors are still operating their medical practices in the worst ways possible—as general partnerships or sole proprietorships. We explained why these are terrible ways to run any business, not just a medical practice. We also explained that a Professional Corporation, Professional Association, or Professional Limited Liability Company are steps in the right direction, but still have serious problems. If the structure of your practice resembles any of these examples, you are subjecting yourself to unnecessary lawsuit risk and are sacrificing valuable tax deductions you may be able to receive from a more appropriate business structure. The good news is that, even if you have operated with a general partnership or sole proprietorship for fifty years, it is neither too late nor too difficult to change your structure and start taking advantage of the benefits that alternative structures offer.

If you truly want your practice to operate as a Fortress and a wealth-building Engine, you should first make sure that you are using the right type of entity for tax purposes.

S Corporation, C Corporation Or Both?

If you sincerely want to have your practice be an Engine and explore ways to reduce unnecessary taxes, *and* would like to see how you can do this without having to change any of your insurance provider or Medicare provider numbers, understanding this chapter is crucial. Choosing the form and structure of one's medical practice is an important decision. Most advisors to medical practices believe that the avoidance of potential double taxation makes the S Corporation the logical choice. This "conventional wisdom" overlooks the potential benefits a C Corporation can offer.

The Tax Basics of Corporations

Per the last chapter, there is *no* reason to practice in a sole proprietorship or general partnership. This results in unnecessary lawsuit risk, in addition to the inability to take advantage of many valuable tax-deductible business expenses mentioned in this chapter.

In our analysis, we need to compare and contrast C Corporations and S Corporations (remember that PLLCs and PAs are also taxed as either an S or C corporation). All businesses that incorporate are automatically C Corporations, absent an election to become an S Corporation. Both S and C Corporations have separate tax ID numbers and are required to file tax returns with the federal and appropriate state tax agencies. Both entities have shareholders. Both entities can be created in any state in the country, and while your medical practice will be created in other states where the laws are friendlier to your corporate planning needs.

When a C Corporation earns profit, it must pay tax at the corporate level. Profit is the difference between income and expenses. Compensation paid to physicians, as long as it is reasonable, is deductible by the corporation on its tax return (and is therefore not taxable to the corporation). The salary received by the owner is taxable to the owner as wages. After the C Corporation pays taxes, distributions of earnings already taxed at the corporate level can be paid to the physician-owners in the form of dividends. These would generally be taxed to the physician-owners as qualified dividends, thus leading to the "double taxation" of such earnings. As you will see below, this "drawback" can be easily overcome and will not be a drawback at all.

An S Corporation is also a separate entity that must file its own tax return. However, the S

Corporation is often referred to as a "pass through" entity. Rather than paying tax at the corporate level, all income and deductions pass through to the shareholders and the shareholders must pay tax on any S Corp income at their individual rates. Whether the income of an S Corp is paid to the physician-owners as salary or as a distribution will not impact the federal or state income tax rates that will be applied to that income for the physician. There is never any tax to the corporation, therefore there is no "double taxation" in an S Corporation. However, physician salaries are subject to FICA and other employment-based taxes, whereas distributions are not.

Double Taxation—Much Ado About Nothing

Mistakenly, most physicians think of S and C Corporations as having exactly the same benefits. Since the C Corporation has a potential double taxation, most doctors and their advisors elect to form an S Corporation to avoid one more potential problem. First, the double taxation problem can be easily avoided by reducing practice profits to zero, or close to zero, at the end of the year. This is done by thousands of medical practice C Corporations that exist today. Second, after you review the next sections you will see the increased benefits C Corporations offer medical practices, including the cost (in time, not money) of using and zeroing out a C Corporation far outweigh the benefits of an S Corporation.

Additional Deductible Benefits of a C Corporation

Contrary to much "conventional wisdom," a C Corporation can be the right choice for many small entities because of the deductions it allows. The corporate deduction for fringe benefits paid to employees is generally limited for shareholders owning more than 2% of an S Corporation. However, a C Corporation enjoys a full deduction for the cost of employees' (including owner employees) health insurance, group term life insurance of up to $50,000 per employee, and even long term care premiums without regard to age-based limitations. The C Corporation can also deduct the costs of a medical reimbursement plan. If the practice owner has a small C Corporation and a lot of medical expenses that aren't covered by insurance, the C Corporation can establish a plan that results in all of those expenses being tax deductible. Fringe benefits such as employer-provided vehicles and public transportation passes are also deductible.

In contrast, health insurance paid by an S Corporation for a more than 2% shareholder is not deductible by the corporation. The shareholder must generally take a self-employed health insurance deduction on his personal return. Long term care premiums paid through an S Corporation are also not deductible with regard to these shareholders. The shareholders, in deducting them personally, are subject to age-based limitations.

Digging Deeper on the Potential Benefits of a C Corporation (over an S)

Before some of the authors were educated on the potential benefits allowed for C corporations, we too often advised doctors to use S Corporations. However, when we realized that the potential tax benefits to many doctors can be hundreds of thousands of dollars over a career by using a C Corporation rather than an S, we changed our minds.

The two most financially significant benefits allowed by law for C corporations are the following:

1. **Only C Corporations can offer Section 79 plans**
   As you will read in chapter 5-5, Group Term Life plans, also called "Section 79" plans for the tax code section that authorizes them, are only available to C Corporations. These plans can be utilized *in addition* to qualified plans like pensions, profit-sharing plans/401(k)s or IRAs. While the specifics of Section 79 plans are described more specifically in Chapter 5-5, it is important to note a few of the following important benefits:

   - These plans can be utilized *in addition* to a qualified plan like a pension, profit-sharing plan/401(k) or IRA.
   - Because regulations permit "permanent" insurance as well as term insurance, the funds in these plans can grow in the top (+5) asset protection environment in Ohio.
   - Maximum contribution levels are $100,000 per doctor in practices with 10 employees or less. In larger practices, these levels can be even higher.
   - In a group practice, not every doctor need contribute the same amounts—this is extremely beneficial for group practices with doctors who want to "put away" differing amounts.

2. **Only C Corporations Can Offer Doctors Full Deductibility for Long-term Care Insurance**
   As you will see in chapter 7-4, long-term care insurance—coverage vital to preventing your family's forced "spend down" and loss of assets—can be deductible to a corporation. However, it is not deductible for an S corporation as to the 2%+ owners. This means that for 99% of medical practices operating as S corporations, the insurance would not be deductible. Using the C corporation, however, such policies would be 100% deductible. As the total premiums on this type of insurance can be over $100,000 over ten years, the total tax saving could be $40,000 or more per doctor—typically, well worth the time of creating year-end bonuses to avoid double taxation.

Changing from an S to a C Corporation

If you are already operating as an S corporation and are interested in converting to a C, the good news is that it is extremely easy. A simple revocation of the S election can be made instantly for an S corporation. This can be done until March 15th for that calendar year and any time for the next calendar year.

Get the Best of Both Worlds—Why Not Use Both an S and a C?

If you are already using an S corporation and it is after March 15th and you do not want to wait until the following year for these benefits, you could consider what many practices have done—for this, and general asset protection reasons—that is, to create a 2nd entity as a non-medical management company.

In fact, many practices can take advantage of both the C Corporation and the S Corporation by setting up two distinct entities to operate different aspects of their practice. Perhaps the S Corporation will be used for the operating side of the practice (professional practice of medicine) while the C Corporation will be used for management functions (billing and administration). In this way, the practice as a whole can take advantage of both the tax deductions and benefits afforded a C Corporation and the "flow through" advantages of an S Corporation. See the diagram below. This may also provide some additional asset protection. As long as all formalities of incorporation are followed, as well as compliance with rules for employee participation in all benefit plans, medical practices can benefit from this "dual" corporate structure.

Medical Practice: Multiple Entities

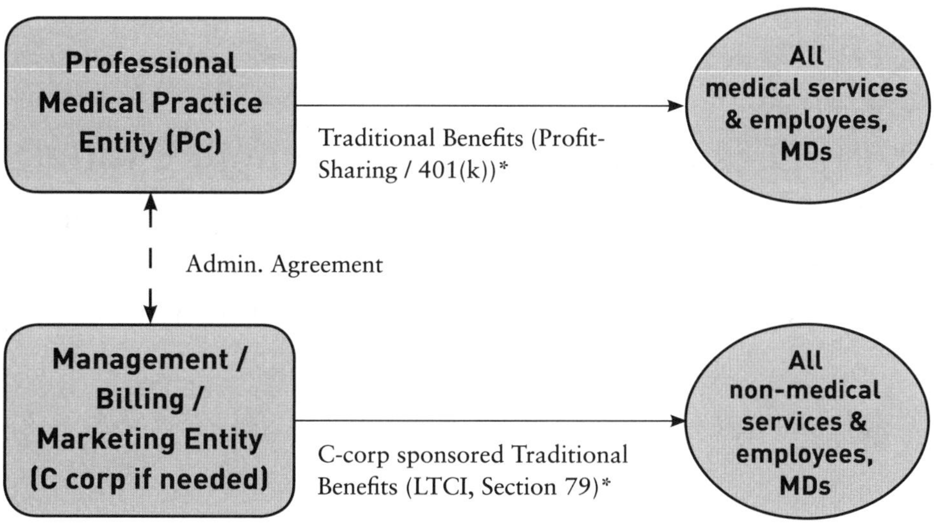

* *Affiliated Service Rules Apply*

The Diagnosis

In this chapter, we pointed out that many Doctors may be using the wrong type of legal entity for their practice. If wealth creation and asset protection are priorities in the practice, a C corporation should be strongly considered—and the special benefits C corporations allow should be closely examined. For doctors using S corporations, it is easy to convert to a C Corporation, and to use a 2-entity structure as well. In the next chapter, we will explain other ways to use multiple entities for medical practice asset protection.

5-3

Using Multiple Entities For Asset Protection

In the last chapter, you learned how a C corporation can make more financial sense for a medical practice than an S corporation. You also learned that, if you have an S corporation now, you can easily convert to a C corporation—or use both an S and C corporation in a multi-entity structure. The strategy of using multiple entities goes beyond the tax and financial benefits of S and C corporations, as you will see here. In this chapter, we will explain additional multiple entity asset protection concepts that can help you better shield practice assets from lawsuits (Fortress) and earn more without seeing more patients (Engine).

Protecting Practice Assets By Using Multiple Entities

We understand that it is a tremendous risk to put all of a practice's "eggs" into one basket, but what's the solution? For your practice, it may be as simple as using multiple baskets. In fact, using multiple entities to run a business is quite common in many types of business outside of medicine. Consider:

- Most restaurant businesses use different entities if they expand beyond one location.
- Most real estate developers or investors use multiple entities for different pieces of property.
- Many owners of taxicabs use one entity to own each taxicab.

Why do these business owners use multiple entities in this way? They do so primarily because they want their businesses to be Fortresses—shielding different business units or assets from claims against their other businesses or assets. If one restaurant location performs poorly or there is a lawsuit at one property, the restaurateur does not want the other locations to be held responsible. If one taxicab is in a terrible accident, the owner of the taxicab business does not want the income from the other taxicabs to be exposed to the lawsuit creditor. Doctors can use the same tactic for the exact same reason.

How should a Doctor use multiple entities to protect a medical practice? The most common way is to separate the practice's assets into various entities. Typically, the practice's accounts receivable (AR) is its greatest asset. We will deal with this asset in its own chapter later in this Lesson. After AR, many practices own the real estate where the practice operates, as well as some valuable equipment. Here, we will deal with the real estate—but note that the same "lease back" concept can be applied to equipment as well.

There are three asset protection goals of separating the ownership of the real estate (RE) from the operating practice.

1. First, the RE is a valuable asset that should be isolated from any liability created by the practice. By isolating the practice from the real estate, you may have isolated malpractice or employment liability created by the practice from the valuable RE.

2. Second, the RE itself may cause liability, such as slip-and-fall claims from those coming and going on the premises. If the RE and the practice are operated by the same legal entity, all the "eggs" are in the same "basket." This means that the claim will be against an entity that has something to lose—all of those valuable assets. By separating the RE from the practice, you have also insulated the practice from these risks.

3. If there is a claim against the Doctors personally, an LLC formed in the proper jurisdiction (often Nevada, Wyoming or Delaware) can provide (+2 to +3) protection of the assets in the separate LLC from such claims due to the charging order protections that you can read about in Lesson #6 on personal asset protection.

Separation Involves LLCs And Lease-Backs

The actual tactic of separating ownership simply involves creating a new Limited Liability Company (LLC) and transferring ownership of the real estate or equipment to the new LLC. Because the RE is no longer owned by the operating practice, claimants suing the practice have no claim against the LLC that owns the RE. For this arrangement to be respected and to ultimately protect the assets, Doctors must:

1. Properly create the LLC, with the right language in its Operating Agreement and all formalities being followed by the owners.

2. Respect and observe all entity legal and accounting formalities.

3. Transfer title of the RE to the LLC.

4. Create fair market value lease documentation between the practice and the LLC(s) and make actual rental payments.

5. Ensure proper tax treatment for all parts of the transaction.

6. Transfer all insurance policies for the RE to, and premiums paid by, the LLC.
7. Comply with all other formalities that evidence the ownership of the RE by the LLC.

Your Financial Incentive

As we noted at the outset of the chapter, there is also a way the LLC lease-back tactic can be part of your "practice as Engine" strategy as well. In other words, the LLC lease-back can actually allow you to create more wealth while also protecting the RE. In fact, it can help you build wealth without requiring you to work additional hours or see more patients.

For simplicity's sake, we will assume that you have a one-Doctor medical practice (although these techniques work equally as well for group practices). Let's assume today that you own the practice's office building in the same practice entity (PC). Tomorrow, you follow our advice and use the LLC lease-back technique for the practice office and follow all the proper formalities.

We would use an LLC that is initially owned by you and your spouse. Over time, you can gift ownership interests to children while maintaining 100% control of the LLC and the RE the LLC owns. Once the children are over the age of 18 (or age 24 if they are full-time students), their percentage of the LLC income will be taxed at their (likely) lower income tax rates. If you can take full advantage of this opportunity for tax bracket sharing (see Chapter 7-3), you can save tens of thousands of dollars in income taxes each year. Stretched out over a career, the savings (and growth on saved dollars) can reach well into the six figures.

LLC Lease Back for Office Property

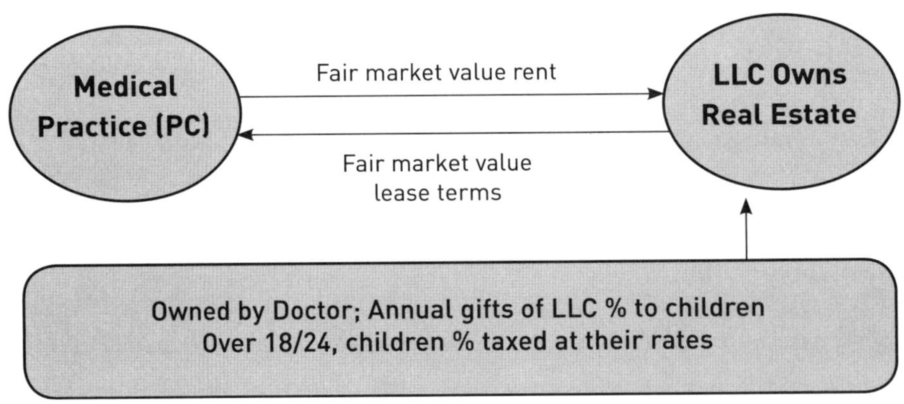

The Diagnosis

After learning that the way you manage your practice is likely inappropriate, you may have been chagrined. This chapter showed you one way to resolve this issue. By using multiple entities to protect business assets, you can take advantage of a strategy that millions of businesses worldwide have used for decades. Don't be discouraged that very few Doctors are familiar with this technique. Many Doctors are too busy seeing patients—working *in* their practices—to spend enough time *on* their practices to make them better Fortresses and Engines. Just because few of your colleagues use multiple entities doesn't mean that you have to forfeit an opportunity to turn your practice into a Fortress and an Engine. To continue your education on transforming your practice into a Fortress and an Engine, you should consider another strategy that few Doctors implement—protecting accounts receivable. This is the topic of the next chapter.

5-4

Protecting Your Practice's Accounts Receivable

Since a medical practice's Accounts Receivable (AR) is typically its largest and most vulnerable asset, one would think that most Doctors would focus on protecting it (Fortress) from the many lawsuit risks that Doctors, medical practices, and any operating business with employees and customers face. Unfortunately, this isn't the case. Also, since the Doctor earns the right to be paid weeks and often months before the AR is ultimately collected, one might think that most Doctors would try to apply the concept of Leverage to this unproductive asset (Engine) to get more out of the asset. Again, you would be wrong.

In this Chapter, we will explain the exposure of a practice's AR to claims against the Doctors and employees of the practice. Then we will compare and contrast two options for protecting the AR and leveraging this asset for further wealth creation.

How Doctors Lose Their Accounts Receivable

A medical practice's accounts receivable (AR) is the Doctor's most vulnerable asset when it comes to losing wealth in any claim against the practice (or, if a Doctor is operating in the wrong type of entity, claims against the Doctor or a member of the Doctor's family). These claims can be medical malpractice claims, employment claims, healthcare related suits, or any number of financial risks to the practice. This financial risk exists because every case against a physician or the practice will include the medical practice as one of the defendants in the lawsuit. When there is a successful lawsuit against the practice, attorneys will look to corporate assets to satisfy the corporate debt. What is the biggest (and possibly only) liquid asset a practice has? The Accounts Receivable (AR).

The accounts receivable has already been earned by your practice. You are only awaiting payment. Most medical practices "turn over" their AR every 60-90 days or so. This means the creditor only needs to wait 2 or 3 months, at most, to get access to your AR. It doesn't matter that the AR is used to pay salaries and expenses. Once there is a lien against the AR, it becomes the property of the creditor and you have to find other ways to pay salaries and expenses.

Protecting Accounts Receivable

It is important to understand how you can protect your AR. Basically, what you need to do is find a way to "encumber" the AR to protect it. In both of the techniques we will examine, there will be a loan to the practice where the AR will become the collateral or "security" for the loan. In this way, the AR will be encumbered. This means that the AR is owned by the lender until the debt is repaid. By implementing one of these two accounts receivable financing strategies, you may not only shield your AR, but you will turn a non-productive asset (the AR balance) into a productive asset that can be immediately invested. This can lead to financial Leverage that may result in greater retirement income for you and greater death protection for your family. This is another example of how the practice can help build assets (Engine) while protecting existing and future assets from claims (Fortress). Let's examine the basics of accounts receivable financing and the two different types of strategies you can use.

Accounts Receivable Financing

Accounts Receivable Financing or "AR Financing" is an arrangement where a lender makes a loan to a practice that pledges the AR as collateral for the loan. This way, the practice has a liability (the loan) that offsets the asset (the AR). Typically, the lender will file an official UCC-1 form to give notice to the world that their security agreement exists and that the lender is first in line as a creditor to the AR. This means that any future creditors, including claimants who eventually get any judgments against the practice, would not be able to successfully attack the AR. In this way, the practice can create an arrangement that would successfully dissuade any future creditor from going after the AR that rightfully belongs to someone else. This is an example of an asset protection "debt shield."

This is similar to what a bank does when it gives you a first mortgage on your home. Once the bank files their security interest, all subsequent mortgages come behind the bank's interest. If you have a home worth \$1 million with a \$1 million previously filed first mortgage, no creditor (including a lawsuit plaintiff) would see any value in your home. This is because there is no equity for the creditor to attack.

The above description applies to both types of AR financing protection we will discuss in this Chapter. Beyond this basic similarity, there are substantial differences between the two strategies that significantly impact the Doctor's ability to practically apply the techniques in a cost effective manner. Let's consider the nuances of the two strategies so that you can make up your mind as to which might work best for you and your practice.

AR Financing Type 1: Unrelated Lender

In the unrelated lender AR financing structure, an outside lender (typically, a bank) makes a loan to the practice and takes the security agreement against the AR. There are a number of vendors for this type of AR financing in the U.S. Most of the programs we have seen work the same way, although there may appear to be significant differences among them. Let's examine a number of factors involved in these types of programs:

1. **Protection of the AR**
As above, because the lender is an unrelated bank, the protection of the AR will be at the highest (+5) level of protection. However, this assumes that all the formalities are respected and followed. The most important formalities are that the collateral and security agreement make the AR the primary collateral for the loan and that the proper UCC filings are made. While all promoters of these techniques claim that they "do it right," we have reviewed many of these arrangements where we disagree with both the structure and the method of following the formalities.

2. **Borrower**
In most of the properly structured arrangements, the borrower is the medical practice. In some, the individual Doctors are the borrowers. It's a "facts and circumstances" determination.

3. **Use of loan proceeds**
There is a great deal of variability here. In most of the arrangements, the practice gets the loan and then creates a deferred compensation arrangement for the Doctors. If the practice owns the deferred compensation agreement, this may not protect the loan proceeds at all. In other arrangements, the deferred compensation agreement can trigger immediate ordinary income tax to the Doctor, even though the AR has not yet been received (discussed in point #4 below). How the funds get out of the practice, how they are taxed, and what the Doctor does with the funds are all very important considerations. Make sure to discuss this with experts who understand the nuances of tax law before agreeing to participate in such a plan.

   In almost all cases, the proceeds of the loan will eventually be invested in some type of cash value life insurance policy. You will learn in Lesson #8 that insurance policies can significantly outperform mutual funds and other brokerage accounts when the investor is a high-income taxpayer. In addition, in the states where cash values in life insurance policies are given the highest (+5) level of asset protection this is a great way to achieve full (+5) protection of the AR. Ohio is one of the states that fully protects the cash value in life insurance policies.

4. **Tax issues**
Often, the promoters of AR financing arrangements make ill-founded and inaccurate claims. Although some arrangement promoters have improved their promotional materials or structures, this is not always the case. The two key tax issues here are the deductibility of the interest paid to the bank and, if there is a deferred compensation plan as part of the arrangement, the tax treatment of that plan. It is imperative that

Doctors get independent review of these issues and not rely solely on the promoter or bank, or any tax attorney or accountant who has a relationship or financial incentive to work with the program promoter or bank.

5. **Protection of loan proceeds**
As above, in many of the AR financing structures, the loan proceeds are invested in (+5) state-exempt assets like cash value life insurance policies and annuities. While Ohio protects cash value life insurance policies (+5), annuities are not protected. If the proceeds are invested in annuities, the protection of the proceeds is more challenging and may typically involve (+2) LLCs. Of course, this assumes that the loan proceeds are properly removed from the practice. Any assets that remain in the practice will not be protected.

6. **Economics**
This is the area where promoters were especially aggressive when initially selling these plans a decade or so ago. The promoters would sell these techniques based on projections of very low interest rates on the loans and very high rates of return in the policies and annuities. For the most part, the reality of the past decade has been returns that were nowhere near these rosy projections. Nonetheless, there is the potential for some wealth creation in these techniques. Because interest rates and investment returns vary greatly from year to year, there will always be a significant opportunity for appreciation and a substantial risk of lost principal. This needs to be understood before you agree to any such arrangement.

7. **Overall cost/benefit**
We recommend that you look at the unrelated lender AR financing arrangement more specifically as a protection tool and less as an arbitrage play that will create significant wealth in retirement. We understand that the stock market has outperformed the prime rate over time, but we cannot be sure how these two indices will perform between today and the day you need the money. If the arrangement can be structured to protect the Doctor's financial downside and shield the AR effectively, that would be ideal. The additional valuable insurance protection these programs can afford (which most Doctors and their families need) can become the "icing on the cake."

AR Financing Type 2: Related Lender

In the related lender AR financing structure, a related lender (often, an irrevocable trust for the benefit of non-physician family members) makes the loan to the practice and takes the security agreement against the AR. Because the trust and family members (spouse and children, typically) are being paid market-comparable interest, the overall family economics are superior to the unrelated lender arrangement.

Let's examine a number of factors involved in these types of programs:

1. Protection of the Accounts Receivable

As above, because the lender here is a related entity, the protection of the AR will be examined more closely. Nonetheless, if done properly, this technique could afford protection at levels of (+3/+4). This also assumes that all of the formalities are followed. Most important are that the collateral and security agreement make the AR the primary collateral for the loan, that the proper UCC filings are made and that the loan is at a market-comparable rate (at no less than the Applicable Federal Rate, or AFR, when dealing with family members). Making sure your arrangement follows the necessary guidelines is the job of the attorney who structures the arrangement.

2. Borrower

In these arrangements, either the practice or the Doctor could be the borrower.

3. Use of loan proceeds

In most arrangements, the funds are ultimately invested directly into a cash value life insurance policy, which enjoys absolute asset protection (+5) in Ohio

4. Tax issues

If the Doctor is the borrower, there will not be a deferred compensation arrangement. That means that the tax issues are much simpler. If the practice is the borrower, the same deferred compensation tax issues exist as they do with an unrelated lender. In both situations, interest deductibility is still an issue that needs to be addressed with your tax advisors.

5. Protection of loan proceeds

As above, the loan proceeds may be invested in (+5) state exempt assets like cash value life insurance policies.

6. Economics

Because the trust and family members (spouse and children, typically) are being paid interest, the overall family economics are superior to the unrelated lender arrangement. This is because the practice will pay interest to family members instead of to a bank. This means that the funds stay "in the family." This technique will work in high or low interest markets, while the previous technique's success will be contingent on a long-term, low-interest rate environment. Also, this arrangement may be combined with a related debt shield of the home (see asset protection Lesson #6), and an estate plan, to become a centerpiece of the Doctor's asset protection plan.

7. Overall cost/benefit

The related lender AR financed structure, though a bit more complex at the outset, can be much more rewarding to the Doctor and his or her family. The main reason is that the interest payments are not "lost" to the bank. Rather, they are paid to a trust for the benefit of the family. In addition, this structure can also protect the Doctor's home. For this reason, the authors often work with attorneys who have experience with this technique and introduce them to our clients when appropriate.

AR Segregation

In this transaction, there is no loan at all. Instead, essentially, the AR is provided a (+2) shield by having the practice transfer the ownership of the AR to limited liability companies (LLCs). While there may be adjustments to employment agreements and a collection agreement involved, the day-to-day operations of the practice stay the same. The attorney co-authors of this book work closely with an attorney who has pioneered this technique and implemented it for many physician practices throughout the U.S. Please call us if you would like to delve further into this topic further.

The Diagnosis

For most practices, the single largest asset is the outstanding Accounts Receivable. This generally represents between 16% to 25% of a practice's annual revenue and 30% to 50% of a practice's annual profit. A single successful lawsuit against the practice resulting from the actions of any of the partners or employees could wipe out up to six months of income for ALL of the partners. This significant risk necessitates the protection of Accounts Receivable.

In this chapter, you learned that related and unrelated lender AR financing strategies, as well as AR segregation, are viable for protecting this valuable practice asset. If you meet with your advisory team, they should be able to explain the differences between each plan and help you determine which plan is right for your situation.

5-5

Using Qualified & Non-Qualified Plans

This chapter discusses two topics which are related and can contribute to the practice being both a Fortress and an Engine. However, the chapter is unique in that almost every Doctor takes advantage of the first option—qualified plans—while almost none utilize non-qualified plans. We will discuss both the common qualified retirement plans and the less common non-qualified plans here, so that you can be aware of options available to you and, hopefully, get more out of your hard work, build greater wealth and enjoy the fruits of your labor.

Qualified Retirement Plans

A "qualified" retirement plan describes retirement plans that comply with certain Department of Labor and Internal Revenue Service rules. You might know such plans by their specific type, including pension plans, profit sharing plans, money purchase plans, 401(k)s or 403(b)s. Properly structured plans offer a variety of real economic benefits, such as:

- The ability to fully deduct contributions to these plans
- Funds within these plans grow tax-deferred
- Funds within these plans are protected from creditors

In fact, these benefits are likely the reasons why most medical practices sponsor such plans.

For this chapter, we will include IRAs as "qualified plans" even though, technically, they are not. We are doing this because IRAs have essentially the same tax rules as qualified plans and have the same attractions to Doctors who can use them.

As you will learn in Lesson #6 on asset protection, qualified plans and IRAs enjoy (+5) protection in bankruptcy—for asset protection purposes.

You can learn more about their tax benefits (and drawbacks) in Lesson #7. You will see that the obvious tax benefits may be outweighed by the less obvious tax drawbacks.

Qualified plans (not IRAs), must be offered to all "qualified" employees (within certain restrictions). For a Doctor owner, there may be some economic costs to having a plan that you must offer to, and contribute to, for everyone at the office or at related businesses. With these mixed benefits and drawbacks, it is surprising how many Doctors (nearly 100%) use qualified plans and ignore their cousins, non-qualified plans, which are far less restrictive. Review the following chart so you can better understand the pros and cons of qualified plans.

Benefits & Drawbacks of Qualified Plans

Benefits	**Drawbacks**
Tax deductible contributions	You must contribute to plan for all eligible employees
Highest level of asset protection (+5)	All withdrawals subject to ordinary income tax rates
Tax-deferred growth	Penalties for access prior to age 59½
	Must take minimum distributions at age 70½
	You are "betting" that future income tax rates are the same or lower
	May be taxed at 72% or more at death

Your Qualified Plan "Bet" on Future Tax Rates

In other parts of the book, we cover most of the benefits and drawbacks of qualified plans in more detail. Here, we want to make sure you understand the bet you are making on future tax rates when you rely on qualified plans heavily for your retirement. Since all amounts that come out of qualified plans (and SEP and roll-over IRAs, of course) are 100% income taxable, there is no way to know how good (or bad) a financial deal such a plan could be for you until you know the tax rates when you withdraw funds.

In other words, if you contribute funds to a qualified plan today (when the top federal income tax rate is 35%) and withdraw funds when income tax rates are at the same or a lower level, the deduction today and tax-free growth over time is likely a "pretty good deal" for you. However, if you withdraw funds from your plan and the top federal tax rates are 40%-50% or higher, then the qualified plan/IRA may be a "bad deal" for you. Certainly, future federal income tax rates of 50% or more could make qualified plans a very negative long-term investment proposition for you. At the time this book was sent to press, all forecasters agree that income tax rates—local, state and federal—are headed up.

[Clarification Point: Some folks may argue that, in retirement, doctors are likely to have less income and thus the plan distributions will be taxed at lower rates. While this may be likely for

95% of taxpayers, many doctors will build enough wealth in retirement and non-retirement assets to be in the top marginal tax rates in retirement. The second highest marginal income tax rate (2% less than the highest rate) goes into effect when a married couple earns TOTAL income of only $208,850 in 2009. If you are single, divorced or widowed, that second highest rate applies to income above $171,550. Do you think that your total income will be less than $171k or $208k when you add in retirement distributions, Social Security, rental income, and any investment gains from non-pension assets? In many cases, doctors are going to retire only when their retirement assets will generate incomes equal to their last year's salary. For most of our clients, this is the retirement game plan—retire only when they can maintain the lifestyle to which they have become accustomed.]

With this is mind, review the history of US income tax rates chart below. Putting aside politics, you must understand that it is certainly a possibility that tax rates can return to the levels they were for most of the 20th century. If they do, qualified plans utilized today by most doctors may turn out to be "losing bets" in the long run. Since we cannot know what future tax rates will be, we need to at least acknowledge the bet we are making and ask how we can reduce our risk and perhaps hedge against such a losing bet.

Federal Income Tax Rates

Year	Top Marginal Federal Income Tax Rate
1920	73.0%
1930	25.0%
1940	81.0%
1950	91.0%
1960	91.0%
1970	71.0%
1980	70.0%
1990	28.0%
2000	39.6%
2008	35.0%
2011 on	39.6%

Source: Citizens for Tax Justice, May 2004.

A New Concept for Investing—Tax Treatment Diversification

Does the fact that our qualified plans today may turn out to be losing bets mean that we should abandon them? In most cases, the answer is "no." These plans generally have the strongest asset protection available and provide significant incentives for employees. We would strongly recommend, however, that EVERY doctor make investments that offer a hedge against potential tax rate increases.

The concept here is that you should have various "buckets" in which to grow wealth—and each bucket should be subject to a different tax treatment. Consider it a second, but equally important, diversification technique for your wealth—along with investment class diversification.

We spread our investments across different classes of assets so that, in the event something bad happens impacting one industry or investment type, the total portfolio is not affected. With tax treatment diversification, a similar theory applies. If you have some investments that may be taxed as ordinary income, some that may be taxed at capital gains or dividend tax rates, and some assets that may not be taxable at all, you have flexibility. When ordinary income tax rates are very high, you may choose to spend assets that are taxed at low capital gains tax rates or not taxed at all. When rates are low, you may choose to pay those taxes now. For example, some real estate investors in the last few years have NOT made 1031 exchanges. They volunteered to pay the 15% federal capital gains taxes. Others deferred the tax and may have to pay future federal rates of 20% or 28% when they sell (if rates, as expected, increase). The goal is to have flexibility so you are never at the mercy of one legislative change. Some savvy investors exchange and later fund their charitable remainder trust with the replacement real estate in order to avoid the capital gains taxes. This technique is explained in Lesson 9-8.

How to Hedge Your Qualified Plan "Bet" with Tax Treatment Diversification

Above, we have recognized that, if history is any indication of the future, federal income tax rates may rise, perhaps significantly. We also understand that our qualified plans are, in fact, a bet on future tax rates staying close to the rates today or decreasing in the future. Because such a bet is risky at best, we would all like to find a way to hedge against it. We can hedge against federal tax increases, using tax treatment diversification. Such diversification can be accomplished in two ways: (1) by accumulating non-qualified plan after-tax investments and (2) by using non-qualified benefit plans that are taxed differently from traditional qualified plans. Let's examine each here:

1. **Using After-Tax Investments**
   Most doctors use this technique. It is simply investing one's after-tax savings in a liquid asset class (securities, savings, CDs, etc.) that can be accessed in retirement. Because these assets can be sold without significant income tax—stock sales will typically trigger "capital gains" taxes, while savings, bonds and CDs trigger income taxes on relatively small interest payments—they are much better protected against a high future income tax than qualified plan distributions that are 100% income taxable. In this way, if income tax rates are very high for a period of retirement, you

could use these types of assets to live on and not significantly draw down the qualified plan assets at that time. Even more importantly, by having this asset class as part of your retirement game plan, you are not as exposed to the risk of ordinary income tax rates increasing in the future.

While this technique is certainly crucial, it still has one tax risk—that capital gains tax rates rise significantly. In fact, while we call this technique "after tax investments," this is actually a misnomer. That is because such assets will trigger capital gains taxes when they are sold and—for certain assets, like mutual funds—capital gains taxes are levied along the way as well.

Again, study the chart below. You will see that, at the time of publication, US federal capital gains tax rates are at the LOWEST point in the history of the tax. Putting politics aside, we do not think that it is unrealistic to expect that such rates will be higher at any point in the future. Again, does this mean that we should abandon this asset class? Absolutely not. However, it does make sense for most Doctors to examine a third tax asset class that can eliminate the risk of future income tax rate AND future capital gains tax rate increases.

Top Federal Capital Gains Tax Rate

Year	Top Federal Capital Gains Tax Rate
1940	30.0%
1942—1967	25.0%
1970	32.3%
1977	39.9%
1980	28.0%
1990	28.0%
2000	20.0%
2009	15.0%
2011 on	20.0%

Source: Citizens for Tax Justice, May 2004.

2. Using Non-Qualified Benefit Plans

Non-qualified plans are relatively unknown to Doctors, despite the fact that most Fortune 1000 companies make non-qualified plans available to their executives. This type of plan should be very attractive to Doctors, as employees are not required to participate AND allowable contributions for the owners and executives (Doctors, in the case of a medical practice) can be much higher than with qualified plans. Because there are numerous types of non-qualified plans—from split dollar plans to 162 Executive Bonus plans among many others—we will keep our discussion here to one type of plan that has both qualified and non-qualified traits and that can provide you with excellent tax diversification—the Group Term Life Plan authorized by tax code section 79, also known as a "Section 79 Plan."

A Section 79 plan is a very flexible plan that has numerous benefits for a medical practice. As relevant here, the contributions are partially deductible and partially taxable at the outset—which is much better today than the "after tax investments" asset class and not as good as the qualified plan. The funds grow tax-deferred, which is the same as the qualified plan and better than the "after tax investments" class. Finally, in the future, when funds are accessed in retirement, they can be reached without tax—better than the "after-tax investments" and far superior to the qualified plan. In this way, the Section 79 plan avoids the risks of future income and capital gains tax rate increases in a substantial way—and can act as an ideal "hedge" against future income and capital gains tax increases.

In addition to playing the role as a future tax increase hedge, the Section 79 Plan has the following benefits:

- These plans can be utilized *in addition* to a qualified plan like pension, profit-sharing plan/401(k) or IRA.
- The funds in these plans can grow in the top (+5) asset protection environment in Ohio.
- Maximum contribution levels are $100,000 per Doctor in practices with 10 employees or less. In larger practices, these levels can be even higher.
- In a group practice, not every doctor need contribute the same amounts—extremely beneficial for group practices with Doctors who want to "put away" differing amounts.
- The plan funding can be flexible.
- Employee participation requires a minimal funding outlay.
- There are no minimum age requirements for withdrawing income (no early withdrawal penalties).
- The transfer of assets at the Doctor's death is income tax-free to heirs.

The Diagnosis

Most Doctors in the U.S. utilize some type of qualified retirement plan, including an IRA, as part of a benefit plan. Certainly, these plans can serve both as a protective (Fortress) and wealth accumulation (Engine) tool. On the other hand, too few Doctors use, or even investigate, non-qualified plans. This is unfortunate given the tax bet that qualified plans require—a bet that could be a losing one in the future. We hope that you make it a priority to hedge such a bet—and investigate other tax asset classes such as the plans described above.

5-6

The One Contract Your Practice Must Have

Although the odds of a premature death of a practice partner are not high, the same cannot be said about a life changing disability. Because both of these risks can have such devastating effects on the finances of the practice and the future income of the remaining healthy partners, we find it troubling that so few Doctors properly address this risk.

A medical practice is a business. As such, it is created for the purpose of generating financial benefit for its owners. Practice CEOs are supposed to take calculated risks and manage these risks to maximize long-term after-tax income. There is no excuse for them to completely ignore the potentially devastating risk of disability or death of physician-partners. Are you the de facto CEO of your practice? If so, how are you protecting against these risks?

Compared to a regular business owner, a Doctor building a medical practice is not generally building wealth for his or her family. If you want to ensure that you do build wealth for the family through your practice and actually turn your practice into a "Wealth Building Engine" for your family, you must draft, fully-execute, and properly fund a Buy-Sell agreement.

In this chapter, we will discuss the reasons why a premature death or disability of a partner is such a big risk and what the financial repercussions are of failing to address this issue. We will then discuss the "medicine" for such an ailment—the Buy-Sell Agreement. We also address the importance, and method, of funding the agreement and how to work with the right team of advisors. With all of this knowledge, you should be motivated and prepared to address this important issue in your practice.

Always Expect The Unexpected

As owners of a professional practice, Doctors can spend 10 hours per day, six or seven days per week getting their practices to the point where the practice provides a measure of security for their families. We know, because we have been there ourselves. Nonetheless, those who ignore one fundamental legal contract jeopardize all of their hard work. This very important legal contract is the Buy-Sell agreement. This is an agreement that all owners sign, agreeing on the definition of disability and how the practice will be valued at the time of one partner's death or disability, and how the purchase of the shares will be paid.

Without a Buy-Sell agreement, partners and remaining families have no guidelines as to how a practice will deal with the disability or an early death of a physician-owner. At a time when the family is grieving or caring for a disabled family member and possibly struggling to pay bills, they will look to the remaining partners' practice to help them in their time of need. At the same time, the remaining partners may be struggling to get by without the services of a valuable partner. The last thing either of these two groups need is a struggle over money. In too many cases, the absence of a Buy-Sell agreement at the time of death or disability can cause bankruptcies for the families of all of the partners.

Let's consider some of the questions that Doctors should ask themselves:

- What would happen to my family if I become permanently disabled or die? Is it fair that I worked so hard to build the practice and all my family will get will be my outstanding accounts receivable?
- What happens if and when any of my partners becomes permanently disabled or dies? How will their families fare?
- If I have another business and a partner becomes permanently disabled or dies, do I want the surviving family members as new partners? How will I buy them out at that time?
- What happens to my share of the practice if I decide I want 'out' of the practice or I decide to retire? (We will discuss exit buy-outs at the end of this chapter.)

Let's look at a quick case study of Steve and David, involving only one of the many situations where a Buy-Sell agreement has great utility. As you'll see, their story of a two-person practice losing one partner is a pretty typical case.

Case Study: Steve and David

Steve and David are owners of a very successful surgery center. Steve has the clinical expertise that patients want, while David runs the operations and marketing. Their overall profitability results from their joint efforts. If Steve were to die prematurely, David would have to find a Doctor capable of doing what Steve does. With the new hire, it's unlikely that the person could duplicate Steve's skills and contributions to the success of the surgery center.

At the same time, Steve's widow would want to continue to take the same money out of the practice that the family received before Steve's death. In fact, if Steve's widow is raising a young family or has children in college, she may have to force a sale of the surgery center at a distressed price just to meet her needs. Maybe Steve's son fancies himself a savvy businessman and has his own ideas on how things should be run. Perhaps Steve's spouse wants to see Steve's son take over his father's place.

It wouldn't matter that Steve Junior is incompetent. So many problems can arise. Needless to say, it may be impossible for David to continue a profitable practice under such circumstances, and he certainly doesn't want to be forced into a partnership with Steve's wife or son.

Special Issue For Medical Practices: Why The Buy-Sell Is Needed For The Engine

Notice that the case study above was for a surgery center—not a professional medical practice. In the case of a professional medical practice, non-physicians generally cannot own the practice. So, at the time of a physician's death or disability, the remaining family has no right whatsoever to any of the practice's assets or future income.

This restriction means that a Doctor can work hard over a career to build a practice that can never be left to remaining heirs. In fact, this creates a huge "gap" in the wealth planning for most Doctor families when compared to clients who have similar sized businesses in other areas. The business owner builds the value of the business while building net worth for the family. The Doctor, on the other hand, is generally not doing that. The only way to accomplish this goal is to convince all partners to agree to a Buy-Sell Agreement and to fund that agreement. This is why the Buy-Sell Agreement is essential to making your practice a financial "Engine" as well as a "Fortress." Let's dig into the details of Buy-Sell Agreements so you can see how they should be used in your situation.

The Buy-Sell Agreement

A Buy-Sell agreement is an agreement that all practice owners sign agreeing how the practice will be valued at the time of one partner's disability or death, and how the purchase of the shares will be paid. There are various ways to structure Buy-Sell agreements, depending on the goals and circumstances of the owners and the structure of the practice. In all arrangements there are some basics regarding the agreements that can apply to any type of practice. Specifically, the benefits different stakeholders and their families can gain from a Buy-Sell agreement are universal.

Practically speaking, Buy-Sells can be used for medical and non-medical corporations (PCs, PAs, and PLLCs all qualify whether they are "S" or "C" corporations for tax purposes), partnerships, limited partnerships, Limited Liability Companies (LLC), and other forms as well. To simplify the text, we will use the words "practice owner" generically to mean any type of physician practice, including shareholders in a corporation, partners in a partnership, and members in an LLC. In the following discussion, we will address the benefits to the living owners, to the practice and its remaining owners after a death or disability, and to the surviving family members who have lost a loved one.

Benefits To All Living Partners

From the standpoint of a healthy practice owner, the Buy-Sell agreement can provide the individual partner with an opportunity to negotiate and obtain the fairest or best price for his share of the practice. In the case of retirement or disability, the agreement can be an additional source of funds for each owner.

Benefits To The Practice And Remaining Owners

There are various benefits of the Buy-Sell agreement for both the practice and its remaining owners when one partner dies or becomes disabled:

A. Provide Continuation and Control

First, from the standpoint of the practice and its remaining partners, a properly planned Buy-Sell agreement will provide for orderly continuation of the ownership and control of the practice. This continuation should survive the disability, divorce, bankruptcy or death of any owner and should provide for a seamless transition in the event any owner wants to retire and sell his or her ownership share.

B. Keep out Unwanted Owners

Second, the Buy-Sell agreement can prevent unwanted outsiders from becoming owners and can eliminate the need for negotiation with remaining spouses and children. The agreement may also perform the role of a succession plan by providing for continuity or orderly succession of practice management. As above, this is not as relevant for the professional practice as it is for surgery centers and other medically-related businesses where non-Doctors can be owners.

C. Provide Liquidity to Buy Out Surviving Family Members

Third, the Buy-Sell agreement is often used in conjunction with life and disability insurance policies to effectively provide liquidity for the practice to purchase the outstanding ownership interests of the disabled or deceased partner.

Benefits To Surviving Family Members

The Buy-Sell agreement benefits the family members of disabled or deceased partners in various ways:

A. Provide Liquidity to Surviving Family Members

For a deceased or disabled owner's family, the existence of a properly funded Buy-Sell agreement can assure the family a liquid asset rather than an illiquid minority interest in a privately-held practice that would be extremely difficult, if not impossible, to sell and which would have little, if any, real financial value to the family. As mentioned earlier, this can be extremely important as the remaining family may be burdened with estate tax payments or additional expenses to care for a disabled family member. The agreement itself may provide a valuation of the practice interest, which can be used for estate tax filing purposes. This may save the survivors the additional headache and expense of securing another valuation and fighting the IRS on that value.

B. Eliminate Practice Risks to Surviving Family Members

If one owner becomes disabled or dies, the Buy-Sell contract guarantees that the disabled owner's family does not have to become involved in the practice in order to protect the total family's interest. The Buy-Sell agreement frees the disabled or deceased owner and his or her family from the risk of future practice losses and creates funds that may be used to pay medical bills and living costs of his or her family.

Funding The Agreement

Because the Buy-Sell agreement contemplates a Buy-Sell transaction at the time of an owner's disability or death, insurance policies are generally recommended to fund the transaction. There are many reasons for this, including the following:

- Insurance policies pay a predetermined amount with proceeds that are available at exactly the time when they are needed. This means there will be no liquidity concerns for any of the involved parties who need money at this time.
- Proceeds will be available regardless of the financial state of the practice at that point (so long as premiums have been paid).
- The practice "Leverages" the cost of insurance premiums to create the proceeds. Therefore, it costs the practice less to buy insurance than it would cost to save money in a special buy-out side fund.
- The economic risks of premature disability or early death of any owner are shifted from the medical practice to the insurance company.
- Insurance proceeds are paid to the owner or owner's family income tax-free.

If the payment to the owner or the owner's family is not fully satisfied in a lump sum cash payment or is not being made by an insurance company through a disability insurance policy, it is important to consider some type of security arrangement for the departing owner. The security arrangement is necessary to protect the owner or the owner's family in the event that the medical practice fails to make future payments. These agreements might include personal guarantees from remaining owners, mortgages or security interests in real estate, a bank standby letter of credit, or even collaterally-assigned life insurance policies.

The Need For A Coordinated Team

Creating a Buy-Sell arrangement that fits a particular practice's circumstances requires expertise and experience. Expertise in areas of corporate and health care practice law, tax law, insurance products, and the valuation of practices are all absolute requirements. Just as important is experience in dealing with different owners and being able to negotiate and draft an agreement that meets the needs of all parties involved.

Too often, practice owners make one of two key mistakes in deciding who should oversee the creation of a Buy-Sell arrangement. These include:

1. Choosing a friend who is a lawyer, rather than an expert with experience in this area, to create the strategy and draft the document.
2. Failing to work with a coordinated interdisciplinary team of financial and legal specialists to implement the plan.

Once you realize that you need a coordinated interdisciplinary team of financial and legal specialists to administer the Buy-Sell arrangement, you have to find the right team. This team would involve the following:

- An *attorney* who has experience creating these types of arrangements.
- A *life insurance professional* who has worked on these issues many times.
- A *disability insurance professional* who is familiar with these issues.
- A *practice appraisal firm*, whose expertise may be needed in the future for annual practice valuations.

The Diagnosis

As with any legal or insurance planning, the early bird is richly rewarded. Nowhere in practice planning is this truer than in the Buy-Sell agreement. The reason is not so much economic, but political. If this planning is done before any owner encounters a disability, divorce, retirement, or death, all owners will be better prepared. That makes the negotiation of a standard deal for all owners a much easier and smoother process. Planning early for a Buy-Sell agreement will truly benefit you, your family, and your practice. In order to avoid financial disasters, the agreement should be an essential part of your financial planning.

5-7

Captive Insurance Companies—The Ultimate Practice Tools

Many Doctors will build their wealth primarily through their professional practice. Typically, the practice is not only the vehicle that allows the client to use Leverage, but also the vehicle that creates the bulk of the client's annual income and long-term wealth accumulation. Given this fundamental importance, it is essential that Doctors do everything possible to protect the practice and maximize its Leverage potential. The best tool for achieving such protection and Leverage is the one we will discuss in this chapter—the captive insurance company (CIC). In this chapter, we will discuss what a CIC is, what benefits it offers, and how Doctors can use it to maximize the benefits they get from their practice planning.

The CIC

Early in the book, we stressed the importance of using tools that have multiple benefits. By using tools that offer multiple benefits, Doctors can compound their Leverage and achieve a number of planning goals more efficiently than if they tried to reach their goals one at a time. Of all the tools discussed in this book, the CIC can be the most efficient. For clients who own successful businesses or professional practices, the CIC often becomes the cornerstone of the ascent to a desired level of affluence. This is because the CIC affords the following benefits:

- Superior risk management for the practice
- Reduction in the practice's insurance expenses to third-party insurers
- The ability to capture profits on insurance policies
- Highest levels (+4 and +5) of asset protection for CIC assets
- Superior income tax treatment for CIC income (when the CIC is properly structured and maintained)
- Significant estate planning benefits (when the CIC is properly integrated with estate planning tools)

- Creation of a potential buy-out mechanism for older owners of the practice upon retirement

The CIC we will discuss here is a fully licensed insurance company domiciled either in one of the states that has special legislation for small captive companies or in an offshore jurisdiction which has similar captive legislation. Whenever a CIC is established offshore, it is critical that the CIC be compliant with all US tax rules and must be handled by captive managers, tax attorneys, or CPAs experienced in these matters.

CIC As A Risk Management Tool

The CIC must always be established with a real insurance purpose—that is, as a facility for transferring risk and protecting assets. The transaction must make economic sense. Beyond this general rule, there is a great deal of flexibility in how the CIC can benefit its owner(s).

First, clients can use the CIC to supplement their existing insurance policies. Such "excess" protection gives the client the security of knowing that the company and its owners will not be wiped out by a lawsuit award in excess of traditional coverage limits. As Doctors, you should be concerned with all types of lawsuits—from medical malpractice to practice risks to employment liability—and this protection can be significant. Further, the CIC may even allow the client to reduce existing insurance, as the CIC policy will step in to provide additional coverage if needed.

Using one's own CIC gives the client flexibility in using customized policies which one would not easily find when using large third-party insurers. For example, many clients would like a liability policy that would pay the client's legal fees (and allow full choice of attorney), but would not be available to pay creditors or claimants (what we call "Shallow Pockets" policies). This prevents the client from appearing as a "Deep Pocket" (a prime lawsuit target). Avoiding this appearance is a necessary asset protection strategy in today's highly-litigious society.

In addition, the CIC has the flexibility to add coverage for liabilities excluded by traditional general liability policies, such as wrongful termination, harassment, or even ADA violations. Given that the awards in these areas can be over $1 million per case, Doctors should understand the value of the CIC for this benefit alone. Let's see how two such clients used a CIC by looking at the Case Study of Justin and Harry:

Case Study: Justin and Harry Use CICs

Justin and Harry are Doctors who each own successful practices and surgery centers. Justin feels like he is paying too much for his group's medical malpractice and commercial liability insurance policies. After our firm introduced Justin to an attorney and actuary who specialize in CICs, he hired them to create a CIC to issue policies that cover the least significant, most common medical malpractice and commercial liability claims (under $100,000 per occurrence). These self-insured policies significantly reduced his existing insurance premiums because he then had much higher deductibles for his third-party insurance policies.

Justin believed he could reduce his insurance premiums to commercial insurance companies, implement successful risk management programs, reduce the claims of the center, and reduce his total overall payments and costs. Ultimately, he hoped that the CIC would help him increase the profits of the center. He was right. While a significant portion of the $1.5 million in total payments was paid out to cover claims, there was still over $1 million in his CIC reserves after five years.

Justin also created the CIC owned by a Trust for his family. This way he was able to build, outside of his taxable estate, the wealth created by the CIC.

Harry had a different approach. He established a CIC to insure lesser risks that were not covered under commercial insurance. These policies included Medicare fraud defense, HIPAA litigation expense, and malpractice defense policies (which are available only to pay for the company's legal fees, but not to pay claimants). After five years, Harry's CIC did not pay any claims. At this point, the premiums are still growing *income tax free* as reserves of the CIC to be used to pay future claims.

Harry is also considering bringing younger partners into his practice. He plans on using the CIC as part of an exit strategy for his practice as well, with each new partner responsible for paying some of his buyout—from both the practice and the CIC.

The purpose of the case study is to demonstrate that clients can purchase policies from their CIC that are similar to policies offered by traditional third-party insurers or can purchase less common policies. In either case, CIC owners have an opportunity to enjoy powerful asset protection, tax, retirement, and estate planning advantages from using a CIC. In essence, the question for the client becomes:

If you are going to use insurance to protect against risk, why give away the potential profits, asset protection, and tax and estate planning benefits when you do not have to?

Let's more closely examine a few of the benefits of having a CIC.

CIC Compared To Self-Insuring—The "Rainy Day Fund"

Because our society has become so litigious, many Doctors have been "self-insuring" against potential losses like the ones named above. These clients have simply saved up funds to be used to pay any expenses that may arise from a risk. This is the proverbial "rainy day fund." While a rainy day fund may prove wise, the client would be better off using a CIC to insure against any risks. This is because premiums paid to the CIC enjoy the highest levels of asset protection (+4/+5), can be structured to grow outside the taxable estate, can be structured to layer into a practice exit strategy, and can enjoy tax advantages as well. None of these benefits are found with the "rainy day fund."

By definition, anything you don't insure, you self-insure. With a CIC, you are able to insure some of what you are now self-insuring, but are paying tax-deductable premiums to your own insurance company.

Avoiding Land Mines

The CIC structure must be properly created and maintained. If not, all risk management, asset protection, estate, practice and tax benefits may be lost. For these reasons, using professionals who have expertise in establishing and managing CICs for clients is critical. It is especially important that the right attorneys and insurance managers are involved. While using such experts and a real CIC structure may be more expensive than some of the cheaper alternatives being touted on the Internet or at fly-by-night seminars, this is one area where "doing it right" is the only way to enjoy the CIC's benefits and be 100% compliant with Federal and local laws and regulations.

Who Can Afford A CIC?

Setting up a CIC requires particular expertise. As you might expect, the professionals most experienced in these matters charge significant fees for both the creation and maintenance of CICs. Set-up costs can be from $70,000 to $100,000 and annual maintenance costs another $30-50,000 per year. While these fees are significant (and often fully tax-deductible), the CIC's potential risk management, tax, practice, estate planning, and asset protection benefits often combine to make it a very attractive option for very successful Doctors. There is no better way for successful practice owners to Leverage their advisors than to work with them to create such a flexible and efficient planning tool as a Captive Insurance Company.

The Diagnosis

Doctors face various financial threats that range from operational problems to exit strategy challenges and from lawsuit threats to increasing operational costs. Astute Doctors not only want to mitigate these risks, but to do so in an efficient manner. For these reasons, Doctors who own very successful practices use captive insurance companies (CICs). A CIC can be a valuable tool in addressing many of a Doctor's planning challenges at one time. In fact, perhaps no other tool described in this book can impact a client's overall wealth protection and long-term accumulation as much as a CIC. Once you read the rest of the book and understand all of the available planning options, you will have a greater understanding and appreciation of the value of a CIC.

5-8

Creating Your Practice's $1 Million Retirement Buyout

One of the most common complaints we hear from Doctors is that they are frustrated that their decades of hard work are not building anything of concrete financial value. In other words, Doctors are frustrated that their practice will not be "worth anything" when they retire. As a result, they cannot "sell it" and enjoy a lucrative exit from the practice of medicine the way other business owners can with their non-medical businesses.

It is certainly true that the days of an outside practice management firm coming in and purchasing a Doctor's practice for millions of dollars are long gone. On the other hand, there are a number of tactics a Doctor can employ to create a $1 million "buy-out fund." We are not talking about the funded Buy-Sell arrangement that applies to unforeseen circumstances such as a disability or premature death of a partner. The buy-out funds we will discuss here are mechanisms to exit a practice at the Doctor's chosen retirement time and take more than $1 million out at that point. Of course, this would also be in addition to whatever the Doctor has in qualified retirement plans and other personal assets.

Buyout Funding Options

As you will see below, each of these tools require periodic funding over time. With the compound growth over an entire career, a Doctor can create significant retirement buy-out funds over 10, 20, or 30 years. A nice bonus is that the funds can grow on a tax-deferred or tax-free basis in most of these arrangements. With all of these tools, Doctors have two potential ways of funding them:

A. Solo Practice Model
Here, the Doctor in question simply takes advantage of one or more of the tools below and funds them from the practice. This approach is certainly better than not funding them at all, thanks to the asset protection and potential tax benefits that many of these tools afford. These options force the Doctor to build the buy-out fund with dollars that might otherwise be spent on personal consumption. Therefore, any and all of these tools can be used in the one-Doctor model.

B. Group Practice Model

In this model, in addition to the potential tax, asset protection, and forced savings benefits, Doctors enjoy another crucial benefit described earlier on in the book. They get to use other people's money (OPM) to achieve a long-term goal. OPM is involved here because each of these tools can be Leveraged in a way that older Doctors of the practice require the younger Doctors (partners or not) to contribute into these vehicles. While the contributions go partly to their own buy-out fund, part of it could also fund the buy-out of older Doctors. When these younger Doctors become more senior, they too will benefit from this arrangement and the funding by younger Doctors at that time. This "pyramid" model is common in professional firms outside medicine, such as consulting or law firms.

Buyout Funding Tools

As you will see below, all the major buyout funding tools are arrangements that we have already described earlier in this Lesson. Let's examine each of them again briefly and review how they apply to the goal of creating a buyout retirement fund.

1. LLC Lease-Back

A valuable piece of equipment or the practice's office can be transferred to an LLC and then leased back to the practice entity. As explained before, this provides asset protection for the practice (vis-à-vis claims from the property or equipment), the property/equipment (from claims against the practice), and for the Doctors (from both).

The LLC lease back works as a buyout funding tool through the rent paid by the practice to the LLC. Each month the practice will pay tax-deductible rent to the LLC. In the solo practice model, the Doctor could utilize a gifting program for the LLC interests and, over time, get the benefit of lower tax bracket "borrowing" of children or grandchildren. Proceeds remain inside the LLC, asset protected at a (+2) level. They can be managed by professionals in a tax-favored way and built up over time to create a buyout fund.

Even better, in the group practice model, the Doctors gain additional shares in the LLC for each year of service. This way, the older Doctors have more of an interest in the LLC accounts as they remain with the practice, and the younger Doctors help fund their value (as the rent can be an expense they all share equally). When the Doctor retires, he or she can redeem LLC interests for cash. The cycle continues as new Doctors join the practice and become young partners.

2. Unrelated AR financing

In the unrelated lender AR financing structure, an outside lender (typically a bank) takes the security agreement against the AR. This is typically in return for a loan to the practice. Often, the loan proceeds are invested in a creditor-protected life insurance policy as part of a deferred compensation arrangement for the Doctors.

In the solo practice structure, the opportunity for a buy-out fund comes from the deferred compensation arrangement. However, as cautioned before, because loan interest must be paid to the bank, the investments of the plan should be conservatively structured to meet the loan interest and principal obligations. Sometimes, it is difficult to generate a return that exceeds the interest costs of the loan. Taking too much risk here in an attempt to generate income to offset the loan payments is extremely unwise and can lead to further negative financial consequences. Remember, the reason you are entering into this transaction in the first place is to reduce—not increase—financial risks.

For the group practice model, there may be more of an opportunity for a buy-out fund, even if the policy is a very conservative one. This is because of the OPM factor. If younger Doctors share the burden of funding the policy of older Doctors, there is a greater opportunity for buy-out funds accumulating beyond the loan obligations.

3. Related AR Financing

In the related lender AR financing structure, a related lender (often an irrevocable trust for the benefit of non-physician family members) makes the loan to the practice and the trust takes the security agreement against the AR. Because the trust and family members (spouse and children, typically) are being paid interest, the overall family economics are superior to the unrelated lender arrangement.

This buyout fund arrangement generally only works with solo or two-person practices because the lender is related to the Doctor. It becomes too complex to have multiple trusts loaning funds to a practice with more than one or two Doctors. However, in the small practice scenario, this arrangement can provide solid asset protection and create beneficial buy-out funds within an LLC or exempt life policy as well.

4. Non-Qualified/Hybrid Plan

Non-qualified plans (or hybrid plans) are benefit plans not required to be offered to all practice employees. While the contributions to the plan are typically not tax deductible, the funds in the plan can grow tax-deferred.

The non-qualified plan works as a buy-out funding tool through the contributions paid by the practice to the plan. Each month or year, the practice will make contributions to the plan for each participant. The funds can then grow in the plan tax-deferred. At retirement (no age restrictions as with qualified plans), the Doctor can withdraw his or her plan funds. The tax at that time depends on the plan. In the solo practice model, the Doctor simply has the practice make contributions to the plan and enjoys the tax-favored build up over time to create a buyout fund.

Even better, in the group practice model, the Doctors gain additional benefits by using the contributions of the practice to fund the plan based on years of service. This way, the older Doctors have more of an interest in the fund as they remain with the practice. The cycle continues as new Doctors join the practice and become young partners.

5. **Captive Insurance Company (CIC)**
As explained in the last chapter, CICs are real insurance companies that insure the medical practice for a host of risks. In many cases, the Doctor's CIC can be just as profitable over their career as the medical practice. Thus, whether the Doctor owns the CIC himself (solo model) or all the Doctors in the practice own it, the CIC can create an enormous potential buy-out fund when any Doctor retires. In fact, the superior structure is one where the CIC is owned from the outset by one or more Trusts for the Doctors' families and the CIC establishes some type of benefit plan for the Doctors' buy-out fund. This creates estate planning benefits as well as buy-out funding benefits.

The Diagnosis

Doctors cannot simply rely on a "white knight" firm to come in and buy their practices for $1 million on the day they want to retire. On the other hand, the idea that they "can't get anything for their practice" misses the point entirely. Doctors who plan for an exit can have a lucrative one—but they need to focus on the goal of creating a buy-out fund years before they retire and be diligent in their funding of one of more buy-out tools over time.

In this Lesson, you learned how not to structure your practice and how to utilize multiple entities to protect valuable real estate, equipment and accounts receivable. You also learned how retirement plans provide asset protection and why your practice MUST have a fully executed and funded Buy-Sell agreement. You also learned how successful practices benefit from captive insurance companies and million-dollar buyout programs.

5-9

What You Must Consider if Your Practice is Acquired by a Hospital

A common trend in the Ohio medical landscape today is the acquisition of medical practices by hospitals. We are seeing this more and more, throughout the state, in a variety of settings and legal structures. If you are a doctor whose practice has recently been acquired by a hospital, or one who is considering the move, this chapter is a must-read.

Types of Transactions: A Background

There are essentially 2 types of transactions where a doctor's practice becomes part of the hospital:

1. **Outright Acquisition**
   This is the most common and well-known transaction and is fairly simple. Here, the practice is acquired by the hospital. The physician becomes a hospital employee, paid as any other W-2 employee.

2. **Physician Enterprise Model** (PEM)
   A lesser-known transaction has begun to take hold in certain areas of the state. This transaction, relatively new to the field, is called the "Physician Enterprise Model" (PEM). In a PEM, the following occurs:

   1. Hospital or health system employs physician through a separate entity that is a "group practice" for regulatory purposes. This is known as the **Physician Enterprise.**

   2. Hospital does not purchase the practice. Physician retains ownership of the practice as before. This is known as the **Practice Entity**.

   3. Practice Entity serves as the manager of the Physician Enterprise. It provides necessary package of services, i.e. non-physician support staff, facilities, equipment, record keeping, etc.

4. Practice Entity and Physician Enterprise enter into any safe harbor management agreement for these services.

Outright Acquisition: Pros & Cons for the Doctor

The traditional outright acquisition model has distinct positives and negatives for the Doctor. The principal positives are the following:

A. Reduced legal exposure for the Doctor, as he/she is now a hospital employee

B. Reduced overhead expenses—most often, rent, administration and liability insurance

C. In some circumstances, increased financial security for the practice—as the hospital may support it financially or guarantee it a certain flow of patients

The significant negatives include:

A. Loss of autonomy—the Doctor is now an employee that must report to hospital executives

B. Loss of control of his/her financial package—including qualified plan and other benefit planning

While the first negative may be more frustrating on a personal level, the second negative can be quite costly to the Doctor over his/her career.

Case Study: Orthopedic Surgeon Oscar Sells Out to Hospital

At 45 years old with a healthy practice, Oscar would likely have either one, or both, of the following Qualified Retirement Plans to help him save for retirement, and reduce his current taxable income. These plans would include:

A Defined Contribution Plan, also referred to as a Profit Sharing Plan. In this plan, Oscar can defer up to $49,000 in 2009. This contribution limit is typically increased each year to keep pace with inflation. Oscar's investment will accumulate on a tax-deferred basis as well, but every dollar withdrawn in retirement will be taxed as income.

A Defined Benefit Plan is also funded with tax-deferred dollars. The annual contributions are calculated each year based on conservative growth assumptions, and a specific amount to be attained at a specific age, for example, $1,000,000 at age 62. For the purposes of our case study, let's say Oscar is making tax-deferred annual contributions of $45,000 into his Defined Benefit Plan. These funds will also accumulate on a tax-deferred basis, and withdrawals during retirement will be taxed as income.

For purposes of the analysis below, we will assume that Oscar maximizes his profit-sharing contribution but does not presently take advantage of a defined benefit plan in addition. More savings-motivated physicians will give up even more by becoming a hospital W-2 employee.

When Oscar becomes a hospital W-2 employee, he will lose the more tax-beneficial qualified plans above—both the profit-sharing plan and/or the defined benefit plan. Even in a "likely hospital scenario," Oscar would have access to a 403b, which will allow him to defer only $16,500 in 2009. In a "best case" hospital scenario, Oscar would also have access to a 457b plan, which is very similar to a 403b, and would allow Oscar to defer another $16,500 in 2009.

In addition to his Qualified Retirement Plans, as a practice owner, Oscar also enjoys the ability to deduct business related expenses, such as a portion of his car lease and home office expenses.

Let's say Oscar pays $800/month for his car lease, and claims he uses his vehicle for business purposes 70% of the time. This would result in an annual deduction of $6,720. *As a W-2 employee of the hospital, Oscar will lose this deduction.*

Oscar would also be able to deduct business related expenses, such as computer and electronic equipment, software, office furniture, office supplies, travel expenses, etc. For this example, we'll assume Oscar is deducting $4,000/year for these expenses. *As a W-2 employee of the hospital, Oscar will also lose the ability to deduct these expenses.*

Assuming Oscar's gross annual income is $500,000, let's look at how the two scenarios currently compare below. Again, we will assume here that Oscar only participates in a profit-sharing plan—for doctors who also have a defined benefit plan, these numbers would look even more dramatic:

Oscar's Private Practice Scenario

	Gross Annual Amount	Income Tax Savings @40% Tax Bracket
Deferred Contribution into Profit Sharing Plan	$49,000.00	$19,600.00
Deduction as a Result of Auto Lease	$6,720.00	$2,688.00
Office Expense Deduction	$4,000.00	$1,600.00
	Total Annual Tax Savings:	**$23,888.00**

Oscar's Scenario as a W-2 Employee—Best Case

	Gross Annual Amount	Income Tax Savings @40% Tax Bracket
Deferred Contribution into 403b Plan	$16,500	$6,600.00
Deferred Contribution into 457b Plan	$16,500.00	$6,600.00
Total Annual Tax Savings:		**$13,200.00**

Oscar's case is not unique. In fact, it is quite typical. The reality is that a Doctor gives up the entire benefit of being a business owner when he/she becomes a hospital employee. As above, the ability to implement aggressive retirement plans, fringe benefit plans, and the tax savings that goes along with them has a direct impact on a Doctor's long-term wealth creation. Giving that ability up is significant—whether the hospital falls into a "likely" or "best" case scenario.

A Potential Solution: A Hybrid Benefit Plan Ideally Suited for Hospitals

While the reality of what Oscar gave up may be startling, there is good news. Hospitals around the country are beginning to learn about, and adopt, a particular type of benefit plan that can provide Oscar with a way to capture all of his lost benefits, and more. Further, this plan costs the hospital nothing! It is not surprising that hospitals are starting to see the fit here—it helps their existing and soon-to-be-recruited doctors significantly and costs them nothing. A major teaching hospital in Ohio, in fact, is in the process of layering this plan into their benefits package as this book goes to press.

A few brief facts about this type of benefit plan:

a. This benefit plan is authorized by a particular section of the Internal Revenue Code ("IRC") that has been in the IRC for over 30 years, an extremely long and stable legislative history.

b. Nearly 5 years ago, the IRS issued rules that made the plan more conservative from a tax perspective, creating "safe harbor" rules, giving us specific "black and white" guidance of exactly how the plan needs to be established to get the benefits desired. This should give any hospital counsel or HR office comfort to move forward with the plan.

c. The hospital can offer this plan in addition to their 403(b) or other qualified retirement plan.

d. The hospital can decide to offer this to all employees, just Doctors, or some other classification tied to employment

e. The plan is asset protected at the highest (+5) level in Ohio (you will learn about what the (+5) designation means in Lesson 6)

While a full description of all the tax and retirement benefits are beyond the scope of this chapter, feel free to contact the authors for more on this at (800) 554-7233. We would be happy to present this concept to any hospital in Ohio.

Case Study: Oscar's Hospital Offers This Benefit Plan

Let's return to Oscar's situation above. Now let's assume that Oscar's hospital adopts this benefit plan as part of their package and offers it to Oscar as a hospital Doctor employee. Now, in addition to the 403(b), he is able to contribute another $50,000 into this benefit plan. He funds this plan for 5 years and then stops. How does Oscar now benefit? Let's see:

- This plan saves him an additional $6-8,000 in taxes per year—for a total of $30,000-$40,000 in tax savings over the 5 years.
- The contributions into his plan grow totally (+5) asset protected under Ohio law.
- If Oscar ever leaves the hospital employment, he takes 100% of his funds in the plan with him, the hospital will receive nothing.
- Presuming an 8% return in the market, Oscar would be able to take out $38,531 per year *tax free* in retirement, ages 65 thru 84. These numbers would be even larger if he waits longer to retire.
- All of the above benefits (and others) Oscar will enjoy—in addition to the hospital's 403(b) and/or 457 plan that he also funds.

Given the implementation of this plan, let's take another look at Oscar's Scenario Comparison:

Oscar's Private Practice Scenario

	Gross Annual Amount	Income Tax Savings @40% Tax Bracket
Deferred Contribution into Profit Sharing Plan	$49,000.00	$19,600.00
Deduction as a Result of Auto Lease	$6,720.00	$2,688.00
Office Expense Deduction	$4,000.00	$1,600.00
Total Annual Tax Savings:		**$23,888.00**

Oscar in "Best Care" Hospital Scenario

	Gross Annual Amount	Income Tax Savings @40% Tax Bracket
Deferred Contribution into 403b Plan	$16,500.00	$6,600.00
Deferred Contribution into 457b Plan	$16,500.00	$6,600.00
Deduction Based on $50,000 Contribution into the Hybrid Plan	$17,512.00	$7,004.80
Total Annual Tax Savings:		**$20,204.80**

With the Hybrid Plan, Oscar has been able to reduce his "lost deductions" by $17,000+ per year, getting him almost to "even" with his deductions when he owned his practice. Even more importantly, the plan contributions are flexible. In other words, Oscar could contribute up to $100,000 per year into the Hybrid Plan, in addition to the 403(b) and 457 plans, giving him another $17,000+ of deductions. By doing this, not only would he then be better off deduction-wise than he was in his practice, but he would be funding a plan that was (+5) asset protected in Ohio and acts as a tax hedge against future income and capital gains tax increases.

If increasing his deductions so that he is at least break-even as he joins the ranks of W-2 employees—as well as tax-beneficial retirement income and asset protection—is important to Oscar, then he should work with his other physicians, the board and the HR department to get this benefit plan added to the hospital's benefit package. As noted above, this plan can be structured with no cost to the hospital, so it shouldn't be hard to get approved.

Physician Enterprise Model: Pros & Cons for the Doctor

The newer Physician Enterprise Model also has distinct positives and negatives for the Doctor. The principal positives are the following:

1. The Doctor can maintain control of his/her benefits package through the Physician Enterprise. This entity can often implement the Hybrid benefit plan described above as well.
2. He/She can continue to manage the practice as they did before hospital employment.

The principal negatives are the following:

1. This model is relatively new and untested. If the business relationship sours, or there is liability to third parties, it is unclear how these arrangements will be treated. This can cause unforeseen legal costs and potential liability.
2. Many hospitals may simply not be open to this model, thereby removing it as practical option.

The Diagnosis

In this rapidly shifting medical economic landscape, many Doctors have sought the "security" of having their practice acquired by a local hospital. Many more may be considering it. In this chapter, we have shown you a number of options for making this "jump" and the pros and cons of each. The book's authors can consult with Doctors, hospitals and their boards about the benefit plans that are available to make such a "jump" more financially rewarding to the Doctor without any cost to the hospital. Now, we will focus our attention on personal asset protection strategies that every Doctor must consider.

LESSON 6

Protect Personal Assets from Lawsuits

Throughout history, the affluent have availed themselves of the comforts of asset protection. Kings built impressive castles to shield their wealth from invading armies or rival kings. Some built walls around the towns that surrounded their castles. Others even built moats around those walls. Today, this is exactly what Doctors need to do with their wealth. The threats may not be rival kings or armies, but the importance of protecting assets has not changed.

Over the last twenty-five years, a period of significant wealth accumulation in this country, the need for asset protection has exploded, as have the tools of asset protection and the availability of professionals who can design and implement asset protection plans and strategies.

The endeavor of asset protection is quite easy to define: "the structuring of one's assets in a way to shield them from lawsuits and other creditor threats." Defining asset protection may be simple, but planning and achieving this goal can be quite difficult.

Implementing asset protection strategies and tools is completely legitimate and legal, provided that one does not engage in transfers or conveyances of their property that results in defrauding their creditors. Defrauding one's creditors typically falls into two broad categories: 1) intentional fraudulent conveyances/transfers, or 2) constructive fraudulent conveyances/transfers also referred to as "badges of fraud." Intentional fraudulent conveyances are conveyances done or made in such a manner as to actually defraud, hinder, or delay one's creditors.

Examples of constructive fraudulent conveyances or badges of fraud are transfers of one's property in which one does not receive in return a reasonably equivalent value for the transferred property, or engaging in transfers which leaves one insolvent or with minimal amounts of property. In this case, intent is not necessary. It is essentially inferred from the totality of the circumstances of the transaction(s). One of the most effective ways to avoid an assertion of a fraudulent conveyance or constructive fraudulent conveyance is to engage in asset protection planning sooner rather than later.

As will be explained later in this section, the use of exempt assets is typically an ideal technique because this rarely can be considered a "transfer for less than fair value."

Designing and implementing an asset protection plan requires expertise from a number of disciplines and must be managed on an ongoing basis to be successful. As a family's situation or asset mix changes, so too will the plan need to change to adequately protect its wealth.

The field of asset protection itself is very dynamic and fluid and is constantly undergoing changes. Court decisions and legislative asset protection laws vary greatly from state to state and nation to nation. In many ways, the asset protection environment has progressed to the point that states and countries are now competing for asset protection business by virtue of the laws they pass or court decisions reached—in short, the laws and legal environments of states and countries are not created equal!

How Does Ohio Stack Up For Asset Protection Planning?

The above discussion leads us to the question, how do Ohio's protection case law and statutes compare to those of other states and other countries? The short answer is, Ohio has both tremendous strengths (exemptions for life insurance as an example and protection of living trust assets from Probate creditors) and significant shortcomings (poor homestead protection). The bottom line is that Ohio physicians may want to consider, as a part of their asset protection planning, jurisdictions than Ohio, whether foreign or domestic.

In this Lesson, we will begin by explaining the importance of asset protection, the sliding scale of asset protection, and common asset protection myths. We will then explain a number of tools and strategies that have helped Doctors protect their assets, such as:

- Business and personal insurance
- State and federal exempt assets
- Family limited partnerships and limited liability companies
- Various types of asset protection trusts
- International planning
- Strategies for protecting your home
- Strategies for protecting against divorce

To see which tools work best for protecting your assets, you will have to work with your Advisory Team and make sure there is at least one member who, like the authors of this book, is a specialist in asset protection. Just as a general practitioner recognizes the need to refer a patient to a medical specialist, so too should you and your Advisory Team recognize the need to enlist an asset protection specialist when planning the protection of your assets.

6-1

The Importance of Asset Protection

Until the last part of the 20th century, it might have seemed excessive to be concerned with protecting assets from potential lawsuits. Lawsuits were not particularly common and jury awards were reasonable. In the 1980s, the number of lawsuits in the United States skyrocketed and outrageous jury awards became commonplace. This has been especially the case in employment and medical malpractice claims—two areas where Doctors are attractive targets for plaintiff's lawyers. As such, Doctors have realized that protecting their assets from lawsuits needs to be the focus of any financial plan.

The Lawsuit Explosion

Why are there so many more lawsuits today? It may be because many Americans see a lawsuit as a way to "get rich quick" rather than as a way to make someone whole and ultimately achieve justice for being wronged by another. In our society, many people believe that misfortune is an opportunity to place blame and seek financial reparations—even if that person wasn't at fault for the misfortune. Unfortunately, juries routinely adopt the idea that someone must pay for alleged wrongdoings and often disregard the facts of the case when reaching a verdict. Through emotion and bias, juries sometimes give away large sums of money to unfortunate victims, even when the defendants were not to blame for the misfortune.

To illustrate this point, let's consider the decisions reached in some cases you may have read about in your daily newspaper:

Claim: A woman sues a franchise eatery because the coffee she spilled in her lap was too hot.
Decision: Woman receives $2.6 million.

Claim: A trespasser is injured while burglarizing a home.
Decision: Burglar receives thousands of dollars.

After reading the large settlements these ordinary people receive, it seems rational that other people might ask themselves, "Why not me?" The more press these cases receive, the greater the reinforcement of this belief. The greater the number of people who try to "work the system," the greater the number of people who will eventually succeed. Each new outrageous success gains more press, and the vicious cycle of lawsuits continues.

Knowledgeable Doctors realize that this lawsuit trend cannot be ignored. They insist on having their advisors devise financial plans that address the protection of their assets. They realize that they have something to lose if they are sued, and that the plaintiff often has nothing to lose. This is especially true in the United States legal system.

Current Status of Ohio Medical Malpractice and Tort Reform

Ohio has had its ups and downs with medical malpractice and tort reform laws. In 1996, the Ohio Legislature passed legislation that attempted to provide among other things "limits" on the amount of money that could be awarded Plaintiffs in medical malpractice actions and other tort cases. But, the Ohio Supreme Court determined that the legislation was unconstitutional. Shortly after this, many of Ohio's physicians, especially those in the higher risk fields of obstetrics, neurosurgery and orthopedics faced skyrocketing malpractice insurance rates. In fact, the American Medical Association, due to the hardships that Ohio's physicians faced in obtaining fair and reasonable malpractice insurance rates, placed Ohio on a list of states considered "in crisis." In response, the Ohio State Medical Association (OSMA) helped formulate legislation that resulted in the passage of S.B. 281. This legislation and its progeny have provided much needed relief from the medical liability crisis.

The highlights of this law (S.B. 281) are the following:

$350,000 cap on "pain and suffering" awards which helps make the system more predictable for insurers and medical providers;

Statute of Repose which limits the time frame in which any liability claim can be filed to four years from the last date of treatment;

Proportionate liability which means Doctors only pay damages proportionate to their share of the medical negligence;

Affidavit of Merit signed by an expert witness in the same specialty as the defendant that attests to the merit of any liability lawsuit;

State Medical Board jurisdiction over out-of-state physician expert witnesses that gives the board the ability to discipline any physician that provides false or completely baseless medical testimony;

"I'm Sorry" law that enables physicians to express apology, sympathy or condolence regarding an unanticipated patient outcome, and protects such expressions or statements from being used as an admission of liability in a subsequent lawsuit;

Peer Review Protection that ensures any information disclosed in peer review is protected from discovery in a subsequent medical liability claim;

Prejudgment Interest Reform that limits calculations to the time when a defendant first received notice of a claim and not when the injury first occurred; prejudgment interest is also now prohibited from being applied to future damages;

Good Samaritan Law extends liability protection to any physicians that care for indigent patients in their offices;

Notice of Requirements holds insurance companies accountable by requiring that they explain the reasons behind non-renewals or premium increases, and increases the time period that they provide physicians of non-renewals or significant premium increases from 30 to 60 days.

The Bottom Line

In some respects tort reform is working in Ohio. In a recent report released by the Ohio Department of Insurance (3rd annual Ohio Medical Liability Closed Claim Report-January 2009), the report cited that medical malpractice liability premium rates are decreasing (down nearly 20% in the last three years) and medical liability lawsuits are also decreasing (34% in the last three years).

However, in other respects there remain concerns: The new law retained some parts of the previous law, which was determined to be unconstitutional. As of the date of this publication, S.B. 281 has not been reviewed by the Courts for constitutionality. Also, despite the fact that the number of lawsuits filed is decreasing, the "monetary" amounts of the medical malpractice jury verdicts and settlement award amounts are increasing. For example, since June of 2008, one medical malpractice firm in Ohio has obtained medical malpractice settlements/awards ranging from $3.8 million to $5.3 million dollars for plaintiffs in two non-death cases. Also, since 2000, this same firm has obtained medical malpractice settlements/awards in Ohio totaling more than $10 million.

It is critical to recognize that tort reform does nothing to limit jury awards related to a catastrophic injury or economic damages. The caps do not apply in cases of catastrophic injury. More importantly, the caps do not apply to economic damages, which include medical care and expenses, loss of earnings, and earning capacity.

Tort reform offers no comfort in cases involving catastrophic injury or injured individuals with high earning capacity. Relying solely on malpractice insurance coverage limits to protect your practice and personal assets may have unwelcome consequences. Just as patients need to take proactive steps to help safeguard their health, doctors need to recognize the risks to their financial security and take proactive steps to help safeguard their wealth.

(*Note: The sources for the above-referenced material also includes, The Ohio State Medical Association,"OSMA Medical Liability Reforms" and American Academy of Orthopaedic Surgeons, Maglione, "How Well Does Tort Reform Work?"*).

American Rule Of Legal Fees

Did you know that in virtually every other legal system in the world, a plaintiff who sues unsuccessfully has to pay the defendant's legal bills? That is correct. This rule, called the "British Rule," effectively keeps people from suing others unless they truly think they have a case with merit. If a plaintiff does not have a very good case, he risks not only paying his own attorney's fees, but also the defendant's.

This is obviously not the situation in the United States. In U.S. courts we follow the "American Rule," which dictates that each side pays their legal fees regardless of the outcome of the case. This rule was originally created so that people wouldn't be discouraged from suing big businesses. Though this rule may have some positive impact, it creates two negative consequences:

1. As a plaintiff, you have a lot less to lose if you bring a meritless case. In fact, with the prevalence of contingency fee attorneys, plaintiffs are literally in a no-lose situation as they have no "skin in the game." This is because contingency fee attorneys do not charge their clients hourly fees. Their only compensation is a percentage of the judgment awards of the cases they win.

2. As a defendant, a winning outcome is still a losing proposition. We say this because a successful defense of a lawsuit still results in significant out-of-pocket defense costs and legal fees. In addition, mounting an effective legal defense requires time away from work and an unquantifiable amount of stress.

Evidently, the American Rule of legal fees encourages civil lawsuits. Proponents of the system still claim that it allows the poor access to the legal system and is a method for Americans to redress injustices. They may be correct, but an unwanted side effect of this rule is that it also allows thousands, if not millions, of frivolous and dubious lawsuits to be filed each year.

People Abuse The Legal System

Whether it is caused by the American Rule of legal fees or not, it is clear that many people simply abuse the legal system for personal gain. This trend is so severe that many states have passed laws to prevent individuals from abusing our legal system. In June of 2002, Ohio passed the Vexatious Litigators Act ("the Act"). The Act establishes a list of people who routinely abuse the legal system by filing too many frivolous lawsuits. There are currently over 70 individuals in Ohio who have been adjudged to be "vexatious litigators." These same individuals cannot be denied their constitutional right to sue. However, the Act strictly regulates the manner in which they may file suits or continue a suit that has already been filed. The "vexatious litigators" list is available for review on the Ohio Supreme Court's website.

The Diagnosis

At this point, we hope you realize what the wealthy have known for years. The American Rule of law has afforded people an opportunity to protect themselves through the courts, but many people have taken advantage of the system and a lawsuit frenzy has resulted in our country. In this litigious society, asset protection planning must be an integral part of any comprehensive financial plan. For Doctors with greater liability than the average person, asset protection planning couldn't be more important. Luckily, it can be integrated into a financial plan to protect assets from lawsuits, allow Doctors to spend more time making money, and provide peace of mind. In the following chapters, you'll learn various tools and techniques you can implement to shield your wealth from lawsuits and other claims.

6-2

The Sliding Scale of Asset Protection

The most common misconception among Doctors regarding asset protection is the idea that an asset is either "protected" or "unprotected." This "black or white" analysis is no more accurate in the field of asset protection than it is in the field of medicine. In fact, asset protection advisors are very similar to physicians in how they approach any client or patient. In this chapter, we will discuss the way in which advisors measure a client's assets by using a sliding scale. Then we will suggest ways in which Doctors can protect assets, avoid high-risk assets, and achieve a high level of protection.

The Sliding Scale And Scores

To measure the assets of a client, advisors use a sliding scale that indicates the client's "good" and "bad" financial habits. Like Doctors, asset protection professionals will first try to get a client to avoid "bad habits." For a medical patient, bad habits might mean smoking, drinking too much, or maintaining a poor diet. For a client of ours, bad habits might include owning property in their own name, owning property jointly with a spouse, or failing to maximize the percentage of exempt assets in an investment portfolio.

Like a Doctor who judges the severity of a patient's illness, asset protection specialists use a rating system to determine the protection or vulnerability of a client's particular asset. The sliding scale runs from—5 (totally vulnerable) to +5 (superior protection). As you have probably already guessed, our goal is to bring a client's score closer to (+5) for each of their assets (see diagram below).

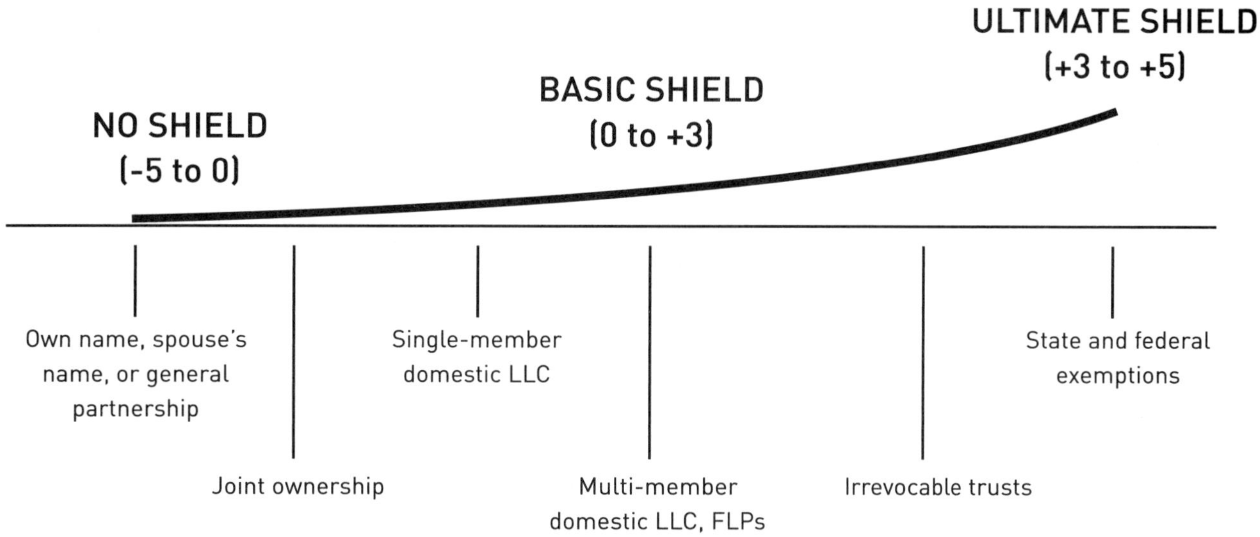

When most clients initially come to see us, their asset planning scores are overwhelmingly on the negative side of the scale. The reason for this score varies. Typically, personal assets are owned jointly (-3) or in their individual name (-5). Both of these ownership forms provide little protection from lawsuits and may also have negative tax and estate planning implications.

Many medical practices themselves also have asset planning scores that are overwhelming negative. For practices, the worst way to operate a business or title assets is a general partnership (-5). For all other business entities, liability from operations is always a concern. For this reason, owning any business assets within an operating business is extremely unwise (-5).

Before asset protection specialists can achieve a high level of protection for their clients, they must first eliminate the high risk assets. There are many ways to protect assets, but the most efficient way to avoid high risk assets and achieve a high level of protection is to utilize exempt assets. This is mentioned briefly in the next section and then discussed in greater detail later in the Lesson.

The Best Protection: Federal & State Exempt Assets

Each state law identifies assets that are absolutely exempt from creditor claims in that state. Federal law also exempts certain assets. Because these assets are inherently protected by law, they enjoy the highest level of protection, a (+5) score on the sliding scale. These will be discussed in detail in Chapter 6-6.

Good examples of how state laws can protect assets are found in Texas and Florida (and currently five other states), where the homestead exemptions are unlimited for personal residences (within certain rules) and the cash value in life insurance policies is completely protected. In Ohio, as you will see, our rules are not as protective—in short, Ohio again, is very average. At the federal level, bankruptcy law affords (+5) protection for qualified retirement plans, like pensions and 401(k) plans.

Basic Domestic Legal Tools

In many states, the list of state exemptions is not very generous. Even in those states where the exemptions are broad, we need to make sure that the asset protection goals are balanced with wealth accumulation and investment goals. For these reasons, there will almost always be non-exempt assets in a client's asset mix. For these assets, we must use other protection tools.

In such a situation, the basic asset protection tools are, domestic asset protection trusts ("DAPTs") family limited partnerships (FLPs), limited liability companies (LLCs). DAPTs, FLPs and LLCs provide good to excellent asset protection against future lawsuits, allow you to maintain control, and can provide income and estate tax benefits in certain situations. For these reasons, we call DAPTs, FLPs, and LLCs the "building blocks" of a basic asset protection plan.

DAPTs, FLPs and LLCs afford asset protection scores somewhere between (+1) to (+4), depending on the circumstances. It may be possible to increase these scores for some of your assets by employing the laws of other states to protect them (read Chapters 6-7 and 6-8 for additional insight on this topic).

Other Protection Strategies

Most Doctors can achieve the majority of their asset protection planning with a combination of exempt assets and legal tools (like FLPs, LLCs, and DAPT's). However, Doctors who are worth more than $3,000,000, or who earn more than $500,000, almost always need additional planning strategies to help them protect their assets. More successful Doctors may utilize advanced techniques like:

Non-Qualified Plans

Certain Non-Qualified Plans or "Hybrid" Benefit Plans used in a medical practice may provide asset protection benefits vis-à-vis creditors of the physician. In addition, these tools can offer tax-deferral and estate planning benefits. Most Doctors find these tools attractive because employees need not be covered in these plans to be successful. Revisit Chapter 5-4 for more on these tools.

Captive Insurance Companies

Structured offshore or domestically, Captive Insurance Companies can also reach the (+5) status when the shares are owned by a second entity like an irrevocable trust. Successful businesses can use such insurance companies to provide superior asset protection, risk management, efficiently fund a partner buy-out, and potentially reduce income and estate taxes. This strategy was discussed in greater detail in Chapter 5-6.

Debt Shields And Collateralization

Debt Shield and Collateralization strategies are ideal for protecting equity in real estate, especially the personal residence and the medical practice's Accounts Receivable (AR). This technique helps achieve a (+1) to (+5) rating. The exact score depends on the funding vehicles used in this technique. When structured properly, after-tax wealth can be built while protecting the real estate equity or Accounts Receivable in a superior way.

The Diagnosis

Asset protection planning, like any sophisticated multi-disciplinary effort, has degrees of success. Nothing in life is 100% certain (except perhaps death and taxes—both of which are discussed in Lessons #9 and #7, respectively). For asset protection planning, this adage holds true. You can protect each personal or practice asset to different levels. Exempt assets offer the greatest level of protection with the least cost. Legal tools generally fill in the rest of the plan for the average Doctor. Successful Doctors may choose to add Debt Shields, Captive Insurance Companies, or Non-Qualified Plans to complete the planning.

In your asset protection plan, make sure you understand the benefits and consequences of the various tools you employ. Your asset protection advisor can help you weigh the pros and cons of each potential strategy. Your advisory team can help explain how each asset protection strategy or tool may be integrated into your comprehensive financial plan. By addressing your asset protection concerns as part of a comprehensive planning process, you will not only protect the wealth you have already built, but you may find more efficient ways to build greater after-tax wealth for your retirement and for future generations.

Asset Protection Myths

Every day, we speak to Doctors about how they can achieve the protection they desire in order to maintain their wealth. In these conversations, we hear many common myths. Perhaps you also hold some of these false beliefs. Five common myths are:

- "My assets are owned jointly with my spouse, so I'm okay."
- "My assets are owned by my spouse, so I'm okay."
- "I am insured, so I'm covered."
- "I can just give assets away if I get into trouble."
- "My Living Trust (or Family Trust) provides asset protection."

These myths are dangerous because they lull the individual or family into a false sense of financial security. This, in turn, may prevent the Doctor from taking necessary steps to truly protect the assets. Let's examine each of these common myths and dispel them.

Myth #1: "My Assets Are Owned Jointly With My Spouse, So I'm Okay."

Most Doctors hold their homes and other property in joint ownership. Unfortunately, this ownership structure provides little asset protection in both community and non-community property (aka "separate property") states.

In separate property states like Ohio, jointly held property or assets are typically at least 50% vulnerable to the claims against either spouse. In other words, 50% of jointly held or jointly titled property involving a medical doctor and his spouse would be vulnerable to the debts or business claims associated with or related to either the spouse or the medical doctor. Examples of such claims or debts would be those resulting from a medical practice, income-producing assets (a real estate loan or lawsuit), or an automobile accident.

Even in community property states like California, community assets will be exposed to community debts regardless of title. Community debts include any debt that arises during marriage as the result of an act that helped the community.

Myth #2: "My Assets Are Owned By My Spouse, So I'm Okay."

One of the most common misconceptions about asset protection is that assets in your spouse's name cannot be touched. We cannot tell you how many Doctors have come to us with their assets in the name of one spouse and assumed that those assets were totally protected from claims against the other. This often happens when one spouse has significant exposure as a Doctor and one does not.

Unfortunately, often times, simply transferring title of an asset to the non-vulnerable spouse may not protect the asset. The creditor can often seize the assets owned by the spouse of the debtor by proving that the income or funds of the debtor were used to purchase the asset or by asserting a fraudulent conveyance or constructive fraudulent conveyance (i.e. badge of fraud). To determine if the asset is potentially reversible, three questions can be asked:

- Whose income was used to purchase the asset?
- Has the vulnerable spouse used the asset at any time?
- Does this spouse have any control over the asset?

If the answer is "yes" to any of these questions, then the creditor may be able to assert a claim against these assets.

We have generally categorized putting assets in a spouse's name as a "potential asset protection myth." However, because Ohio is a separate property state, there may be some circumstances in which putting assets in the low-risk, non-vulnerable spouse's name may be worth examining. Obviously, this determination will turn on the particular facts of each situation. For example, if there were a two physician couple, putting assets in the sole name of either spouse would probably not make sense from an asset protection standpoint. Even if you believe a spouse is non-vulnerable, consider what would happen if that spouse caused a terrible car accident in which the injury awards exceed insurance limits.

Myth #3: "I Am Insured, So I'm Covered."

While we strongly advocate insurance as a first line of defense, an insurance policy is 50 pages long for a reason. Within those numerous pages there are a variety of exclusions and limitations that most people never take the time to read, let alone understand. Even if you do have insurance and the policy does cover the risk in question, there are still risks of underinsurance, strict liability, and bankruptcy of the insurance company. In any of these cases, you could be left with the sole financial responsibility for the loss. Lastly, with losses that fall within the plan's coverage limits, you still may see your future premiums go up significantly.

Myth #4: "I Can Just Give Assets Away If I Get Into Trouble."

Another common misconception of asset protection is that you can simply give away or transfer your assets if you ever get sued. If this were the case, you could just hide your assets when necessary. You wouldn't need an asset protection specialist. You would only need a shovel and some good map-making skills so you could find your buried treasure later.

In recognizing the potential for people to attempt to give away their assets if they get into trouble, there are laws prohibiting fraudulent transfers (or fraudulent conveyances). In a nutshell, if you make an asset transfer after an incident takes place (whether you knew about the pending lawsuit or not), the judge has the right to rule the transfer a fraudulent conveyance and order the asset to be returned to the transferor, thereby subjecting the assets to the claims of the creditor.

If you have been sued or suspect that you may be sued, there are other ways you can protect yourself. Much like other aspects in our lives, the timing of when asset protection is employed can mean everything. Typically, the sooner you employ asset protection strategies (assuming an incident that would invoke the prohibitions in Ohio's fraudulent conveyance law has not occurred) the better, as reactive last minute strategies are not very effective and may be much more expensive than the highly successful strategies that can be implemented when there are no creditors lurking.

Myth #5: "My Living Trust (Or Family Trust) Provides Asset Protection."

There have been countless instances where clients have come to us with the impression that their revocable Living Trust provides asset protection. While you are alive, this is simply not true. Revocable Trust assets are fully attachable by any creditor as the trust is a grantor trust. Later in this Lesson you will read about Irrevocable Trusts and how they provide varying levels of asset protection for you and your heirs in addition to the estate planning they are primarily designed to achieve. A Living Trust may provide some asset protection, but that protection does not exist until one spouse dies.

The Diagnosis

Many Doctors develop a false sense of security as a result of dangerous asset protection myths. Owning assets jointly with a spouse or in your living trust will not protect them. Titling all of your assets in your spouse's name does not work. Relying on your ability to move assets when a problem arises is a terrible plan that can easily be overturned and may result in disastrous consequences. Relying on insurance to protect you will leave too many risks to your financial well-being.

Do not be concerned or alarmed if you believed any of these asset protection myths. Do not be disappointed if your perceived protection has just been proved inadequate. With the myths dispelled, you can now follow the proper steps to implement the right type of asset protection plan for you. The next chapters should be very helpful in this regard. We will start with a philosophical discussion, and some practical examples, of the best way to protect assets.

6-4

The Best Asset Protection is NOT Asset Protection

Too many physicians over the last 20 years have sought cookie-cutter asset protection plans to give them some "peace of mind." While we admire these Doctors' commitment to proactively managing their risk, we have to remind the Doctors we speak with that all "asset protection plans" are not created equal. In fact, many of these "plans" will not work if they ever are tested. Why is this? Essentially, it is because of a basic tenet of asset protection: for any asset protection plan to truly stand up to a challenge, it *must have economic substance*.

Looking at it from a different viewpoint, superior asset protection planning would involve tools that are primarily used by people for non-asset protection purposes. In this way, the best asset protection plan involves tools typically not thought of as "asset protection tools;" instead, they are "business planning tools." Stated another way, "the best asset protection is not asset protection."

Similar To Tax Planning

While few physicians realize this crucial fact of asset protection planning, leading attorneys in the field know it quite well. In fact, we are not alone, as tax attorneys and CPAs know this adage is just as true when it comes to tax planning.

Simply put, when determining whether or not a particular transaction with significant tax benefits was an illegitimate tax shelter or not, the IRS or tax court typically uses a simple test: "Would a taxpayer have done this deal if not for the tax benefit?" In other words, they are asking whether or not this transaction was simply done to save taxes or if it had another economic purpose. If there was such a purpose, the transaction stands. If the transaction was only tax-motivated, it fails.

This same test applies when evaluating whether or not a credit protection tactic will be upheld if ever challenged down the road. Here, the question is "did this transaction have an economic purpose, or was it simply done for asset protection purposes?" If you are using tools that millions of Americans use on a daily basis for non-asset protection purposes, you can convincingly answer yes.

Why This Is So Important

Over the last decade, many courts throughout the U.S. have become increasingly frustrated with "asset protection planning." Reading judges' decisions in this area, it is obvious what has created their frustration—the prevalence of firms marketing themselves as "asset protection" experts, promoting the idea that the judgments of U.S. courts can be frustrated by their planning. Is this surprising? No. Of course judges are not going to be happy about an area of planning that is designed to circumvent the execution of a judgment that their court rendered, and prevent a successful plaintiff from getting paid on a judgment.

The courts' frustration is most severe when the defendant has made transfers or engaged in transactions that seem "fishy," even if the transaction at issue was made well before the beginning of the lawsuit process. If the transaction comes too late, the judges can resort to remedies to undue "fraudulent transfers." However, even in cases where the transaction came well before any plaintiff's action, we have seen judges strain to circumvent the asset protection planning.

In fact, there are certain cases where courts have given more leeway to a claim of fraudulent transfer based on a "foreseeability" argument. On the logic of one particularly noteworthy case, a medical malpractice case could always be seen as "foreseeable." Taken to its logical conclusion, this position could support the argument that a Doctor who does procedures daily is aware of the possibility of mistakes. If this were true, a plaintiff suing a Doctor could attack asset protection transfers made years prior to the case.

By using "non asset protection" asset protection, you are not as vulnerable to this emerging trend in the law. The techniques explained in this chapter do not involve "transfers" at all. Given this, and "non asset protection" techniques with tangible and concrete economic substance, these tools and tactics are certainly among the strongest protection you can implement for the long term.

Asset Protection That Isn't

The best asset protection tools were not created as asset protection tools. They are tools that have other primary benefits and offer outstanding creditor protection as a secondary benefit. Which asset protection tools are not asset protection tools? Let's examine a few of them briefly here. They will all be developed further in other parts of the book.

Qualified Retirement Plans

The term "qualified" retirement plan means that the retirement plan complies with certain Department of Labor and Internal Revenue Service rules. You might know such plans by their specific type, including pension plans, profit sharing plans, money purchase plans, 401(k)s or 403(b)s. Properly structured plans offer a variety of real economic benefits: you can fully deduct contributions to these plans, and funds within them grow tax-deferred. In fact, this is likely why most medical practices sponsor such a plan. Keep in mind that distributions may be subject to tax and a 10% penalty if withdrawn prior to age 59.

What you may not know is that under federal bankruptcy law and the laws of nearly every state, these plans are protected against lawsuits and creditor claims—enjoying (+5) protection status. Yet the overwhelming majority of millions of Americans who use qualified plans are not using them for asset protection purposes. This, then, is a great example of an attractive economic tool that just so happens to have tremendous asset protection benefits as well.

Non-Qualified and "Hybrid" Benefit Plans

Non-Qualified and Hybrid plans are relatively unknown to physicians, even though most Fortune 1000 companies make these types of plans available to their executives. These types of plans should be very attractive to physicians, as employees are not required to participate and allowable contributions can be much higher than with qualified plans, although not deductible. Once again, these plans are generally not used for asset protection purposes, but they may have such benefits. Read more about them in Chapter 5-4.

Captive Insurance Companies (CICs)

CICs are used by many of the Fortune 1000 for a host of strategic reasons. In this technique, the owners of a medical practice actually create their own properly licensed insurance company to insure all types of risks of the practice. These can be economic risks (that reimbursements drop), business risks (that electronic medical records are destroyed), litigation risks (coverage for defense of harassment claims or HCFA audits) and even medical malpractice (keeping some risk in the captive and reinsuring the rest). If it is created and maintained properly, the CIC is an insurance company—established in a real economic arrangement with its insured. Also, CICs enjoy tremendous creditor protection—although they are almost never created for this purpose. This was covered in depth in Chapter 5-6.

Cash Value Life Insurance (CVLI)

CVLI policies are purchased by millions of Americans each year for their tax benefits (generally tax-free growth, tax-free access, and pays income tax-free to heirs), for family protection and for estate planning purposes. Nonetheless, in many states, including Ohio, the cash value can enjoy the top (+5) protections. In this way, a physician can purchase a product that is widely recognized as a part of a financial plan and enjoy (+5) protections easily.

The Diagnosis

When asset protection is a by-product of other primary goals, the courts look more favorably on the planning. In this way, asset protection planning is very similar to tax planning (which is discussed in Lessons #7 and #9). Qualified Plans, Non-Qualified Plans, Captive Insurance Companies, and Cash Value Life Insurance are just a few of the tools that have primary benefits other than asset protection, but offer Doctors outstanding asset protection.

If you have an "asset protection plan" that has no value other than creditor protection, you should be concerned. To help you analyze your situation and to see how well your asset protection plan would hold up to an attack, the authors offer a free phone consultation to everyone who purchases our book. If you visit us at www.ojmgroup.com and click "Free Consultation," you can schedule yours today.

6-5

The Mixed Blessing of Property and Casualty Insurance

As principals of a financial firm that provides all types of financial planning, business consulting, insurance analysis, and product implementation, a number of the authors of this book, including the attorney co-authors, are very familiar with the benefits of insurance.

We all see Property and Casualty (P&C) insurance as an important part of any asset protection plan—both for the practice and personal assets. In this chapter, we will define P&C insurance coverage and discuss its uses and limitations in the context of asset protection planning.

What Is P&C Insurance?

There are two "categories" of insurance: Life and Health (L&H) and Property and Casualty (P&C). L&H insurance includes all life insurance and health insurance, as well as disability insurance and long term care insurance. P&C insurance is designed to protect against property and casualty losses. Often, P&C insurance is referred to as "property and liability" insurance because it protects people from all types of liabilities. Examples of P&C coverage include: automobile, homeowners and renters, umbrella liability, professional liability, medical malpractice, general liability, flood, earthquake, premises liability, errors and omissions, products liability, and others.

P&C insurance is designed to "indemnify" the insured. The insurance industry's definition of "indemnify" is to "make whole" or to restore the status quo. In other words, if you suffer a loss and have P&C coverage, you will be "put back" into the same financial place you were before the loss (minus any applicable deductibles or co-payments). As such, P&C coverage will cover your legal bills and other loss adjustment expenses, as well as the actual loss. These other expenses may include the costs of adjusters, estimates, expert testimony, or other associated costs.

P&C insurance coverage is very important given today's litigious society and the "American Rule" of legal fees. As mentioned before, there is no out of pocket cost (or deterrent) to the plaintiff under this system, yet the defendant is responsible for the actual loss and associated fees. Therefore, if you didn't have P&C insurance but still won your case, you still might have tens—if not hundreds—of thousands of dollars in legal fees and related expenses. As such, it is usually worth buying insurance to avoid these costs and the inconvenience and aggravation associated with a claim, let alone the potential judgment or loss.

Best Uses Of P&C Insurance

As we mentioned above, there are various types of P&C insurances. The most common P&C insurances are homeowners (or renters) and automobile insurance. Average Americans generally have these forms of coverage because they have a mortgage on their home or because they have a loan or a lease on a car. Yet, in a way, one does not own the home or car yet—the bank or credit department does. As such, the lender requires collateral. Buyers must insure the asset while they are paying for it. Once the debt on a home or car is paid off, there is no bank or finance company requiring insurance protection. Of course, we would never recommend completely dropping all insurance on the home. The odds are very slim that they will suffer a house fire or burglary, but the costs of insurance are very small relative to what clients could lose.

Another common type of P&C insurance is the umbrella liability policy. For a very reasonable premium, you can get an additional one to five million dollars of excess liability insurance on top of the liability protection you may have from your homeowners or auto policies. You should seriously consider an umbrella policy.

Other popular P&C coverage includes professional liability insurance and premises and products liability insurance. As a physician, medical malpractice insurance, premises liability insurance, and other overhead insurances are wise options, if not requirements.

Four Limitations Of P&C Insurance

While some P&C insurance always makes sense as part of the asset planning for every Doctor, there are limitations to this tool. That is why we typically recommend using the other asset protection tools we describe in this Lesson, in addition to any insurance. Let's examine these limitations individually.

1. Policy Exclusions

Often we find that clients are completely unaware of the "fine print" P&C exclusions and policy limitations. Of course, they often become aware of such exclusions after it is too late. For example, many clients fail to realize that their "umbrella" policy only applies if certain underlying insurance coverage amounts are in effect. If your liability limits on your homeowner's policy or auto policy are too low, then you'll have to pay out of pocket before the umbrella coverage is in effect.

Case Study: Andy's Daughter's Car Accident

Andy was sued for more than $150,000 when his teenage daughter was involved in a car accident while using his car. Andy was certain that his insurance policy covered his daughter. Only then did his insurance agent tell Andy that the policy no longer covered his daughter, since she had recently moved out of the house. There was an exclusion from coverage for child drivers if they did not reside in the same residence as the parents. Now, Andy alone faced a lawsuit that cost him over $150,000.

The lesson to be learned from Andy's story is simple: Know your policy and the limitations contained therein!

2. Inadequate policy limits

Even if your insurance policy does cover you on a particular lawsuit, the policy coverage may be well below what a jury will award. You must pay any excess above the coverage out of your own pocket. If you were hit by a large judgment, would your policy cover you completely?

3. Insurance forces you to lose control of the defense

Even if your insurance policy covers against a specific claim, you must consider the consequences of filing a claim. You have lost negotiating power because your insurance company will dictate when the case is settled and how much the case settlement will be. While this may not matter with a personal injury car accident lawsuit, a case against you professionally is another matter. Here you may not want to admit liability and settle, while your insurance company does.

On the other hand, if the claim involves your professional reputation, you may want to settle the case out of court and away from the public view. There is no guarantee that your insurer will see things the same way. In these situations, if you rely solely on insurance, you lose all ability to negotiate effectively.

4. Claims bring ever-higher premiums

An additional consequence of relying solely on insurance to protect you from lawsuits is that, once you make claims on the policy, your premiums rise. Given the dismal statistics, you will probably endure a number of lawsuits over your life—and your cost of insurance will rise with every claim, even if you are not at fault.

Recommendations To Manage Limitations

To manage the four limitations of P&C insurance as outlined above, we recommend the following preventive measures:

1. Know your policy
2. Don't skimp on coverage
3. Consider an umbrella policy
4. Utilize other asset protection tools
5. Own your own insurance company if you have significant risks in your practice or business (read Chapter 5-6 for more information).

The Diagnosis

Like every tool discussed in this book, Property & Casualty insurance has its place in a Doctor's comprehensive financial plan. Certain types of coverage, such as homeowner, auto, umbrella, and medical malpractice for physicians, are compulsory. However, we caution Doctors not to rely on insurance for all of their protection. Much more must be done if you want to adequately shield assets and discourage claims from the outset. There are various exclusions within every policy and many risks (like employment liability) that are not covered in traditional insurance policies. You want to integrate insurance into your plan, but this is only one piece of the puzzle. In the next chapters you'll learn about powerful tools that you can use to protect all assets and potentially enjoy significant tax benefits at the same time.

6-6

Maximizing Exempt Assets

In the following chapters, we will explain a number of legal entities and techniques we use to protect the assets of our Doctor clients. This chapter on maximizing exempt assets precedes the following chapters because, in our view, clients should always maximize their use of exempt assets before moving on to legal tools, legal entities, and other techniques.

Despite their superiority to other asset protection strategies, most Doctors do not adequately use exempt assets. This chapter will explain why many advisors don't recommend exempt assets as often as they should. Then we will discuss all of the exempt assets that can be valuable components of a comprehensive financial plan. Throughout the book, you will revisit many of these exempt assets as they provide additional benefits to asset protection. In a later Lesson, you will learn how sophisticated Doctors save time and money by leveraging exempt assets that offer additional benefits. For now, let's begin discussing why exempt assets are considered the "best" asset protection tool and then discuss the reasons why they remain underutilized in asset protection planning.

Exempt Assets: The "Best" Asset Protection Tools

We consider exempt assets to be the "best" asset protection tool for the following reasons:

1. **No legal/accounting fees.** Most of the tools in subsequent chapters involve the creation of legal entities that require set up and ongoing legal fees, state fees, accounting fees, and even additional taxes. Using the exempt assets described in this chapter involve *none of these significant costs* and affords better protection as well.

2. **No loss of ownership or control.** The legal tools of the following chapters typically require giving up some level of ownership or control to family members or even third-party trustees. *By using exempt assets, you can own and access the asset at any time while enjoying the highest (+5) level of protection.*

3. **Superior Protection.** The legal tools explained later offer protection that ranges from (+1) to (+5). *Exempt assets always enjoy the top (+5) protection up to their exempt amount.*

Why Exempt Assets Are Underutilized

Given the clear benefits of exempt assets, one would think that exempt assets would be preferred over other tools in an asset protection plan. Surprisingly, this is often not the case. The reason for this may be that most asset protection planning is implemented by an attorney who is not familiar with the financial tools a multi-disciplinary team could offer.

There are various planning pitfalls that can arise when you do not have the benefit of a coordinated, multi-disciplinary team to help implement your plan. Attorneys generally do not understand many of the exempt asset classes, such as cash value life insurance and annuities. You cannot expect an advisor to recommend something he doesn't understand.

This doesn't mean that one attorney could not recommend an adequate asset protection plan. What it does mean is that the plan created by one attorney may not be efficient, because the plan may be limited only to legal solutions. If you were more skeptical, you might point out that attorneys are generally not licensed to sell such financial products. Is it unrealistic to expect an attorney to have a bias against the use of exempt assets for asset protection when the implementation of those assets does not require any legal work?

Is it unreasonable to expect attorneys to focus their asset protection recommendations around the use of legal documents that may generate thousands of dollars in legal fees? This is not a conspiracy against, nor is it an indictment of, attorneys—we, as an author group, include a number of attorneys. However, we are attorneys who appreciate multi-disciplinary planning and recognize the value of financial, as well as legal, solutions. *The reason we wrote this book with attorneys and the consultants of the OJM Group is that we believe 100% in a multi-disciplinary approach to asset protection planning.*

The lesson here is simple. Your asset protection plan, like the rest of your financial plan, MUST be handled by a coordinated, multi-disciplinary team that carefully considers all planning options to help you efficiently achieve your goals. The absence of exempt assets in a plan is always a warning sign that the planning is not coordinated.

Federally Exempt Assets and the 2005 Bankruptcy Act (BAPCPA)

Federally exempt assets are those assets that are protected under federal bankruptcy law. In 2005 Congress enacted the Bankruptcy Abuse Prevention and Consumer Protection Act (BAPCPA), which brought about sweeping changes to debtor and creditor law. Federal law protects certain assets from creditors and lawsuits if the defendant is willing to file bankruptcy to eliminate the creditor. However, in a Chapter 7 Bankruptcy filed in Ohio, a debtor needs to engage in a two-part analysis: (1) the debtor must review if there is a federal law exemption applicable to the asset(s) and (2), the debtor must then determine how the Ohio state statutes covering exemptions (Ohio Revised Code Section 2329.66 etc.) will impact, if at all, the particular asset in a bankruptcy filing. The reason for this two part analysis is that BAPCPA and the U.S. Bankruptcy Code generally allow individual debtors to exempt certain property from creditor claims based on exemptions under either federal law or state law. Exemptions may vary from state to state. However some states, like Ohio, are permitted by the Bankruptcy rules to adopt their own set of bankruptcy exemptions that are used in place of the federal exemptions, but are also used for non-bankruptcy state debtor/creditor purposes (Ohio opted out of the federal bankruptcy statute via ORC 2329.662 and chose to utilize its own state exemptions for Ohio residents who are filing bankruptcy). Amended Ohio Senate Bill 281, which was signed into law on July 1, 2008 and became effective September 30, 2008, sets forth the updated Ohio exemptions, which are codified in Ohio Revised Code Section 2329.66 and are to be used in bankruptcy filings and non-bankruptcy state law debtor/creditor matters.

Two significant asset classes that federal law protects are qualified retirement plans (QRPs) and most IRAs. The term "qualified" retirement plan means that the retirement plan complies with certain Department of Labor and Internal Revenue Service rules. You might know such plans by their specific type, including profit sharing plans, money purchase plans, 401(k)s or 403(b)s. Most IRAs are very similar to such plans with several technical differences, and for the most part (with a couple exceptions) are now given exempt status under the federal law as well.

While this protection is (+5), you must recognize that this federal protection only applies if you are in a bankruptcy setting. If you were simply sued and a creditor was trying to take the funds in your pension or IRA, bankruptcy protection would not apply. You would have to take the step of filing for bankruptcy to shield the asset. This might be too great a cost for the protection.

If you do not file for bankruptcy, this federal bankruptcy protection would not apply. However, the amount of value in the QRP or IRA that would be protected outside of bankruptcy will be governed by applicable federal law and Ohio debtor/creditor state law.

Let's look at the applicable federal law first. In 1992, the U.S. Supreme Court, in Patterson v. Shumate, 504 U.S. 753 (1992), held that a participant's interest in an ERISA (Employee Retirement Income Security Act)-qualified pension plan was excluded from the participant's bankruptcy estate and could not be used to satisfy the participant's creditor claims.

Outside of bankruptcy, if a Doctor's retirement plan is an ERISA-qualified pension plan, so the logic goes, creditors should not be able to reach that asset either under the laws of Ohio.

State of Ohio Exempt Assets, Statutory and Case Law Protections

In Ohio, state exemption leveraging, together with certain statutory and case law protections, are a fundamental part of a financial plan and every Doctor client should take them seriously.

The most significant exemptions in Ohio are:

1. Qualified Retirement Plans (QRPs) and Individual Retirement Accounts (IRAs) including those under ERISA (excepting SEPS and Simple IRAs)
2. Primary Residence (or Homestead) (albeit a very weak exemption)
3. Life Insurance
4. Annuities
5. Statutory and Case Law Spendthrift Protections for Beneficiaries

Qualified Retirement Plans and IRAs:

Exemption Planning with Qualified Retirement Plans (QRPs) and IRAs can be a powerful asset protection tool. However it is also an area of the law that is in flux and is highly technical. Therefore, it is suggested that an asset protection diagnostic be conducted regarding the type of Qualified Retirement Plan(s) and IRA(s) that a doctor has in order to determine what type of asset protection is provided by the particular Qualified Retirement Plan(s) and/or IRA(s).

Outside of bankruptcy, protection for QRPs and IRAs is provided by a combination of Federal Law and/or Ohio Law. Provided below is a general overview of the type of asset protections that may be available for various QRPs and IRAs.

ERISA Based Retirement Plans-Most Pension, Profit Sharing Plans, 401(k), 403(b) Retirement Plans.

Simply put, an ERISA pension plan is one that provides retirement income to its employees and under federal ERISA and IRS laws, provides certain "anti-alienation" (i.e. asset protection) provisions that "preempt" state collection laws. With regards to state attachment, execution and garnishment laws, ERISA based retirement plans are exempt. These typically include, most pension, profit sharing, 401(k), 403(b) and other ERISA based retirement plans. Therefore, if a retirement plan is a plan covered by ERISA and meets the qualifications under the Internal Revenue Code, a Doctor's benefits under the plan will be protected from creditors' claims. Exceptions to the ERISA exemption include qualified domestic relations orders (QDROs), federal tax levies and judgments, federal criminal penalties, and restitution arising from crimes. Beyond these limited exception, no creditor can touch a Doctor's ERISA plan account.

Traditional IRAs, Roth IRAs and Rollover IRAs.

These types of retirement plans are not ERISA based plans and therefore do not have ERISA protections. However, under Ohio law they are accorded superior exempt asset protection, which can be comparable to ERISA protections. As a general rule, there is no cap on the amount that can be exempted. However, as a prerequisite to being able to exempt all of the amounts in a Traditional IRA, Roth IRA, or Rollover IRA, a Doctor must have followed the contribution rules for a Traditional IRA (i.e. contributions did not exceed the "applicable limits on deductible contributions for a given tax year"), a Roth IRA (i.e. "contributions did not exceed the contribution limits for a given tax year"), and a Rollover IRA (i.e. "contributions did not exceed the stated rollover limits as set forth in the applicable sections of the Internal Revenue Code").

SEP IRAs and SIMPLE IRAs.
On account of two federal case law decisions (*Lampkins v. Golden* case 202 U.S. App. LEXIS 900 (6th Cir. 2002) and *Garratt v. Walker* 164 F. 3d 1249 (10th Cir.1998)) and Internal Revenue Code Section 408, these two types of IRAs fall in between the protections afforded by ERISA and Ohio law. SEP IRAs and SIMPLE IRAs are considered ERISA "established" and "employer sponsored" pension plans (see ERISA code sections, 4(b) and 201), therefore, they preempt state law (i.e. there is no state law exemption applicable). However, the ERISA asset protection provisions (i.e. anti-alienation asset protection provisions) under ERISA code section 206(d) don't fit or apply to these types of pension plans. Due to this fact, all plan assets in a SEP IRA and SIMPLE IRA are entirely exposed to state law creditor actions. One possible solution to this quandary is to roll the assets contained in a SEP IRA or SIMPLE IRA to a rollover IRA. In this situation the assets would no longer be considered assets of an ERISA based plan and instead could take advantage of the favorable Ohio state law exemptions available to rollover IRAs (i.e. in most cases, complete protection with an unlimited monetary cap as described in the preceding paragraph).

Pension and Retirement Plans that are not classified as ERISA or IRA plans.
For those Retirement and Pension Plans which do not fit into the ERISA or IRA category, the amount that can be "exempted" under Ohio law for proceeds contained in these types of pension and retirement plans is not unlimited. Instead, the exempt amount is based upon what is "reasonably necessary for the support of the person (i.e. the debtor) and any of the person's (the debtor's) dependents." Ultimately, the amount that a debtor is to receive will be determined by a Court on a case by case basis taking into consideration such factors as the debtor's age, education, ability to work, and other relevant information.

Qualified Retirement Plans (QRPs) that Benefit only an Owner or Owner's Spouse.
If a Doctor has a QRP that only benefits himself and his spouse (which can include business retirement plans, certain tax-exempt plans, Keoghs etc.) and none of the Doctor's employees, it will not receive any ERISA asset protection. Due to the unique nature of these types of plans, it is strongly suggested that a separate asset

protection diagnostic be undertaken to determine the possible exemption(s) and creditor protections that may be available with these types of plans.

Primary Residence: Homestead

Many Americans consider the home to be the family's most valuable asset. You may have thought you knew the laws that protect your home. Perhaps you have previously heard the term "homestead," and assumed that you could never lose your home to bad debts or other liabilities because of this homestead protection. The reality is that few states provide a total (+5) shield for the home. This is certainly true for Ohio Doctors. In Ohio, the homestead protection is a paltry $20,200 dollars. In essence, Ohio law will not provide any meaningful protection for your home. You must consider other techniques to protect this asset.

Life Insurance in Ohio A True Exempt Asset

One of the most powerful exemptions in Ohio is the cash value of life insurance. In Ohio, the cash value of life insurance is completely exempt (i.e. unlimited), so long as certain rules are followed and certain beneficiaries are designated. This Ohio exemption "conforms to the underlying purpose of life insurance which is to compensate the policy beneficiary for the loss of life of the insured."

As a general rule, if a Doctor has a life insurance policy upon his or her life (i.e. they are the insured person), the cash value is exempt. To enjoy this exemption, the "beneficiaries" of the insurance policy must be: a spouse, child, a person dependent upon such insured Doctor or a trustee for the benefit of such spouse, children, dependent persons, or a charitable entity described in ORC 3911.09. If this is the case, all of the cash surrender value of the insurance policy, whether it be $100 dollars or $10,000,000, is exempt from the creditors of the Doctor (i.e. the insured person).

Annuities in Ohio

Annuities may provide another potential exemption under Ohio law, which if properly structured and certain beneficiaries are designated, can result in the total cash value of the annuity being exempted. The analysis of whether the cash value of an annuity is exempt from a Doctor's creditors is somewhat similar to life insurance. However, a review of the type, characteristics, and purpose of the annuity must also be undertaken. This is because by their very nature, annuities are considered investment tools and are typically defined as a contractual right to receive periodic payments over a specific period of time. They are not often designed to compensate a beneficiary for loss of life of the insured. Because of these typical characteristics, an annuity must have substantial life insurance (i.e., death benefits) attributes to achieve exempt status in Ohio.

Courts interpreting Ohio laws have held that the mere existence of an annuity does not automatically permit it to be claimed as exempt. The cash value contained in annuities that were designed for pension, retirement, and compensation for injuries, have been found not to qualify for the exemption. Instead, in order to qualify, the annuity must be in the nature of life insurance.

As a general rule, if a Doctor is an annuitant and has cash value built up in an annuity with death benefit attributes, the cash value is exempt. To enjoy this exemption, the "beneficiaries" of the annuities must be: a spouse, child, a person dependent upon such Doctor or a trustee for the benefit of such spouse, children, dependent persons, or a charitable entity described in ORC 3911.09. In that case, all of the cash value contained in the annuity whether it be $100 or $10 million, are exempt from the creditors of the annuitant Doctor.

Statutory and Case Law Spendthrift Protections for Beneficiaries

Ohio Revised Code Section 3911.14-Statutory Protection.

Spendthrift clauses contained in estate planning documents (wills and trusts for example) and contracts (such as insurance policies and annuity contracts) can provide powerful asset protection for third party beneficiaries. A third party beneficiary is typically a spouse, child or entity. A spendthrift clause prevents the beneficiary from voluntarily or involuntarily disposing of his or her interest in the trust, such as by assignment, and limits the rights of creditors to reach it, such as by attachment. These clauses in trusts and contracts prevent a creditor from being able to sue, attach or collect the proceeds or assets contained in either a trust for a third party beneficiary or contained in an insurance policy or annuity for a third party beneficiary. In order to protect these proceeds or payments from creditor claims of third party beneficiaries, the life insurance policies or annuity contracts must include a specific spendthrift clause, which is set forth in ORC 3911.14 and reads as follows:

"...the proceeds... or payments .... shall not be subject to transfer, anticipation, commutation, or encumbrances by any beneficiary, and shall not be subject to the claims of creditors of any beneficiary..."

Therefore, if a Doctor establishes a $30,000 annuity contract that contains the appropriate spendthrift clause for the benefit of his daughter, and the Doctor's daughter has a Court judgment rendered against her for $10,000, the creditor cannot attach the proceeds and assets contained in the annuity contract.

Case Law Established Spendthrift Protection and These Protections Have Been Codified in the Ohio Trust Code.

As was stated above, a spendthrift clause protects the interests of beneficiaries from their creditors and prevents the beneficiaries from transferring their interests. Ohio law provides superior asset protection for trusts which contain spendthrift clauses and which have been established for the benefit of third party beneficiaries (typically a son, daughter or other relative). According to a number of long standing Ohio

Supreme Court decisions (*Scott v. BankOne Trust Co.*, and *Domo v. McCarthy*), if a trust established for a beneficiary contains a spendthrift clause, the trust assets for the beneficiary will be protected from the beneficiary's creditors and from legal collection measures attempted by the beneficiary's creditors. Additionally, the State of Ohio recently passed a new law in 2007 that provides statutory spendthrift clause protection for trusts.

As will be described later in this Lesson, spendthrift protection in Ohio is something that can be established for a third party that the third party cannot establish for himself or herself. As a general rule, a Doctor cannot establish a trust for himself in Ohio and obtain spendthrift protection.

The Diagnosis

The easiest and cheapest way to achieve the highest level of asset protection is to use exempt assets. For this reason, it makes sense that every Doctor who is interested in asset protection should attempt to maximize his or her use of exempt assets. However, to use exempt assets properly within a comprehensive financial plan, you may need an insurance product, home loan, qualified plan, and tax and asset protection expertise. This is another example of why you need a multi-disciplinary team to help you achieve your financial goals.

Practically, the laws in Ohio usually do not afford you enough exemptions to place every dollar of your wealth into exempt assets. For this reason, you will have to utilize legal strategies as part of your asset protection planning. The following chapters, 6-7 and 6-11 will discuss the three most common asset protection tools—the Family Limited Partnership, the Limited Liability Company and the Domestic Asset Protection Trust.

6-7

Family Limited Partnerships and Limited Liability Companies

While (+5) exempt assets may be the most effective asset protection tools, most clients will need to go beyond the use of exempt assets in their quest to protect assets. They will make use of legal tools as well. Of all the legal tools we use to shield assets, the three we use most are Family Limited Partnerships (FLPs) Limited Liability Companies (LLCs), and Domestic Asset Protection Trusts (DAPTs). Domestic Asset Protection Trusts are covered in Chapter 6-11. Of course, having family members play a role in these tools is common—that's why we use the "F" in front of the "LP." However, using family members in this way is NOT required. Whether you use family members or non-family members, these entities can provide you solid asset protection. In this chapter we will discuss the similarities of the two tools, how they protect assets, and three tactics Doctors should use to incorporate FLPs and LLCs into their plans to build and preserve wealth.

FLPs and LLCs: Similarities and Differences

We have combined FLPs and LLCs in this chapter because they are very similar. You can think of them as closely related, like brothers and sisters, as they share many of their best characteristics. In fact, unless we make the point otherwise, we will use these tools interchangeably—if a case study refers to a FLP, you can generally assume that an LLC could have been used and vice versa. Similarities between the FLP and LLC include:

1. They are both legal entities certified under state law.
Both FLPs and LLCs are legal entities governed by the state law in the state in which the entity is formed. Many of these laws are identical, as they are modeled after the Uniform Limited Partnership and Limited Liability Company Acts, which have been adopted at least partially by every state. As state-certified legal entities, state fees must be paid each year to keep an FLP or LLC valid.

2. They both have two levels of ownership.
FLPs and LLCs allow for two levels of ownership. We'll call one ownership level

"active ownership"—that is, the active owners have 100% control of the entity and its assets. In the FLP, the active owners are called "general partners", while in the LLC the active owners are called "managing members" (Note Well: Managers of LLCs do not have to be "owners.")

As you may have guessed, the second ownership level is "passive ownership"—the passive owners have little control over the entity and only limited rights. The passive owners are called "limited partners" in the FLP and "members" in the LLC

This bi-level structure of ownership allows a host of planning possibilities because clients can use FLPs and LLCs to share ownership with family members without having to give away any practical control. Why is it optimal to be able to give away ownership but still maintain control? Asset protection reasons will be discussed in great detail in this chapter and estate planning benefits will be explained in Chapter 9-5.

3. They both have beneficial tax treatment.

In terms of income taxes, both tools can elect for "pass through" taxation, meaning neither the FLP nor the LLC is liable for income taxes. Rather, the tax liability for any and all income or capital gains on FLP/LLC assets "passes through" to the owners (partners or members). Also, as discussed in the income tax and estate planning Lessons, both entities allow the participants to take advantage of "income sharing" and "valuation discount" techniques in the same ways.

Two Differences Between The FLP And LLC

1. Only the LLC can be used for a single owner.

Most states, including Ohio, now allow single-member (owner) LLCs, while a limited partnership in every state must have at least two owners. Thus, for single clients, the LLC is often the only option. However, there have been a number of recent legal decisions that have weakened the liability protections provided by one-person LLCs. The formation of a one-person LLC needs to be reviewed in light of these recent court decisions. Also, if a Doctor is considering having an FLP or LLC protect a home, then the single member LLC is one possible alternative. Since the home is a significant asset, both financially and emotionally, there is an entire chapter devoted to protecting it, in Chapter 6-8.

2. The FLP's general partner has liability for the FLP.

While a general partner has personal liability for the acts and debts of the FLP, a managing member has no such liability for his/her LLC. For this reason alone, asset protection experts always recommend using an LLC rather than an FLP when the entity will own "dangerous" assets, i.e., those likely to lead to lawsuits.

"Safe" assets, conversely, are those that are unlikely to lead to lawsuits. Common safe assets include cash, stocks, bonds, mutual funds, CDs, life insurance policies, checking or savings accounts, antiques, artwork, jewelry, licenses, copyrights, trademarks and patents, among others.

"Dangerous" assets are those that have a relatively high likelihood of creating liability. Common dangerous assets include real estate (especially rental real estate), cars, RVs, trucks, boats, airplanes, and interests in closely held businesses.

How FLPs And LLCs Protect Assets and the Emerging Trends for FLPs and LLCs

The discussion of this section assumes that, in transferring assets to an FLP or LLC, you do not run afoul of fraudulent transfer laws. We discussed these laws in the introduction of this Lesson. It also assumes that one remains in compliance with state laws and does not use the FLP/LLC as an alter ego of one's personal business affairs.

This section will review in particular: (1) the general asset protection rules (including a brief legislative history) of FLPs and LLCs, (2) the charging order remedy, (3) the practical effect of the charging order protections offered by FLPs and LLCs (4) the emerging trends of asset protection for FLPs and LLCs (5) judicial foreclosure of LLC or FLP interest and (6) the options available for debtors regarding FLP and LLC asset protection.

1. The General Asset Protection Rules for FLPs and LLCs. As a general rule, FLPs and LLCs are fairly good asset protectors because the law (both statutory law and judicial case law) prescribes the specific remedies which creditors are permitted to exercise when coming after assets in either entity. The legislative basis for the FLP laws in most states comes from the 1976 and 2001 Revised Uniform Limited Partnership Act (RULPA).

   Similarly, there is a Uniform Limited Liability Company Act for LLCs, but most states have not followed this Act, and instead have drafted their own LLC laws. However, when it comes to creditors rights, many of the LLC laws in these states have adopted the 1976 RULPA concepts, so the creditor remedies for LLCs and FLPs are very similar. When a personal creditor pursues you and your assets are owned by an FLP or LLC, the creditor typically cannot seize the assets in the FLP/LLC. Under the limited partnership laws (governing FLPs) and LLC laws of several states, a creditor of a partner (or LLC member) cannot reach into the FLP/LLC and take specific partnership assets.

2. The Charging Order Remedy for FLPs and LLCs. Creditors can generally force the liquidation of corporations, but not so an FLP or LLC. If the creditor cannot seize FLP/LLC assets, what can the creditor get? The law normally allows a unique remedy: the "charging order." A charging order is something a creditor

can obtain against a debtor, allowing the creditor to "step into the shoes" of the debtor. In other words, if the debtor was entitled to distributions from the FLP or LLC, the creditor may legally receive those distributions. The charging order is meant to allow the business to continue operating without interruption and provides a remedy for creditors to be paid. This also can create the beginning of the "waiting game."

3. What are the practical effects of the waiting game involving a charging order with a FLP or LLC? The practical effect of a charging order is that by making the creditor wait for its monies (i.e. wait for a distribution from the FLP or LLC to the limited partner of the FLP or the LLC member), the debtor may be able to negotiate a more favorable settlement amount (i.e. a reduced settlement amount instead of the full amount of a judgment). Realistically, the debtor may need to access the monies or distributions in the FLP or LLC. So what happens then? In that situation, according to typical charging order rules, the creditor is entitled to receive the monies or distribution first (up to the amount of the creditor's judgment amount). So depending upon the personal financial situation of the debtor, the FLP or LLC charging order protection, can provide a short term, medium term, or long term solution.

4. What are the emerging trends involving creditors' remedies with FLPs and LLCs? In the past it was generally accepted that the charging order was the "exclusive" remedy for a creditor when dealing with LLCs and FLPs. After a monetary judgment was obtained against a debtor, the charging order was normally the only collection option permitted and chosen by a creditor. However, creditors have increasingly attempted (with some success) to expand the creditor remedies that they can utilize against LLCs and FLPs (see also "Special Ohio Rules Regarding FLPs and LLCs"). The emerging trend is to permit other remedies including the assertion of fraudulent transfers, alter-ego piercing of the business entity shield theories, various trust theories, and creditor's bills. However, the most powerful remedy is judicial foreclosure of FLP and LLC interests by creditors. If a court judicially forecloses on a physician owner's interest, the physician owner's interest is sold to raise cash for the creditor. The buyer (who is oftentimes the creditor) effectively becomes the owner and the physician loses all rights in the entity. The bottom line regarding the emerging trends is that creditor's remedies are expanding and foreclosure of a debtor's interest is becoming one of the accepted remedies that a creditor may pursue.

5. What occurs in the foreclosure of a limited partnership interest or LLC membership interest? The following is an example of what can occur on the foreclosure of a debtor's limited partnership interest or LLC membership interest. Assume

that Doctor Smith contributes $500,000 to a 3 member LLC that owns a commercial real estate development. A couple of years after later, Doctor Smith is sued by a creditor and the creditor obtains a judgment against him for $100,000. If Doctor Smith has formed his LLC in a state where the LLC laws provide that the "sole and exclusive remedy" for a creditor is to only obtain a charging order against the debtor's interest, then the creditor would have to wait for distributions, "when and if" they were ever made from the LLC. If the creditor could wait for the distributions and if the distributions from the LLC would total at some point, $100,000, then the creditor's judgment would be satisfied. If the creditor wanted to satisfy the judgment earlier, he or she could negotiate with the debtor and receive a "negotiated" lesser amount to satisfy the judgment. This is why some legal commentators feel that the LLC or FLP can either be a short, medium, or long term asset protection tool—it often depends on how soon the creditor wants to get paid.

Assume the same set of facts, but the debtor is in a state in which a creditor is permitted not only the right to charge a debtor's interest in the LLC, but also permits a creditor to foreclose the debtor's LLC interest. If the creditor chooses the remedy of foreclosing the debtor's interest, and let's say the same creditor purchases the debtor's LLC interest, the creditor would potentially be entitled to all distributions made from the LLC without regard to the amount of the judgment. This could mean that the creditor would be entitled to all profits, surplus and equity in the partnership property of the original debtor including the return of the debtor's original capital contribution of the $500,000.

Assume the same facts, but instead of the original creditor purchasing the LLC interest of the debtor at the foreclosure sale, a "different" creditor purchases the LLC interest. In this instance, the proceeds of the foreclosure sale go to the first creditor holding the charging order and if the proceeds were not enough to satisfy the creditor's judgment, the debtor has potentially two creditors to deal with—the first creditor with the charging order and the second one who has purchased all of the "economic rights" of debtor's LLC interest (profits, surplus, equity etc.).

6. Based upon the emerging trends of expanded creditor rights including the laws of states (like Ohio) that permit foreclosure and other possible creditors' remedies, what other options are available for debtors regarding FLP and LLC asset protection? The answer to this question requires you to focus on, analyze, and consider forming business entities in the states that offer the charging order as the "sole and exclusive" remedy to creditors. The leading states in this area are Delaware, Texas, Alaska, Nevada, and South Dakota. Because of changing laws and judicial activism, it is becoming increasingly clear that in order to enhance the asset

protection of FLPs and LLCs should be utilized in combination with other asset protection tools such as domestic asset protection trusts.

The Typical Limitations Of The Charging Order

As mentioned earlier, the charging order is a court order that instructs the FLP/LLC to pay the debtor's share of distributions to his/her creditor until the creditor's judgment is paid in full. The debtor's share of distributions is legally also considered an "assignment" (to the extent granted) of the debtor's interest. In this context, the debtor may also be referred to as an assignee. When and if a distribution is made, it is made to the creditor. More important, *everything we will describe below assumes that your FLP or LLC operating agreement is properly drafted and all formalities are followed*. With such drafting and administration, the charging order ***does not***:

- Gives the creditor FLP/LLC voting rights
- Force the FLP general partner or LLC managing member to pay out any distributions to partners/members.

While the charging order may seem like a powerful remedy, you do need to understand and consider its status and its limitations. It is a temporary interest that may have to be renewed. In addition:

1. It Is Only Available After a Successful Lawsuit.
The charging order is only available after the creditor has successfully sued and won a judgment. Only then can the creditor ask the court for the charging order. It must be noted that once the threat of a charging order exists, and even while a lawsuit is proceeding, FLP/LLC assets are completely untouchable by creditors and are available for you to use (so long as you avoid fraudulent transfers).

2. It Does Not Afford Voting Rights—So You Stay in Complete Control.
Despite the charging order, you remain the general partner of your FLP (or managing member of the LLC). You make all decisions about whether the FLP/LLC buys assets, distributes earnings to its partners or members, shifts ownership interests and so forth. Judgment creditors cannot vote you out because they cannot vote your shares. Thus, even after creditors have a judgment against you, you still make all decisions concerning the FLP/LLC, including whether to pay distributions to the owners.

3. It Does Not Grant to the debtor/assignee any Management Rights in the FLPor LLC.

4. It Does Not Grant to the debtor/assignee any Partner or Membership Rights in the FLP or LLC.

5. It Does Not Create, in favor of the debtor/assignee, any Fiduciary duty in theGeneral Partner of the FLP or the manager of the LLC.

6. It Does Not Permit a debtor/assignee to force a dissolution of the FLP or LLC.

7. The Creditor May Have to Pay the Tax Bill.
The real "kicker" is how the charging order may backfire on creditors for income tax purposes. Because taxes on FLP/LLC income are passed through to the parties who are entitled to the income, the FLP/LLC does not pay tax. Each partner/member is responsible for his/her share of the FLP/LLC income. This income is taxable regardless of whether the income is actually paid out.

Depending upon how aggressive the creditor is and the extent to which the creditor "charges" the interest of the debtor or the extent to which the creditor is granted a "charge" of the interest of a debtor, the creditor could be faced with a tax bill even though no distribution was actually received. If a creditor obtains from a Court a charging order for just the debtor's proportionate share of the FLP or LLC distributions (i.e. the profits), this "charging order" will probably be considered similar to a garnishment order and the debtor/owner will be stuck with any tax bill generated by the FLP or LLC distribution, even after the distributions to the creditor.

However, if a creditor with a charging order against an FLP partner or LLC member goes to the step of "foreclosing" on the charging order (i.e. the creditor in such case would be the owner of this FLP or LLC interest), the creditor's interest will then become more permanent. This could also have the effect of making the creditor potentially liable for all of the income attributable to the charged interest of the debtor. At this point, it could be argued that the creditor "steps into the shoes of the debtor" for income tax purposes with respect to the FLP/LLC interest—resulting in receipt of the debtor's tax bill for income taxes on the debtor's share of the FLP/LLC income (see Revenue Ruling 77-137 and Evans v. Commissioner 447 F.2nd 547 (7th Cir. 1971)). This tax liability could exist even though the creditor will likely never receive any income. Once this occurs, aggressive creditors may become even more motivated to settle—as they have swallowed the tax "poison pill" without even realizing it.

Case Study: William and Donna are Protected By FLPs

Let's examine spouses William and Donna. Assume that William is an oncologist. After two years of employment, William's assistant, Maribel, sues William for sexual harassment and wins an award of $750,000. William's general business insurance package does not cover this type of lawsuit. Once Maribel discovers, through a debtor's examination, that William and Donna's personal assets are owned by their LLCs, what can she do?

She cannot seize the vacation home, stocks or cars owned by the LLCs. State laws prohibit that. She also has no fraudulent transfer claim because the LLCs were created in advance of her claim. She can get a charging order on William's 39% share of the LLCs, but William and Donna would still control the LLCs and they would make no distributions. Maribel would therefore not receive any distributed profits, only a tax bill on stock dividends that William and Donna never distributed. This charging order will not sound too inviting to Maribel, will it?

Maribel could look only to William's assets not owned by the LLCs. Because William had an incomplete asset protection plan and retained personal ownership of copyrights and business interests in a film company worth about $75,000, William settled the judgment for just that—$75,000 cash. William and Donna's LLCs helped them avoid financial disaster and settle the claim for pennies on the dollar. Moreover, they never lost control of their assets.

You may wonder why we have such protective laws for limited partnerships and limited liability companies. The charging order law, which can be traced back to the *English Partnership Act of 1890*, is aimed at achieving a particular public policy objective—business activities of a partnership should not be disrupted because of non-partnership related debts of the individual partners. The rationale for this objective is that if non-debtor partners and the partnership were not at fault, why should the entire partnership suffer? American law has adopted this policy for over 100 years, culminating in the charging order law of the Uniform Limited Partnership and Uniform Limited Liability Company Acts. (Note Well: The same is not true for general partnerships!)

The One-Person LLC—Is it Slowly Becoming a Dinosaur?

The LLC statutes of most states permit the formation of one-person owner LLCs. One-person LLCs are very popular and commonplace because they are fairly easy to set up and manage and they can also be treated as a "disregarded entity" for tax reporting purposes (i.e. the owner continues to use his or her social security number for tax reporting purposes and the LLC is not required to file its own tax return). However, the viability of their asset protection status could slowly be eroding, especially in states that permit judicial foreclosure of LLC and FLP interests as well as other creditor remedies. This reasoning is based on a 2003 Bankruptcy case (*The Albright case*) involving a one-person LLC. The Bankruptcy Court permitted the bankruptcy trustee of the debtor the right to take over all ownership and control of the debtor's LLC membership interest and the LLC. The Court reasoned that this was proper because with a one-person LLC there was no reason to grant charging order protection, when there were no other innocent members to protect. Additionally, there was no major ongoing business enterprise that the charging order would protect. The *Albright* LLC merely held title to a passive real estate investment. Although the *Albright* case was decided under the Colorado LLC statute and in a bankruptcy context, the reasoning used by the Bankruptcy Court, combined with the rights of creditors under the law of states in which LLCs are formed) need to be analyzed when reviewing whether or not to form a one-person LLC.

If you are the owner of a one-person LLC and a creditor obtains a judgment against you, the LLC will provide little or no protection—the creditor will in all likelihood be able to take control of the assets inside the LLC. However, the one-person LLC still provides protection from personal liability created by "Dangerous" assets described earlier in this Chapter. If the one-person LLC owns rental real estate and there is a slip and fall claim, the injured party will in general, only be able to make a claim against the LLC assets and not your personal assets. This is often referred to as protection from "inside" liability.

Corporation Conversions (S or C) to LLC options

It is commonplace for Doctors to be utilizing both "S" corporations and "C" corporations in their practice. One of the concerns with "S" corporations or "C" corporations is that if a Doctor is sued and a judgment is rendered against him/her, the judgment creditor can, as a creditor remedy, "levy upon and attach" the corporate stock of the corporation. In this instance, unlike LLCs or FLPs, if the debtor's corporate shares amount to a majority or controlling interest in the corporation, the creditor can take over or seize the stock (through the Court judgment process), manage the corporation, inspect books and records, attend meetings, vote themselves as officers of the Corporation, and even start a dissolution or winding down process to sell all assets of the Company. One of the ways to avoid this and provide LLC type asset protection for the corporation's assets, is to convert the S corporation or C Corporation to an LLC and at the same time "maintain" the S corporation or C corporation tax status. This is commonly called an "F reorganization" (Internal Revenue Code section 368(a)(1)(f) etc.). Generally, the end result of this type of business entity reorganization is that for "IRS tax purposes," the new LLC entity is considered the same business entity (i.e. keeping the same tax basis, keeping the "S" election and even keeping the same federal identification number) as the former "S" corporation. However, for asset protection purposes, the owners of the new entity can now avail themselves of the business entity protections an LLC can offer. This strategy is very technical and an in depth review should be undertaken in advance with the corporation's and owners' accounting, tax and legal team to definitively ascertain whether or not this conversion for asset protection purposes can be successfully accomplished. This is another example of the critical need for you to have a multidisciplinary team working to optimize your financial success.

Three Tactics For Maximizing FLP/LLC Protection

You now understand the basic strategy for using FLPs/LLCs: Personal assets are placed into an FLP/LLC to protect them from personal creditors. This is basic "outside" asset protection. You can also be protected from claims arising from assets "inside" the FLP/LLC. Beyond this, there are four basic rules:

1. Don't put all your eggs in one basket.

Life is full of uncertainties. One never knows when a court of law is going to make a surprise departure or deviation from accepted legal norms or precedents. One never knows when an asset within a single FLP/LLC could cause a lawsuit. Because our clients understand that they cannot control court decisions or the litigious nature of society, they protect their assets by titling them in multiple FLP/LLC arrangements (among other tools discussed in this Lesson), often in states outside of Ohio, to title their assets. Titling your assets in different legal entities makes it more difficult for creditors to come after your entire wealth because they may have to conduct more investigations, file more motions with the court, and, perhaps, even travel to different states and hire lawyers licensed to practice in each of those states. The more entities used, the more difficult it will be for your creditors to attack your wealth and be more likely to negotiate more favorable settlements.

2. Segregate the dangerous eggs from the safe ones.

Separating safe assets from dangerous assets increases the "inside" asset protection for the safe assets. In other words, since no dangerous assets are within the same entity as the safe assets, a lawsuit arising from a dangerous asset will not threaten the safe assets if the safe assets are in their own LLC. As we explained in the beginning of the chapter, dangerous assets should be owned by an LLC rather than by an FLP because LLCs give better "inside" protection. The general partner of an FLP can be personally liable for acts within an FLP but the managing member of an LLC cannot be personally liable for the acts within the LLC.

3. If possible, use LLCs or FLPs in the most protective states.

Not all LLCs and FLPs are created equal. They vary greatly in their asset protection, estate and tax benefits based on the experience and expertise of the attorney drafting the operating agreement and the states in which they are formed. Some states offer much more protective language in their LLC or FLP statutes than others, and it would be unwise to form an LLC with an attorney who is unfamiliar with the differences from state-to-state.

Some state statutes are much creditor-friendly, while others are more debtor-friendly. In addition, many states have adopted uniform language. However, each state's courts may adopt different interpretations of similar statutes. Further, over time, courts within a state may have a change of opinion. Thus, our Doctor clients use legal entities domiciled in jurisdictions that offer the best laws, and they make sure that a member of their team is an asset protection expert, keeping an eye on developments in the field so that they can switch state domiciles if necessary.

4. If possible, combine the LLC and FLPs with other asset protection tools.
As we discussed previously, in order to enhance the effectiveness of the LLCs and FLPs, they should be used in combination with other asset protection tools such as, domestic asset protection trusts.

Ohio FLPs and LLCs: A Review

The analysis of whether or not to form an LLC or FLP under Ohio law should focus on the following: (1) What level of asset protection do Ohio's FLPs and LLCs provide an owner/debtor? (2) Is a "charging order" the only remedy that a creditor is entitled to receive? (3) What direction is Ohio heading with regards to the remedies available to creditors against FLP and LLC interests?

Response to Question #1
The level of asset protection that Ohio's FLPs and LLCs provide an owner/debtor are typical of many states. The bottom line is that Ohio's FLP and LLC laws are average at best.

Response to Question #2
Ohio's FLP statutes (ORC 1782.40, 41 and 42) and LLC statutes (ORC 1705.18 and 1705.19) state that a creditor can charge an owner's membership interest or limited partnership interest. The statutes (both the Ohio LLC and Ohio FLP) also contain language that the judgment creditor has "only" the rights of an assignee with regards to a membership interest or limited partnership interest.

Response to Question #3
While on its face the language of the Ohio Statutes would seem to indicate that Ohio is an "exclusive remedy" state (i.e. the creditor can only charge the interest of the debtor and then only has the rights of an assignee), this type of statutory language has been and is being interpreted in case law as permitting a creditor the right to pursue other collection and creditor remedies. These can even include judicial foreclosure of the debtor's membership or limited partnership interest and other legal actions such as veil piercing, creditor's bills and other direct actions. This appears to be where Ohio is headed, due to the language of its LLC and FLP statutes, and the emerging case law. The bottom line is, at present, Ohio's LLC and FLP statutes provide only an "average" level of asset protection. Other jurisdictions are more favorable, and Doctors should take advantage of the more favorable laws in those states.

The Diagnosis

Since exempt assets generally can't protect 100% of your assets, other techniques must be used to achieve optimal asset protection. FLPs and LLCs are two of the most frequently employed asset protection tools we use to manage the wealth of Doctors and their families. We would be surprised if you did not use at least one as part of your new comprehensive financial plan. These tools not only protect assets, but they also can offer income and estate tax benefits. Taxes and preservation of estates will be discussed in depth in Chapter 9-5.

FLPs and LLCs certainly have their limitations and are not cure-alls. This is why we need to consider other tools as part of our comprehensive planning. Trusts are another set of tools that offer asset protection, tax, and estate planning benefits. These asset protection tools are discussed in the next chapter.

6-8

Using Trusts to Shield Wealth

In addition to exempt assets, FLPs and LLCs, there is another tool that can be used to protect Doctors' assets and maintain their wealth—a Trust. A Trust is a legal entity that is often misunderstood by many Doctors. In this chapter, we will explain what a Trust is and the asset protection role Trusts can play in physicians' planning.

What Is A Trust?

A Trust is merely a special type of contract created by one or more persons or entities. It creates a legal arrangement where a person or entity holds property for the benefit of another.

The person who holds the property is the Trustee. The trustee "holds" the property for the benefit of one or more beneficiaries. The Trust document establishes the terms of how the Trust should be administered and how the Trust assets should be distributed during the lifetime of the Trust as well as after the Trust is terminated.

The following definitions and classifications should help you understand a Trust and how it functions.

1. **Grantor:** The Grantor is the person who sets-up the Trust. He or she is usually the person who transfers property into the Trust. A Grantor may also be called the *Trustor* or *Settlor*.

2. **Trustee:** The Trustee is the legal owner of the Trust property. The Trustee is responsible for administering and carrying out the terms of the Trust. He or she owes a fiduciary duty to the beneficiaries—the utmost duty of care that he or she will follow the terms of the Trust document and manage the Trust property properly. A Trustee may be a person, such as a family member or trusted friend. The Trustee can also be an institution, such as a professional Trust company or the Trust department of a bank. When there is more than one Trustee, they are called *co-Trustees*.

   The Trustee is the legal owner of any assets owned by the Trust and has "legal title" to the assets owned by the Trust. For example, assume that Dad wants to set-up a Trust for his Son and Daughter. Dad wants his brother, the children's uncle, to serve as Trustee. If Dad transfers his house into the Trust, the deed will provide that the house is owned by "Uncle, as Trustee of the Dad Trust."

3. **Beneficiary:** The beneficiary (or beneficiaries) is the person (or persons) for whom the Trust was set-up. (In the example discussed above, the beneficiaries would be Son and Daughter.) While the Trustee has legal title to assets owned by the Trust, the beneficiary has *equitable title* or the right to the Trust property. The beneficiary can sue the Trustee if the Trustee mismanages the Trust property or disobeys specific instructions in the Trust. The beneficiary may be the same person as the grantor, and can possibly be the same person as the Trustee. In a living trust for example, the grantor, trustee, and beneficiary are usually the same person. If asset protection is the goal of the trust, then the Trustee, beneficiary and grantor cannot all be the same person.

4. **Funding:** Funding the Trust means transferring assets to the Trust. A Trust that is "unfunded" has no property transferred to it. It is completely ineffective. You must title assets to the Trust if you want Trust protection as with any other legal entity/ asset protection tool discussed previously. To title real estate to the Trust, you must execute and record a deed to the property to the Trust. Bank and brokerage accounts can be transferred by simply changing the name on the accounts. Registered stocks and bonds are changed by notifying the transfer agent or issuing company and requesting that the certificates be reissued to the Trust. Other assets, such as household items, furniture, jewelry, artwork, etc., are transferred by a simple legal document called an *Assignment* or *Bill of Sale*. Your asset protection specialist can transfer assets simply and quickly.

Revocable Living Trusts: Illusory Asset Protection

Revocable Living Trusts (also called "Family Trusts" or "A-B Trusts") allow the grantor of the Living Trust the flexibility to make changes to an estate plan and to avoid unnecessary probate expenses. Probate is an unnecessary expense and hassle for Doctors and is discussed in detail in Lesson 6. Revocable Living Trusts also effectively sidestep the hidden dangers of joint tenancy, which is also discussed in Lesson 6. However, many people mistakenly assume that these Trusts provide asset protection benefits.

During your lifetime, Living Trusts provide absolutely no asset protection. This is because Living Trusts are revocable. While revocability and flexibility are valuable characteristics for almost all financial planning tools, these characteristics render the Revocable Trust useless for asset protection purposes, at least during the lifetime of the grantor. Remember this simple rule: *Revocable Trusts are vulnerable to creditors*. Let's explore the main reason why Revocable Trusts offer no protection.

Creditors Can "Step Into Your Shoes," Revoke the Living Trust, and Seize Trust Assets

Revocable Trusts are useless for asset protection because Revocable Trusts allow the grantor to undo the Trust. If you wanted to unwind a Revocable Trust and use the funds for yourself, you could do so. Because of this, a creditor can essentially force the grantor of the Trust to do this. If the grantor's creditors want to seize assets owned by a revocable Trust, they need only petition the court to "step into the shoes" of the grantor and direct the funds of the Trust back to the debtor. The Trust assets will no longer be owned by the Trust, but by the debtor personally. The creditors then have all the rights and privileges to seize these assets now owned by the debtor.

Irrevocable Trusts: The Asset Protectors

While Revocable Trusts offer no asset protection, Irrevocable Trusts are outstanding for asset protection. Once you establish an Irrevocable Trust, you forever abandon the ability to undo the Trust and reclaim property transferred to the Trust. With an Irrevocable Trust, you lose both control of the Trust assets and ownership.

Of course, this discussion assumes that in transferring assets to any Irrevocable Trust, you do not run afoul of fraudulent transfer laws. We introduced the concept of these laws at the beginning of this Lesson. Now, let's discuss why and how Irrevocable Trusts can protect assets. What follows below is an overview of certain terms and provisions that we recommend an irrevocable trust should include. An additional analysis of irrevocable trusts and the asset protection features they can offer for estate planning purpose is covered in Lesson 9. Because transferring assets to an irrevocable trust may have serious repercussions involving gift tax issues, please consult a tax expert. This is why the authors recommend a team of experts including a tax planning expert to help clarify these issues.

Why Irrevocable Trusts Protect Your Assets

Irrevocable Trusts protect assets for the same reason that Revocable Trusts do not. As mentioned earlier, Revocable Living Trusts do not provide asset protection because creditors can "step into your shoes" and undo such a Trust. The logic here is that if you have the power to undo your Revocable Trust, so do your creditors.

Irrevocable Trusts results in the opposite. Because an established Irrevocable Trust cannot be altered or undone (except in very limited circumstances, and not by the trustmaker), your creditors cannot "step into your shoes" and undo the Trust any more than you can. Assets in an Irrevocable Trust are immune from creditor attack, lawsuits, and other threats against the grantor (the person who created the Trust).

Provisions,Terms and Trust Designs That Your Irrevocable Trust Should Have

There are a number of provisions, terms (clauses) and trust design options that should be included in an Irrevocable Trust so you can properly protect your assets and those of your beneficiaries. These clauses are not necessarily important to protect the Trust creator, but work to shield the Trust beneficiaries from their creditors.

Spendthrift Clause

Spendthrift clauses allow Trustees to withhold income and principal—which would ordinarily be paid to the beneficiary—if the Trustee feels that the money could or would be wasted or seized by the beneficiary's creditors. This clause accomplishes two goals.

First, it prevents a wasteful beneficiary from spending Trust funds or wasting Trust assets. This is especially important to many Doctors who set up Trusts with their children as beneficiaries. If you worry that money in a Trust for your children would be wasted if not controlled, then use a spendthrift clause, allowing the Trustee to reduce or stop payments if your child spends too quickly or unwisely.

Second, the spendthrift clause protects Trust assets from creditors of the beneficiaries. Beneficiaries may be young now, but as adults they will face the same risks we all face: lawsuits, debt problems, divorce, a failing business, etc. The spendthrift clause protects Trust assets from your children's creditors by granting the Trustee the authority to withhold payments to a beneficiary who has an outstanding creditor. If the beneficiary and Trustee are at "arm's length," the creditor has no power to force the Trustee to pay the beneficiary. The creditor only has a right to payments actually paid by the Trustee. He cannot force the Trustee to make disbursements.

As we described in Chapter 6-6, Ohio law recognizes the protection provided by spendthrift clauses and the protection is significant.

Anti-Alienation Clause

The anti-alienation clause also protects Trust assets from the beneficiary's creditors. Specifically, the anti-alienation clause prohibits the Trustee from transferring Trust assets to anyone other than the beneficiary. This, of course, includes creditors of the Trust beneficiary. Thus, while the spendthrift clause allows the Trustee to withhold payments if a creditor lurks, the anti-alienation clause goes one step further—it prohibits the Trustee from paying Trust income or principal to anyone but the named beneficiary.

Dynasty Trust or Perpetual Trust Clause

In many circumstances adding a dynasty trust or perpetual trust clause to an irrevocable trust should be considered when creating an irrevocable trust. Ohio is one of a handful of states that permits an irrevocable trust to "exist, or carry on" in perpetuity as opposed to being limited to a number of years. This is also commonly referred to as "an irrevocable dynasty trust or simply, a dynasty trust." However, under Ohio law, the creator of the irrevocable dynasty trust must follow the statutory rules set forth in Ohio Revised Code sections 2131.08—.09 when creating the Ohio dynasty trust. If this right to create an irrevocable dynasty trust is properly exercised and is combined with other related asset protection and estate tax planning strategies, the dynasty trust can eliminate forever any future transfer taxes and be held in a protective manner for successive generations.

The Trust Protector-Adding Flexibility to the Irrevocable Trust

Every irrevocable trust should have a trust protector. The position of trust protector is created in the trust document and typically permits the trust protector to protect the interests of the trust and the trust beneficiaries from unforeseen changes in the law or other unforeseen circumstances that could be detrimental to the trust or the trust beneficiaries. By its very nature, the terms of an irrevocable trust typically cannot be changed. In some circumstances a Court can make changes to an irrevocable trust, however, this can have unpredictable results and is not the preferred method. Further, irrevocable trusts are also typically long term trusts that can go on for years and years and even in perpetuity. To address these concerns and create flexibility, the role of trust protector was introduced. The legal concept of a trust protector has been around for years and originated with offshore trusts. Trust protectors are now increasingly being included in irrevocable trust documents throughout the United States. There is generally no downside to making provision for a trust protector in an irrevocable trust. The trust protector is typically an attorney, accountant, financial advisor, or an individual that has excellent business acumen and understands trusts and is not related to or subordinate to the trustee(s) of the trusts or the beneficiaries.

Domestic Asset Protection Trusts ("DAPTS")— An Irrevocable Trust Tool That Can Provide an Asset Protection Shield

A domestic asset protection trust (DAPT) is an irrevocable asset protection trust formed by a Grantor in one of the 12 states (currently) in the United States that permit these types of irrevocable trusts. They are called "domestic" asset protection trusts because they are formed in various states in the United States and to distinguish them from "foreign," "offshore," or "international" asset protection trusts. Unfortunately, Ohio is not among the 12 states that permit DAPT's. Therefore, an Ohio doctor must use the laws of another state to create a DAPT.

DAPTs are unique because for years, in all 50 of the United States, there was essentially a universal common law rule that stated a person could not by themselves: (1) create an irrevocable trust for his own benefit, (2) put his own assets in the irrevocable trust, (3) retain the right to access the assets of the irrevocable trust, and (4) at the same time prevent any of his creditors from accessing his assets owned by the irrevocable trust. This was called the rule against "self settled trusts." Traditionally, the common law has been that a creditor could reach the maximum amount that the trustee could distribute or apply for the benefit of the person who established the trust.

However, various offshore jurisdictions have permitted these types of self-settled trusts for years. Then beginning in 1997, two states, Alaska and Delaware, borrowing from the laws of a number of foreign jurisdictions, enacted legislation which permit a person (commonly referred to as a trustmaker or settlor) to create their own irrevocable trust for their benefit and transfer certain amounts of their assets to an independent trustee of the irrevocable trust (it is usually a banking institution or privately bonded trustee). The trustmaker also retains the right to receive discretionary distributions of income and/or principal from the irrevocable trust. As a general rule, so long as the transfers to a DAPT from its inception are not fraudulent and the statute of limitations has run regarding potential or future creditors of the trustmaker, the assets in the DAPT will be protected from any creditors of the trustmaker. Based upon the design of the DAPTs and the state legislation authorizing them, creditors of the trustmaker cannot "pierce" the DAPT and reach its assets.

Some of the common characteristics of a DAPT are: (1) It is formed in a state which permits DAPTs by statute; (2) Transfers of property and/or assets occur from the Grantor to the DAPT; (3) There is an independent "resident" trustee located in the state where the DAPT is formed who is the trustee of the DAPT; (4) There exists a "spendthrift clause" in the DAPT; (5) The Grantor retains numerous rights regarding the DAPT including for example, the discretionary right to receive income or principal from the DAPT, the right to veto distributions as well as others' rights; (6)There are statutes of limitations periods which cut off certain creditor's rights beginning from the date the Grantor makes contributions to the DAPT; (7) There are three classes of "exception creditors" (this may vary somewhat from state by state) which are permitted to possibly gain access to the DAPT assets and these are: (i) spouses and children (for support payments), (ii) proven fraudulent transfers and (iii) existing tort claims (death, personal injury or property damage claims).

Case Study

Harry, a high risk obstetrician, consulted with our planning group a few years ago. He was concerned that his malpractice limits and Ohio's tort reform did not provide sufficient protection for him. We agreed. Harry's net worth at that time was approximately $3.7 million, much of which consisted of Ohio exempt assets (life insurance and qualified retirement plan benefits). However, Harry maintained an investment account with approximately $1 million in it. He asked for suggestions on vehicles to protect his investment account.

We recommended that Harry establish a DAPT in the state of Delaware and transfer his investment account to the trustee. A few years later, Harry is sued for Medicare fraud because of a clerical error made by his staff. Harry's insurance policy does not cover this type of claim and damages amount to $100,000. Medicare is granted a judgment against Harry for $100,000. Medicare may assert a number of arguments to attempt to collect the assets in Harry's Delaware DAPT, but more likely than not, the assets in the Delaware DAPT will be "unavailable" and cannot be accessed or collected by Medicare.

Even though DAPTs are becoming a more popular and acceptable asset protection strategy, it remains a relatively new asset protection tool, and there are a number of legal commentators who feel that there are still many areas in which their effectiveness has yet to be tested. These legal concerns should be thoroughly reviewed with a knowledgeable attorney prior to entering into a DAPT. However, for the most part, if a Grantor follows the proper steps in setting up a DAPT, the DAPT should provide a substantial amount of asset protection. Additionally, the DAPT will provide another set of obstacles that creditors would have to confront when determining what legal remedies, if any, they can exercise against a debtor. Also, the existence of a DAPT could increase the negotiating position and leverage a debtor can have over a creditor.

Combine Irrevocable Trusts with Debt Shields

As you may recall from Lesson #5 (and you will see again in Chapter 6-10), Doctors can protect assets by using "debt shields" or "collateralization" of a valuable asset. Basically, you can protect an asset by making that asset the collateral for a loan. This can be done by using an unrelated lender, such as a bank or credit facility, or by using a "friendly" lender. Often, an ideal "friendly" lender is an irrevocable trust for the benefit of your children. In the case of the "friendly" lender, you would be paying interest to your family, rather than to an outside organization. This way, your debt costs stay in the family—thus making additional debt more palatable for most physicians.

Using an irrevocable trust and a debt shield can be an ideal way to protect a Doctor's home in states, such as Ohio, where homestead protection is limited. This same technique can also protect other real estate and even the accounts receivable of a medical practice.

The Diagnosis

Once Doctors have maximized their investment in exempt assets, they move on to FLPs, LLCs, and Trusts. When trusts are structured properly and funded, they can provide significant estate planning and asset protection benefits. With a strong advisory team Trusts can be combined with LLCs to offer potential income tax benefits and leveraged estate planning benefits as well. When Trusts are combined with friendly loans and LLCs, Doctors can achieve asset protection for otherwise difficult-to-protect assets (like the primary residence or practice accounts receivable). Work with your team of advisors to see how Trusts can be integrated into your comprehensive financial plan to maximize your efficiency when addressing your specific planning goals.

6-9

International Planning

Over the last decade, an increasing number of Doctors—though still a small minority—have looked internationally for solutions to their comprehensive financial planning goals. It isn't necessarily a bad thing that international planning is limited to a small group, as there are numerous pitfalls that can snare naive Doctors. In this chapter, you'll learn what to do (and what to avoid) in international planning, and about specific tools used by top attorneys in their international planning. In addition, we will discuss the major pitfalls some clients experience as a result of inadequate international planning with advisors who lack international financial experience. We will conclude the chapter by discussing how international trusts and LLCs are effective financial tools for protecting assets.

Onshore Partnerships With Offshore Trust Ownership

We often recommend a trust that is known as a foreign integrated estate planning trust (IEPT)—one created by a Doctor who establishes a trust in a country other than the Doctor's domicile. On this subject, the authors recognize attorney Barry Engel, who was very helpful to the following discussion. The Doctor's domicile is referred to as the home jurisdiction. For most physician clients, this is the United States.

One of the reasons a foreign IEPT is one of the strongest asset protection vehicles available is that, if it is properly structured and properly administered, the final legal battle can be forced into one or more foreign jurisdictions with favorable asset protection laws and court systems.

Under the typical foreign IEPT, there are two trustees, one of whom is an individual domiciled in the home jurisdiction (a.k.a. the domestic trustee). The second trustee is usually a corporate trustee (a.k.a. the foreign trustee), domiciled in a jurisdiction of the foreign IEPT's applicable law. The foreign IEPT agreement provides the domestic trustee with the power to take binding action so long as the foreign trustee is notified by the domestic trustee of any action taken.

As long as the Doctor's legal seas are calm, the foreign trustee's duties and activities are relatively passive. However, in the event of a legal threat against the Doctor, the foreign trustee has the express power and authority to fire the domestic trustee and take assets out of the reach of U. S. courts.

To obtain charging order protection and discounts for federal gift tax purposes, and allow the Doctor to have control over certain designated assets, many planners combine a foreign IEPT with a domestic family limited partnership (FLP). The foreign IEPT is usually the 99 percent limited partner and the Doctor is the one percent general partner. Typically, a Doctor will establish a foreign IEPT at the same time that he or she creates a domestic FLP.

Once the FLP is formed, the Doctor gifts the 99 percent limited partnership interest to the foreign IEPT. However, since the Doctor retains full control over the assets and the investment decisions of the FLP as the general partner, the Doctor retains full control over the assets and the investment decisions of the FLP.

There is a common misconception that a foreign IEPT must invest most or all of its assets abroad. This is not true. While there are a number of good reasons for at least a portion of the assets of a foreign IEPT being invested abroad, more typically the bulk of the assets remain invested within the U.S. while there are no threats against the Doctor or the foreign IEPT assets, which is usually all of the time for most physician clients.

Dangerous International Pitfalls To Avoid

As you might imagine, in our business, we see too many Doctors who use international planning for the wrong reasons. Often, people are so anxious to avoid taxes, shield assets improperly, or get rich quick that their otherwise reasonable judgment is clouded. Consequently, people engage in planning which they would never do here in the U.S. Combine these desires with the virtually unregulated international jurisdictions (i.e., no reporting to the IRS, no SEC or NASD disclosure requirements, no state attorney generals remedying fraud, etc.), and one has an area ripe for potential abuse.

Offshore Planning Strategies

As explained in this Lesson, (+5) asset protection can be achieved in the U.S. through the use of exempt assets. Beyond this, a variety of strategies and legal tools are needed. Although the tools and structures are essentially the same here and abroad, sometimes there are better laws available outside the United States, and American attorneys and financial advisors who are not experts in asset protection planning are unfamiliar with foreign laws and unable to practice in countries where they are not licensed. Those of us who practice regularly in this arena have relationships with attorneys and trust companies in countries with the best asset protection laws and court systems.

Unfortunately, while creating legitimate international asset protection plans is not difficult for experienced advisors, many Americans forego such planning and simply try to "hide" wealth in these international centers. Rather than use an entity like an LLC, they simply set up bank or brokerage accounts in countries where there is little, if any, reporting. No one is the wiser, right?

The problem with this "no entity" approach is that in any litigation—civil lawsuit, divorce, or even a governmental case—there will eventually be some type of formal inquiry of assets. This might occur by way of a "debtor's exam" after a successful lawsuit, a bankruptcy filing, a list of assets for a divorce settlement, etc. For the "no entity" approach to work, the client would have to omit the international assets or lie about their existence. This amounts to perjury, bankruptcy fraud, or obstruction of justice, depending upon the forum of the case. Thus, the ultimate success of many "hidden" offshore planning strategies relies on the clients' ultimate decision to commit perjury or some other crime. Smart clients realize this potential pitfall and have a group of advisors who help ensure that this will not happen.

Going Offshore to Avoid Tax Is Illegal

As explained above, Americans are liable for taxes on all income worldwide, no matter how or where it was earned. However, it is true that many international banks, mutual funds and other financial institutions will not report earnings/interest to the IRS. This is the chasm where many greedy clients—or unscrupulous advisors—operate. This is also where tax evasion—a federal crime—is committed.

While the client is required under U.S. law to make the necessary tax reporting on income earned internationally (and advisors should instruct their clients to do so), many clients may keep quiet and hope they are never caught. Failure to report offshore income can subject a client to substantial penalties and interest expenses. This "hide the ball" strategy is used not only by knowing clients, but also by shady advisors who concoct ever more sophisticated schemes, like moving money from one Trust to another company to a third foundation and so on, in hopes of avoiding detection.

Although the pitch may seem complex and impressive, astute Doctors know to always ask the following question: If the income will eventually accrue to my benefit, how come I don't have to report it to the IRS? They know that they must steer clear of these schemes unless they want the cloud of a possible tax evasion indictment hanging over them for years to come.

Going Offshore To "Get Rich Quick" Can Lead You To Scams And Frauds

The desire to get rich quick leads many clients into problems most pervasive in the investment arena. Here, scam artists and fraudsters abound, poised to take advantage of the next client who wants to "get rich offshore." The savvy Doctor understands that any investment that offers truly outstanding returns is on the radar screen of the world's most sophisticated financial institutions and their super affluent clientele. Those investments are reserved for the financial institutions' billionaire clients. They know that the only thing that can be achieved from chasing fantastic returns in international markets is a significant, if not complete, loss of principal. Let's explore how some of these mistakes happen.

International LLCs And Trusts

Used properly, these tools can be used to achieve a high (+4/+5) level of protection. Compared to exempt assets, which do not have professional, government or accounting fees, these tools are expensive. However, they may be the best non-exempt options for Doctor clients who must have the top level of protection.

A number of jurisdictions have adopted or enhanced asset protection LLC legislation over the last decade, most notably in this hemisphere the island nation of Nevis. Also, many jurisdictions have international Trust (IT) laws as well. Common uses of these tools include:

To Own International Insurance Policies

One of the leading international financial planning strategies today is purchasing a permanent (cash value) life insurance policy offshore. In terms of tax planning, if the policy is U.S. tax-compliant, all of the growth within the policy will accumulate tax-free. Further, the proceeds will pay out to the beneficiary income tax-free and the client can take loans against the accumulated cash values during his life, tax-free. This is similar to the benefits of a domestic cash value life insurance policy, which you can read more about later in this book.

For Multi-Generational Planning For An International Family

Let's say the goal of a client is to create a nest egg for future generations like children, grandchildren, and beyond. And let's say it is important that the nest egg be asset-protected in an ironclad way. In this circumstance, an international Trust would be an ideal tool. This would be especially appropriate if the trust was created in a country where the law does not limit the duration of Trusts under the "rule against perpetuities," found in many of the states. By using an IT, a U.S. client could literally secure the family's ability to enjoy the fruits of the gift for hundreds of years, as long as other tax issues were addressed by an experienced tax expert.

The Diagnosis

We live in a global economy. There are worldwide financial options for all of us. With developments in technology and communication, it is possible (if not easy) to access international vehicles. The benefits of international planning in our global economy can be significant. These benefits can come in the form of increased levels of asset protection (+4 or +5) or intriguing investment opportunities that may offer excellent diversification for your portfolio (see Lesson #8). However, there are a number of scams and frauds to be avoided offshore. Even if you avoid scams and frauds, you are not "out of the woods" just yet. International tax and reporting laws are highly complex. There are many areas where an individual or advisor could make a mistake.

Though all areas of planning require the assistance of advisors, no area of planning requires greater expertise than international planning. Make sure your team of advisors has an asset protection expert who can help you navigate the tricky waters of international planning and that your tax advisors are familiar with international tax laws. With the right expertise and strategy, international planning can help protect liquid assets, real estate and possibly your home. For solutions to protect the home, you should read the next chapter.

6-10

Protecting Your Home

Along with retirement accounts, the family home is often the most valuable asset of most Doctors. Even beyond its pure financial value, the home has great *psychological* value as well. In fact, we find that most of our clients who engage in asset protection planning often begin with the question: "How can I protect my home?" That is why we thought it important to dedicate an entire chapter to discussing this asset and how to protect it from outside threats.

This chapter will discuss the pros and cons of state Homestead Law, LLCs/FLPs, and the Debt Shield. You may be surprised to find out that something you always feared could actually be your ally in your quest to protect your most valuable asset.

State Homestead Law

As you learned earlier, in Ohio, the amount of the homestead exemption is $20,200 per person.

Homestead protection is often automatic, but may require additional action in some cases. Each state has specific requirements for claiming homestead status. In some states, you must file a declaration of homestead in a public office. Other states set a time requirement for residency before homestead protection is granted. In Ohio however, homestead protection is automatic. Unfortunately, this exemption is virtually worthless for nearly all Ohio residents and in particular Ohio doctors.

LLCs And FLPs

LLCs and FLPs are two tools that could potentially protect a primary residence. In fact, many advisors regularly recommend these techniques to their clients who want to protect their homes. The drawbacks of these methods are perfect examples of why multidisciplinary planning is a necessity for Doctors. Let's look at some of the problems with doing asset protection planning in a vacuum with respect to the home.

LLCs And FLPs For The Home

In Chapter 6-7, we discussed LLCs and FLPs in detail. We will assume that this is fresh in your mind so you can see why owning real estate in an LLC would be attractive. However, when it comes to the primary residence, these entities are not very common choices of clients.

Unlike other assets, the family home has unique tax attributes—most notably, the deductibility of the mortgage interest and the $250,000 per person ($500,000 per couple) capital gains tax exemption. By owning the home within an LLC or a FLP, both of these tax benefits may be lost. However, this seriously impacts the asset protection of the structure as well—so the asset protection and tax issues must be balanced.

A One-person LLC For the Home—An Option Worth Exploring

As was stated previously, the residence or home can represent one of the larger sources of net worth for a Doctor, so protection of the residence is usually a high priority. Due to the fact that Ohio has a very paltry residential exemption ($20,200), alternative asset protection strategies need to be explored. Also, as previously indicated, there are tax benefit considerations that factor into the asset protection strategies of shielding the home from creditors and these include, preserving the Internal Revenue Section 121 sale proceeds exemptions (i.e. $250,000 exclusion on capital gain for a single person and $500,000 for a married couple), as well as the tax deduction for mortgage interest. One such strategy that may be viable for a Doctor, and worth exploring is:

1. Having either the Doctor or his spouse (the spouse would be preferred if the spouse is in an occupation or career that has less liability exposure than the Doctor) form a one-person/one member LLC;

2. The one-person/one member LLC would be formed under the laws of a state that has favorable debtor charging order protection (see previous discussion in Chapter 6-7), for example, Delaware.

3. The one-person/one member LLC would elect to be treated from a tax standpoint as a "disregarded entity." The IRS permits one-person LLC's to be treated as a "disregarded entity." From a tax standpoint, the LLC does not exist and is not required to file its own tax returns. In other words, the single owner continues to report taxable items of the LLC (e.g., mortgage interest) on his or her personal 1040 for tax reporting purposes.

If a Doctor implements this strategy, the Doctor may be able to receive increased asset protection for the home, preserve the ability to deduct mortgage interest and preserve the $250,000 per person ($500,000 per couple) capital gains tax exemption.

A number of legal commentators and legal scholars believe this strategy is not viable, due to the fact a Doctor would be utilizing a business entity to protect personal assets and the business entity in this situation does not have any legitimate "business" purpose. This strategy falls into the category of "may or may not work, but worth a try," if acquiring asset protection for the home is an important goal.

Qualified Personal Residence Trusts

The "Qualified Personal Residence Trust" (or QPRT) is primarily an estate tax planning tool, but as with most such tools, also provides asset protection. After creating a QPRT, the owner deeds ownership of the home to the QPRT irrevocably. While this is certainly effective for both asset protection and estate planning purposes, it comes with a significant cost—you no longer own your home. In fact, when the term of years is up (typical range of years for a QPRT is 5 to 20 years), you have to pay rent to the Trust to continue living in the home. Also, homes with mortgages on them present tax difficulties. For these reasons, while the QPRT is a strong asset protection tool, we typically do not advise using it for most younger clients whose main concern is asset protection, rather than estate tax planning. Nonetheless, if it can be implemented correctly, and there are no fraudulent transfer issues, a QPRT can receive a rating of (+4).

The Debt Shield Concept

The debt shield can be the most effective way to shield the equity of the home. Essentially, using a debt shield means getting a loan against the equity in your home. For many clients, this is counter-intuitive—they want to pay down the mortgage as much as possible. While this may have an emotional appeal, for asset protection purposes, it is the exact opposite of what you want to do in states like Ohio, where home equity is exposed and homestead protections are minimal.

For most Doctor clients, using a "debt shield" does not mean taking a new loan on their home at all—rather, understanding that they may not want to rush to pay down their existing mortgages quickly. Here, the decision on whether (or to what extent) to pay down a mortgage they already have is examined from the asset protection perspective (could the funds be invested in another better-protected asset?) and wealth accumulation perspective (could the funds be invested in another better-performing asset?). When getting a new loan is involved, the analysis is identical.

Types of Debt Shields

As you will read in the Lesson on practice strategies, and earlier in this Lesson on trusts, "debt shields" can be implemented by using an unrelated lender, such as a bank, or by using a "friendly" lender. Often, an ideal "friendly" lender can be an irrevocable trust or a family LLC. While the asset protection may be slightly stronger for an unrelated lender debt shield, the economics can be much greater, and risks much reduced, when using a related lender.

Asset Protection

From an asset protection perspective, the transaction is simple—use the debt shield to move the equity from the vulnerable asset (the home) to a better-protected asset (e.g., exempt asset, LLC, FLP, etc.).

Economics

From an economic perspective, the transaction is also simple. Is the cost of the equity move (the after-tax interest cost) higher or lower than the yield on reinvestment of the loan proceeds? Also, how "safe" is the investment of loan proceeds? Of course, paying interest to a related entity, such as a Trust for the benefit of family members, is certainly a lot different than paying it to an unrelated bank.

Your economic analysis for an unrelated lender might be to ask, "What if the funds I gain by shielding my home could be invested in such a way that I had the opportunity to earn more within the investment than the loan interest would cost?" In this way, you would make money by shielding the home—through the concept of leverage we developed in the second Lesson.

The Diagnosis

For most Doctors, there is no more financially valuable and psychologically important asset than the family residence. Some states offer great homestead protection, but most, including Ohio, offer inadequate protection of this valued asset. If homestead does not protect your home adequately, you should focus on this as part of your plan or accept the fact that your most valued asset is completely exposed. For older clients who are most concerned with estate planning, a one-person/one member LLC or QPRT may be an option.

For Doctors who are not ready to give away their homes to their children, some type of debt shield will likely be the most appropriate strategy. For Doctors who already have attractive loan rates on their homes and don't want to refinance their homes, the "friendly" debt shield that essentially pays children the interest may be the most attractive option. For more on this technique, speak to your advisors or contact the authors.

Divorce Protection

Of all the risks to Doctors, the most common threat to financial security may be divorce. According to the United States Census Bureau's 2002 statistics, only 33% of marriages in the United States will last 25 years. *Divorce Magazine* reports that remarriages end in divorce 60% of the time. Undoubtedly an emotionally devastating experience, divorce can be a financially disastrous experience as well.

Divorce protection is not about hiding assets from a soon-to-be ex-spouse. Nor is it about cheating or lying to keep your wealth. Rather, it involves resolving issues of property ownership and distribution before things go sour. By agreeing in advance what will be yours and what will be your spouse's, you save money, time, and emotional distress in the long run. In fact, this type of asset protection planning inevitably benefits all parties, except the divorce lawyers of course.

Divorce planning is also about shielding family assets from the potential divorces of children and grandchildren. Given the statistics enumerated above, it is almost a certainty that either a child or grandchild of yours will get divorced. Thus, for purposes of intergenerational financial planning, this is a crucial topic, unless you want to give half of your legacy to the ex-spouses of your heirs. This is a lesson wealthy families have known, and addressed, for decades. Wealthy families do not have a secret to avoiding divorce. Wealthy families do have a secret to avoiding the financial losses that can be associated with inevitable divorces. This chapter will discuss why divorce can be so financially devastating, the pros and cons of prenuptial agreements, irrevocable Trusts, and ways to protect your children from divorce.

Why Divorce Can Be A Financial Nightmare

Most Doctors do not have to read newspapers to see how financially devastating a divorce can be. While high-profile divorces involving tens of millions of dollars illustrate the point dramatically, most of us need only look to family or friends to see how a divorce turns into financial upheaval. The prevailing attitude toward divorce can be illustrated by a scene from the movie, *The First Wives Club*. In the film, Ivana Trump explains her theory of divorce to three ex-wives, played by Goldie Hawn, Diane Keaton, and Bette Midler. "Don't get even," she says. "Get everything!"

Combine this fight-for-everything attitude with the terrible odds of facing a divorce, and you have a very serious threat to financial security. In fact, a divorce threatens not only former spouses, but also their families and possibly their business partners as well. To truly understand how a divorce affects the finances of the participants, you must first understand how property is divided when the marriage is dissolved.

Ohio is a Separate Property State

As a general rule throughout the United States, there are "community property" states, such as California, and "separate property" states such as Ohio. Because Ohio is a separate property state, the law in Ohio recognizes that between a husband and wife, each spouse *can* have their own separate property and this separate property of a spouse will not be considered marital property.

On the other hand, domestic relations law in Ohio has developed over time to the point where the legal "line" between separate property and marital property can also be dependent upon a myriad of factors. Those factors can include: the length of the marriage between husband and wife, what assets were accumulated during the marriage, whether or not there are children of the marriage, what role did either spouse play in the raising of the children, the educational differences between husband and wife, did a prenuptial agreement exist, and whether or not separate property that either one or both of the spouses brought to the marriage was commingled with the martial property or became so intertwined with the marital property that the separate property lost its "character" as separate property. These issues are hard to prove in court, and most Domestic Relations judges have little patience for the arguments,

Assume that a husband (Doctor) and wife who were married fresh out of medical school for over 30 years decide to get divorced. The wife files for divorce. The Doctor built a successful medical practice, and the wife raised the children. The Doctor brought some separate property (i.e. cash) to the marriage initially and contributed this to the purchase of the marital residence 30 years ago. In this situation, a domestic relations court would most likely determine that the separate property became converted to marital property and the residence along with most of the other assets, including the value of the Doctor's practice, would be "marital property" of the married couple (i.e. property accumulated during the marriage) and would be divided in half (50/50) by the domestic relations court. There are ways to keep separate property (i.e. property inherited, property developed or created by one spouse) separate. One of the most effective and commonplace strategies is a prenuptial agreement.

Can A "Pre-Nup" Protect You?

A premarital agreement (a.k.a. prenuptial agreement, premarital contract, ante-nuptial agreement, etc.) is the foundation of any protection against a divorce. The premarital agreement is a written contract between the spouses. It specifies the division of property and income upon divorce, including disposition of specific personal property, such as family heirlooms. It also states the responsibilities of each party with regard to their children after divorce. Finally, these agreements lay out the respective responsibilities during marriage, such as the financial support each spouse can expect or which religion will be used to raise future children. The agreement cannot limit child support because the right to child support lies with the child and not the parent.

Because a premarital agreement is a contract, the parties can customize the agreement to their particular situation, and mutually determine what property is to remain the separate property of either spouse. In short, a premarital agreement should not be looked upon as an "all or nothing" planning strategy. For example, the Doctor spouse may determine that all he wants to have his prenuptial agreement cover is his medical practice and the real estate that he owns which is associated with the medical practice. In this instance all other property would potentially be considered marital property.

Irrevocable Spendthrift Trusts: Ideal Tools To Keep Assets "In the Family"

As mentioned earlier, Irrevocable Trusts are very effective asset protection tools because the grantor no longer own the assets owned by the Trust. In other words, the grantor has transferred the property with no strings attached. Because the grantor neither owns nor controls the property, future creditors, including an ex-spouse, cannot claim the property. Moreover, the grantor can make children, grandchildren, and even future great-grandchildren, beneficiaries of an Irrevocable Trust. However, even though they can benefit from Trust assets, the Trust can be drafted so that their creditors, including divorcing ex-spouses, cannot get to Trust assets.

Nonetheless, using an Irrevocable Trust should not be taken lightly. Giving away assets forever with no strings attached can prove to have serious consequences when protecting against divorce, lawsuit, or other threats. When would such a strategy make sense? It would make sense in circumstances where you would have inevitably given away the assets to certain beneficiaries anyway. For example, the Trust might be used for assets that (1) you will leave to your children or grandchildren when you die; and (2) you do not need for your financial security. For a more detailed example, consider Irving's case study.

Case Study: Irving's Trust Protects His Summer Home

Irving, a plastic surgeon, bought a summer home by a lake. He and his first wife had three small children. Unfortunately, they divorced about six years into their marriage. In the settlement, he received the summer home.

Fifteen years later, Irving was ready to marry again, now in Santa Fe, New Mexico (a community property state). Both he and his prospective spouse had been married previously and understood divorce. Irving considered a premarital agreement to keep the summer home as his separate property. He had planned to give it to his three children, but wondered whether working on the home would jeopardize this plan if he later divorced.

After speaking with Irving, we noted three important points:

1. Irving's handiwork on the home might make it marital property;
2. Irving's children and their families used the home throughout the year; and
3. Irving had a lawsuit from a failed real estate venture.

Given these points, it was clear that the best strategy for Irving was to have an Irrevocable Trust own the summer home, which would give beneficial interests of the home to all three children equally (which already occurred).

By using an Irrevocable Trust to own the summer home, Irving protected the home against possible future divorce and also shielded it from other creditors and lawsuits. By including spendthrift provisions, Irving protected the home from his children's creditors, as well. This will insure that the summer house stays in the family for generations.

Protect Your Children From Divorce

When your children or grandchildren come to you, giddy with exciting news about their recent engagements, the last thing they want to hear you ask is "Are you going to sign a pre-nuptial agreement?" In fact, if you weren't paying for the wedding, you might lose your invitation for making such a statement.

As you learned earlier, the secret to protecting assets from divorce is keeping them as "separate property" and not commingling them with community or marital property. You can't trust your children to do this, so you are going to do it for them—without requiring the consent of your child or the future (or existing) spouse.

By leaving assets to your children's Irrevocable Trusts, with the appropriate spendthrift provisions, rather than to them personally, you can achieve this goal. They can even act as trustee of the trust you create for them. Of course, if the children take money out of the Trust and use it to buy a home or other property, that property will be subject to the rules of their state. To illustrate this point, let's look at the example of Rob and Janelle.

Case Study: Janelle's Divorce and Her Inheritance

Rob and Janelle were college sweethearts who got married right after graduation. Within a few years, their romance quickly turned sour and Rob could no longer handle the physical and emotional abuse. However, during their three-year marriage, Janelle received a sizeable inheritance and used it to pay off the couple's home. When they filed for divorce, Rob's attorney successfully argued that his time and labor on the house, and the fact that he lived in it except when Janelle occasionally kicked him out and he had to stay at his mother's, made half of the equity in the home (or $100,000) Rob's fair share. Though Rob and all of his friends will argue the $100,000 was a small consolation for what he endured, Janelle's grandparents certainly didn't intend for Rob to receive their inheritance.

What could Janelle have done differently to ensure that she protected her assets? Her grandparents could have left her the inheritance through an Irrevocable Trust that only allowed her to take out so much money per year. In that case, she would have used the interest from the inheritance to pay the mortgage down each month. If she did so, the corpus of the inheritance would have remained separate property and would not have been part of the divorce settlement. In the short three years of their marriage, they would have had next to no equity in their home and Rob would have left the divorce with what he brought into the marriage and his wounded pride—but none of Janelle's grandparent's life savings. It is left to the reader to determine what is equitable—we aren't marriage counselors. We are only trying to help you reach your desired objectives.

In a nutshell, a little proactive financial planning can go a long way to making sure that a divorce doesn't completely disrupt a family's financial situation.

Divorce Protection from *Your* Parents

Inherited assets that are segregated and not comingled with marital assets are protected from divorce in Ohio. If you have the potential to receive a consequential inheritance from your parents—and especially if you are concerned about the durability of your marriage—you should want to receive your inheritance in trust.

It is often wise for our Doctor clients to spend time and energy (and maybe even money) on their parents' estate and financial planning to make certain they receive their inheritances in a protected form. Inheritances received in properly designed and drafted lifetime irrevocable inheritance trusts—even if the doctor becomes the trustee of that inheritance trust upon his or her parents' deaths—are protected from divorce and can be exempt from the claims of personal and professional lawsuit creditors.

In other words, if the relationship with your parents permits, you can ask them to do for you that which you are doing for your own children.

The Diagnosis

In this Lesson, we discussed the importance of asset protection in our litigious society and how the sliding scale of asset protection can help you assess how protected (or unprotected) your assets may be. We dispelled myths that may have given you a false sense of security, then discussed the ways you can protect your assets. We explained philosophical requirements for any asset protection plan and shared information about exempt assets and legal tools. We explained how FLPs, LLCs, Trusts, and international planning could be part of your planning. We even discussed how to protect your home and how to protect your family from divorce.

Now that you are well informed in the area of asset protection, you are ready to learn how to build wealth. In the next Lesson, you will learn how to legally reduce taxes. Then, you will learn how to invest wisely, how to avoid estate taxes, and how to move forward with your planning. If, while on your educational journey, you have questions about anything you read, feel free to email us at odell@ojmgroup.com or mandell@ojmgroup.com. We can forward questions on to our co-authors.

LESSON 7

Legally Reduce Taxes

You don't have to be a Doctor to want to legally reduce your taxes. Judge Learned Hand once said: "Anyone may arrange his affairs so that his taxes shall be as low as possible... There is not even a patriotic duty to increase one's taxes." The difference between moderately and highly successful physicians is that the latter group always considers the tax impact of anything they do.

Doctors should understand that every additional dollar earned will be decimated by federal, state, and local taxes that may approach 50 cents. Physician families should also know that up to 50% of the family's after-tax net worth will be subject to federal estate and state inheritance taxes every time wealth transfers from one generation to the next. The Internal Revenue Code (IRC) is structured in a way that makes it almost impossible to accumulate wealth and pass it to future generations without significant friction. This is why your ability to work less and enjoy more of your hard earned dollars is directly related to your ability to manage taxes throughout your career, into retirement, and at your death.

You can't expect to manage taxes unless you understand taxes first. Every Doctor should read the next chapter, "Uncle Sam's Pieces of Your Pie," to learn exactly what taxes threaten wealth accumulation. This will help you better understand the motivation for, and benefits of, the strategies in subsequent chapters. These are tools that may help you reduce, defer, or even eliminate some taxes while providing you, your family, or your practice additional financial benefits. By learning and implementing the techniques in this Lesson, you will be able to reduce unnecessary taxes and build wealth more quickly. If you and your family can reduce taxes and enjoy more of every hard-earned dollar, you will be able to work less and get more out of your career in medicine.

7-1

Uncle Sam's Pieces of Your Pie

You can't expect to successfully overcome any challenge until you fully understand the challenge itself. In this chapter, we will explain how great an impact taxes have on your finances. We will also share techniques successful business owners have used to reduce unnecessary taxes for decades. If you need any additional motivation to save taxes, we know dozens of families that have been able to save tens of thousands to hundreds of thousands of dollars per year during their lifetimes, and millions of dollars in taxes at the time of death, by integrating these strategies into their comprehensive financial plans. Let's get started by examining where and how all of this tax revenue is generated by looking at four types of taxes:

- Incomes Taxes
- Taxes on Investments or Capital Gain Taxes
- Estate Taxes
- Income In Respect of a Decedent (IRD)

Income Taxes

Every citizen pays income taxes on salaries and other income. Do you know exactly how income taxes are computed? Most people believe they move from income tax bracket to income tax bracket—increasing the percentage they pay on each dollar earned as they move forward. The truth is that every individual (in the same filing category) pays the same tax rate on the first $16,700 of income. As a taxpayer's income crosses a threshold into the next tax bracket, only the dollars earned within that bracket are taxed at the higher rate. The next table illustrates how income tax is determined for married couples that filed jointly in 2009.

2009 Federal Income Tax Table—Married Couples Filing Jointly

If taxable income is over:	But not over:	The tax is:
$0	$16,700	10% of the amount over $0
$16,700	$67,900	$1,670 plus 15% of the amount over $16,700
$67,900	$137,050	$9,350 plus 25% of the amount over $67,900
$137,050	$208,850	$26,637 plus 28% of the amount over $137,050
$208,850	$372,950	$46,741.50 plus 33% of the amount over $208,850
$372,950	no limit	$100,894 plus 35% of the amount over $372,950

To better understand how income tax is tabulated for families, let's look at the example of Mike and Gina.

Mike and Gina are married and file jointly. Mike makes $240,000 per year, while Gina runs an in-home business that generates $10,000 per year. For simplicity, the table below assumes they have no deductions and they live in a state with 0% state income tax. If they lived in Ohio, they would have paid state income taxes of $9,090 plus 5.925% of every dollar earned in excess of $200,000. For income of approximately $250,000, that is over $12,052.50 of state income taxes in addition to the federal taxes described below. Based on their salaries, they have $250,000 of total adjusted gross income that generates federal income tax liabilities as follows:

On the first $16,700 of income they pay 10%	$1,670
On the next $51,200 (up to $67,900) they pay 15%	$7,680
On the next $69,150 (up to $137,050) they pay 25%	$17,287.50
On the next $71,800 (up to $208,850) they pay 28%	$20,104
On the next $164,100, they pay 33%	$13,579.50
Total tax	**$60,321**
Marginal Tax bracket	33%
Effective Tax Rate ($100,894.50/$250,000)	24%

Let's also assume that Mike and Gina spend $12,000/month on their expenses and they save the rest.

Gross income	$250,000
Income Tax	$60,321
After-Tax Income	$188,771
Expenses	$144,000
Savings	$44,771 for retirement

If Mike and Gina put away $40,000 of his salary into a tax-deductible vehicle (like a retirement plan), it would look like this:

Gross income	$250,000
Deduction	$40,000
Taxable income	$210,000
Taxes	**$47,121**
Net income	$162,879
Expenses	**$144,000**
Savings	$18,879

Gina and Mike have $40,000 in pretax retirement savings to add to the $18,879 of after-tax savings for a total of $58,879 in total savings instead of the $44,771 they had before!

Beware: Present Income Tax Rates Are Very Low and May Rise

As we write this book, federal income tax rates are at one of the lowest points in the history of the U.S. income tax. See the following table.

Federal Income Tax Rates

Year	Top Marginal Federal Income Tax Rate
1920	73.0%
1930	25.0%
1940	81.0%
1950	91.0%
1960	91.0%
1970	71.0%
1980	70.0%
1990	28.0%
2000	39.6%
2008	35.0%
2011 on	39.6%

Source: Citizens for Tax Justice, May 2004.

Doctors need to understand the information presented in the table above and what it means. In short, tax rates are currently at a historical low and will likely rise (possibly significantly) in the future. You may recall when the highest marginal federal income tax rates were as high as 70%+. Could the largest U.S. deficit in history lead to higher rates sooner rather than later? Are you willing to bet your hard earned money that rates will not increase again?

Taxes on Investments

Once you earn money and pay income taxes, you aren't done with tax payments. This is only the tip of the tax iceberg. You may spend the money you earn (after taxes) on purchases and have to pay sales tax; or buy real estate and pay annual property taxes. Another possibility is that you save the money and invest it in some type of investment. Common investment choices include savings accounts, certificates of deposit (CDs), money market funds, stocks, bonds, mutual funds, cash value insurance policies, and real estate. A detailed discussion of investments is offered in Lesson #8.

Most investments can generally be classified as either income or growth vehicles. In some cases, an investment may offer both. Income investments are those that offer some type of regular return (income) to the investor. Your bank accounts, CDs, and money markets give you an interest payment each year. If you own traditional bonds, you receive a coupon every six months or year. If you own rental real estate, you may collect rental income. All of these interest payments, bond coupon payments, and rent checks are added to your income for the purpose of calculating taxable income discussed above. If you are in a 33% marginal federal income tax bracket, then you will have to pay federal tax of 33% on those payments. If you are in a 35% marginal tax bracket, you will pay 35% of the investment gain in taxes on that investment income. Of course, if you are not in an income tax-free state (most are *not*, like all of us in Ohio), you could pay up to 5.925% in additional state income taxes as well.

Not all investors require immediate income from investments. When you don't need current income from investments, you can afford to invest in riskier investments in search of greater long-term appreciation. Many of these investments are discussed in great detail in Lesson #8. We will offer a short discussion here to help you understand why it is so important to manage taxes on investments.

When you invest in a particular company by buying stock, your money is used to help grow that firm. The company receiving your investment will reinvest the proceeds to potentially increase the net worth (value) of the company. As the value of the company increases, the value of your shares in the company will also increase. You do not receive a regular check from the company. Rather, you have the right to sell your shares of the company. If you realize profit on your investment when you sell your shares, you are responsible for taxes on your "capital gains."

For tax purposes, capital gains can be categorized as long term or short term. Short term is defined as realized (sold) appreciation of an asset that you owned for less than one year. If you have a short-term gain, it is treated exactly the same way (for tax purposes) as interest, coupons, and rental income. If your income puts you in a marginal federal tax bracket of 33%, your short-term capital gains would be taxed at 33% (plus any applicable state income taxes). Of course, you only need combined earned income and investment income of $208,850 to qualify you for the 33% federal tax rate. Most physicians will pay federal taxes of 33% or 35% or even 39% in 2011 (or sooner if tax rate hikes become law).

If you hold an asset for more than one year, the government gives you a benefit. You can pay long-term capital gains tax rates, which are lower than short term capital gains rates, on your realized appreciation. Presently, these federal rates are 10% of the growth (for individuals who are in the lowest tax bracket—not physicians) and 15% for all other taxpayers (plus applicable state taxes). This benefit gives an incentive to investors to keep their funds invested. This stability is much better than the constant buying and selling that could significantly disrupt business. This tax incentive also acts as a deterrent to potentially unethical short-term trading.

Back to the example of our happily married couple who filed jointly—Mike and Gina. Let's say that Mike and Gina invest $70,000 of savings into a 5% money market. This generates a $3,500 interest payment annually. They must add this $3,500 to their income. Because they are in a 33% marginal tax bracket, the additional federal income tax liability will be $1,155. The $3,500 growth will only really be worth $2,345 (a real 3.33% return, instead of the 5% they thought they were getting) after-taxes.

Beware: Present Capital Gains Tax Rates Are Very Low and May Rise

As we write this book, capital gains tax rates, like ordinary income tax rates above, are at the lowest point in the history of the U.S. capital gains tax. See the following table:

Top Federal Capital Gains Tax Rate

Year	Top Federal Capital Gains Tax Rate
1940	30.0%
1942-1967	25.0%
1970	32.3%
1977	39.9%
1980	28.0%
1990	28.0%
2000	20.0%
2008	15.0%
2011 on	20.0%

Source: Citizens for Tax Justice, May 2004.

Like the table presented earlier in the chapter, Doctors need to understand the information in the table above as well. Tax rates are low now and could easily become much higher in the relatively near future. Since your planning is long term, you must take the high probability of an increased capital gains tax rate into account in your planning.

Is Uncle Sam's triple dip enough? No, it isn't. After you pay your income taxes, sales taxes for your purchases and property taxes on real estate, and taxes on all of your investment gains, there is still more tax to be paid.

Estate Taxes

When you pass away, Uncle Sam levies an estate tax on those of you who might be worth more than $1,000,000 at the time of your death, assuming you live until at least 2011 (Please visit http://www.forohiodoctors.com for up-to-date legislation, as Congress may be changing these rules as we go to press). That $1,000,000 includes the combined value of your home, retirement plans, real estate, brokerage accounts, and insurance policies. While the rates might be between 40% and 55%, for estimation purposes, we will assume the estate tax rate to be about 50% for ease of calculation throughout the book. That means that half of what you think you will leave your children could go to taxes. For a complete description of the estate tax, how it works, why the supposed "repeal" is a fairy tale, and how to avoid the unnecessary costs associated with it, please read Lesson #9, which focuses on estate planning.

IRD: The Only 70%+ Tax Trap

Lastly, there is a combination of taxes that severely threatens those of you who hope to be worth over $1,000,000 and who might die with a retirement plan or an IRA you would like to leave to your children. There is something called "income in respect of a decedent" (IRD).

No tax discussion is complete without mentioning IRD. IRD means the taxation of income earned by a deceased person who didn't pay tax on the income before passing away, or hadn't received the money before passing away. This is income that would have been taxable to the decedent had the decedent lived long enough to receive it. These income items include unpaid salaries, bonuses, and commissions, as well as retirement plans and IRA balances and variable annuity appreciation. Statistically, retirement plan and IRA balances are by far the most significant assets that may be subject to IRD.

The following pie chart shows an example of how a retirement plan may be distributed at the time of death:

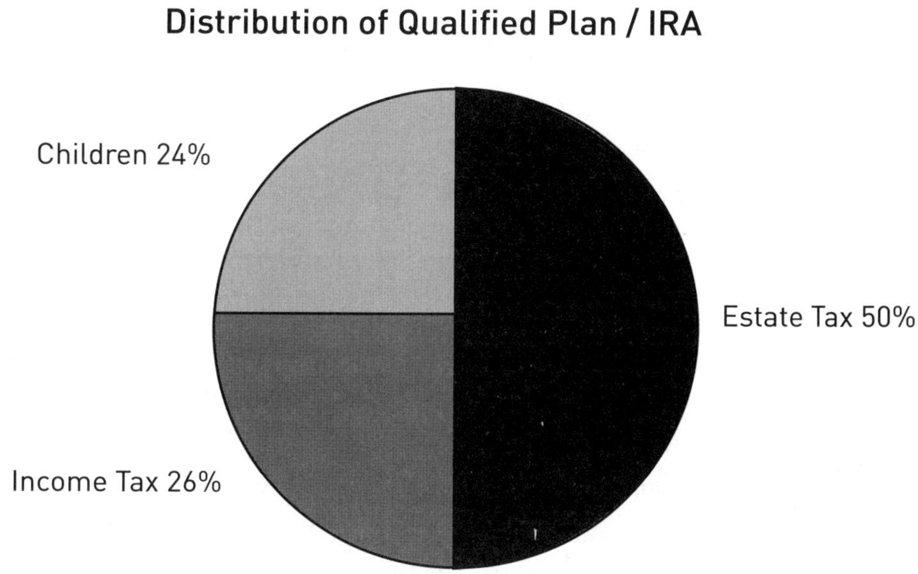

Based on this figure, you should be aware that it is possible for less than $250,000 of a $1,000,000 retirement plan or IRA to reach your children after all taxes are paid.

The Diagnosis

It may seem crazy that there are so many ways you can lose your wealth to taxes. Our tax law is the most complex system of rules created by mankind. We will never master them. The best we can hope to do is attempt to manage assets within the system. It is hoped that you understand how much money is at stake and will take this section very seriously. Managing taxes may prove to be the most important lesson for Doctors to master. In the next chapter, we will learn practical ways to legally reduce taxes.

Use Retirement Plans

There are socially beneficial reasons for the creation of tax incentives surrounding qualified retirement plans. If you see a long history of tax benefits being afforded to a particular behavior or asset, this is generally because Congress believes that the behavior or asset provides some economic benefit to society as a whole. We will revisit additional tax benefits for investments later in this Lesson and in Lesson #8. In the case of retirement vehicles, the theory is that by encouraging people to fund their own retirement, the government (and the rest of us taxpayers) will not have to support them in retirement.

Two retirement tactics for Doctors to consider are:

1. Maximizing available qualified retirement plan contributions for all members of the family.

2. Maximizing investments in vehicles that are similar to qualified retirement plans for all members of the family.

As you learned in Lesson #1, Doctors must leverage assets, capital, and advisors if they want to work less and build more. By creating separate business entities to own real estate, equipment, and liquid assets, Doctors are able to create employment opportunities for members of their family. By creating income opportunities for family members, you can accomplish two things:

1. Generate effective wealth transfers to junior generations.

2. Create opportunities for such family members to make tax-deductible contributions to their own retirement plans.

Maximizing The Use of Qualified Plans

Since tax deductible retirement plan contributions are limited for each person, having additional family members earning income within a family business or practice allows multiple tax-deductible contributions. This technique reduces the total tax liability for the family. In an earlier

Lesson, you learned that qualified retirement plans were afforded the highest level of protection from creditors (+5). The use of multiple contributions also affords physician families a greater level of asset protection for their total wealth, as more money will be invested into this exempt asset class. In addition to the reduced taxes and increased family savings, this strategy helps protect those savings from lawsuits (see Lessons #5 and #6). All of these benefits are integral for long term, sustainable affluence.

There are many types of tax-deductible retirement vehicles. They fall into one of two categories: defined contribution plans or defined benefit plans.

> **Defined contribution plans** restrict the amount you can contribute to the plans on an annual basis. These include all forms of IRAs (individual retirement accounts), profit sharing plans, money purchase plans, 401(k) plans, 403(b) plans and others.

> **Defined benefit plans** restrict how much can be in the plan at any time. The broader category of defined benefit plans includes fully insured defined benefit plans which are also known as 412(i) plans. Typically, defined benefit plans are used to help older individuals catch up on lost contributions.

The choice and implementation of the right plan for the situation will be determined by your planning team. The benefits of that planning will vary widely depending on each family's circumstances and the ages and salaries of the employees.

Maximize The Use Of Vehicles Similar To Qualified Plans

Another tactic Doctors should employ is to use tools and techniques that mirror many of the benefits of retirement plans. Since retirement plan contributions are limited, Doctors need to utilize alternative saving and investment methods to meet their significantly higher long-term retirement needs. A common strategy to enhance long-term retirement income and reduce taxes on investment gains is to invest in cash value life insurance. This will be discussed in detail in Lesson #8 where we discuss how certain investments offer important benefits to Doctors. If you want to maximize long term, tax-efficient retirement income, you should definitely take time to review Lesson #8.

The Diagnosis

Retirement plans are a great way to achieve a high level of asset protection, while reducing current tax liabilities. In addition, the use of vehicles like cash value life insurance policies can help Doctors avoid taxes on investment gains and enhance retirement income while protecting assets from lawsuits all at the same time. Other vehicles, like Family Limited Partnerships and Limited Liability Companies, can also offer tax benefits. These are discussed in the next chapter.

7-3

"Borrow" Lower Tax Rates

In the last chapter, you learned that by creating income opportunities for family members you increase the family's total capacity for tax-deductible retirement plan contributions. This reduces a family's total income tax burden. By shifting the ownership of income-producing assets to family members in lower marginal income tax brackets, you can also reduce total family income taxes even further.

How FLPs And LLCs Reduce Taxes

In the asset protection Lesson (#6), you learned that family limited partnerships (FLPs) and limited liability companies (LLCs) are effective asset protection tools when exempt (+5) assets will not suffice. In addition, if used properly in the right situations, FLPs and LLCs can save tens of thousands of dollars in income taxes each year.

By gifting interests of the FLP or LLC to family members who are in lower marginal income tax brackets, parents are effectively "income sharing." A percentage of the income generated within the FLP will be taxed at the lower rates of the partners who are in lower marginal tax brackets. Typically, these are children or grandchildren. As long as the child is over 18 years old (or 24 if a full-time student), the child's share of the income will be taxed at a rate that is presumably lower than that of the working parents. (For more detailed information on this topic, revisit Lesson #5). Let's see how this works by reading the case study of Danny and Rina.

Case Study: Danny and Rina's LLC Reduces Income Taxes

Danny and Rina had annual taxable income of $100,000 from their rental real estate, which was worth $1 million. In a 40% combined state and federal tax bracket, their total income tax on this income came to $40,000. To reduce their taxes, they set up an LLC.

The LLC was funded with the real estate. Danny and Rina appointed themselves as managing members, so they would have 100% control. They gifted a 3% membership interest to each of their four children (Zach, Elgin, Earvin & Jerry) for a total of

12% removed from their estate. Because each child's interest would be valued at about $20,000 (3% x $1,000,000, less the minority valuation discount), no gift tax applied to the transfers to the children. Danny and Rina made these 12% transfers to their children annually for 5 years.

Under the LLC agreement, the children were taxed on their share of the LLC's income; which, after five years, became 60%. Thus, in year five, 60% of the LLC's taxable income would be taxed at the children's lower tax rates. So, when the LLC assets earn $100,000 in income, 60% of that income was taxed at the children's rate—15%. Thus, their tax bill for operation of the LLC was $16,000 (40% on $40,000, the parents' share) plus $9,000 (15% on $60,000, the children's share). Danny's family tax savings would therefore be as follows:

Total tax with the LLC, Year 5:	$25,000
Total tax without the LLC, Year 5:	$40,000
Year 5 family income tax savings with the LLC:	**$15,000**

It must be remembered that there were also savings in years one through four! What's more, under the LLC agreement, the managing members were not required to distribute any LLC income to the members. This was totally within the discretion of Danny and Rina as managing members. Thus, Danny and Rina could pay all LLC taxes (at the lower rates) with the income and reinvest the remaining proceeds.

Use Tax-Efficient Investments

Tax-efficient investments are used by wealthy families across the country to build wealth and protect assets. In the beginning of this Lesson, you learned that taxes on investment gains could significantly stunt long-term appreciation. You also learned that taxes on investment gains in states with state income taxes, like Ohio, could be as high as 41% of the short-term growth and 21% of the long-term growth. To explain how a small differential in after-tax returns can have a significant impact over a long period of time, we would also like to add a simple law of finance to help you.

"The Rule of 72" states that 72 divided by the annual after-tax rate of return of an investment will give you the number of years it takes an investment to double in value.

Under the Rule of 72, an investment that returns 9% per year doubles in value every 8 years. In 24 years, a $100,000 investment that grew by 9% per year would be worth $800,000. What would happen if this investor paid less attention to taxes? Would it make that much of a difference? Let's see. $100,000 invested at 6% (because 33% of the 9% pretax gain was lost to taxes) would take 12 years to double in value. At the end of 24 years, this investment would only be worth $400,000. ***If your investments lose 33% of the return to taxes, you could end up with half as much money in your investment account at the end of 24 years.*** Half? That is a significant reduction indeed! Is the possibility of doubling your savings reason enough to pay attention to taxes on your investments now?

Savvy Doctors have always focused on after-tax investment returns. This is why some have so much more money than others. Sometimes, tax management means investing in vehicles that are tax-exempt. Other times, it means hiring advisors who take a more active role in managing taxes within an investment portfolio. It can also mean investing to generate losses to offset gains. These are important Lessons Doctors must master to get the most out of their investments.

The Diagnosis

In Chapter 6-7, you learned that Limited Partnerships and Limited Liability Companies are favorite asset protection tools of asset protection specialists who advise Doctors. In this chapter, you learned how to use these same tools to "share" income with family members in lower tax brackets. In Lesson #9, you will learn how these tools can be valuable estate planning tools as well. This is an example of how one tool can offer numerous benefits. You will learn more about this important philosophy in Lesson #8. For now, let's focus on more ways to save unnecessary taxes by getting the government to pay for some of your health insurance costs. This is the topic of discussion in the next chapter.

7-4

Let the IRS Subsidize Your Long-Term Care Insurance

In this chapter, you'll learn how to reduce taxes while providing an important financial planning tool for your family—long-term care insurance (LTCI).

Conventional financial planning wisdom tells us that the reasons for buying long-term care insurance are twofold:

1. To make sure you have enough money to pay for potentially devastating medical costs later in life and still have enough money to support your retirement (covered in Lesson #4).

2. To protect your estate from high medical costs, so you can leave an inheritance to your children and grandchildren (covered in Lessons #4 and #9).

What's more, you can also deduct your long-term care insurance premiums and reduce your taxable income. As an individual taxpayer, you can deduct up to the eligible amount of the LTCI premium. The following table shows the eligible tax-deductible premium in 2009.

Eligible Tax Deductible LTC Premium in 2009

Attained Age	Limitations on Premiums
Age 40 or less	$320
Age 41—50	$600
Age 51—60	$1,190
Age 61—70	$3,180
Age 71 and older	$3,980

Source: Internal Revenue Code §§213(d)(1)(D), 213(d)(10))

If you have your own practice entity, you can possibly take much larger deductions for LTCI than indicated in the table above. A C-corporation can deduct all LTCI premiums for owners and employees. If you do not have a C-corporation (i.e., you have an S-corporation, LLC or partnership), you can only deduct additional LTCI expenses by covering employees and their spouses. Theoretically, you could employ your spouse and achieve the maximal tax deduction you desire by offering LTCI to your spouse (as an employee) and you (as the spouse of an employee). This way, you can get a 100% deduction for LTCI premiums without having to change your practice to a C-corporation. The basic guidelines regarding LTCI paid through a business by the employer are:

- Employer provided LTCI treated as accident and health plan. IRC §7702B(a)(3).
- Deductible by employer (subject to reasonable compensation). IRC §162(a).
- Total premium excluded from employee's income (not limited to eligible premium). IRC §106(a).

The reason deductions for long-term care insurance are allowed is because LTCI is considered to be a form of health insurance that pays for a variety of health costs, which may or may not be covered by Social Security, Medicare, or Medicaid. The details of long-term care insurance and our recommendations on what to look for in an LTCI contract are covered Chapter 4-4 on LTCI, which should be read to get a full understanding of how LTCI will help you and your family.

You may wonder, "Doesn't Ohio or Medicaid pay these expenses?" The answer is yes, and no. That is, the State of Ohio will pay for a senior's medical bills, but only after that individual has depleted all but $1,500 of the patient's net worth. This means that if a retirement plan or any investments are titled to an individual, or have been titled in the individual's name in the last 5 years, the state will require those assets to be sold to pay for medical costs. In addition, the state will then take all but $40 per month of the individual's income as reimbursement for the coverage.

Given the currents costs of caring for our aging population, it isn't hard to imagine how quickly a "spend down" to obtain Medicaid eligibility could deplete someone's assets. In many cases, it would even be prudent to purchase long-term care insurance for your parents. Such a decision would protect your parent's assets, avoid the governmental bureaucracy and uncertainty associated with the program, and remove the possibility of limiting your parents to an allowance of $40 per month.

CAUTION: The numbers above refer only to Ohio (Medicaid) paying for your LTCI. You should keep in mind that Medicare has separate requirements unrelated to Medicaid. At the present, Medicare will pay 100% of an individual's stay in a skilled nursing facility for the first 20 days only after a 3-day minimum inpatient hospital stay for a related illness or injury. Moreover, a doctor must certify that the individual needs daily skilled care, not long-term care or custodial care. For days 21-100, the individual must share in the cost of staying in the skilled nursing facility, which is currently $133.50 per day. After 100 days, Medicare will cease paying for the skilled nursing facility and the individual will be expected to use other means to pay for his or her continued stay.

For more detailed information on Medicare, please visit www.medicare.gov.

The Diagnosis

Because of the work of Doctors like you, we are living longer. The longer we live, the more likely we are to develop a condition that may require sustained, costly medical attention. Unfortunately, government programs will not adequately protect us. As a result, we have to protect ourselves with long-term care insurance. If we structure our business affairs properly, we can get a tax deduction for helping ourselves. The tax code also allows us to use deductions for helping others. This is covered in the next chapter on charitable planning.

7-5

Use Charitable Planning

The desire to give is strong in many people. As a society, we cherish the right to give to the charitable institutions of our choice. This interest in giving is what we refer to as "charitable intent." We all want to give something back. Legendary Ohio State football coach Woody Hayes even exhorted his students to "give forward." Often, the biggest hurdles to giving are that we do not know how to give or we assume that our family will suffer as a result of our giving. Our goal in this chapter, and in Chapter 9-8 on charitable planning, is to show you a few ways to make charitable gifts that benefit the charity and your family at the same time. This is possible because of the tremendous tax benefits the IRS grants for charitable gifts. Before we examine the ways to use charitable giving to reduce income taxes, let's take a look at the basic—albeit complex—tax rules regarding charitable giving. The following explanation will be rather simplistic, but offers a good foundation for understanding the strategies that follow.

Direct Gifts

Direct gifts are gifts that are made to a charitable organization for their immediate use. The federal tax code provides for current income tax deductions for gifts to charities that have qualified under IRC Section 501(c)(3) as a charitable organization.

The IRS distinguishes between "public charities" (universities, hospitals, churches, etc.) and "private charities" (private family foundations are the most common). What's the difference? If the gift is given to a public charity, you can deduct the amount of the gift against your adjusted gross income (AGI) up to a maximum of 50% of your AGI. If the gift exceeds this amount, you can apply the excess as deductions against future year's income for 5 additional years.

If the gift is to a private charity, then you can only deduct a maximum of 30% of your AGI, which can also be applied forward 5 years. Let's see how public and private charities differ in the case study of Charitable Chris.

Charitable Chris: Give to Foundation or Alma Mater

Chris is a retired cardiologist who created a small private family foundation a few years ago to give something back to the community. He involved his children in the foundation and realized significant tax benefits. Now Chris has $60,000 of highly appreciated stock he doesn't need to support his retirement needs. As a result, he would like to make a gift to charity. His annual AGI is only $30,000 per year from the consulting work he does. Chris is considering gifting the stock either to his family foundation or to his alma mater where he sits on the board.

If he gifts the stock to the foundation, he will only be able to deduct $9,000 per year from his tax return (30% of AGI). If he gifts to the university, he will be able to deduct $15,000 (50% of AGI). Because he can only carry the deduction forward 5 years, he'll only be able to apply $54,000 (6 years x $9,000) worth of deductions using the family foundation but he'll be able to use all $60,000 (4 years x $15,000) of deductions if he gifts to the university.

Indirect Gifts

Indirect Gifts are often called "split interest" or "planned gifts" because some of the benefit from the gift is for the benefit of the charitable organization and some of the benefit of the assets being gifted will be retained by the grantor (or donor) and his or her family. The real beauty of charitable giving from the family perspective is that the IRS also allows tremendous tax benefits for "indirect gifts"—those left to charity through a trust or annuity. In fact, the IRS also allows deductions for indirect gifts through irrevocable charitable remainder or lead trusts, and through charitable gift annuities, which provide lifetime income to the donor as guaranteed by the charity and monitored by the state. By using an indirect gift, charitable planning can truly be a win-win-win situation: you win, your family wins and your favorite charities win.

Common Charitable Giving Scenarios

The following are the most common charitable giving scenarios, where it can make financial sense for a family to consider charitable planning because of the tax benefit:

Sale of a highly appreciated asset: Many Doctors or their parents, especially those over 60, hold highly appreciated assets—usually real estate or stocks that have grown enormously in value over time. Sometimes there are few assets making up the bulk of someone's net worth. This is often the case where there is a closely held family business or a family farm. Regardless of the asset, you may want to sell the asset but don't want to pay the capital gains tax, thus reducing the after-tax value of the asset by up to 20+%. Through the use of charitable planning strategies, you may be able to unlock some of the appreciation and significantly reduce the capital gains tax while benefiting a favorite charity as well.

Need to generate family income from investment assets: When clients seek to shuffle their asset allocation to produce more income and diversify their portfolios, they may be hit with a substantial tax on their gains. By giving to a charity they have the chance to be creative, converting paper gains to cash flow, saving taxes, and turning non-deductible items into tax deductible ones while addressing charitable objectives at the same time.

Estate Planning: The most powerful benefits of charitable planning can be enjoyed when used as part of a multi-disciplinary financial plan. As you'll learn in Lesson #9 (Estate Planning), when you die, your family could pay as much as 40-60% in federal and state estate taxes, plus income tax on IRD assets such as pensions and IRAs. Charitable giving mitigates many of these taxes. In Chapter 9-8, we'll address in more detail charitable planning as it pertains to estate planning.

The Most Common Charitable Tool: The Charitable Remainder Trust

Let's assume you have one highly appreciated asset you would like to sell but are reluctant to do so because of the significant capital gains taxes you would incur. At the same time, you are looking for ways to reduce your current year's taxable income and would like to receive an ongoing income stream. Moreover, you would like to diversify your overall investment portfolio. Usually, this would mean selling the highly appreciated asset, paying the high taxes, and reinvesting a substantially reduced amount. In this situation, the Charitable Remainder Trust (CRT) may be an ideal option for you.

Used properly, a CRT can potentially:

- Reduce current income taxes by creating a current income tax deduction.
- Eliminate immediate capital gains taxes on the sale of appreciated assets, such as stocks, bonds, or real estate.
- Increase disposable income throughout the remainder of your life.
- Create a significant charitable gift.
- Reduce estate taxes that your estate may be required to pay upon your death, leaving more for your heirs.

- Avoid probate and maximize the assets your family will receive after your death.
- Protect your highly appreciated property from future creditors.

Think of a CRT as a tax-exempt trust that provides benefits to two different parties. The two different parties are the individuals receiving income and the chosen charity or charities. The "income beneficiaries" (usually you or your family members) typically receive income from the trust for either their lifetimes or a specified number of years (20 years or less). At the end of the trust term, the chosen charity will receive the remaining principal to use for its charitable purposes.

How A CRT Works

A CRT is an irrevocable trust that makes annual or more frequent payments to you—typically until you die. What remains in the trust then passes to a qualified charity of your choice.

A number of tax saving advantages may flow from the CRT. First, you will obtain a current income tax deduction for the value of the charity's interest in the trust. The deduction is permitted when the trust is created even though the charity may have to wait until your death to receive anything. Second, the CRT is a vehicle that can enhance your investment return. Because the CRT pays no income taxes, the CRT can generally sell an appreciated asset without recognizing any gain or paying any tax on the sale. This enables the trustee to reinvest the full amount of the proceeds from a sale and thus generate larger payments to you for the rest of your life.

Using Life Insurance For "Wealth Replacement"

Many people would be more motivated to make gifts to charities, but are afraid they won't leave an adequate inheritance to their heirs. Doctors need to understand that they can make donations during their lifetimes, save income taxes, and find a way to leverage the tax deduction to produce a similar, or sometimes larger, inheritance for their heirs than if they hadn't utilized charitable planning. This concept of using life insurance for "wealth replacement" will be discussed next.

A CRT is eligible for the estate tax deduction if it passes assets to one or more qualified charities at the time of one's death. If you wish to replace the value of the contributed property for heirs who would otherwise have received it, you could use some of your cash savings from the charitable income tax deduction to purchase a life insurance policy on your life held in an irrevocable life insurance trust for the benefit of your heirs. This is called a "wealth replacement trust."

Often, through the leveraging effect of life insurance, it is possible to pass on assets of greater value than those contributed to the trust. In this way, your heirs are not deprived of property they had expected to inherit. In fact, your heirs may find it advantageous to receive cash proceeds from an insurance policy, as opposed to a more complicated asset that they did not wish or know how to manage. Let's see how this works:

1. You gift a highly appreciated asset to the CRT. You receive a current income tax deduction that you can use to reduce your income tax liability for up to 5 years.
2. The CRT sells the asset. Neither you nor the CRT pays any taxes on the sale. 100% of the value of the asset is preserved and invested in a tax-free environment.
3. You receive a larger annual distribution from the CRT than you would have received if you had paid taxes on the sale of the asset and invested the proceeds in a taxable environment.
4. Although the annual distribution is taxable, it is taxed in accordance with how it was earned in the trust. This form of taxation is beneficial given the lower dividend and capital gains tax rates. The income beneficiary will save a significant amount in taxes each year.
5. After the death of all income beneficiaries, the remaining assets from the CRT go to your selected charity.
6. A "wealth replacement trust" can be funded with insurance to replace those assets given to charity and give the family even more than they would have received if no charitable planning been done.

The CRT's "Cousin"—The Charitable Lead Trust (CLT)

When it comes to charitable trusts, CRTs seem to get all the attention, especially when interest rates are high. But the cousin of the CRT, the charitable lead trust (CLT), also can provide significant charitable and tax benefits, particularly in an environment of lower interest rates.

With a CLT, sometimes called a "charitable income trust," you transfer cash or income-producing assets to the trust. The trust then pays out income earned by the assets to a designated charity or charities. The payout may be an annual fixed dollar amount set at the time of the transfer—called "an annuity trust"—or an amount based on a percentage of the assets in the trust at the end of the year prior to the payout year—called a "unitrust."

At the end of a specified number of years, the remaining assets in the trust are distributed to the non-charitable beneficiary, usually someone other than you or your spouse. It could be your children, grandchildren, other family members, or a trust for the benefit and protection of any of these heirs. This timing is, in effect, the opposite of the CRT, in which the donor receives current income from the trust assets and the assets go to the charity at the end of the designated time.

Gift tax may be due at the time the assets are transferred to the trust, because non-charitable beneficiaries (your family) will ultimately receive the assets. However, this can often be planned so that no gift tax will be due. This is because (1) the gift is discounted because the beneficiaries won't receive the gift for some time; and (2) you receive a gift-tax deduction because a charity is receiving the income from the assets (the deduction is based on the amount transferred into the trust and the amount of time the assets are to remain in the trust). Furthermore, the gift won't be taxed at all if its discounted value is less than your remaining applicable gift tax exclusion.

Keep in mind that CRTs and CLTs can be established not only during life, but also after death, i.e., testamentary. Your team of advisors can help you determine whether it is better to establish CRTs/CLTs during your life or after your death.

The Diagnosis

If you have charitable intent and want to reduce current income taxes, capital gains taxes, or even estate taxes, you should seriously consider charitable planning techniques. Often, you and your family will stand to benefit as much as the charity itself. The right team of advisors can help you understand the costs and benefits of charitable planning and manage all of the complex issues. If you want to find out ways to more efficiently invest for the other people you take care of—your children—you should read the next chapter on tax-efficient educational funding.

7-6

Tax-Efficient Educational Planning

In Lesson #1, you learned Doctors all use leverage when they leveraged their education to increase their earning potential. This increased level of education is directly responsible for your significant income. From our experience, most highly educated professionals would like to give their children every opportunity to gain as much education as possible. Why not do this in as efficient a manner as possible?

The average cost of a 4-year education at a private college for a student graduating in 2000 was $85,356. With a 6% inflation estimate, the estimated cost of a 4-year private education for the graduating class of 2020 will be over $273,000. Of course, if your child goes to an Ivy League school, like many children of physicians do, the total cost of the undergraduate degree could be well over $500,000. If you consider that most physician families pay almost 44% in income taxes AND between 15% and 44% in taxes on capital gains and dividends, it may seem almost impossible to save for a child or grandchild's education while also putting away funds for retirement. In this chapter, we will discuss five types of tax efficient college investment options that you should consider to preserve your wealth.

Tax Efficient College Investment Options

If you have children or grandchildren who might go to college, graduate school, medical school, or law school, there are tax efficient ways to save for this future expense. The short list of potential tax-efficient investment options includes:

1. 529 College Savings Plans
2. 529 Prepaid Tuition Plans
3. Uniform Gifts to Minors Act/Uniform Transfers to Minors Act (UGMA/UTMA) Trusts
4. Cash Value Life Insurance
5. Coverdell Plans (formerly Education IRAs)

Because the Coverdell plan contribution limits are $2,000 per year and that amount is completely inadequate for high-income earners like physicians, we will exclude it from our analysis. To compare and contrast the first four plans, we want to consider each of them across a number of metrics. Then, we will offer a qualitative discussion about the contribution limits, tax benefits, access, and flexibility of each plan to help you understand why Doctors should use some plans more than others.

To do so, let's consider the following table.

Comparison of Tax-Efficient Educational Funding Options

	529 Savings Plan	529 Prepaid Plan	UGMA / UTMA	Cash Value Insurance
Income Litations	None	None	None	None
Maximum yearly contributions per beneficiary (all numbers double when gifts come from two parents or grandparents)	Annual federal gift tax exclusion (up to 5 years in advance)	Annual federal gift tax exclusion (up to 5 years in advance	Annual federal gift tax exclusion	Umlimited as policy is owned by parents
Account earnings	TAX-FREE, if used for qualified expenses	TAX-FREE, if used for qualified expenses	Taxable	TAX-FREE
Ability to change beneficiaries	Yes	Yes	No	Yes
Contol of withdrawals	Owner of account	Owner of account	Transfers to child when child reaches legal age	Owner of policy
Investment options	Ready-made portfolios of mutual funds	Tuition units guaranteed to match tuition inflation	Wide range of securities	Various. Depends on policy chosen
State tax deductible contributions	Varies by state—up to $2,000 in Ohio	Varies by state	No	No
Qualified use of proceeds	Any accredited post-secondary school in the U.S.	Varies by state (Currently un-available in Ohio)	Unlimited	Unlimited
Penalties for nonqualified withdrawals	10% penalty withheld on earnings	10% penalty withheld on earnings	No	No
Taxation of qualified withdrawals	Tax-free	Tax-free	A portion may be exempt; income may be taxed at child's rate	Tax-free
Ownership of assets for financial aid purposes (may vary by institution)	Account owner	Student	Student	Exempt for student aid

Reducing the Comparison to 3 Plans

The first thing we want to make clear is that we are skeptical of prepaid tuition plans. Though these plans allow parents to "lock in" tuition rates at the state universities and colleges when they make contributions, we see the inflexibility of the plans as a major issue. If it is so hard to get children to clean their rooms or take out the trash, we find it hard to base the success of a plan with hundreds of thousands of dollars in it on our ability to convince our children to attend one of a few colleges we chose for them when they were two years old. We can't make that assumption. Practically speaking, we will compare 529 plans (not prepaid tuition plans) to UGMA/UTMA plans. Then, we will compare 529 plans to cash value life insurance.

Basics of 529 Plans

529 plans allow an individual to make annual tax-free "gifts" of $13,000 to any person. It also allows a couple to make such gifts of up to $26,000 per year to each child. With the 529 College Savings Plan, an individual can make 5 years worth in advance. Total benefits include:

- Contributions over $26,000 for a married couple (and $13,000 for an individual) are allowed—gift tax-free.
- You, the donor, control the withdrawals.
- You may change the beneficiaries.
- You receive any tax benefits.
- You direct the type of investments (from a short list of choices).
- The money grows tax-free.

Contributions Over $26,000 May Be Allowed—Gift Tax-Free

You may already know that an individual can make annual tax-free "gifts" of $13,000 to any person and that a couple can make such gifts of up to $26,000. With the 529 College Savings Plan, an individual can make 5 years worth of gifts in one year without paying a gift tax. The 529 plan allows you to allocate those gifts over the next five years. Thus, a couple can gift $130,000 tax-free in one year to a 529 plan for each child or grandchild.

Total proceeds in a 529 plan are capped. The amount differs from plan to plan but many caps range from $220,000 to $260,000. This means that a set of parents could gift $130,000 to a 529 plan AND a set of grandparents could gift an additional $130,000 to the same child's 529 plan and no gift taxes would be paid. Larger amounts could be gifted, but gift taxes would apply.

When you compare the 529 plan to the Educational IRA (now called a Coverdell Plan) whose annual contribution limit is $2,000, there is no question which is the better choice.

YOU Control The Withdrawals And Beneficiaries

Unlike an UGMA account or Education IRA, you control the withdrawals and may change the beneficiaries of a 529 plan. If one child doesn't go to college or receives a scholarship, you may change the Plan to benefit someone else. You can also make these changes as often as you like, as long as the beneficiaries are related. In fact, you can even name yourself the beneficiary if you plan to go back to school.

If you change your mind and want to withdraw the funds and use them yourself, you may do so. The only penalty is that you must pay a 10% penalty in addition to ordinary income taxes on any growth of the funds in the plan.

YOU Receive The Tax Benefits

The funds in a 529 plan grow on a tax-free basis. Because annual capital gains and dividends are not taxed in the 529 plan, the account balance has the potential to grow faster than if invested in comparable taxable investments. If you consider that dividends and short-term capital gains are taxed at rates that may be as high as 41% in states like Ohio, the 529 plan could grow twice as quickly as a UGMA or UTMA that offers no real tax deferral benefit.

You may also be able to reduce estate taxes by using a 529 plan. The plan's high contribution limit provides a convenient way to effectively lower the taxable value of your estate. As you'll learn in Lesson #9, federal estate taxes can be as high as 55% for Doctor families for wealth passing to the next generation after 2011. In light of this fact, the ability to reduce your taxable estate while providing educational funding for family members should be very attractive.

You Direct The Type Of Investments

Some 529 plans allow you to invest in a variety of stock, bond, and money market funds. You may have a choice of a growth portfolio or a balanced portfolio. There's even a company that offers an "Age-Based Portfolio" that focuses on growth in the early years of the child and automatically re-balances every few years to focus more on capital preservation as college approaches. There is no extra fee for this added service.

Shortfall Of The 529 Plan

If you make your scheduled contributions, don't mind the risk of the stock market and don't die, the 529 plan is a much better alternative than just saving money in your brokerage account with the intention of cashing it in to pay the bills later. However, we can't guarantee that you will live to see all of your children go to college or graduate school and we can't invest in a 529 plan without subjecting our funds to market risk. For these reasons, you may want to consider some type of life insurance as part of your college savings plan. There are two plans to consider. If you are going to invest in a 529 plan, you should also invest in a decreasing term life insurance policy. If you need $1,000,000 because your two young children will someday attend Ivy League schools, then you should buy a $1,000,000 decreasing term policy that reduces by your annual contribution amounts. To illustrate this point, let's refer to the following:

Year	Children's Ages	Amount in 529 Plans	Amount of Term Insurance
1	2 & 4	$40,000	$1,000,000
2	3 & 5	$84,000	$950,000
3	4 & 6	$132,400	$900,000
5	6 & 8	$244,200	$800,000
10	11 & 13	$637,500	$500,000
15	16 & 19	$1,279,000	$0

If you are very concerned about the stock market's volatility and don't want it to have a significant impact on your children's educational funds, you should consider a whole life policy with a AAA-rated insurance company. This is a relatively stable investment and will grow at a steady rate. Even in 2001, one of the worst years in recent stock market history, one AAA-rated insurance company paid over 7.5% on its whole life policies. In addition to the tax-free cash accumulation inside such a policy, there is also a minimum death benefit to protect against an early death. When your children eventually attend college, you can then use tax-free loans to withdraw money from the policy and keep the death benefit intact. We will develop this idea in the next section.

Unconventional Wisdom—Life Insurance As An Investment

The last few pages focused on the benefits of 529 plans versus UGMA and UTMA plans. Now, let's compare the 529 to cash value life insurance. The only benefit the 529 has over the insurance policy is that, in some states, the 529 plan offers a state income tax deduction. Generally speaking, this could give the 529 plan a grade of an A+. Ohio residents who contribute to an Ohio 529 plan receive a state income tax deduction of up to $2,000 "per beneficiary" with no limitation on the number of beneficiaries that can be deducted in one year.

The tax pendulum could swing back the other way when using a 529 plan if your children earn academic or athletic scholarships, choose to attend a less expensive school, or don't attend college at all. Let's look at an example of how this could create a tax problem for the parents.

If the parents invest $100,000 into a 529 plan that grows to $200,000 and they don't want to spend the funds for a child's education, they could be subject to income taxes and penalties that total $50,000 or more. The flexibility of a 529 plan is excellent if you are talking about transferring funds from one child's plan to another child's plan. However, the flexibility of using the funds for things other than education is quite poor.

Let's look closely at how life insurance fairs in a comparison to the 529 plan. First, let's look at contribution amounts. Unlike all of the other college funding options, there is no practical maximum on how much a parent can invest in a life insurance contract. We have seen affluent clients invest over one million dollars per year into insurance policies. There are financial underwriting guidelines, but there should be very little problem contributing much more than the $13,000 or $26,000 per year limit of the 529 plan.

Second, let's look at the tax benefits of the life insurance policy. Like the 529 plan, the funds grow without taxation. Also, if you compare withdrawals from the 529 that are used for educational expenses to policy withdrawals and loans, those are also equal. The big difference occurs if you want to use the 529 values for something other than qualified college costs. Where the 529 plan is fully taxable plus a 10% tax penalty, there is no tax on any withdrawals from an insurance policy if you don't violate modified endowment contract (MEC) guidelines or lapse the policy (which the insurance professional on your team should be able to help you easily avoid). This tax benefit leads into a discussion of flexibility below.

Third, the life insurance policy offers you much more access and flexibility. Not only can you use the funds for anything you like, but you can also protect your children at the same time. If you contribute $100,000 to a 529 plan and die, your children will get no more than $100,000. If you contribute $100,000 of premiums to a life insurance policy and die, your heirs may get $2,000,000 or more. When you compare this to the sole tax penalty-free use of 529 plans, it is obvious that life insurance can be a much more valuable component of your financial plan. When you finish reading this book, you will have seen a handful of uses for life insurance, some of which may never have occurred to you.

To look at a review of the different options, please consider the following:

	529 Savings Plan	**529 Prepaid Plan**	**UGMA/ UTMA**	**Cash Value Insurance**
Contribution Limits	B+	B+	B-	A+
Tax Benefits	B- to A+	B- to A+	B-	A-
Access (reversibility)	B-	C-	F	A
Flexibility of Plan	B-	C-	F	A+

The Diagnosis

If you have children, grandchildren, or nieces and nephews whom you would like to assist in funding their education, or if you or your spouse might go back to school, you may consider a 529 College Savings Plan. If you are looking to build an efficient, flexible financial plan that can easily be altered to manage different issues as they arise, you should consider funding cash value life insurance as a funding vehicle for college savings planning. There is much more detailed discussion of insurance policies for this and other purposes in Lesson #8.

7-7

Avoid the Only 70%+ Tax Trap—Pensions and IRAs

There is one type of asset that can generate a tax as high as 70%+—your retirement plan. This results from a combination of income and estate taxes being applied to retirement plan balances at death. By leaving less than 25% of your retirement plan assets to your heirs, it will be very hard to achieve a high level of affluence for future generations of your family.

One of the "common sense" lessons you will hear repeated in the financial media is that you should contribute as much as you can to your retirement plans (pensions, profit-sharing plans, IRAs, 401(k) plans, etc.). The conventional wisdom is that because you get an income tax deduction and tax-deferred growth, these plans are a huge win for the taxpayer.

In Chapter 9-6, we will offer an in-depth discussion of qualified plan taxation, including the following: tax rates may be higher when you finally retire, you may not need the funds in retirement; how double taxation on retirement plan assets; and how to avoid this terrible tax trap.

For those who have not followed the estate tax legislation saga in Washington the past few years, you may be under the impression that there is "good news" on the horizon. While nothing has been decided, all signs point to the fact that assets at death will continue to be subject to an estate tax, and ongoing planning will be essential. Indeed, for most physicians, the area where such taxes will hurt the most remains pensions and IRAs, where 70%+ taxation may still occur.

Legislative Update

As this book is going to press, federal estate tax legislation is being addressed by Congress. Visit our website at http://www.forohiodoctors.com for up-to-date information on federal and Ohio estate tax rules.

Taxes on Pensions/IRAs at Death

Qualified retirement plans, such as pensions, profit sharing plans, 401(k)s, 403(b)s, and IRAs (excluding Roth IRAs) are characterized as items of "IRD" or "income with respect to a decedent" under the tax law. As such, when a taxpayer dies, these assets are not only subject to federal (and state, as above) estate taxes, but they are also subject to federal and state income taxes.

Because federal and state income taxes can total as high as 45% in some states, the combined taxes (federal/state and estate/income) can escalate quickly. *In fact, with these four different taxes to be assessed, the total tax on assets characterized as IRD assets can reach levels of over 70%+.* Let's see how this can work:

Case Study: Jim The Physician

Let's take Jim, a single physician whose non-qualified plan assets exceed the current estate tax exemption. When he retired from his practice, he rolled his profit-sharing plan containing $1 million into a rollover IRA. Let's assume that the federal estate tax rate is 45%.

Jim's estate would first pay $450,000 in federal estate taxes on the value of the IRA. While this seems bad, the real pain comes next.

To pay the federal estate taxes, the estate would likely take the funds from the IRA itself. Let's assume here that all $1 million was taken out of the IRA at once. When each withdrawal is made from the IRA, federal and state income taxes would be due. Given the size of these withdrawals, and the income tax situation of Jim's heirs, the estate could very well reach the top federal (35%) or state (6.24%) income tax brackets. With these taxes also levied on the IRA, Jim's heirs could get less than 24% of the IRA. While this may seem egregious, Jim's situation would actually be worse in many states, like New York, where the state estate tax is much higher (16%). Let's examine how these numbers are calculated:

Jim's IRA: Estate/Income Taxes Exceed 70%+

IRA Value	$1,000,000
Less Federal Estate Tax (45%)	($450,000)
Less State Estate Tax (7%)	($70,000)**
Total Estate Tax	$520,000
Income With Respect To A Decedent	$1,000,000
Less Federal IRD Deduction	($450,000)*
Taxable IRD	$550,000
Less Federal Income Tax (35%)	($192,500)
Income With Respect To A Decedent	$1,000,000
Less State Income Tax (6.24%)	($62,400)**
Total Income Taxes	$254,900
TOTAL TAXES ON IRA	$774,900
EFFECTIVE TAX RATE (ESTATE AND INCOME)	77.49%
Amount for beneficiaries	$225,100

**the IRD deduction will be even less (and the income tax consequences more severe) for taxpayers subject to the Section 68 phase-out*

***these are approximate amounts*

How to Avoid the Tax Trap

There are a number of ways you can avoid this tax trap, or diminish its impact on your estate. These include:

1. Consider non-qualified plans

Non-qualified plans have been used by most Fortune 1000 companies for more than 30 years, yet few physicians or their advisors know how to implement them properly for medical practices. This is a serious mistake, as non-qualified plans are much more flexible than qualified plans such as pensions, profit-sharing plans and 401(k) s when it comes to how they can be structured for IRD and estate tax treatment. In addition, non-qualified plans can be discriminatory and may have much higher contribution limits than traditional qualified plans.

2. Use the Capital Transformation Strategy (CTS)

This strategy essentially "transforms" wealth from the worst IRD/estate tax position to a position where the taxes are not as onerous. This may involve the use of a rollover and/or the creation of a special purpose qualified plan. It may also involve the use of investments and/or insurance vehicles that are not income taxable. It may also involve the use of a particular type of irrevocable trust that may allow funds to pass to heirs with a reduced or eliminated estate tax liability. While the details are beyond the scope of this article, this technique can often reduce the tax bite by 50% or more—without sacrificing your quality of life in retirement.

3. Use an Enhanced Liquidate & Leverage Strategy

This technique was initially laid out in our book Wealth Protection, MD. This essentially involves distributing the amount from the IRA likely not needed in retirement, paying the income taxes, and then, through a combination investment/premium financing structure (using one of the largest financial institutions in the U.S.), making up those lost taxes in an investment for heirs. Typically, this technique generates 2 to 5 times more for your heirs, net of taxes, than leaving funds in the retirement plan. This technique is also ideal if you fear that income tax rates may increase over your lifetime and you wish to eliminate this risk. If you want more information on this technique, contact the authors.

The Diagnosis

If you are participating in a retirement plan and may someday have a sizeable pension balance, you should be concerned that your heirs may unnecessarily have to pay the 70%+ tax on IRD assets. No tax discussion is complete without mentioning IRD. No financial plan should disregard this potential tax trap. When you are finished reading this tax Lesson, you should make a point of reading Lesson #9 to learn more about protecting your hard earned money from this avoidable and unnecessary tax.

7-8

Determine When Your Tax Advisor is Helping or Hurting You

As previously highlighted in the Case Study for Chapter 3-3, some years ago, David Mandell's former law firm was retained by a long time client to perform a self-audit. The client, an extremely successful businessman, had reason to believe that his firm may have made a mistake in tax reporting. If he had underpaid taxes, he wanted to review the situation and bring it to the attention of the IRS and volunteer to pay any missing taxes to avoid some potential penalties. He hired the firm to do an audit of his personal and corporate income tax returns for a period of five years. What the firm found was shocking.

Even though this client had used four different accounting firms for his various returns (including a well-known 500 person firm), the taxes he had paid were far from what he actually owed. Luckily for him, it was an overpayment—in the neighborhood of over $2 million!

That is correct. Because of the self-imposed audit, the client learned that he could legally file amended tax returns and claim a multimillion-dollar refund. Lucky for him, he was concerned about poor tax advice and spent the money to hire David's former firm to perform the audit (even though he thought he would owe more, not less tax).

Lessons To Be Learned

While the above case is extreme, it is not unusual. It demonstrates the two ways millions of taxpayers get in trouble with tax planning by relying on tax professionals who (1) incompetently cause unjustified underpayments of tax; or (2) are so conservative or close-minded that they actually "cost" the client through gross overpayments of tax.

When you add the federal, state and even municipal taxes, Doctors pay marginal income taxes at the rate of 40% to 45%. At these rates, the following question becomes very important: *Does your tax advisor—CPA, attorney, or other professional—suffer from one of the drawbacks below?*

Incompetence: Not Admitting When an Area is Beyond His or Her Expertise: This is the most obvious issue for any advisor. While it may be obvious that you should avoid incompetent advisors, the signs of incompetence are not necessarily apparent. When you do realize it, it is often too late.

Lack of Multi-disciplinary Skills: Skilled in One Area, but Not the Other: More common is the situation where the client's advisor is skilled in one area of practice but not knowledgeable about another. This is understandable. Tax planning is like medicine. Each area has become so complex that one can only hope to become an expert in one specialty or sub-specialty. In the medical arena, most patients and physicians realize this and readily accept the idea that patients are regularly referred to other specialists. A gastroenterologist would no sooner make diagnoses of skin conditions than a dermatologist would handle a digestive disorder. Yet this is what happens all the time in the tax arena.

When an advisor is faced with an issue beyond his expertise, he tends to do one of the following:

1. Admit his lack of knowledge and refer the client to another expert.
2. Try to quickly get up to speed on the issue (on the client's dime).
3. Simply reject any recommendations he does not understand.

Most often, we see tax advisors resort to the third option, rejecting a potentially beneficial strategy for their client because it is out of the advisor's area of expertise. We also see accountants and attorneys who refuse to work as part of a multi-disciplinary team. Often, this is because they fear losing the client to another advisor if they admit that what the other advisor recommends actually makes sense. While these advisors will never actually tell the client not to listen to another professional, their behavior speaks for them when they reject another professional's suggestions with arcane arguments and references that they know the client will not be able to evaluate on his own.

The Diagnosis

There is no easy answer to the dilemma of how to choose a competent tax advisor who has a great deal of experience working with the Doctor clients, can handle complex planning, and is balanced between overly-aggressive and overly-conservative. We are not suggesting that you abandon your present CPA or tax attorney. We are merely suggesting that you take an active role in your tax and estate planning, bringing new solutions to your advisor and/or bringing in other professionals to assist your advisor in a coordinated team approach. Since you are the client who will ultimately pay your advisors for the planning (or lack of it) that is implemented, it behooves you to make sure that your planning fits your needs and tax goals, taking full advantage of the many available, and sometimes little-known, tools and strategies.

LESSON 8

Avoid Poor Investment Outcomes

Just as avoiding poor medical outcomes is an obvious goal for physicians, so too should be avoiding poor investment outcomes. Similar to medicine, the application of this obvious financial goal is much more complicated than you would think. One reason for the difficulty is that wisdom and luck are often hard to differentiate. Historically, many unwise investments have performed well, at least in the short term. Do you remember Enron? It once was the investment community's darling. To measure the wisdom of an investment strategy, one needs to measure the strategy's performance over a complete market cycle—which is defined as a bull high to a bear low and back again, or vice versa.

Let's look at this another way: If you applied the modified Machiavellian concept of "the ends justify the means" to an investment scoring philosophy, you would say that the person who purchased a lottery ticket and won $25,000,000 was a smarter investor than the millions who spent the same $1 on losing lottery tickets. You should instead look and compare the probabilities of success with the risks, complexity of the investment and interaction with the other elements of the plan to determine the wisdom of the investment philosophy. Doing this, you might come to the more reasoned conclusion that none of the investments in lottery tickets were wise—one was simply lucky. Picking individual high-risk equities in hopes of finding one that "hits it big" is another example of a lottery mentality with similar appeal to the unwise. Like the lottery, this strategy has a very low probability of success.

The applications of the numerous principles discussed throughout this book are the keys to successful investing. Lesson #6 on asset protection showed you how to protect your investments from lawsuits. Lesson #7 on tax planning showed you how to reduce unnecessary taxes. Lesson #9 on estate planning will show you how to pass your wealth onto your heirs with as little tax and complication as possible.

This specific Lesson is going to explain how to avoid bad outcomes so you can preserve as much of your principal and investment gains as possible. This Lesson will help you avoid the most common physician investment mistakes by teaching you some important investment fundamentals, explaining how these may or may not apply to Doctors, and explaining some common and not-so-common, investment alternatives. More specifically, this Lesson will explain the limitations of a Nobel Prize winning investment theory that most investment firms follow, the real costs of taxes and inflation, the pitfalls of mutual funds for the wealthy, and discuss alternative investment strategies that address these concerns. This Lesson will also discuss specific investments that address all of these concerns, making them a cornerstone of your Fortress for building and protecting wealth.

8-1

A Nobel Prize Is Not Enough

Many investment advisors may boast that their strategy is based on a Nobel Prize-winning theory. Though this statement may seem impressive, it has two faults:

1. `Nearly everyone's strategy is based on that same theory.
2. `The theory itself has a number of limitations that were acknowledged by the Nobel Laureates themselves.

The purpose of this chapter is threefold. First, we will give you a very basic understanding of this Nobel Prize-winning investment theory. Second, we will point out the limitations of the theory. Third, we will suggest how to make the theory work within a Doctor's comprehensive financial plan.

The Modern Portfolio Theory and Capital Asset Pricing Model

In 1990, the Nobel Prize in Economics was awarded to Harry Markowitz, Merton Miller, and William Sharpe for their Modern Portfolio Theory ('MPT') and Capital Asset Pricing Model ('CAPM'). With apologies to Messrs. Markowitz, Miller, and Sharpe, we would like to offer simplistic summaries of MPT and CAPM. There are three concepts you must understand before you can put them together to form the MPT and CAPM. Those are:

1. Types of Risk;
2. Risk vs. Reward; and
3. Diversification of Investments.

Types of Risk

CAPM divides the risk of any investment into two types of risk—specific risk and market (or systematic) risk. Specific risk is unique to an individual investment; while systematic risk affects all investments in the "market" and is also known as "market risk." Let's look at examples of each:

Specific Risk: Do you remember the Tylenol scare of 1982? Someone tainted a number of bottles of Tylenol with cyanide. This obviously affected the stock price of Johnson & Johnson, the maker of Tylenol. The risk of this type of occurrence is an example of specific risk because it didn't have an effect on all makers of analgesics in the market, just Johnson & Johnson.

Market or Systematic Risk: You've no doubt heard or read about the stock market crash of 1929. That incident affected all investments in the market. The risk of a crash is certainly the most extreme example of market risk. A more current example is what has happened between January 2, 2008 and March 3, 2009. The Dow Jones Industrial Average was down 49% (from 13,261.82 to 6,764.81). In this time, very few stocks saw a rise in value.

When you make an investment, that investment is subject to both market and specific risk. In a portfolio of investments, you are subject to market risk, which affects the whole portfolio, and a combination of specific risks that affect each individual investment distinctly.

Risk vs. Reward

Over an extended period of time, rewards are generally higher for those who take more risk. Individuals who start their own businesses and are ultimately successful will probably make considerably more money than those individuals who took the less risky route and went to work for someone else. The entrepreneur risked his time and money. If successful, he will be rewarded handsomely for the risk he took.

Doctors and lawyers bypass the opportunity to make money right out of college. Instead, they spend more money going to medical school or law school and delay their income-producing careers by another 3 to 7 years. For this risk of time and money, they are generally rewarded with higher income opportunities than other college graduates. Within the medical field, for example, some Doctors pursue even more education and defer income to become surgeons. Within the surgical field, there are plastic, neurological, orthopedic, and dermatologic surgeons who undertake additional training. Within those specialties, there is additional training as orthopedic surgeons may become spine specialists or dermatology surgeons may go on to learn the Mohs surgery procedure. Usually, an increased investment in time and money (risk) leads to greater income potential (reward).

Diversification Of Investments

Diversification is a business school term for "not putting all of your eggs in one basket." When applied to investments, it has two meanings. First, it means diversifying among asset classes. This is more popularly known as asset allocation. Asset allocation involves investing in a combination of stocks, bonds, real estate, cash, and other investment classes. Diversification also applies to the individual investments made within each asset class—not investing in just a few stocks, just a few bonds, or in one or two parcels of real estate. As an example, most investment managers recommend a portfolio of at least thirty securities to achieve a minimally acceptable level of diversification.

Earlier, we explained the idea that an investment portfolio is subject to (1) market risk and (2) the specific risks of each of the assets in the portfolio. One interesting finding of the CAPM & MPT is that in a "well-diversified portfolio," all specific risks cancel each other out. In other words, specific risk can be diversified away. Investors can reduce the overall risk in their portfolios by spreading their risk across and within different asset classes. At face value, this makes perfect intuitive sense. More significant, the mathematical proof for this statement and the subsequent model for creating the "most efficient" set of portfolios were worthy of a Nobel Prize.

How Do The CAPM And MPT Work For You?

CAPM and MPT provide a mathematical model for minimizing systematic risk in any investment portfolio. Once an investor determines the level of risk he or she is comfortable assuming (we call this risk tolerance), he or she can follow the mathematical model to construct a portfolio that will optimize the risk-reward balance. In other words, by following this theory, the investor can maximize his expected returns for any level of risk. All such "maximized" portfolios exist on what financial people call "the efficient frontier."

Certainly, we are not going to contend that the findings of three Nobel Laureates are incorrect. Rather, we are going to point out the acknowledged limitations in their theory and offer additional insights that might help you.

As acknowledged by the laureates, CAPM and MPT are designed to work in a simplified world where:

- There are no taxes or transaction costs.
- All investors have identical investment time horizons.
- All investors have identical perceptions regarding the expected returns, volatilities, and correlations of available risky investments.

As there is no such thing as a simple world, these three components actually present the limitations of CAPM and MPT as financial tools that provide wise investment advice. We will now discuss these problems and suggest ways that Doctors can overcome them in an effort to avoid bad investment outcomes.

Problem #1: All Investors Pay Different Taxes & Transaction Costs

The first limitation of the theory involves taxes and transaction costs. Obviously, we consider tax to be a significant concern of Doctors. If we didn't, we wouldn't have devoted an entire part of this book (Lesson #7) exclusively to this topic. If all of your investments are in a non-taxable account, like an IRA, you don't have to worry about taxes until you begin taking distributions. You could look to maximize the pretax returns on your portfolio for a given amount of risk because taxes have no impact until you take withdrawals.

A more common situation is to have a portion of the total investment portfolio in a retirement account and a portion in a taxable account. If this is true for you, you will need to determine which investments will be made in the tax-favored accounts and which investments will be made in taxable accounts. If you are in your prime earning years and are in the 30% to 35% federal income tax brackets, the following rules should suit you well:

1. Hold all interest-bearing and dividend-producing assets within a tax-favored account. Otherwise, as much as 44% of the earnings will go to paying income taxes each year. You are better off deferring the tax and earning money on the government's dime.

2. Hold all long-term growth assets in your taxable accounts. If you don't intend to sell these assets for at least one year, you will only pay 15%-24% capital gains taxes when you sell. You can control the deferral of taxes by controlling recognition of gains. If you hold these assets in a pension account, you would be taxed at up to 35% federal (plus up to 5.925% State of Ohio) when you make withdrawals. Why pay the government twice when you don't have to do so?

These are just basic strategies to supplement the CAPM and MPT when taxes are an issue. There is much more to be learned about taxes in the chapters within Lesson #7.

Problem #2: All Investors Do NOT Have Identical Investment Time Horizons

Another obvious problem with the CAPM and MPT is that all investors do NOT have identical investment time horizons. Some investors need their money in 30 days and some don't need it for 30 years. The investor who needs his money in less than a month would be well served by a CD or money market. When an investor doesn't need the money for 30 years, he should have nearly 100% of his investments in equities (stocks) and other long-term investments.

If you have assets that you do not need for five years, you can afford to take some risks with those assets and should seriously consider investing in the stock market. If you need the money in less than a year, cash equivalents are your best option. For the assets that need to be accessed in 1 to 5 years, some combination may work well.

Problem #3: All Investors Have Very Different Perceptions Of Risk And Expected Returns

In English, the environment where the CAPM and MPT work best is one where everyone has the same knowledge of all assets and the same access to purchasing assets. Yet, investors have very different perceptions of expected returns, volatilities, and correlations of available risky investments. For stocks and bonds, where there is more research available than you could possibly read, perceptions of the risk of any given stock are broad. People can't even agree on the value or the risk of certain stocks.

As far as availability, there is also a very wide gap. If you are only investing $100,000, you may be restricted to mutual funds that can have very high transaction costs and taxes. If you have more than $500,000 to invest, you have access to unique products that have considerably lower transaction costs than the investments that are available to smaller investors. If you have $5 million or more, you can access products that others can only dream of buying. These may include small businesses and initial public offerings, to name a few.

For those of you with real estate investments, you know the gap in knowledge between buyer and seller is a key competitive factor for the investor. Many professional real estate investors have admitted that over 50% of their profits are a direct result of a buyer or seller not understanding the real estate market. The CAPM and MPT call for a percentage of your portfolio to be invested in real estate assets. However, for the real estate expert who understands this market better than most, we would deviate from the strategy and recommend he (or she) stick with what he (or she) knows best to maximize profit from the advantage in this arena.

For the investor with little knowledge of real estate, we would avoid investing in real estate (other than your home)—unless you hire professional real estate advisors as part of your team. There are two reasons for this. First, the time necessary to manage the property or the costs to pay someone else to do so will reduce the earnings the property generates. Second, there is no reason to jump into a market where you have a distinct disadvantage. This adds risk to your portfolio instead of reducing it as you had hoped by utilizing the CAPM and MPT.

In addition, the recent real estate and credit crashes have demonstrated two reasons why leverage is so important—especially in real estate. If you had very little equity in a property, you could have walked away from your debt and the property with a very small loss. If you had a lot of equity in a property, it has been very difficult to get it out lately. Many institutions just are not lending. Unless you have a lot of leverage, your real estate investments can be very illiquid. These are all points that your team of financial and legal advisors should be sharing with you.

Doctors need to understand what they know and what they don't know. By understanding the investment landscape (if not the investments themselves), Doctors can avoid unnecessary risk in an investment portfolio. In the next chapter, you will learn how to avoid decimation of wealth by taxes and inflation.

The Diagnosis

CAPM and MPT have contributed greatly to the field of portfolio selection. In fact, these theories are the basis for a significant percentage of institutional investors and mutual fund managers. They have also played a large role in the field of financial risk management. However, as you saw from this chapter, there are problems with the practical application of these theories. You should work with an experienced financial planner and investment advisor who can help you apply these theories to your particular situation while integrating them into your comprehensive financial plan by working with the other members of your advisory team. As you will learn from the remainder of the book, you may wish to invest in a vehicle that offers you other benefits in addition to capital appreciation—like asset protection, tax deferral, or protection against a premature death. These are the types of investments the remainder of this Lesson will address.

8-2

Taxes, Inflation & Your Investments

In Lesson #2, you learned that most printed material and consulting firms focus their efforts toward Average Americans. Doctors need to understand that this has never been truer than in the world of finance. Though most of the money in the world is owned by a very small percentage of the people, almost all of the advertising is directed at the Average American. As such, it can be very misleading and detrimental to the uninformed Doctor. Consider the following.

"XYZ fund returned 18.6% last year." "My money manager has beaten the S&P consistently for 5 years." "In this magazine, we'll profile the 'best returning' mutual funds." As financial professionals, we read and hear these types of statements on a daily basis. Why? Because everyone looks at the investment returns as the "currency" of investing. This is the popular way of comparing money managers, mutual funds, CDs, bonds, and other investments. What most people fail to consider is the impact that taxes and inflation have on those investments as well as the risk involved in each investment. When you consider that ALL investments and financial professionals report their Pre-Inflation/Pre-Tax returns, it is easy to see why some people realize no additional purchasing power from their investments—they simply don't understand what they are really getting out of their investments!

Uncle Sam Back For Another Helping: Taxes

The last chapter discussed how taxes were not considered in Markowitz and Sharpe's Nobel Prize winning Capital Asset Pricing Model of investments. A new development in the mutual fund arena is that mutual funds may have to report AFTER-TAX gains, not Pre-Tax gains. How much will that change the numbers? A lot! Consider what Lipper, a mutual fund tracking firm, concluded:

> **"Over the past 20 years, the average investor in a taxable stock mutual fund gave up the equivalent of 17 percent to 44 percent of their returns to taxes."***
>
> **_*CNN/Money.com 4/17/07_**

Without boring you with the math, this number means that some mutual funds sell most of their holdings within one year of purchasing them. This is also called "portfolio turnover" and can be used to compare different investments. This means you get much more short-term capital gains tax treatment (28%-44%) on your appreciation than you do long-term capital gains tax treatment (15%-24%). For example, if your mutual fund appreciated by 11% last year, it probably cost you close to 4% in taxes. Which number is more important to you, the 11% the investment firm reported or the 7% you actually received?

Mutual funds are not the only tax problem. Do you have CDs, money markets, or bonds? All of the income from these vehicles will be taxed as ordinary income. This will likely be taxed at rates between 27% and 35%, not to mention up to 5.925% for State of Ohio income tax. For this reason, 5% to 6% in dividend or interest income may only be worth 2.5% to 4.0% after taxes. While this is depressing, it isn't the end of your problems.

Inflation: When A Dollar Is Only Worth 50 Cents

You would always rather have a dollar today than a dollar tomorrow, right? There is an area of finance and economics that deals with this simple concept. It is known as the "time value of money." Time value of money allows us to compare the value of a dollar over different periods of time. When determining the present value of future dollars, many people want to know what a dollar in the future will buy them in today's dollars. What they are really talking about is inflation and how it impacts one's ability to purchase items.

Obviously, things become more expensive as we get older. We have all heard our parents talk about a Coke costing a nickel or a movie costing a quarter. That a movie costs close to $10 today is because of inflation (though many might call it highway robbery given the quality, or lack thereof, of films today!). The average annual inflation rate over the past 70 years has been approximately 3.1%. This means that approximately every 22 years, things cost twice as much.

Calculating The Impact Of Inflation

The after-tax return that an investment achieves is called the "nominal return." This does not take inflation into account. When you divide the nominal return of an investment over time by the rate of inflation over that same period of time, you get the "real" rate of return, or inflation-adjusted rate of return.

Think back to the mutual fund mentioned earlier—where an 11% pre-tax return meant a take-home 7% after taxes. That 7% return is actually more like a 3.8% REAL return (1.07/1.031 = 1.038), after inflation is factored into the results.

Invest Wisely While Planning For Inflation

If Doctors want to reduce taxes, they should invest in the stock market through tax-managed investment accounts, variable annuities, various types of life insurance policies (variable universal life, equity-indexed universal life, or private placement life insurance) or managed accounts if the funds are inside of tax-deferred retirement plans. Within these investment accounts, you can work with the money manager to design a portfolio that will adequately manage inflation risk.

The Diagnosis

When it comes to investing, there is no sure-fire method to avoiding taxes or inflation. However, there are a number of tools that are discussed in this Lesson. The more you know about your options, the easier it will be for you to understand what you are really getting from your investments. Of course, there is no substitute for having a strong team of advisors that includes an investment advisory firm that understands tax management and other advisors who are tax-savvy to help you meet all of your needs. One way to avoid unnecessary taxes on investments is to avoid mutual funds. This is explained in the next chapter.

How Doctors Outgrow Mutual Funds

If you are like most physicians, you likely have over $250,000 in cash or mutual funds. These investments may be inside or outside of your tax-deferred retirement plans. In the previous chapter, we discussed alternatives to taxable mutual fund accounts ideal for your non-retirement plan accounts. Some of these alternatives offer asset protection, tax-deferral, and death protection. In this chapter, we will discuss an alternative to mutual funds both inside and outside of retirement plans. Before we compare mutual funds to individually managed accounts, we must first explain what both of them are.

Mutual Funds ("MFs") and Individually Managed Accounts ("IMAs") represent two of the most popular investment programs used by individuals to create wealth. On the surface, at least, one could argue that they are not all that dissimilar. Both offer investors a professionally managed portfolio of securities generally comprised of stocks, bonds, or a combination of the two. They are both tailored to provide ample diversification.

When looking beneath the surface, however, two distinctly different approaches emerge. Each offers particular advantages depending upon one's needs. Which is the more prudent choice? Which ones will help you make wise investments? These are questions properly answered only by the individual investor. The information that follows is designed to help you make a wise investment decision, one with which you are comfortable, and, we hope, will prove over time to be the "right" choice for you.

Mutual Funds

A MF is a company that invests in stocks, bonds, and other securities on behalf of individual investors with similar financial goals. A "no-load" mutual fund is one that is sold directly to investors without an initial sales charge or "load."

Many financial advisors now provide access to no-load funds as part of a comprehensive range of services. However, the charge for the advisor's assistance tends to offset the lack of an initial sales charge, effectively minimizing any cost differences between load and no-load funds. Of course, you get the assistance of an advisor that you would otherwise have to pay anyway.

For purposes of this discussion, therefore, "no-load funds" will refer to funds purchased directly from the company without the help of an advisor.

Both load and no-load MFs are essentially "cooperatives" of investors who pool their money for a common purpose. Investors contribute to the pool by buying shares in the fund. Each share represents an equal percentage of ownership in the fund's assets.

The fund draws from the pool not only to make investments but also to pay for the services of a fund manager (who decides when and if to buy and sell securities for the fund based on its stated objective), marketing and distribution costs, custodian fees, and transaction costs. MFs are not limited but generally hold a hundred or more different securities. No matter how many shares of the fund the investor holds, the investor cannot control the buying and selling of these securities inside the fund. You can only buy or sell the basket of securities the fund has by buying or selling your shares of the fund.

Individually Managed Accounts

An IMA is an account that is individually managed by a professional investment manager who decides when to buy and sell securities based on *your* stated investment strategy or individual goals.

Unlike mutual fund investors, managed account investors do not pool their money. Rather, they own the securities in their account directly. They may have many similar holdings with a number of their clients, but each portfolio is isolated. The investor can direct the manager to buy only certain types of stocks or to avoid certain stocks (perhaps no tobacco stocks for moral reasons or no healthcare stocks because you work as a physician and enough of your income is already tied to healthcare). This obviously gives you greater flexibility and control than you would have with a mutual fund.

There is no doubt that mutual funds are easy. Their forms are easy. Their marketing materials are readily available. The companies are household names with all the advertising they do. These materials and advertising would have you believe that the mutual funds offer better returns with lower fees. Let's see if this is true.

Are Managed Accounts Worth The Money?

One of the most common problems we see with clients is that they are obsessed with the fee associated with any type of planning. If you took this approach to everything you bought, you'd only eat 99-cent Big Macs at every meal. There is truth to the saying "you get what you pay for." You should not be quick to dismiss the advantages of one investment strategy over another based purely on price. The recent popularity of no-load mutual funds is proof that many investors, particularly those who like a no-frills approach to investing, are doing just that.

You invested your time in reading this book in hopes that it would help you. That was time well spent, right? You are considering asset protection, insurance, estate planning, and retirement strategies that undoubtedly will cost you something. Why? Because these strategies offer you something of greater value in return. A prudent investor considers differences in:

- The quality of service provided in return for the fee.
- How the accounts treat capital gains and losses relative to your situation.
- The effect that other investors may have on an investment manager's decisions.
- The methods used to report information.
- The way in which fees are handled.

These are very important factors to consider when comparing investment options because the fee is not important. What you earn net of the fee and taxes is what is most important.

Is Your Tax Situation A Consideration?

With IMAs, you pay taxes only on the capital gains you actually realize. Because you own the securities in your account directly, you can work with your tax advisor to implement planning strategies that mutual fund investors may not be able to duplicate. There are actually IMA firms who will call YOU to ask you how you want them to manage the account at the end of the year. You may want to maximize investment account gains because you have other investment losses to offset the gains. You may want the advisors to generate losses to offset other investment gains you may have. You may just want the investment manager to buy or sell securities to balance your annual tax liability from your portfolio to zero out the tax.

With mutual funds, you pay taxes on your pro rata share of capital gains experienced by the fund, whether you benefit from the sale of the security or not. The following hypothetical example serves to illustrate this point.

Assume that a fund purchases stock at the beginning of the year for $25 per share. Over the next few months, the stock's price rises to $50 per share. Coincidentally, an investor buys shares in the fund just as the stock's price reaches this peak.

Later in the year, the stock's price falls to $40 per share, and the fund sells its position. At the end of the year, the investor is allocated a pro rata share of the fund's gain on the stock (the difference between the purchase price of $25 and the sale price of $40), even though the investor did not fully benefit from the gain; in fact, the stock actually declined in value after the investor purchased shares in the fund at $50.

Over time, investors who own IMAs and mutual funds who hold their investments for the same period and whose portfolio managers follow identical strategies will report little, if any, difference in capital gains taxes on those particular investments. For the mutual fund investor; however, the point at which the gains are realized may be moved forward and that can affect the investor's tax planning strategy. The table below illustrates this point.

Comparing Individually Managed Accounts and Mutual Funds

	Individually Managed Account	Load Mutual Fund	No-Load Mutual Fund
Investment Portfolio	Tailored to meet investor's particular needs	Two-way communication, including in-person discussions with Financial Advisor. Can also call toll-free number.	One-way communication: Call toll-free phone number and talk to sales representative.
Establishing Investor's Goals	Investor benefits from Financial Advisor's help.	Investors benefits from Financial Advisor's help.	Investors determine their own goals.
Investment Manager Selection	Chosen by investor with Financial Advisor's help.	Chosen by mutual fund.	Chosen by mutual fund.
Investment Manager Evaluation	Screened and evaluated by investor and Financial Advisor.	Screened and evaluated by investor and Financial Advisor.	Investors must screen and evaluate on their own.
Performance Monitoring	Financial Advisor monitors on investor's behalf.	Financial Advisor monitors on investor's behalf.	Investors must monitor on their own.
Tax Planning	Investors have some control over the timing of capital gains.	Investors have little control over the timing of capital gains.	Investors have little control over the timing of capital gains.
Redemption Requests	Investors are not affected by the actions of others who use the same manager	Manager may be forced to sell securities at undesirable prices to raise cash to meet redemption requests.	Manager may be forced to sell securities at undesirable prices to raise cash to meet redemption requests.
Reporting	Detailed monthly or quarterly statements; monthly letters; quarterly newsletters; periodic investment literature from manager.	General quarterly statements; semi-annual investment reports; possibly periodic newsletters.	General quarterly statements; semi-annual investment reports; possibly periodic newsletters.
Up-Front Costs	$0	Up to 6% of investment or an additional 1% per year added to the annual cost.	$0
Annual Costs	On average for a stock-based portfolio, between 2.5% and 3% of total investment.	On average for a stock-based portfolio, between 2% and 3% of total investment.	On average for a stock-based portfolio, between 1.5% and 2% of total investment.

The Cost Of IMAs

So, what do IMAs really cost? Investors who open IMAs usually do so with a minimum investment of at least $250,000. Some firms have minimums that can be as high as $10,000,000. Depending on the client's particular situation, most firms will make exceptions. As an example, the primary authors' firm (www.ojmgroup.com) invests through their registered investment advisor The O'Dell Group (TOG). TOG has a published account minimum of $500,000. However, they will aggregate family accounts (all IRAs, 401(k)s & other assets of parents and children) to reach that minimum account size. They will also take a smaller account of an investor who has a high income and who is likely to reach that minimum in a few years. This isn't uncommon in the industry.

Fees for IMAs can vary greatly. A common estimate in the industry is about 1-2% of assets, paid quarterly. Now, a smaller account may have higher fees and a larger account always pays lower fees. Some special private placements, private equity, and hedge funds can have significantly higher fees. All fees will be disclosed either in the firm ADV (Uniform Application for Investment Adviser Registration) for registered investment advisory firms, a prospectus for a registered security or a private placement memorandum for private placements. You should never invest in anything before receiving an ADV, prospectus, or private placement memorandum.

Subsequent transaction costs are paid either by paying commissions on individual trades or by paying an asset-based fee on a quarterly basis. In addition to covering transactions, these fees encompass reporting, custody, and the services of a financial advisor as well. For a stock-based portfolio, on average, total fees range annually from 1.3% to 3% of the assets under management. There are no additional charges.

MFs have lower minimum investment requirements, often $1,000 or less. With a no-load MF bought directly from the company, the entire investment is placed in the fund at the time of initial purchase. With a front-end load fund, on the other hand, the investor's money is placed in the fund only after deducting a sales charge. In the case of a 3.5% load fund, the fund would invest $965 of the investor's initial $1,000.

Beyond the initial sales charge, or lack thereof, the difference in fee structure between load and no-load mutual funds virtually disappears. Management fees, transaction costs, custody fees, and distribution and marketing costs (known as 12b-1 fees) are deducted automatically from the fund's assets. These fees are usually not seen directly by investors, but are instead specified in the fund's prospectus and statements of additional information. MF expenses for stock-based portfolios typically range from 1.5% to 2% per year for no-load funds and from 2% to 3% per year for load funds.

According to Morningstar, a third-party research publication that follows open-end MFs, the average diversified domestic equities fund incurs about 1.63% in annual costs, including a 1.32% expense ratio and 0.31% in transaction costs. Tack on an additional 0.94% annual sales charge on average for load funds, or an estimated 1% annual charge for no-load funds purchased through a financial advisor, and that annual cost figure rises to approximately 2.6% for all funds.

Investment	Investment Minimum	Annual Fees	Tax Treatment of Gains
Mutual Funds (MFs)	$1,000	1.6% to 2.6%	Capital gains or ordinary income tax rates. Varies by fund. No control for investor.
Indiv. Managed Accounts (IMAs)	$500k to millions	1%—2%	Varies. Look for tax-management in a firm so taxes can be avoided.
Hedge Funds	$1 million	3% or 25% of gain	Primarily ordinary income tax rates (35% to 44% for MDs)

Investors should note that transaction costs tend to vary depending on the type of securities in the fund. Trading foreign securities, for instance, can cost almost twice as much as trading domestic securities.

Doctors should accept the philosophy that "off the rack" mutual funds are not likely to fit into their planning as well as custom-made individually managed accounts.

The Diagnosis

While you may appear to be building your fortune by purchasing no-load funds, such savings may not be enough to offset the loss of the value-added services that normally include investment planning, monitoring, and communication that only a financial advisor can provide. Beyond perceived cost differences, MFs limit investors' tax planning choices and offer individual investors no control over securities in the fund.

Doctors should use IMAs to build wealth and protect their assets because of the tax benefits and the additional benefits. They avoid the MF trap of losing 17-44% of their returns to taxes. Another benefit of IMAs is that they offer the ability to add alternative investments to the portfolio. The explanation of these investments and the benefits Doctors should look for from these investments are explained in the next chapter.

8-4

Alternative Investment Strategies for Doctors

In the last chapter, you learned that IMAs can be more valuable to Doctors than MFs because IMAs are much more flexible. This flexibility offers tax management benefits and customization to better fit the investor's situation. Traditionally, most IMAs purchase stocks and bonds that are readily available to anyone (publicly traded securities). Though IMAs are valuable options, Doctors need to realize that the investment world does not end with stocks and bonds. There are additional classes of investments that cannot be made available to the public because of their complexity or level of risk. These investments can offer greater levels of diversification, inflation hedging, and potentially higher returns.

In this chapter, we will discuss who can legally access these alternative strategies, why investors may wish to purchase them, and the inherent risks within these investments. Then, we will discuss a few favorite alternative investment strategies. Many successful investors can credit the knowledge and utilization of the material in this chapter as the secret for their significant increase in net worth.

Accredited Investors

Alternative investment strategies can be offered to Doctors who have the financial means to survive the significant losses that can accompany riskier transactions. These investments are only available to a class of investors known as "accredited investors." One definition of this term, can be found on the TIAA-CREF website:

> To qualify as an accredited investor, an investor must either be: a financial institution; an affiliate of the issuer; or an individual with a net worth of at least $1 million or an annual income of at least $200,000, and the investment must not account for more than 20% of the investor's worth.

Why Invest In Alternative Investments?

In Chapter 8-1, we explained that greater risk was generally accompanied by a potential for greater return in financial markets. This increased risk can help investors who are willing to take greater risk to earn higher returns. Alternative investments, by definition, are riskier than traditional investments. As an asset class, alternative investments traditionally offer a significant risk premium (added expected return) to investors to convince them to invest in these riskier investments. Since most Doctors have the financial means to wait out down markets and can survive lost investments, they are ideal candidates for these investments. In addition to the expected returns, there are other reasons to consider alternative investments. A partial list includes:

- *Increased diversification of holdings* by expanding a portfolio to include items not within the traditional portfolio.
- *Decreased volatility* by investing in strategies not correlated to the stock or bond markets.
- *Preserved capital* can also be managed through an alternative allocation.
- *Increased access* alternative investments are sometimes called an asset class for the reasons mentioned above about accredited investors.

The Risks Of Alternative Investments

We mentioned that alternative investments have a higher risk than traditional investments. What are those risks? A partial list includes:

- **Lack of regulation:** Alternative investments are not required to be registered with the SEC. Though many hedge fund managers choose to do so to gain access to institutional investors that require it, many still do not register these securities. This is the old-fashioned caveat emptor, ("let the buyer [or investor] beware") situation.
- **Lack of transparency:** Assets held by hedge funds may not have a price quoted each day. Think of your personal residence or car as an example. This also means there is less liquidity so investors may be stuck with these investments for a while even if they want to sell them.
- **Excessive Leverage:** Some managers borrow money and others borrow money against borrowed money, thus exponentially increasing risk.
- **Fraud:** There are people who are not qualified to manage your money but are able to build trust and confidence in an attempt to steal your money.

- **Manager selection risk:** Not all managers are equal. In fact, there is evidence that the difference in manager performance is greater than the benefit of using alternative investments.

Savvy physician investors do not just accept these risks. They work with their investment team to analyze investment alternatives and find investments that fit into the strategy they have developed for their portfolio.

Alternative Investment Strategies

Behind the press reports of big payouts, high returns, and bankruptcies, there are sound investment strategies that are grouped together under a category called "hedge funds." One broad-brush term is typically used to paint the picture for over two dozen investment strategies. Instead of using the term "hedge fund," we recommend you view these funds as alternative investment strategies. There are literally hundreds of ways to invest outside of the traditional channels. We will break this down to make it easier to follow. We will begin by giving you a categorical list of investments that traditional managers are often prohibited from offering to clients who are accredited investors:

- **Short-selling securities:** This is selling someone else's shares in return for the promise to replace them later at what you believe will be a lower price. This is a way for an investor who speculates that a stock value will depreciate to benefit from the devaluation of the stock. The risk of short selling is unlimited since every dollar increase to a shorted stock is a dollar the investor loses and there is no theoretical limit to a stock's appreciation. For long investors who buy and hold a stock, they can only lose the original investment since the stock price can't fall below zero.

- **Buying on margin:** This is buying shares with borrowed money. This is a way for someone to leverage someone else's money. If the stock appreciates by more than the interest on the loan, there is a chance to earn money. If the stock price decreases, you may face a 'margin call,' requiring you to invest more of your own money or the lender will sell your stock to cover your debt.

- **Option trading:** These are individual options to buy or sell 1,000 shares of a stock at a particular price. There are options to buy or sell the security at that price and the investor can buy or sell the option.

- **Investing in any unregistered security:** This includes private placements and other worldwide investments that were not registered within the United States.

We have compiled a list of alternative investment strategies that are available to accredited investors. There is not enough space in this book to review them all. If you are interested in learning more about any of them, feel free to contact the authors.

Partial List of Alternative Investment Strategies

- Absolute Return Strategies are designed to achieve a steady rate of return in up or down markets, thereby minimizing volatility. Categories include:
  - Equity Market Neutral
  - Convertible Arbitrage
  - Fixed Income Arbitrage
  - Statistical Arbitrage
  - Risk Arbitrage
  - Multi-Strategy
  - Merger Arbitrage
  - Credit Arbitrage
- Opportunistic Equity Strategies seek to achieve above-market returns by anticipating market inefficiencies before they occur. Categories include:
  - Long / Short Equity
  - Global Macro
  - Short Only
  - Long / Short Specialty
  - Long / Short International
- Enhanced Fixed Income Strategies seek to return income above the market rate of return for a given risk profile. Categories include:
  - Capital Structure Arbitrage
  - Distressed Securities
  - Global / Emerging Market Debt
- Energy and Natural Resource investment strategies direct the purchase of oil, coal, timber, and other natural resources. These may have tax benefits as well.
- Real Estate Strategies include direct or leveraged purchases of commercial real estate properties.
- Private Equity includes the purchase of stocks not registered with the Securities and Exchange Commission. This is also called a private placement.

"If You Can't Stand the Heat..."

It is important to point out that not all strategies are successful all the time and not all investors in alternative investments achieve their goals. However, there is a formula that has worked over the years. Ironically, large endowment funds of some of America's premier universities turned to these strategies due to the shortcomings of traditional investing and successfully reduced their risk exposure while preserving the endowment capital in perpetuity.

An endowment is expected to provide a certain level of income, usually at an increasing amount, each and every year. Down years and performance under the required income level will wipe out the corpus of the endowment. Managers of these funds didn't really care what the stock market did. They had to ensure the endowment grew each year. They turned to alternative investments and have not looked back. This is an excellent example of wealth management as opposed to wealth building or accumulation strategies. For the individual investor, the endowment model of multiple alternative strategies would be used for the portion of your portfolio sometimes called the "stay rich pocket" as opposed to the "get rich pocket."

When Doctors are hiring an asset manager to manage an investment portfolio, the secret to long-term success is to find an investment advisor who can also help find, review, and possibly purchase other investment classes to round out the total portfolio. There are countless hedge funds, private placements, options, and currency and commodity based investments. To expand your options, you may want to make sure your investment advisor is accustomed to helping successful Doctors with their unique needs. Another way to look at the overall investment portfolio is to review it for Leverage and efficiency. This is discussed in the next chapter.

The Diagnosis

So far, you have learned that diversification is not enough to give you the best possible portfolio. You have learned that attention has to be paid to taxes and inflation and that mutual fund investments may be inappropriate for Doctors with investment accounts of $250,000 or more. You have even learned that the inclusion of alternative investments is an important piece of Doctors' investment planning.

As you learned in Lesson #1, you need to Leverage your team and your investments to achieve wealth. You also need efficiencies to make this work. The best way to do this within your planning is to try to "kill two birds with one stone." By hiring advisors who are experts in multiple areas, you will realize additional benefit. More important, focusing on planning tools and strategies that solve multiple planning problems and are flexible enough to be used in different ways is a great way to gain Leverage and efficiency. In the next few chapters, we will look at investments that do just that.

8-5

Life Insurance as an Investment for Doctors

Before you roll your eyes or dismiss this and the next three chapters, oblige us and read the rest of this paragraph for the sake of your own financial success. The authors of this book collectively hold multiple MBAs in Finance, law degrees, CPA designations, and securities licenses, in addition to having managed over $100 million for doctors since 1992 and bringing actuarial experience. We have a very strong working knowledge of financial analysis and don't take such strong positions without proof. The next four chapters will illustrate how life insurance can be used as an investment, how life insurance might benefit high-income taxpayers, and how life insurance might compare to other investments.

Life insurance is a contract between you and an insurance company. The most common term of the contract is that the insurance company will pay your named beneficiaries the "face amount" or "death benefit" of the policy when you die. Some life insurance policies accumulate cash over time (permanent policies) and some do not (term policies). For the next few chapters, we will be focusing on all types of life insurance *except* term insurance. To help you better understand some of the different types of insurance, we have put together a brief description of the different categories of life insurance and then discussed the pros and cons of each type. The different categories we will discuss include:

- Term Life Insurance
- Whole Life Insurance (WL)
- Universal Life Insurance
- Variable Life Insurance (VL)
- Variable Universal Life Insurance (VULI)
- A Hybrid: Equity-Indexed Universal Life Insurance (EIUL)
- Private Placement Variable Universal Life Insurance (PPVUL)

Term Life Insurance

Given its affordability, term life insurance is the most common type of life insurance policy. However, because it does not have a cash value (wealth accumulation) component, term insurance can only play a very limited role in your financial plan. It can provide temporary death protection for your family or for business partners as part of a buy-sell agreement.

The premium on a term policy is low compared to other types of life insurance policies because it carries no cash value and provides protection for a limited period of time (referred to as a "term"). This limited time frame is usually 10 to 20 years, though some companies offer a 30-year term product. A term life insurance policy pays a specific lump sum to your designated beneficiary upon your death. The policy protects your family by providing money they can invest to replace your salary and to cover immediate expenses incurred as a result of your death. Term life insurance is best for young, growing families, when the need for death protection of the breadwinner is high and excess cash flow is especially low.

Pros: Affordable coverage that pays only a death benefit. Term life insurance initially tends to cost less than other insurance policies because it has no cash value.

Cons: Term life insurance premiums increase with age because the risk of death increases as people get older. Some term premiums may rise each year, or after 10, 20 or 30 years. Over the age of 65, the cost of a new term insurance policy becomes very expensive, often unaffordable. Term insurance is not available beyond a certain age. It is a terrible tool for estate planning because the coverage cannot be continued at a reasonable price as you approach life expectancy.

Whole Life Insurance (WL)

Whole life insurance pays a death benefit to the beneficiary you name and offers you a cash value account with tax-deferred cash accumulation. The policy remains in force during your entire lifetime and provides permanent protection for your dependents while building a cash value account. The insurance company manages your policy's cash accounts.

Pros: Whole life insurance has a savings element (cash value), which is tax-deferred. You can borrow from this account free of income tax or cash-in the policy during your lifetime. It has a fixed premium which can't increase during your lifetime (as long as you pay the planned amount), and your premium is invested for you long-term. Because it has the cash accumulation component, whole life insurance can offer benefits such as tax reduction, wealth accumulation, asset protection, estate planning, and even reduction of the retirement plan tax trap.

Cons: Whole life insurance does not allow you to invest in separate accounts (i.e.

money market, stock, and bond funds). Thus, your policy's returns will be tied to the insurance company's ability to invest its capital. It also does not allow you to split your money among different accounts or to move your money between accounts and does not allow premium flexibility or face amount flexibility.

Universal Life Insurance (UL)

Universal life insurance is a variation of whole life insurance. The insurance part of the policy is separated from the investment portion of the policy. The investment portion is invested by the insurance company—generally, in bonds, mortgages, and money market funds. This investment portion grows and is tax-deferred. The cost of the death benefit is paid for out of the investment fund. A guaranteed minimum interest rate is applied to the policy's cash values. This ensures that a certain minimum return on the cash portion of the policy will be paid no matter how badly the investments perform. If the insurance company does well with its investments, the interest return on the cash portion could increase.

Pros: The product is similar to whole life insurance, yet has more flexible premiums. It may be attractive to younger buyers who may have fluctuations in their ability to pay premiums. Because it is so flexible, universal life insurance can offer benefits like tax reduction, wealth accumulation, asset protection, estate planning, and even reduction of the retirement plan tax trap.

Cons: If the insurance company does poorly with its investments, the interest return on the cash portion of the policy could decrease. In this case, less money would be available to pay the cost of the death benefit portion of the policy and future premiums may be necessary in addition to the premiums originally illustrated.

Variable Life Insurance (VL)

Variable life insurance provides permanent protection to your beneficiary upon your death. The term "variable life" is derived from the ability to allocate your dollars to various types of investment accounts (within your insurance company's portfolio), such as an equity fund, a money market fund, a bond fund, or some combination of funds. Hence, the value of the death benefit is "variable" and the cash value may fluctuate up or down, depending on the performance of the investment portion of the policy.

Although most variable life insurance policies guarantee that the death benefit will not fall below a specified minimum, a minimum cash value is typically not guaranteed. Variable life insurance is a form of whole life insurance and because of investment risks, it is also considered a securities contract and is regulated as a security under the Federal Securities Laws and must be sold with a prospectus.

Pros: Variable life allows you to participate in various types of investment options without being taxed on your earnings (until you surrender the policy). You can apply interest earned on these investments toward the premiums, potentially lowering the amount you pay. Because of the ability to invest in more aggressive assets (mutual funds, etc.), variable life insurance is an ideal tool for accumulation and retirement planning, especially if you are looking for growth over a longer term.

Cons: You assume the investment risks. When the investment funds perform poorly, less money is available to pay the premiums, meaning that you may have to pay more than you can afford to keep the policy in force. Poor fund performance also means that the cash and/or death benefit may decline, although never below a defined level if the policy so provides. Also, you cannot withdraw from the cash value during your lifetime.

Variable Universal Life Insurance (VUL)

Variable universal life insurance pays your beneficiary a death benefit. The amount of the benefit is dependent on the success of your investments. If the investments fail, there is a guaranteed minimum death benefit paid to your beneficiary upon your death. Variable universal life insurance gives you more control of the cash value account portion of your policy than any other insurance type. As a form of universal life insurance, it has elements of both life insurance and a securities contract. Because the policy owner assumes investment risks, variable universal products are regulated as securities under the Federal Securities Laws and must be sold with a prospectus.

Pros: Variable universal life enables you to make withdrawals or borrow from the policy during your lifetime, and it offers separate accounts in which to invest. Because it combines the flexibility of universal life with the ability to invest in mutual funds of the variable policy, variable universal can be the ideal tool for tax reduction and retirement wealth accumulation over a long time horizon. It also affords you another opportunity to invest in the equities markets on a tax-deferred basis.

Cons: It requires the policyholder to devote time in managing the policy's accounts. The policy's success is dependent on the investments you make. Premiums must be high enough to cover your insurance and your accounts.

A Hybrid: Equity-Indexed Universal Life Insurance (EIUL)

Equity-indexed universal life insurance (EIUL) pays your beneficiary a death benefit. The amount of the benefit is dependent on the success of the investments of the insurance company. In this case, the investments are contractually obligated to be equal to a market index. If the investments fail, there is a guaranteed minimum death benefit paid to your beneficiary upon your death. EIUL gives you more upside than a traditional UL policy because the insurance company contractually agrees to credit the policy's cash value with the same return as the stock market index the policy holder chooses (typically, the S&P 500 Index, but it can be the Dow Jones or NASDAQ) realizes over the same period of time—subject to a cap. The cap on the upside for two carriers we like, for example, are 12% per annum and 14% per annum, respectively. In return for taking away a piece of your upside, they offer a minimum annual return of 1% or 2% annually.

Pros: EIUL enables you to make withdrawals or borrow from the policy during your lifetime and it offers the investor the upside of the market (with a cap). It also, unlike variable life and variable universal life, offers the investor downside protection so the cash value will always see a positive crediting rate—even in a bad market. Studies have been done by insurance companies showing an investment in a portfolio with the upside cap and downside protection actually outperformed the straight pre-tax S&P 500 Index over every 10 year period in the last 70 years.

Cons: EIUL policies vary from carrier to carrier. Some only allow for 50% or 75% participation (others offer 100%) of the rate of return from the S&P. This means that if the S&P 500 returns 10%, you may only get 5% or 7.5%. The policyholder must pay particular attention to the carrier's contractual obligations. Also, the minimum guaranteed returns are typically 1% to 2%, which is much lower than most traditional insurance products that offer minimum crediting rates of 3% to 4%. EIUL is another instance where you have to give up something to get something. Like all insurance policies, you need to understand what you are getting before you can make an informed decision.

Private Placement Variable Universal Life Insurance (PPVUL)

Private Placement Variable Universal Life insurance (PPVUL) shares most of the characteristics of VUL discussed earlier. However, PPVUL differs from the VUL in a few ways. Some of these differences make it very attractive for wealthy Doctors. These differences are:

1. PPVULs are only available to accredited investors.
2. PPVULs do not generate materials that are available to the public. They must be requested by a bona fide accredited investor.
3. PPVULs have higher minimum premium requirements (differ by company and minimum premiums generally range from $500,000 to $5,000,000 of premium in the first five years).

4. PPVULs have lower fees than traditional insurance products.
5. PPVULs offer more investment flexibility. Policy owners typically choose among hedge funds or can suggest their own investment management firm to manage the funds within PPVUL if premiums are large enough.

Pros: PPVULs allow the client to choose hedge funds or, if the premiums will total $5,000,000 over 5 years, suggest their own independent financial advisor to manage the funds within the insurance contract. Commissions tend to be much lower than traditional insurance policies. PPVUL enables you to make withdrawals or borrow from the policy during your lifetime, and it offers separate accounts in which to invest. Because it combines the flexibility of variable universal life with lower fees, more investment flexibility, and investment gains within the sub-accounts are not taxed, PPVUL is the ideal tool for tax reduction and retirement wealth accumulation over a long time horizon for clients who are in high marginal tax brackets. It also affords another opportunity to invest in the equities markets on a tax-deferred basis.

Cons: Very high minimum premium requirements. Limited to accredited investors only. Because this is a private placement, there is very little written marketing material to review. Very few insurance companies do enough of this type of work to be considered efficient. Most insurance agents don't, or won't, sell it. The policy owner bears all the risk of the investments within the investment sub-accounts.

There is an emerging class of insurance policies that offer the lower costs of PPVULs but do not have the same accredited investor requirements and sizable minimum investments. Contact the OJM firm (www.ojmgroup.com) for more on this developing market trend. At the time of the writing of this book, we were negotiating with two insurance companies to release PPVULs with smaller minimum premium requirements.

The Diagnosis

There are many different types of life insurance policies. All of them have their place in planning for Doctors. What is important to realize is that all policies offer wealth accumulation benefits and tax-free death benefits as well as asset protection in most states. As discussed earlier, Ohio provides the top (+5) asset protection for cash value, making this asset class even more attractive for Ohio doctors. The Leverage opportunities of life insurance are discussed in the next chapter.

8-6

Getting More Out of Your Investments = Efficiency & Leverage

If you have read the entire book so far, you have learned the important philosophical keys to wealth accumulation and asset protection—efficiency and Leverage. The reason these two concepts are so important is that there are only 24 hours in a day and everyone wants to work less and build more. As stated in Lesson #1, efficiency and Leverage are the keys to reaching this goal. In this chapter, we will discuss an investment secret that combines Leverage and efficiency better than any others. This much-maligned investment is life insurance.

Why do we call this very popular investment a "secret" when everyone in America has heard of, or even purchased, life insurance at one point or another? The reason is that many Doctors don't think of life insurance as an investment. Rather, they perceive life insurance as a very costly necessity. This is a result of the inappropriate advice that is directed at low income Average Americans but finds its way to Doctors as well. As an example, most financial advisors for Average Americans discourage the use of life insurance while the wealthiest Americans and their advisors maximize their use of life insurance.

In this Chapter, we will discuss why life insurance is a secret investment of successful Doctors. We will also explain why life insurance is so important to the creation and maintenance of wealth. We will then discuss the basics of life insurance and explain how it achieves Leverage as a very efficient and flexible financial planning tool. At the request of many of the readers of our previous books, we have included Chapter 8-8, which shows a comparison of life insurance to mutual funds as an investment. Then, we end the Lesson by discussing creative applications of insurance as retirement planning and college education savings tools.

Investment Efficiency

The concept of investment efficiency is not one you will find in most finance textbooks. In Lesson #2, you learned that Doctors should embrace their affluence. As part of this acceptance, Doctors must also recognize that general information in books, newspapers, articles, websites, or on television is likely to be inappropriate for them because it is geared toward Average American's financial planning needs. If you can adopt the philosophy that you are different, you can easily expand your planning opportunities to include investments that can give your family greater flexibility, efficiency, and Leverage. A perfect example of this type of investment is life insurance.

The concept of investment efficiency is extremely important in the context of an overall financial plan. In this context, an "efficient" investment is one that:

1. Addresses two or more planning goals at the same time;
2. Helps a client reach a planning goal with less effort or with a smaller investment of time or money than other investments; and
3. Is flexible enough that it can be modified to address different planning needs as the client's personal circumstances change.

The Need For Efficient Investments

There are many reasons why efficient investments are such an important key to acquiring and maintaining wealth. First, efficient investments address multiple planning goals simultaneously. As we will see in this Lesson, the efficient investments described here can build wealth while reducing taxes, providing asset protection, allowing for college funding access, and providing estate planning benefits. These investments become cornerstones of a Doctor's flexible, multi-disciplinary financial plan.

Second, efficient investments have less tax friction than other investments. As we have discussed repeatedly in this book, Doctors must consider tax ramifications in making their investment decisions. Cash value life insurance has tremendous tax benefits that are unmatched by other investment classes.

Third, efficient investments utilize Leverage. Lesson #1 explained how Leverage is necessary for all wealth accumulation. Efficient investments may allow you to meet a planning need by spending $5,000 instead of having to spend $25,000 or $50,000. By utilizing Leverage with efficient investments, you will have more money left over for living expenses or necessary inefficient investments. Since we all want to achieve our own desired levels of affluence as quickly and safely as possible, it only makes sense to consider using Leverage whenever possible. Without the use of efficient investments to achieve Leverage, you are just like the landscaper who only has so many hours of daylight when he can work. You will never get ahead.

Fourth, efficient investments are your safety net. Perhaps you have heard the phrases "Life is Plan B" or "Life Happens." We speak to thousands of wealthy clients every year at our seminars and in our consulting practices. As our specialty is planning and implementation, we have designed and helped execute hundreds of financial plans for clients. Through all of our experiences, we can tell clients one thing with certainty. The plan we help them create "will never go as planned." We know that life will throw them a series of curveballs. We just don't know what those curveballs will be. So, we have to plan with an expectation that we will have to make many changes to this plan. By using flexible investments that can serve different purposes, we create plans that are more likely to fit the clients' future needs with fewer modifications (and costs) than if we had used inefficient investments in the plan.

Life Insurance Leverage

The basic concept of life insurance was built on the shifting and sharing of risk. The benefits of insurance have always revolved around its Leverage. In this chapter, we will break life insurance Leverage into basic Leverage and advanced Leverage. You can think of the basic Leverage as ways to turn small dollars into big dollars. Advanced Leverage is turning a small amount of someone else's small dollars into your big dollars. Because of this significant Leverage, life insurance is seen as the most efficient way to transfer wealth and protect a family or business. Let's look at some applications of life insurance Leverage, including:

- Part1: Death Benefit
- Part 2: Estate Planning
- Part 3: Tax-Free Accumulation

Part 1: Death Benefit

Lesson #4 is to do no financial harm to yourself or your family. In other words, you have to protect your family from financial disasters. Lesson #9 explains how to preserve your estate. The most efficient tool to address both of these concerns is life insurance. By paying small amounts to an insurance company, you can protect your family from lost income and estate taxes. To illustrate this point, let us consider the story of the Rob W., a hard working, 35-year old who has just started a family.

Case Study: Rob and Ronelle

Rob, 35, has a wife, Ronelle, and two young children, Nigel and Dikembe. Rob is a young dermatologist who is trying to help his family get ahead. He works for a clinic during the week and is a professional dancer who makes extra money during the weekends. Ronelle was a singer before she had the kids. Rob owns a house and has just started saving for the children's education. He knows that his family relies on his income and that the music would stop altogether for his family if he died. He recently asked us to help him find a life insurance policy that would help to protect his family's financial future.

With the $2,000 per month he was saving from his dancing, we were able to secure a $3,200,000 life insurance policy on Rob. Because Rob doesn't know how long he can dance, he only wanted to look at policy illustrations that assumed premium payments for 10 years. As such, Rob purchased a $3.2 million death benefit insurance policy. He pays $24,000 per year for 10 years to pay for the death benefit and accumulates cash values to pay for future premiums (after the 10 years). If Rob were to die, the death benefit would adequately cover his mortgages, his children's college funds, and leave Ronelle with enough money to raise the children. Now that Rob has insurance, the beat can go on for his family even if it doesn't for him.

What happens if Rob doesn't die? Some people would say that Rob has wasted a lot of money protecting his family when he could have just bought term insurance. However, that couldn't be further from the truth. If Rob's insurance policy earns 8% before fees and expenses (this assumption is realistic here, as Rob's particular policy offers an investment return that is tied to 100% of the S&P Index, an index that has averaged close to 8% over the last 25 years) for 20 years, Rob will have over $248,000 of cash value at the end of 10 years. In other words, at the end of 10 years, it may look like a Christmas club at the bank. $250,000 paid in, $248,000 left, PLUS he had $3.2 million of protection for his family. Not a bad deal. If Rob had bought term insurance, he would have spent valuable money and would have had absolutely nothing to show for after the term ended.

If Rob keeps his coverage for another 10 years, but does not pay another dollar of premium, he could expect the cash values to grow to approximately $460,000 and still maintain the financial protection for his family. That is a 6.5% after tax return (from a pretax, pre-fee return of 8% within an equity indexed life insurance policy) between years 10 and 20 while offering protection to his family. If Rob had invested that $248,000 in stocks and bonds at 8% instead of keeping the insurance policy, he would have paid at least 15% federal tax on his capital gains and up to 9% of the gain to state taxes (in Ohio, Rob would pay up to 5.925% as ordinary income tax). This means that even if Rob could find an investment manager or mutual fund that didn't charge any fee at all (which is impossible), 22% of the 8% gain would have gone to taxes, giving him a 5.925% gain on his investment. The insurance actually outperformed the market AND it protected his family. Rob looked at this proposal and termed it his "free insurance" plan.

Cash Values in Rob's $3.2 Million Life Insurance Policy after Paying Premiums of $2,000 per Month for 10 Years

Period of Time	Cash Values in Rob's Insurance Policy
After 10 years	$248,000
After 20 years	$460,000
After 30 years	$862,000

Let's assume Rob leaves the policy in place for another 10 years until he is ready to retire. At the end of 30 years, the policy cash value would be approximately $862,000. That equates to a 6.34% compounded rate of return on an insurance policy with underlying investments yielding 8% gross returns. Another way to say this is that the internal costs of administration, fees, and management of the policy are 1.66%. When you consider that Rob would be lucky to find an investment with total underlying fees of only 1%, his taxes on gains would be no less than 1.54%. This means that the internal rate of return for taxable funds or money management accounts could, at best, be 5.46% when the S&P Index returns 8%. An insurance policy with all of its fees and commissions offers an internal rate of return of 6.34%. Rob gets a better return for his investment in an insurance policy AND he is getting protection for his family.

Impact of Taxes, Fees & Commissions over 30 Years

	Mutual Funds	Cash Value Life Insurance
Gross Return	8.00%	8.00%
Fees & Commissions	1.00%	1.66%
Taxes	1.54%	0.00%
Net	5.46%	6.34%

Part 2: Estate Planning

Let's assume that Rob wins $1,000,000 on the reality show *So You Think You Can Dance* or Ronelle's revived singing career finally hits the big time and they are making more money than they need to support their lifestyle. Because they love their children and want to give them every opportunity they didn't have, they want to put money aside for them. Rob and Ronelle meet with their advisory team who explain a number of options. One of the techniques they chose to implement is the creation of an Irrevocable Life Insurance Trust (ILIT). Under the ILIT, Rob and Ronelle will each make $12,000 of tax-free annual gifts to the trust for the benefit of each of Nigel and Dikembe to remove the funds from their estate. Then, the $48,000 will be used to purchase a 2nd-to-die life insurance policy on Rob and Ronelle. When they finally pass away, their children will receive $10,000,000 tax-free. Even if Rob and Ronelle were to die next year, the children would get $10,000,000.

The ILIT is flexible too. Rob and Ronelle can direct the attorney to draft the language of the ILIT in a way that allows the children to get access to cash values of the policies for certain expenses that Rob and Ronelle find important. If the children need money for college or a wedding or dance lessons, the trust can be drafted to allow the children to access the insurance policy's substantial cash value to do so. For example, one 2nd-to-die policy we reviewed had cash values in excess of $600,000 in year 20; over $1.3 million in year 30; and over $2.5 million in year 40. The family could protect themselves from premature death of both spouses, build an estate for future generations, and provide a fund to help pay for college, weddings, first homes, and much more if Rob and Ronelle live. Because life insurance withdrawals, policy loans, and death benefits can all be income tax-free, this life insurance investment offers amazing Leverage and unmatched flexibility.

Part 3: Tax-Free Accumulation

As established in the beginning of this Lesson, most people don't think of life insurance policies as investments. However, large companies have been purchasing life insurance policies in great numbers over the last five years to protect their assets and accumulate more wealth. In addition, Doctors have used these tax-efficient investment tools for years. We have a number of clients who invest over one million dollars per year into life insurance contracts. We also have many clients who invest hundreds of thousands of dollars every year into life insurance policies. These clients have some interest in the death benefit, but they are primarily interested in the wealth accumulation benefits of life insurance.

Let's look at a healthy 35-year-old male, like Rob in the earlier example. He may look at his equity indexed universal life insurance policy as his unlimited "after tax pension." The big differences between the insurance policy cash values and his pension are that he can take all (or none) of the money from the insurance policy before he is 59½ without penalty; he doesn't have to take any funds out of the policy at age 70½ (like he has to take minimum required distributions out of a pension); he doesn't have to contribute for employees; and the insurance policy appreciates at the time of his death instead of depreciating in value by 70% like his pension does when he dies and leaves it to his children (see Chapter 9-6).

The economics of investing into a life insurance policy look like this:

- Beginning at age 35, Rob invests $2,000 per month for 30 years
- The policy grows at 8% per year (before expenses and fees)
- Cash values in year 30, when Rob retires, are approximately $2.2 million
- He takes tax-free policy withdrawals and policy loans of over $220,000 every year from age 65 until age 90! That is $720,000 of investments yielding over $5,500,000 of tax-free retirement income while offering death protection to the family at the same time.

By leveraging the tax-free accumulation and death benefit features of equity indexed universal life insurance, Rob is able to protect his family from his premature death and provide a very tax-efficient investment return for himself at the same time. He can solve two planning challenges with one investment. That sounds pretty efficient!

The Diagnosis

Life insurance offers more Leverage than any other investment tool—even real estate. First, a very small premium payment can protect a family from a premature death; protect a business in a buy-sell arrangement; accumulate wealth without taxes; or efficiently transfer the wealth from one generation to another. Second, life insurance offers tax Leverage as both a wealth accumulator and as a tax-free death benefit for your family. For more detail on the flexibility and efficiency of life insurance, you should proceed to the next chapter. To see a much more detailed analysis that compares this investment to low cost index funds, you should make sure you read Chapter 8-8.

8-7

The Best Investment Option for Doctors

Would you be surprised to read that life insurance is the most important tool in the financial plans of Doctors? If you simply follow the "common sense" advice of the Average American-focused mass media, you certainly would be surprised. On the other hand, if you have been reading the past seven Lessons or if you have advisors who regularly work with high income, high liability or high net worth clients, then you wouldn't be surprised at all. No other financial, tax, insurance, or legal tool can play as many roles in a financial plan as life insurance can.

In this chapter, we will discuss the key characteristics of cash value life insurance—that is, permanent (not term) insurance policies whose excess premium is invested in a tax-efficient manner with a cash value account for the benefit of the policy owner. In subsequent chapters, we will share applications that allow you to Leverage these characteristics.

Key Characteristics That Make Life Insurance So Valuable

Life insurance has many characteristics and offers various benefits. Savvy investors take advantage of life insurance as an investment because it can be such a flexible planning tool that will help you address so many planning challenges in an efficient way. The following attributes that make life insurance a valuable investment apply to permanent (cash value) life insurance and should capture your attention:

1. **Amounts in life insurance policies grow tax-deferred:** While investments outside of retirement plans and life insurance policies are taxed on income and realized capital gains, funds growing within a cash value life insurance policy grow completely tax-free. This is why life insurance is so attractive as a wealth accumulation and tax reduction vehicle. It is seen as the "Unlimited After-Tax Retirement Plan" by the most successful business owners in the United States.

2. **Account Balance values in life insurance policies can be accessed tax-free at anytime:** When you take funds out of a retirement plan (pension or IRA), these withdrawals are always subject to income tax and may be subject to a penalty if with-

drawn before age 59½. With a cash value life insurance policy, you can take tax-free loans against the cash value at any time. There is never a tax penalty and there is no tax on the loan so long as you keep the policy in force and the policy is not a modified endowment contract (MEC).

3. **Life insurance is asset-protected:** In Ohio, cash value life insurance policies, if structured properly, can provide you the maximum amount of asset protection (+5) available. Thus, this asset should play an important role in your asset protection plan. Working with a knowledgeable advisory team, you can use cash value life insurance policies to solidify your Ohio Fortress.

4. **Life insurance has beneficial tax valuation:** In dealing with the 70% tax trap facing pensions and IRAs, life insurance can play a very valuable role. The essence of this rule is that life insurance enables the plan owner, who would otherwise *lose 70%* of his plan holdings to estate and income taxes, to instead pass most, if not all, of those dollars and more to heirs.

As you can see, life insurance can offer so many benefits to policy owners. It can grow tax-free, provide a tax-advantaged death benefit, and is protected from lawsuit creditors. This flexibility is what allows Doctors to use life insurance to meet planning challenges more efficiently. Ohio Doctors would do well to consider integrating this asset into their Engine and Fortress.

The Diagnosis

The most important characteristic of life insurance is that it is flexible. You don't have to decide exactly what you want to use the life insurance for before you buy it. You can add more premium later, gift the policy to a person or entity, sell the policy, save it for the death benefit, use the cash values for lifetime needs and return the money you take out or not. The biggest misunderstanding about life insurance is that most people don't see it as an investment tool. The next chapter illustrates how a cash value life insurance policy outperforms mutual funds.

8-8

Proof That Life Insurance Outperforms Mutual Funds

If you Google the phrase "buy term and invest the difference" you get 11,500,000 results. This is not an unfamiliar phrase for most Americans. What this "common sense" adage means is that, when considering buying cash value life insurance, you will be better off buying the cheaper term life insurance product and investing the difference into the market. The difference is determined by setting aside money every month equal to the premium that a permanent plan would require, then using a portion of this money for the term premium and placing the rest in an investment vehicle. Though not explicitly stated, this generally means that you should invest the difference in mutual funds.

In this chapter, we will prove that life insurance is a wiser investment for building wealth and protecting assets than buying term and investing the difference. To do so, we will provide two examples that illustrate our argument.

The Debate: Life Insurance vs. Buy Term And Invest The Difference

If you think back to Lesson #2, you may remember our explanation of why the popular press focuses on issues of the Average American. The "life insurance versus buy term and invest the difference" commentary is another example of the financial media perpetuating "common sense" for the common people. These are people who generally do not have significant tax and asset protection concerns because they don't earn much, don't pay very high taxes and aren't able to acquire very much wealth to protect. Doctors should be concerned with after-tax investment returns (i.e., what you take home from the investment after all taxes are paid) and asset protection of those investments. If you want to learn these lessons, you must read this chapter. What you will learn may surprise you—unless, of course, you are already a savvy investor getting the most out of life insurance as an investment!

Basic Assumptions For The Comparison

To compare two investments fairly, you have to develop and use similar assumptions. This is often referred to as "normalizing" the data. In all examples, we will assume a 35-year old healthy male makes investments of $4,000 per month for 30 years and then maximizes his withdrawals for 25 years in retirement. This will cause him to run out of money at 90 years of age. This is well beyond his life expectancy. In both the mutual fund and cash value life insurance policy, there are an infinite number of potential combinations of premium payments and withdrawals. So, we chose a reasonable set of assumptions and applied the same constraints to both the mutual fund and cash value life insurance examples so we would have a fair comparison.

A Crucial Benefit Ignored: Asset Protection

In this analysis, we will look only at pure investment performance. We are simply examining the dollar amounts resulting in either scenario, with the same assumptions. This is fine theoretically. However, as a concrete comparison for any of our clients, we would also factor in other elements—including the costs of achieving a desired level of asset protection for the client.

As you learned in Lesson 6, cash value life insurance policies can enjoy the very highest (+5) level of protection. In many states, like Ohio, the entire cash value of an insurance policy can be structured to receive exempt status—meaning a Doctor can't even lose the cash value in the most extreme situations where a bankruptcy is forced by a creditor. When comparing the financial performance of cash value life insurance to individually-owned (-5) or jointly owned (-3) mutual funds for Doctors who have significant liability risks, it is imperative to factor in the additional costs of asset protection to the mutual fund option.

The goal of any comparison is to "normalize" the data so that you are comparing truly equivalent options. To increase the level of asset protection of the mutual funds (to meet the level of protection offered through properly structured cash value life insurance), we would have to add significant costs to the mutual fund investment portfolio. While we would not be able to match the protection level exactly (as exempt assets are always preferable for asset protection planning), we could use rather expensive legal tools to give the mutual funds a (+5) level of protection. The creation of an international trust would be one tool that offers a very high level of desired protection. To compare the financial benefits of investing in cash value life insurance in a state where insurance is exempt to the financial benefits of mutual funds, you would have to reduce the total investment into mutual funds by upwards of $25,000 in year one and $10,000 per year on an ongoing basis to account for those additional costs of your desired protection. In a true comparison of the costs and benefits of both investment options, you must realize that the mutual fund projections offered below are unfairly skewed in favor of mutual funds. If asset protection is important to you, please keep in mind that investing in life insurance policies may be even more attractive than investing in mutual funds than the examples below suggest.

The Comparative Analysis = Stack The Deck In Favor Of Mutual Funds

Notwithstanding the caveat regarding asset protection mentioned above, in this performance-driven comparative analysis, we will offer unrealistic assumptions that will give the mutual funds every opportunity to make a case for being the better investment choice. The purpose of this set of unreasonable comparisons is to emphasize that cash value life insurance is a much better investment than mutual funds even under extreme circumstances that are unrealistically skewed in favor of mutual funds. After we complete this analysis, we will offer a similar analysis with realistic expectations.

In the Mutual Fund Corner...

- We are going to compare an investment in a theoretical no-load mutual fund that has no annual costs or expenses of any kind.
- We are going to assume the S&P 500 Index has an annual return of 8% per year (excluding dividends) for the next 55 years.
- We will assume that every investor lives in a state with no state income tax, even though only 9 states—Alaska, Florida, Nevada, New Hampshire, South Dakota, Tennessee, Texas, Washington, and Wyoming—do not have state income taxes. Note: You could remove New Hampshire and Tennessee from this list because they do tax dividend and interest income.
- We will assume that the tax on all gains will be at the lowest possible capital gains tax rate of 15% for the next 55 years, even though we believe rates will increase significantly at some time (and, as you have seen in past chapters, 15% is the lowest the tax rate has ever been on such gains).
- We are going to assume that the cost of the "buy term" portion of "buy term and invest the difference" is $0. In other words, we will completely disregard the buy term portion and just compare mutual funds to life insurance without any accounting for the friction of the term insurance.

In short, these unreasonable assumptions will yield projections that are not reasonable for actual mutual fund investors who will be paying management fees every year and are likely to have to pay state taxes and certainly will have to pay something for their term insurance.

In the Life Insurance Policy Corner...

- We are going to use an insurance policy from one of the nation's top insurance companies. This company has an A+ rating from the rating firm A.M. Best Company (this is the 2nd highest of 15 ratings offered by this rating organization).

This insurance company is also rated by Comdex (another ratings firm) as being in the top 8% of U.S. insurance companies, in terms of financially stability.

- To prove that this was not an anomaly, we found a second insurance policy from another A.M. Best A+ rated company that was rated by Comdex to be in the top 12%, in terms of financial stability, of insurance companies in the country. The ultimate income results of this secondary policy were within 3.96% of the first one.
- We are going to attempt to compare investments of equal risk by choosing an equity-indexed universal life insurance product that is readily available to the public in most states. This policy's performance is tied to the S&P 500 Index (excluding dividends). Unlike the mutual fund investment, however, the insurance product has a minimum annual investment return of 1% per year. That is, even if the S&P has a return in a given year that is less than 1%, the insurance company will still credit the policy as if the S&P returned 1%. This actually reduces the risk for the insurance policy vs. the index fund, but we will assume they are the same.
- We will assume the same 8% long-term gross return of the S&P 500 Index (excluding dividends) over 55 years.
- The policy also has a cap of 14%, but that does not come into play here as we are assuming the 8% annual return, as above.
- We will assume a fully commissionable insurance policy that has no term insurance blending to reduce commissions and increase cash values.

In this set of assumptions, we are giving a realistic projection of the S&P 500 equity indexed universal life insurance policy. In both this analysis and the subsequent more realistic comparison, the projection for the equity indexed universal life insurance policy will be the same.

The Comparative Analysis With The Deck Stacked For Mutual Funds

Let's examine how the no-fee, lowest possible tax, mutual fund portfolio and a cash value life insurance policy would perform with 30 years of investments at $4,000 per month, followed by 25 years of withdrawals by referring to the table below:

No Fee Funds with No State Tax Paying Investors vs. Cash Value Life Insurance

		Investment in No-Fee, Low Tax Mutual Funds				Investment in Life Insurance			
Year	**Age**	**Annual Mutual Fund Investment**	**6.8% After Tax Growth**	**Retirement Withdrawal**	**Year End Balance**	**Annual Insurance Premium**	**Withdrawals and Loans**	**Value at Death**	**Improvements over Funds at Death**
1	35	$48,000	$1,632		$49,632	$48,000	$0	$1,160,944	$1,111,312
10	44	$48,000	$41,723		$679,294	$48,000	$0	$1,832,780	$1,153,486
15	49	$48,000	$76,669		$1,228,158	$48,000	$0	$2,947,312	$1,719,154
20	54	$48,000	$125,227		$1,990,800	$48,000	$0	$4,241,600	$2,250,800
25	59	$48,000	$192,698		$3,050,487	$48,000	$0	$5,815,060	$2,764,573
30	64	$48,000	$286,448		$4,522,913	$48,000	$0	$7,802,940	$3,280,027
31	65		$283,290	$356,879	$4,449,324		$440,000	$7,401,372	$2,952,048
35	69		$261,138	$356,879	$4,101,409		$440,000	$6,828,168	$2,726,759
40	74		$223,848	$356,879	$3,515,733		$440,000	$6,343,556	$2,827,823
45	79		$172,034	$356,879	$2,701,940		$440,000	$5,888,176	$3,186,236
50	84		$100,038	$356,879	$1,571,181		$440,000	$5,597,232	$4,026,051
55	89		($0)	$356,879	($0)		$440,000	$5,660,016	$5,660,016
Total		$1,440,000		$8,921,974		$1,440,000	$11,000,000		

$2,078,027	Increase in Retirement Income
23.3%	% Increase over Mutual Funds

To save space, we compressed the table above to show a sample of the 55 years of data. Even with the deck stacked against the insurance policy—by considering an index fund with NO fees, an investor with NO state income taxes, and with NO costs of term life insurance—the insurance policy still outperformed the mutual fund investment. The mutual fund investment of $48,000 per year in a no fee, low tax environment yields annual after-tax income of $356,879. The investment in the equity indexed life insurance policy offers tax-free withdrawals and policy loans of $440,000 per year. The investment income from the investment insurance policy was over 23% greater than that of the "too good to be true" mutual fund. In addition, the family of the investor who purchased the insurance policy also has death benefit protection. The benefit in the last column is in addition to the increase in retirement income. In short, ***the investment in a life insurance policy significantly outperforms the investment in mutual funds, even with ridiculously skewed assumptions.***

The Comparative Analysis With More Realistic Assumptions

Now that we have determined that this type of cash value life insurance policy outperforms a "too good to be true" exaggerated mutual fund, let's conduct a second comparative analysis with realistic assumptions. The differences between this analysis and the previous one are threefold. First, we assume that the mutual fund has a total of 0.50% in annual expenses. This is quite low for most mutual funds. Second, we assume that the investors live in a state with 5% state income taxes (which is less than the Ohio tax rate). This is also a very reasonable assumption because 33 states have marginal income tax brackets over 5%. Twenty-four of those states have marginal income tax brackets over 6% and some have rates as high as 9.3%. Third, we assume that the term insurance costs would be approximately $2,000 per year. This is a rough estimate, but it reflects a slight reduction in the investment funds for the "buy term and invest the difference" scenario.

Let's look at how these more reasonable assumptions affect the projections. The table below compares how a low fee, moderate tax, mutual fund portfolio and a cash value life insurance policy would perform with 30 years of investments at $4,000 per month, followed by 25 years of withdrawals.

Low Fee Funds for Low State Tax Paying Investors vs. Cash Value Life Insurance

Investment in Low-Fee, Moderate Tax Mutual Funds						Investment in Life Insurance			
Year	Age	Annual Mutual Fund Investment	6% After Tax Growth	Retirement Withdrawal	Value at death	Annual Insurance Premium	Withdrawals and Loans	Value at Death	Improvements over Funds at Death
1	35	$46,000	$1,380		$1,160,944	$48,000	$0	$1,160,944	$0
10	44	$46,000	$34,048		$1,832,780	$48,000	$0	$1,832,780	$0
15	49	$46,000	$61,120		$2,947,312	$48,000	$0	$2,947,312	$0
20	54	$46,000	$97,352		$4,241,600	$48,000	$0	$4,241,600	$0
25	59	$46,000	$145,840		$5,815,060	$48,000	$0	$5,815,060	$0
30	64	$46,000	$210,724		$7,802,940	$48,000	$0	$7,802,940	$0
31	65	$0	$208,160	$276,432	$7,401,372	$0	$440,000	$7,401,372	$0
35	69	$0	$190,240	$276,432	$6,828,168	$0	$440,000	$6,828,168	$0
40	74	$0	$161,088	$276,432	$6,343,556	$0	$440,000	$6,343,556	$0
45	79	$0	$122,076	$276,432	$5,888,176	$0	$440,000	$5,888,176	$0
50	84	$0	$69,868	$276,432	$5,597,232	$0	$440,000	$5,597,232	$0
55	89	$0	$0	$276,432	$5,660,016	$0	$440,000	$5,660,016	$0
Total		$1,380,000		$6,910,800		$1,440,000	$11,000,000		

$60,000	Term Insurance Premium	$4,089,200	Increase in Retirement Income
$1,440,000	Total Term + Investment	59.2%	% Increase over Mutual Funds

With realistic expectations, the annual after tax retirement income of the mutual fund investment is $69,108 per year. The insurance policy offers tax-free withdrawals and policy loans of $110,000 per year. That is a 59% improvement in income over the mutual fund investing. The death benefit is the same with the purchase of the term insurance, but the income suffers dramatically. The reason the insurance policy outperforms the mutual funds is that the actual expenses and the taxes of the funds, combined with the term life insurance costs, are significantly higher than the "supposedly" high internal costs of the cash value life insurance policy. ***This is one of the most misunderstood comparisons in financial planning.***

Another Case—The 45-Year Old

Insurance doesn't just work for 35-year old Doctors. We also looked at a recent case from a client of ours. This client was a 45-year old physician who wanted to work full-time for another 15 years, then work part time for 10 years, then take retirement plan distributions from ages 71 through 90 (20 years). We were asked to compare after tax investments of $5,000 per month into mutual funds and cash value life insurance under similar investment return assumptions (8% per year for the S&P 500 Index). This is what we found:

Low Fee Funds for Low State Tax Paying Investors vs. Cash Value Life Insurance

		Low-Fee, Moderate Tax Funds			Cash Value Life Insurance	
Year	**Age**	**Annual Mutual Fund Investment**	**6% After Tax Growth**	**Retirement Withdrawal**	**Annual Insurance Premium**	**Withdrawals and Loans**
1	45	$53,750	$1,613		$60,000	$0
10	54	$53,750	$39,784		$60,000	$0
15	59	$53,750	$71,419		$60,000	$0
20	64	$0	$0	$0	$0	$0
27	71	$0	$0	$201,197	$0	$254,358
35	79	$0	$0	$201,197	$0	$254,358
40	84	$0	$0	$201,197	$0	$254,358
46	90	$0	$0	$201,197	$0	$254,358
Total		$806,250		$4,023,942	$900,000	$5,087,160

$93,750	Term Insurance Premium	$1,063,218	Increase in Retirement Income
$900,000	Total Term + Fund Investment	26.42%	% Increase over Mutual Funds

In this example, our client would have over $1,000,000 of additional after-tax retirement funds by investing in a life insurance policy instead of into mutual funds or individually managed accounts. Not surprisingly, the client found this to be a much better alternative.

As we explained above, the life insurance option in Ohio, if structured properly, also provides qualitatively better asset protection—(+5) versus (-5) or (-3) for mutual funds. Thus, cash value life insurance can be a better investment for all Ohio Doctors, even those who are starting this investing at the age of 60 or possibly 70, if in excellent health.

Possible Explanation

We hope it is clear to you that the common sense adage "cash value life insurance is a poor investment" is generally inaccurate. Before we wrote this book, we believed that the taxes were the biggest factor in the success of cash value life insurance policies as wealth accumulation vehicles. Certainly, for Doctors in the higher combined marginal tax brackets, this is absolutely true. Yet, with the analyses above, we saw that the insurance policy was still a better investment for investors who only pay taxes of 15% on their investment gains. This was surprising, as it indicated to us that the taxes couldn't be the primary reason for the insurance policy's superior performance. It must be the type of insurance policy itself.

Before equity indexed universal life insurance policies were invented, the only practical life insurance investment choices were Whole Life, Universal Life and Variable Universal Life policies. Whole Life insurance policies are very inflexible. Further, Whole Life and Universal Life policies typically have returned 4% to 7% over the last 10 years. Though this return is respectable, it did not keep pace with the appreciation of the S&P 500 Index over the same period. In a strong market, the mutual funds could possibly outperform those policies in states with low taxes. If the people who did the original comparison of "buy term and invest the difference" used whole life policies, those results would perpetuate the aforementioned "common sense" myth.

The Variable Universal Life policies that offer mutual fund choices within the insurance contract could theoretically keep pace with a strong market since their underlying investment are mutual funds. However, these policies have always had the highest internal fees of all insurance products. If you have a variable-type policy with high fees being purchased by an investor in a state that had no state income tax on investment gains, the mutual fund investment may outperform the Variable Universal Life policy. This would also further the "common sense" myth.

With Equity Indexed Universal Life (EIUL) policies, one has access to both the tax benefit and lower costs of certain types of policies and the access to the upside potential of the S&P 500 Index. When you combine these benefits with the results from the direct comparison above, you can see why EIUL policies are able to consistently outperform mutual funds for long term investors who are as young as 30 or possibly as old as 70 years of age.

The Diagnosis

The misconception that "buy term and invest the difference" outperforms an investment in life insurance is common. If you continue to seek financial advice through Average American media channels, you may continue to get this kind of inaccurate and inappropriate information. This chapter gave examples of how cash value life insurance policies significantly outperformed realistic mutual funds. Even when we compared the insurance policy to an unrealistic (and unavailable) mutual fund with no expenses and sold it to a taxpayer in a state with no income taxes and gave that investor the term insurance for free, the cash value insurance policy still outperformed the mutual fund.

Throughout this book, you have learned that life insurance would protect against a premature death, serve as a source of liquidity for estate planning, and provide asset protection for your investment dollars. Now you know that the investment in life insurance can be significantly more attractive than an investment in mutual funds. Doctors maximize their investment in life insurance as a way to accumulate more wealth and protect assets. This is likely to be a significant key to your achieving, and maintaining, your desired level of affluence.

The Ultimate After Tax Pension & College Savings Tool

After reading the chapters within this Lesson, you now understand that life insurance is a wise investment alternative worthy of serious consideration. In addition, you have also learned that life insurance offers asset protection, tax and estate planning benefits. With all of these benefits, and the unmatched flexibility of life insurance policies, you can see why insurance is the cornerstone of the financial planning for Doctors. In this chapter, we will show you how you can use life insurance as a wise investment tool. Doctors can utilize creative applications of insurance, which are:

- Unlimited After-Tax Retirement Plan
- Insured College Savings Fund for Children or Grandchildren

In doing so, you can accomplish more than one goal with one single investment tool and create even more efficiency in your financial plan.

In Chapter 7-2, we explained how Doctors can maximize their use of retirement plans. This is desirable because Doctors want to take advantage of three key elements of a qualified retirement plan:

1. Tax deduction for plan contributions
2. Tax-free growth of plan assets
3. The highest level of available asset protection for plan assets

Doctors can combine the benefits in Chapter 7-2 with the philosophy of "Leverage" from Lesson #1 by involving family members in their businesses so that they can make additional contributions to retirement plans for family members as well. Despite this desired Leverage, there are limits to how much Leverage you can achieve through retirement plans.

To increase the amount of "retirement plan-like" benefits their families can enjoy, Doctors can look to investment vehicles that offer similar benefits to retirement plans. Life insurance is the investment vehicle that has the characteristics that are most similar to those of retirement plans. Cash value life insurance always offers tax-free accumulation and, in Ohio, offers the highest level of asset protection. Though life insurance premiums are not tax deductible, the funds come out of the policy through tax-free policy loans and withdrawals. For those of you who are familiar with Roth IRAs, cash value life insurance can be seen as an unlimited Roth IRA that also offers death benefit protection.

The Roth IRA is a type of individual retirement account in which contributions are made with after tax (nondeductible) dollars. If certain requirements are met, earnings accumulate within the Roth IRA tax-free and no federal income tax is levied when qualifying distributions are taken from the Roth IRA. The major restrictions of the Roth IRA are that only $2,000 per year can be invested into a Roth IRA and funds cannot be accessed before age 59½. When compared to a Roth IRA, the benefits of life insurance are that the annual premiums are practically unlimited and the funds can be accessed before age 59½. These benefits make cash value life insurance a very attractive alternative or complement to retirement plans.

The Ultimate College Savings Tool

When we have children, most of us want to give them every opportunity to succeed and protect them from unnecessary pain. Lesson #4 showed you how to financially protect your family from your premature death, yet protecting children from your death is not enough to ensure their financial success. In Chapter 1-3, we discussed the Leverage of effort and education. Obviously, the more education we receive, the greater opportunity we have to succeed. No one knows this better than a highly trained Doctor.

For this reason, a common dream of American parents is to send their children to college to take advantage of this opportunity. Physicians' families often stress the importance of business school, law school and medical school. Their children do not need to go to work right after college to support themselves, so they have an advantage over students who can't afford to continue their education and must begin working right away.

We all want to help our children pay for college and any additional education we can afford. We can make investments to save for college, but that doesn't ensure that there will be enough to pay for college if we pass away. For that reason, we have to buy some life insurance if it is important to give our children every opportunity to succeed.

Doctors should understand that they have to invest for their children's educational expenses and they have to buy life insurance to guarantee the funds will be there even if they aren't alive to see the child off to college. Doctors should also understand the analysis in the last chapter that explained how life insurance outperforms mutual funds after you factor in tax costs. For this reason, Doctors should make investments in life insurance to protect their children from a premature death and to provide a tax-efficient investment alternative for savings for college. This one tool can handle educational expenses whether you live to see your children off to college or if you die prematurely.

The Diagnosis

You have already learned that life insurance is flexible and efficient. It can offer income protection, asset protection, tax-efficient wealth accumulation and liquidity benefits. The applications of the life insurance can range from the traditional buy-sell, estate planning and income replacement options to more creative applications like retirement enhancing and college savings funding.

So far, you have made it through eight Lessons to Working Less and Building More. Within these lessons, there are dozens of practical applications. It may seem very overwhelming to manage all of this within a financial plan. It is overwhelming! This is why you need to work with an experienced team of advisors who can help you analyze the different options that may help you most efficiently Leverage your assets to meet your planning goals.

LESSON 9

Protect Your Family's Wealth from Estate Tax & Fees

For families wishing to preserve wealth as it passes from one generation to the next, estate planning is an important part of the comprehensive financial plan. Hard work, the proper use of Leverage, the protection of assets, and wise investing can all be undone by estate and inheritance taxes. By making estate planning a priority early on, you can avoid unnecessary taxes and ensure that the wealth you build will benefit your family for generations to come.

It is not just estate and inheritance taxes you can avoid by implementing a comprehensive estate plan. Consider that a proper estate plan can help you avoid:

- **Accidental disinheritance of family members.** Each year, millions of Americans title property in joint ownership without realizing that this form of ownership supersedes their Wills, leaving the property to their joint owner rather than to those they named in their Wills. This "disinheritance risk" might be lurking in your estate plan right now.
- **The costs and delays of probate.** These can be significant if not planned for in advance.
- **Future generations losing funds through irresponsibility, lawsuits or divorce.** All of these can be prevented by savvy estate planning today.

In this Lesson, you will learn about tools you can use to reduce—and even eliminate—estate taxes, avoid disinheritance risk, avoid probate and address "problem assets" such as pensions, IRAs, and family businesses. Specifically, you will learn how to preserve your estate by using such tools as Wills and Living Trusts, life insurance policies, Irrevocable Trusts, Family Limited Partnerships, Limited Liability Companies and charitable planning. This lesson includes a brief review and commentary on the status of the federal Estate Tax. At this writing, no one can predict what Congress will do. One thing is relatively certain: The scheduled 2010 repeal of the federal estate and gift tax will not happen. This is one of the more dynamic areas of the law and one that must undergo significant change in the near future. Therefore, the material contained in Lesson 9-1 may become outdated. To obtain the most current information, we encourage our readers to visit our website at www.forohiodoctors.com for the latest legislative changes regarding the estate tax.

9-1

The Truth About the Estate Tax Repeal

It is true in a limited sense that Congress "repealed" the estate tax as part of the 2001 Tax Relief Act. If you die in the year 2010—and only in 2010—the estate tax will indeed be repealed for you (unless, as is likely, Congress acts in late 2009 to "un-repeal" the repeal). Beyond this simple statement; however, there is much uncertainty. There is a strong likelihood that estates will be taxed heavily in the foreseeable future. Let's look at the facts surrounding the supposed repeal so we can understand what challenges we face.

The Estate Tax Repeal

The temporary Estate Tax Repeal has begun and is scheduled to be fully phased in by 2010. Before that time, the law reduces the estate tax on the estates of those who die during the intervening "transitional" period. It does this in two ways. First, in a provision that benefits all estates, it steadily increases the individual exemption amount. The exemption amount was $675,000 per person for 2001. Under the Economic Growth and Taxation Relief Reconciliation Act (EGTRRA) of 2001, it rose to $1 million per person in 2002 and 2003; $1.5 million per person in 2004 and 2005; and $2 million per person in 2006, 2007, and 2008. The exemption amount in 2009 is $3.5 million per person, but the federal estate tax is scheduled to be repealed completely in 2010!

Each taxpayer has one of these federal estate tax exemptions, but one of the cruel tricks in the Internal Revenue Code is that, for married couples, only the exemption of the second to die is automatic. Married taxpayers must affirmatively claim the exemption of the first to die by (a) having wills or trusts properly drafted to invoke the exemption of the first to die, and (b) have their asset ownership and beneficiary designations arranged in a manner that will not sabotage the wills or trusts. Jointly owned assets cannot be exempted.

With proper documents and properly coordinated asset ownership in 2009, a couple with a $7 million estate could die and avoid all estate taxes with relatively straightforward—albeit comprehensive—estate planning. It is important to note that many states still impose a separate state estate tax. Ohio is one such state, and the exemption is only $338,333.

Evaporation Of The Repeal

You may have noticed that we used the term "temporary" in a few places. This was not an accident. The current repeal is only a temporary repeal. If you live another few years, there is likely to be no repeal or tax rate reduction whatsoever. This begs the question, "Is this repeal real or simply a fairy tale?"

In the fairy tale of Cinderella, when she did not return to her home by the time the clock struck midnight, her fine clothes turned to rags and her carriage turned into a pumpkin. Similarly, the estate tax repeal becomes fully effective January 1, 2010. However, unless the entire estate tax repeal is re-approved by Congress prior to 2011, the clock strikes midnight for the repeal and the tax law returns to where it was before EGTRRA was enacted. Of course, Congress and the White House could—and probably will—change the tax law before 2010. No one truly knows whether the repeal will be re-approved before 2010. Doctors certainly should not gamble their family's entire estate plan on this uncertainty.

It is important to understand that, in the absence of a re-approval of the repeal, the estate tax is not simply reinstated at the lower tax rates and larger exemptions enjoyed in 2009. Rather, the exemption amount is returned to the level allowed by the law as it existed in 2001 (a relatively minor $1 million per person exemption) and the marginal tax rates are again raised to a top rate of 55%. In this regard, if the repeal is not re-approved, most of the estate tax reduction gained over the 10-year period will be lost.

When Congress passed this legislation, the budget office was projecting multi-trillion dollar surpluses in the federal government. This was back in the Spring of 2001, before the economy continued to falter, before the terrorist attacks of September 11, 2001 and before the prolonged War on Terror. Beginning in 2007 and continuing for the foreseeable future under the Obama administration and the current Congress, the United States will undoubtedly have some of the largest budget deficits in the history of the country. In addition, the dollar has depreciated against the Euro and other currencies since EGTRRA. The federal government can no longer afford to give away predicted future surpluses. In fact, it may have to take back some of the funds it has already given away just to balance a budget without the expenses of war. With a continued effort in the Middle East, Afghanistan, and other parts of the world, and significant budget deficits, new sources of tax income will continue to be a necessity.

Experts predict that the estate tax arena will be the first one targeted, as the 2001 repeal only helped the wealthiest 1% of taxpayers—a small enough minority that politicians won't be overly concerned about a public relations nightmare. Certainly, a rescission of the estate tax repeal would be easier to pass than a further reduction of social security benefits (which most people over age 65 utilize).

Even if the fairy tale does become reality and the estate tax repeal continues beyond 2010, the gift tax will remain intact. The 2001 Act did not repeal the gift tax imposed on gifts in excess of the lifetime gift exemption. This exemption increased to $1 million in 2002 with no further increases slated. This may seem strange, but it does make some sense. You have to die to trigger estate taxes. We don't think many people would die to take advantage of low estate tax rates in a given year. However, gifts are made during one's lifetime. If you had an ability to make unlimited lifetime gifts without tax, there would be a serious threat to the tax system. People could play a big economic shell game, moving money to taxpayers in lower brackets and reclaiming the funds when it suits them. This could basically eliminate all state income tax revenue and make tracking funds almost impossible.

What did happen in 2001 was that the gift tax rates were scheduled to be reduced to the same tax rates that applied to estate taxes until 2010. Then, in the year where there may not be any estate taxes, gift tax rates will be capped at 35%. Incidentally, 35% was the top marginal income tax rate when EGTRRA was passed. There was good reason for linking the top gift tax and income tax rates. Congress decided to retain the gift tax to discourage taxpayers from making tax-free gifts of income-producing property to family members in lower income tax brackets. Such transfers would be an easy way to reduce the overall income tax burden on the family. Although it will still be possible to make such transfers after the potential estate tax repeal, the continuation of the gift tax will act as a "toll charge" for taxpayers engaging in this type of planning.

Hidden Tax Hikes With The Repeal

Another problem with the supposed repeal is that one new tax appeared while another tax exemption was eliminated. In other words, some families are already paying higher taxes at death under the new law and many other families will pay substantially more tax if the repeal stays in effect. Let's review some of the implications of the repeal so you can see how this repeal may actually cost most families more in taxes.

1. **State estate taxes have re-appeared, so total taxes are higher!** Prior to the "repeal," the estate of a wealthy family was entitled to a federal estate tax credit for state death taxes paid by the estate. Essentially, while the federal estate tax rate was capped at 55%, the federal government kept 39% of the total tax and gave 16% to the various states (this was called a "sponge tax" because the states soaked up their piece of the total tax). Thus, most states had no need to impose their own estate tax other than the amount they would get from the federal return. This scheme was repealed by EGTRRA and effective for individuals dying after 2004.

   The estate tax reduction eliminated the states' piece of the estate tax as of 2004. The states no longer receive any of the federal estate tax. The federal government now actually keeps more of the taxes it collects than it did before the repeal.

   The states were not happy losing out on tax revenue. To fight this tax loss, many states instituted their own version of estate taxes, sometimes called "state inheritance taxes." These states charge a tax on the assets that are left as an inheritance in their jurisdiction. As of 2008, 23 states (including the District of Columbia) currently impose their own state estate (or inheritance) tax, in addition to the federal estate tax. These taxes are imposed at rates up to 16% of the value of the estate. Ohio, of course, already had a stand-alone 7% state estate tax, which it continues to collect, but for which taxpayers no longer receive a credit against their federal estate tax.

As a result, Doctors' families can actually pay combined federal and state taxes of over 50% of the value of the estate at death. Obviously, the only winners in this poorly planned scenario were the federal and state tax agencies. ***Taxpayers are worse off under the "repeal" than before it! Do most people understand this? No!*** Most Americans think it was a good thing for them. The well-informed know better. The well informed also know that every taxpayer will suffer from a repeal when it comes to selling appreciated assets, as seen below.

In Ohio, there is no "state" estate tax for estates under $338,333. However, as shown in the tax table below, estate taxes for estates above $338,333, can be fairly significant. By implementing proper estate tax planning techniques as explained further in this Chapter, the Ohio estate tax "bite" can be reduced.

Ohio Estate Tax Table

Net Taxable Estate	Tax Rate
More than $338,333, but not more than $500,000	$13,900 + 6% of excess more than $338,333
More than $500,000	$23,600 +7% of excess more than $500,000

2. **Any "repeal" means a loss of basis step-up at death.** Currently, whether rich or poor, the 2nd generation does not pay capital gains taxes on the sale of inherited appreciated assets when they sell them. This is because the current law readjusts the income tax cost basis of most inherited assets to their value on date of death; the so-called "step-up" in basis. However, wealthier taxpayers pay the federal and state estate taxes on the total value of the asset (which is a much higher rate than capital gains tax) at the date of death of the decedent.

The *quid pro quo* for repeal of the estate tax was the loss of step-up in income tax basis at death. Before repeal, as stated above, most appreciated property (but not IRAs, retirement plans or annuities) owned by a decedent receives a "step-up" in tax basis equal to its value at the date of death. Under EGTRRA, property acquired from a decedent will generally retain the decedent's tax basis after December 31, 2009. This is known as "carryover" basis. When the recipient eventually sells the property, he or she will be compelled to compute the gain using the decedent's cost basis. In most cases, the decedent's basis will be less than the date-of-death value, resulting in an increased capital gains tax.

EGTRRA, however, contains two major exceptions to carryover basis. These exceptions permit the executor of an estate to "step-up" the basis of certain property. The first exception permits the executor to step-up the income tax cost basis of property passing to a non-spouse beneficiary to $1.3 million; the second exception permits the executor of an estate to step-up the income tax basis of property passing to a surviving spouse to $3 million.

For larger estates, the additional capital gains taxes will take a large bite out of any potential estate tax savings. Moreover, there will be an increase in administrative difficulty and an increased cost in determining the basis of assets purchased 20, 30, 50 or more years ago by now-deceased relatives. Congress has done this before. It eliminated stepped-up basis in the 1980s, creating such a documentation nightmare that it *retroactively* repealed its imprudent action 3 years later.

3. **The "repeal" leaves IRD alone:** In addition to the estate tax, income tax must be paid on certain assets left in a decedent's estate at death, which would have been subject to income tax had the decedent lived. This tax is levied on what is called income in respect of a decedent ("IRD"). The classic examples are amounts left in pensions, profit-sharing plans and individual retirement accounts. Because combined federal and state income taxes—including those characterized as IRD taxes—can be as high as 45%, and estate taxes range from 45% to 49% during the transitional period, the combined tax rate can escalate to more than 70% on IRD! This means less than 25% of certain assets could go to your heirs at death unless you make a plan to avoid this serious problem. Because most doctors accumulate the bulk of their wealth in various types of "qualified plans" subject to IRD, special attention should be given to these types of assets during the estate tax planning process.

4. **Beware of and plan for the Generation Skipping Tax (GST).** The Generation Skipping Tax (GST) is a hefty tax imposed in addition to the gift and estate tax if you leave assets (directly or in trust) for the benefit of your grandchildren or later generations. Congress implemented this tax in 1986 so families could not leave all of their wealth in trust for future generations and avoid federal estate tax forever. The goal of the GST is to impose tax at each generation. For example, if a Doctor and his wife desire to leave assets in their estate plan to their grandchildren, the generation skipping tax could be triggered depending upon the amount of assets left to the Doctor's grandchildren.

In the 2001 Economic Growth Tax Relief Reconciliation Act (EGTRRA Tax Act), Congress established amounts that are exempt from the GST tax so long as proper estate planning is put in place and certain tax elections are made. The GST exemption is equal to the estate tax exemption. In 2009 the GST exemption amount is $3.5 million, but in 2010, as with the estate tax, the GST is repealed. The GST exemption resurfaces in 2011 at only $1,120,000 (indexed for inflation). Assets transferred to "grandchildren" in excess of the permitted GST exemptions are taxed from 45% (2009) to 55% (2011). The GST tax is in addition to the gift and estate tax. If the transfer is subject to both GST and gift/estate tax, the tax could be more than the transfer—yes, you read that correctly—the tax could exceed 100% of the transfer.

The planning necessary to avoid this tax and to leverage your GST exemption can be confusing, but extremely powerful. The goal is to utilize your GST exemption so that we ***skip the tax*** in future generations. A GST-skipping trust can benefit your children, grandchildren, great-grandchildren, etc. and never be subject to estate tax. The goal is not skip your children for purposes of distribution, just to skip them for purposes of estate tax.

As an oversimplified example, assume that your children inherit $1 million from you and that your children and future generations will each be subject to estate tax at 50%. If you leave your $1 million outright to your children instead of in trust, and each generation does the same thing, your $1 million will be eroded to $125,000 in 4 generations simply because each generation paid estate taxes. However, if you planned ahead to properly leverage your GST exemption, the $1 million could stay in trust for your children, then your grandchildren, then your great-grandchildren and NEVER be subject to estate tax.

The bottom line is that the GST is something about which doctors need to be aware when planning their estate because of the potentially high tax rates involved. Additionally, in light of the legislative changes in the estate planning arena taking place in Washington, D. C. at the time this book is going to press, we encourage our readers to visit our website at www.forohiodoctors.com for updates regarding the GST and GST estate planning recommendations.

The Diagnosis

There has been a lot of talk about the estate tax repeal, but for many Doctors the result is a tax increase. And the tax law change is only temporary. Even if it becomes permanent (which is highly unlikely), new taxes have emerged on the state level and capital gains on the federal level that fill the tax void left by a repeal. If you truly want to see that your estate passes on to your family, you must implement an estate plan for your family's benefit and not rely on the government to help you. The following chapters in this Lesson will help you do this.

9-2

Wills & Living Trusts

A Will and Living Trust are the foundation to any estate plan. Without these two tools, your family's wealth will become public information and the government will decide who gets what assets when you die. In this chapter, we will discuss the importance of Wills and Living Trusts and how to avoid unnecessary pitfalls of Living Trusts that can trap unaware families.

The Government's Will

Are you surprised to know that you already have a Will even if you have never written one or had an attorney draft one? It is true. If you die without a Will, your property will pass under the scheme your state government has written for all of its citizens. This is what is known as dying "intestate." While this may seem like a good thing, it probably is not because there is no guarantee that the way the government will split up your estate is the way you would want your property to be divided.

There are various negative consequences of a state government's Will. While the precise rules vary among the 50 states, typically the laws are very rigid and formulaic. Usually, all of your nearest relatives get a piece of your property but no one else does—not friends, cousins, charities or anyone else. Furthermore, no one gets more than the state-allotted share, even if it's seemingly unfair. Often, this ends up hurting the surviving spouse. In this all-too-common scenario, in Ohio and many other states, the decedent's grown children may get some of the money meant for the surviving spouse, even if it means the surviving spouse then has too little to support his or her lifestyle. In larger estates, this could have the very impractical effect of creating an estate tax payable when the first spouse dies if the children's intestate share of the estate exceeds the federal exemption amount.

Moreover, the absence of a Will often leads to expensive and lengthy court battles by family members contesting the division of assets. Sometimes family members produce a questionable Will in court, trying to establish a claim to a portion of the estate. Once again, this can be avoided by having a valid Will in place.

If you have minor children and both parents die without a Will, the courts will decide who becomes the legal guardian of your children. What parents would want to have an unknown judge decide who will care for their children after they pass away? Moreover, your minor children will receive their share of your estate when they turn 18 rather than at some more appropriate later age that you could otherwise specify. Avoid this tragedy and create a valid Will, including an Appointment of Guardian, sooner rather than later. Among other things, under your Will you could leave your children's share in trust for their benefit until age 30 or 35. Better yet, you could leave their share in trust for their lifetimes, allowing them to become trustee at a certain age, so that their inheritance would remain protected from divorce.

The Need For A Will *and* A Living Trust

Having a Will is certainly better than not having a Will. However, your entire estate will be stuck in the probate process if you only have a Will. Probate is the process established by the state under which the Probate Court publicly administers your Will. Probate is time-consuming, a matter of public record and quite costly in Ohio and many other states. In most states, knowledgeable advisors combine a Living Trust with a short Will called a "pour-over Will" when planning for Doctors. This combination ensures the vast majority of the estate will avoid probate and the details of your estate plan will remain private. Before we examine how a Living Trust works, we must first see why it is so important to avoid probate.

The Pitfalls of Probate

Delays. Probate often takes between one to two years to complete. During that time, your beneficiaries must wait for their inheritances. Perhaps worse, the representatives of your estate may have to petition the court for permission to conduct any transactions involving your estate's assets during this time. This can make it unnecessarily difficult to sell estate property or invest estate assets during the probate process.

Costs. Probate can be very costly, incurring expenses that can be avoided. These expenses include additional legal fees, executor's commissions and the costs associated with marshalling assets. In Ohio, like many other states, these probate fees are assessed on your gross estate—not taking into account any mortgages on your assets! For example, if you die owning, say, $1 million worth of real property that has a mortgage of $800,000, your estate could pay probate fees based on the $1 million fair market value, or approximately $50,000. Many county probate courts in Ohio have general guidelines as to how an attorney may charge for probate estate administration services. Some county courts permit attorneys to charge on a percentage basis and others permit an attorney to charge on an hourly basis. As a general rule, probate attorney costs can run anywhere between 4% and 8% of the gross value of the estate and an attorney is generally permitted to also charge an estate for extraordinary services rendered, such as preparation of estate tax returns.

Privacy. Probate is a public process in all states. Anyone interested in your estate can find out who inherits under your Will; how much he or she inherits; the beneficiaries' addresses; and more. While you may not be famous or worry about the newspapers exploiting this information, you should think of your beneficiaries—your surviving family members. They certainly will not appreciate the many financial advisors and telephone solicitors calling them with "hot tips" on investments or the unwelcome efforts of less scrupulous individuals who try to take advantage of recent inheritance recipients. These people find beneficiaries by examining probate records. They know who they are and how much "found money" they have to invest.

What seems fair to some may seem completely unfair to others. This is definitely the case with privacy and probate. Probate is designed primarily to make certain all creditors are paid, and to make sure that all potential beneficiaries are given an opportunity to review the Will and make objections. For this reason, the Will has to be public. When you die, it could take a very long time just to track down all potential beneficiaries (even if they live abroad) to give them formal, legal notice. Not only will your intended heirs have to wait a very long time, but they may also lose a significant part of an inheritance to people you haven't spoken to in decades. Even if the probate process does distribute your assets to the people you intended, they still have to pay the costs of administering this process.

Control. In probate, the court controls the timing and final say-so on whether or not your Will—and the wishes expressed in your Will—are followed. Your family must follow the court orders and pay for the process as well. This can be extremely frustrating.

Double Probate. If you own real estate outside of Ohio, your Will must be probated *again* (in an ancillary proceeding) in each state where real property is located. This is a burdensome proceeding that becomes very time consuming and expensive.

You are probably thinking, "In what sort of situation would anyone choose to use a Will as the estate planning document of choice when probate is this unappealing?" One such situation could be where the relationships among family members are so contentious, that it may make sense to consider allowing a probate judge to preside over some or all of the estate. However, as a general rule we believe it makes far more sense to avoid the time and expense of probate by choosing a Living Trust.

The Problem-Solver: A Properly Designed and Executed Living Trust

As mentioned earlier, a Living Trust is a legal document that provides direction for the use of your assets both while you are alive and at the time of your death. It is called a Living Trust because as long as you are living and competent, it is revocable, meaning you can change it at any time before your death. During your life, the assets transferred to the trust are managed and controlled by you, as the Trustee (or you and your spouse as co-trustees), just as if you owned them in your own name or jointly. When you die, these trust assets pass outside the public probate process to whomever you designated in the trust. Other benefits of the Living Trust include:

- Avoiding the unintentional disinheritance caused by joint tenancy or joint ownership (this happens in most 2nd marriages)
- Preventing court control of assets if you become incapacitated
- Protecting "Special Needs" beneficiaries
- Provide for management of your assets if you are incapacitated, and for the assets of loved ones when you die

"Funding the Trust"

The transfer of assets to the Living Trust—and the preparation of proper beneficiary designations for IRAs, Qualified Plans, Annuities, and Life Insurance—is known as "funding the trust." If you create a trust and don't properly fund the trust, it will not accomplish much of what it was supposed to accomplish. This is like building a car and not putting an engine in it. If you want to obtain the intended benefit from your trust, you must fund it!

When you transfer assets to your Living Trust while you are alive, you maintain 100% control over these assets as though you still own them in your own name. For stocks, bonds, bank accounts, home, and any other assets, the process of transferring an asset to your Living Trust is the same. Many assets can be changed with simple forms. Deeds are needed to re-title real estate. If the asset is jewelry or artwork that has no official ownership record, an "assignment" or "bill of sale" document is used to properly transfer ownership to your Living Trust.

These ownership changes will transfer the name of the registration or deed to "John and Jane Doe, Trustees of John Doe Revocable Living Trust," rather than "John Doe" as it now reads. As Trustee of the trust, you have the same power to buy, sell, mortgage, or invest as you did before. Further, because the trust is revocable, you can always change beneficiaries, remove or add assets, or even revoke your trust entirely.

The transfer of assets to the Living Trust is a necessary activity. While it has no income tax ramifications at all (you are still treated as the owner for income tax purposes and report income on your regular 1040), it is crucial to gain the probate-saving and privacy benefits afforded to you at the time of your incapacity or death. Below is a list of some of the valuable benefits of a trust that allow you to achieve important estate planning goals without any imposition upon your quality of life. The benefits of a trust are:

You may name yourself or someone else as Trustee. You need not name yourself as the Trustee of your Living Trust, although most people do. Many married couples name their spouse as co-trustee. You could name an adult child, another relative, or close friend or even a corporate Trustee, like a local bank or trust company. However, if you do not like the way the outside Trustee is handling the trust, you retain the power to remove him.

When you die or become disabled, your successor Trustee will take over. If you are the Trustee while you are alive, you will name, in your Living Trust, one or more individuals (or possibly a corporate Trustee) as the successor Trustee. That person or entity will take over the Trustee duties when you die or become disabled...and you may define what constitutes disability. Upon your death, the successor trustee's duties involve collecting income or benefits due your estate, paying your remaining debts, making sure the proper tax returns are filed, and distributing your assets according to the trust instructions. This person or entity acts like an executor for a Will. However, unlike a Will, actions under a Living Trust's directions are not generally subject to court interference or supervision, or public scrutiny.

You decide when your beneficiaries receive their inheritances. Another significant advantage of a Living Trust over a Will is that you, rather than the court, decide when and how your beneficiaries get their inheritance. Because the court is not involved, the successor Trustee can distribute assets right after your final affairs are concluded, or even make partial distributions during the administration of your trust.

If you choose, assets need not be distributed right away. Instead, you may direct that they stay in your trust, managed by your individual or corporate Trustee, until your beneficiaries reach the age(s) at which you want them to inherit. One of the advantages to distributing assets in this manner is that while the assets remain in the trust prior to distribution, they are protected from creditors—a feature that may interest you if you have concerns about your heir's creditors or potential future divorce.

The successor Trustee must follow your Trust instructions. Your successor Trustee (as well as your primary Trustee if it is not you) is a fiduciary—a legal term meaning that there is a legal duty to follow the Living Trust instructions and to act in a reasonably prudent manner. Trustees must treat the Living Trust as a binding legal contract, and must use their "best efforts" to live up to the obligations of the contract. If successor Trustees mismanage the trust by ignoring the instructions in your Living Trust, they could be legally liable.

Tax Benefits Of The Living Trust

For many physician (and other wealthy) families, there is a financial blunder hidden in their estate plans. Many couples plan to provide for the surviving spouse by having the first spouse simply leave everything to the surviving spouse. Most Americans, in fact, don't know any other way to leave money to support the survivor. *This mistake may cause your family to pay hundreds of thousands of dollars in unnecessary estate taxes!* Advisors to affluent clients (like Doctors) always suggest the use of a tool that helps affluent clients preserve their estates. This tool is the Living Trust that contains provisions to create "A-B Trusts" upon the death of the first spouse. Because of reasons you will learn later in this chapter, the Living Trust may also be referred to as an A-B Living Trust.

We will now discuss how you can take advantage of tax breaks afforded those who properly utilize the A-B Living Trust. The tax breaks are the Unified Tax Credit (UTC) and the Unlimited Marital Deduction (UMD).

UTC And UMD

To understand why you should not simply leave everything to your surviving spouse, you must first understand the two fundamental creatures of our estate tax system: the unified estate tax credit and the unlimited marital deduction.

The Unified Estate Tax Credit (UTC). The UTC translates into a dollar amount which can be left by a decedent estate tax free (commonly called the "estate tax exemption"). The amount of estate tax—the "unified credit"—avoided by the 2009 exemption is $1,455,800.

We often explain the UTC as a "get-out-of-estate-taxes-free" card, like in the board game Monopoly. Every one of us gets one of these cards to use either during our lives or at the time of our death. However, the card is non-transferable and, if not used at death, is lost forever.

The unlimited marital deduction (UMD). The UMD rule means that a decedent can leave an unlimited amount to a surviving spouse without any estate tax—provided both spouses are US citizens.

Unfortunately, when thinking about their estate plans, too many married couples look at the UMD as their solution. They simply leave everything to their spouse, using the UMD to avoid all estate taxes. While this effectively eliminates all estate taxes at the first death, it is a "penny-wise-and-pound-foolish" mistake. Because they failed to do proper planning, the first spouse wasted his or her UTC, or "get-out-of-estate-taxes-free" card. If it wasn't used at the time of the first death, it is gone forever.

While this seems innocuous when the first spouse dies, the IRS gets you back when the second spouse dies. At that point, the surviving spouse's estate can only use one exemption. That means everything over the single exemption amount will be subject to estate taxes—at a rate of up to 45%.

To illustrate this point, let's take a look at the case-study of Tina and Ike.

Case Study: Tina & Ike

Tina and Ike owned a home with $750,000 equity, have life insurance policies with combined death benefits of $2,000,000, had another $1,000,000 in a retirement plan, a business worth $500,000 and general investments totaling $750,000. They might not think of themselves as "wealthy," but to the federal estate tax authorities their $5 million estate is "estate taxable."

When Ike died in 2007 and left everything to Tina, there was no federal estate tax, because of the UMD. Tina inherited the entire estate and lived off of the earnings until she died in 2009.

As per Tina's will, the entire estate went to her children when she died. In 2009, the children are not taxed on the first $3,500,000 worth of property they inherited from their mother because of the UTC. The children do, however, pay federal estate taxes on the amount in excess of $3,500,000, or in our example, $1,500,000. The top tax rate in 2009 is 45%. This means $675,000 in *totally unnecessary* federal estate taxes!

The terrible fact about the case of Tina and Ike's children is that the entire $675,000 of taxes could have been avoided easily. Moreover, Tina still would have had the use of every dollar Ike left her. This could this have been achieved by implementing an A-B Living Trust.

Why Is It Called An A-B Living Trust?

The A-B Living Trust is a revocable, testamentary trust that contains "A-B" trust provisions. Not all living trusts contain such provisions, and even those that do are often not properly drafted or properly funded. The A-B Living Trust is the building block of estate planning as it helps maximize the exemptions and provides other benefits. When using an A-B Living Trust, the property of the first spouse to die is divided after death into two "buckets"—bucket "A" (or Trust A, often called the "Marital Trust") and bucket "B" (or Trust B, often called the "Family Trust"). Most people transfer assets equivalent to the UTC amount into bucket "B"—which, after the death of the surviving spouse, passes to children or other loved ones free of federal estate tax. The balance of the property, if any, is then transferred to "Trust A," which becomes the "Marital Trust" for the surviving spouse. During his or her lifetime, the surviving spouse can be the full legal owner of Trust A. As Trustee, the surviving spouse can do virtually anything with the assets of the Marital Trust. This trust can be made completely revocable during the lifetime of the surviving spouse.

Trust B is different. The surviving spouse does not technically own Trust "B," but may benefit from it. He or she will have an ability to draw income or interest from the Trust; may be able to use the property (for example, live in the home); may have access to principal for "health, education, maintenance and support" (a special IRS term); and may use up to either 5% of the principal or $5,000 a year, whichever is greater, for any reason whatsoever.

After the death of the second (surviving) spouse, the Trust B assets pass to the beneficiaries without any federal estate taxes and, if properly drafted under Ohio law, with a reduced amount of Ohio estate tax. This is true even if the value of the assets has grown to equal more than the UTC amount.

Trust A, which belonged to the surviving spouse, will also be distributed to the named beneficiaries. First, all the debts and liabilities will be paid. Then depending on the year of the death, the wealth that is equivalent to the UTC amount will be transferred estate tax-free to the beneficiaries. If the value of the Trust A assets, when combined with the surviving spouse's personal assets, exceeds the UTC amount, then that portion of the estate will be subject to estate taxes. After paying the federal and state estate taxes, the assets will be transferred to the beneficiaries.

Case Study Revisited: Tina & Ike

Let's now assume that, during their lives, Tina and Ike hired an attorney to create a joint A-B Living Trust and they funded it properly. When Ike died, the A-B Living Trust created the B Trust and funded it with the UTC amount in 2007, which was $2 million. During the rest of her life, Tina had access to the income and principal of Trust B for her health, education, maintenance and support—nearly anything she needed. The remainder of the property—$3 million—funded the A Trust, which Tina could access and spend for whatever reason she wanted. She could live in the home as well.

When Tina died in 2008, the B Trust paid out directly to the beneficiaries of that Trust—their children. Because the B Trust qualified for Ike's UTC when it was funded, there is no estate tax on what is left in the Trust; regardless of whether it has grown above $2 million or been spent down to less than $2 million.

Any property left in the A trust will qualify for Tina's UTC. Thus, if there is less than $2 million in this trust when she died (and likely there is because she has been living on the interest and a portion of the principal of the $2 million), there would be no estate tax on this portion either. In this way, the A-B Living Trust—properly drafted and properly funded—would have saved Ike and Tina's family $900,000 in estate taxes.

Ohio Estate Tax Planning Options

As was indicated at the beginning of this Chapter, Ohio is one of the many states that has its own estate tax. Under current Ohio estate tax law there are a number of strategies for married couples that can minimize, and in some situations, eliminate the Ohio estate. These Ohio estate tax strategies are typically called the Ohio Life Estate Marital Deduction (OHLEMD) and the Ohio QTIP Deduction (OHQTIP). These estate tax avoidance strategies are unique to Ohio. However, these potential estate tax savings can only be accomplished only if the following requirements are met:

1. The living trust documents of the husband and wife provide for "QTIPable" survivorship trusts upon the death of the first spouse (a QTIP trust simply provides that all income from the decedent's trust must be payable to the surviving spouse), and

2. Upon the death of the first spouse, certain post-death elections are properly made on the Ohio estate tax return filed with the Ohio Department of Taxation.

Following these two steps can potentially reduce the Ohio estate tax of married couples in Ohio. Our experience is that most estate planning attorneys, who are concentrating on avoidance of federal estate tax, fail to put language in their documents that allow for minimization of the Ohio state estate tax despite the fact that a few paragraphs in the living trust can save heirs at least $21,000 in unnecessary Ohio estate tax.

The Diagnosis

Under both the federal and Ohio estate tax rules, any married couple whose total assets might put them above the estate tax exemption amount by the time they pass away (in 10, 20 or 30 years) should consider, at a minimum, an A-B Living Trust. Without such a Trust, one spouse is forfeiting his or her "get-out-of-estate-taxes-free" card. Additionally, a married couple in Ohio should consider including in their estate planning the use of OHLEMD and OHQTIP techniques. The next chapter is going to explain a very common and significant mistake many couples make. You will learn why a couple should never own any assets jointly or in their own names.

9-3

Joint Ownership & Disinheritance Risk

The most common way for married couples to own property is to own it jointly. Though this is very typical, it is completely inappropriate for Ohio Doctors and their families. Not only does this form of titling assets leave your assets unprotected from lawsuits, it also creates estate planning problems. By owning assets jointly, you can negate all the potential benefits from the work you may have done with your Living Trust. This is a serious problem to avoid if you want to build and preserve wealth. In this chapter, we will discuss the dangers of joint ownership.

The Dangers Of Joint Ownership

Joint ownership is the most popular form of ownership for Average Americans' real estate and bank accounts. This is not so for Doctors who know the risks and understand their options. With joint property, when one joint owner dies, property owned in joint ownership automatically passes directly to the surviving joint owner(s). Although jointly owned property passes outside of a Will and avoids the expense of probate, which may be desirable, joint ownership of assets can create serious problems and disastrous results.

Using joint ownership is almost always a big mistake. This is because joint ownership "overrides" Living Trusts and other estate planning. Joint ownership can ruin your estate plan. Let's examine how joint ownership can be harmful.

Joint ownership threatens your estate plan because any property you own jointly will pass automatically by right of survivorship to the surviving joint owner(s). In the eyes of the law, this automatic transfer takes effect the instant you die, before any Will or Living Trust can dispose of your property. In this way, your Will or Living Trust simply has no effect whatsoever on jointly held property. If you designate certain beneficiaries in a Will or Trust to receive your share of jointly held property, they will be "disinherited" as to that property because the surviving joint owner(s) will take title to the property. This avoidable tragedy occurs everyday because (a) people do not realize the dangers of joint ownership and (b) their advisors are not giving them adequate information.

The Other Negative Side Effects Of Joint Ownership

To fully understand the negative consequences of joint ownership, consider these stories:

1. William, a man in his late 60s, marries for the second time. Shortly after the wedding, he puts all of his significant property—his home, his winter vacation condominium and his stock portfolio—into joint ownership with his new wife. Within six months, William dies. The home, the condo and the stocks all go to William's new wife. His three children and eight grandchildren inherit virtually nothing, even though William had made ample provisions for them in his Will.

2. Susan's Will bequeathed her property equally to her son and daughter. Because her son lives near her and he pays her bills, Susan put her house, her safe deposit box and her bank account in joint ownership with him. When she dies, Susan's son will get all of the money in the bank account and deposit box, as well as the house, regardless of the Will provisions. Unless the son is extremely generous, the daughter will get nothing. Do you want to rely on your children's generosity to carry out your estate plan?

3. Assume the same situation as in #2, but add to the facts that the son has serious creditor problems. Overdue on $15,000 in credit card debts and a defaulted loan, the son's creditors can come after the bank account, the safe deposit box contents and, likely, the house the moment Susan dies. The only real beneficiaries of Susan's estate may be banks and finance companies.

4. Becky, a single mother in her thirties, is trying to build a college fund for her ten-year old son, Dylan. Becky has invested some of her excess income to buy old residential multi-family homes, which she and her partner fix-up and rent to owners. While her relationship with her partner has been strained at times, Becky nevertheless takes title to the investment properties in joint ownership with her partner without realizing that, if she dies before they resell the properties, her partner will take them all and leave nothing for Dylan.

Many well-intentioned people get stuck in these predicaments because they do not know any better and their advisors are not doing their jobs. Sometimes, owners may not even realize what type of ownership they have chosen. In other cases, people consciously decide to use joint ownership because they know it will avoid probate. Avoidance of probate is never a reason to use joint ownership. If your goal is to avoid probate, use a Living Trust rather than joint ownership. You will get many more benefits without any of joint ownership's pitfalls.

The Diagnosis

Joint ownership is the most common way to title assets and it does offer a way to avoid probate. However, joint ownership can create significant asset protection and estate planning problems. After reading this chapter, you should now know the dangers of joint ownership and should see the value of using a Living Trust as an alternative.

The next most common estate planning mistake results in the unnecessary wasting of 50% of life insurance proceeds. This problem, and various solutions to it, are explained in the next chapter.

9-4

Estate Planning with Life Insurance Policies and Irrevocable Trusts

This chapter will cover two important estate planning topics, the use of Irrevocable Trusts in estate planning and the use of life insurance.

Every Doctor's financial plan should include cash value life insurance because of (a) its ability to leverage cash, (b) tax-free growth and (c) ability to access cash values tax-free. These benefits of life insurance were discussed in Lessons #6, #7 and #8. This chapter is not going to re-visit how the cash value of life insurance can be a tax-efficient wealth accumulation vehicle, as that was covered in Lesson #8. Rather, this chapter focuses on the death benefit proceeds of life insurance. Many Ohio Doctors maximize their investments in cash value insurance policies for tax-efficient wealth accumulation. Other Doctor clients, who are usually older, often purchase second-to-die (or survivorship) insurance policies purely for the death benefit and without concern for cash value accumulation. That will be the "insurance" focus of this chapter. We will call such policies "estate planning life policies" or "EPLPs".

Similarly, every Doctor's estate plan should include, at some point, the use of Irrevocable Trusts for themselves and/or their beneficiaries. Properly structured Irrevocable Trusts can provide numerous benefits including estate planning, asset protection planning and estate tax planning.

Avoiding EPLP Pitfalls

Estate planning life policies (EPLPs) are life insurance policies purchased for the primary purpose of transferring wealth and creating liquidity for future generations. This is in sharp contrast to the purpose of the insurance policies discussed in Lessons #6, #7 and #8. The life insurance policies discussed in those chapters were created primarily for wealth accumulation, not wealth transfer.

For estate planning purposes, it is important that the EPLP proceeds not be subject to estate tax; that you remove them from your taxable estate. The following are two popular "strategies" for removing the EPLP proceeds from your taxable estate. Both have distinct drawbacks and pitfalls.

- **Having the spouse own the policy or be its beneficiary.** One popular method of sheltering EPLP proceeds from estate tax is to name your spouse as owner or beneficiary of the policy. As you learned previously, the IRS is happy to see you pass everything to the surviving spouse so that you forfeit your "get-out-of estate-taxes-free" card (unified tax credit). This is because when the surviving spouse dies, the IRS gets a piece of everything exceeding one exemption amount rather than only the amount exceeding two combined exemptions.

  A second pitfall of this approach is that you lose all control of the proceeds when you die. The assets will pass to your surviving spouse outright. If he or she spends them down, gets re-married and divorced or gets sued, then your planning just benefited someone other than your family members. As you'll see below, you can control the funds, even after you're dead, and keep them in the family for generations by using a special life insurance trust that dictates exactly how the funds can be used.

- **Having the children own the policy.** Another method of removing EPLP proceeds is to have your children own your EPLP and indicate that they will receive the proceeds at your death. They can apply for the policy, pay the premiums (with money you may gift to them) and receive the proceeds at your death. If the policy and the proceeds are outside your estate, no estate tax will be due at your death.

  However, there are some drawbacks to this strategy:

  - If the EPLP proceeds are paid to children, your surviving spouse may run short of funds to pay bills and support himself or herself. This can be a very big problem in the situation of second or third marriages, as children may not agree to support a step-parent.
  - If the EPLP policy is a cash-value policy (typical in estate-planning situations because it is permanent insurance), your kids may be tempted to borrow against the policy, thus reducing the future death benefit.
  - If any of your children get divorced, the EPLP policy may be considered a marital or community property asset of your children. Some of the cash value could end up going to an ex-son-in-law or ex-daughter-in-law.
  - If your children are still minors, the policy would have to be owned by a custodian or a guardian.
  - If your children own the policy jointly and any one of them is sued and becomes subject to a lawsuit judgment, the plaintiff may seize the entire policy in satisfaction of its debt.
  - Your children's spouses may have different ideas about how "their" money is to be spent.

The Irrevocable Life Insurance Trust

The wealthiest American families know they can avoid many of the pitfalls discussed above by creating Irrevocable Life Insurance Trust (ILIT) to be the owner and beneficiary of life insurance policies. As mentioned earlier, an ILIT is an Irrevocable Trust designed to purchase life insurance for the benefit of your children and grandchildren. Spouses can also benefit if the ILIT is properly drafted.

There are many benefits of having an ILIT. First, if the ILIT owns a policy, the policy is out of your taxable estate. Moreover, a properly structured ILIT can safeguard the proceeds from irresponsible children or their disgruntled spouses or creditors. The funds can then be used to pay estate taxes, provide an income stream, pay off debts, mortgages or notes and keep other valuable and needed assets intact for the family.

In many cases, the ILIT will use the insurance proceeds to buy illiquid assets, such as shares of a closely held business or real estate, from your estate to keep them in the family. A purchase of this type is a tax-neutral exchange, so no tax will be due on the asset itself. Alternatively, the trust can lend money to your estate, securing the loan with estate assets. This is sometimes done to pay the estate taxes that are due on other less liquid assets. Because estate taxes are due nine months after the date of death, this ability to have liquid cash available is crucial to avoid selling assets in a "fire" sale where the family may not get a reasonable price.

In either case, the estate will receive cash that can be used in a variety of ways. Later, the Trustee can distribute the assets to the trust beneficiaries, the surviving spouse and children. This can be done in a lump sum or, if desirable, the assets can be maintained in trust for their later benefit and use. Such trusts can be structured so that creditors of the surviving spouse, children, and even grandchildren will have no access to them—even in the case of potential lawsuits, bankruptcies and divorces. In this way, the ILIT can be an asset-protecting tool for many generations. The bottom line is that all the insurance proceeds are available to help pay estate taxes and provide cash for whatever need might arise. No distress sale is necessary to raise money to meet the tax obligations, and your family maintains control over the assets.

Lastly, we recommend that when designing and establishing an ILIT, a Doctor should consider incorporating some of the design features and protections we recommend for Irrevocable Trusts as set forth in Chapter #6-8, and as set forth further in this Chapter.

Accessing Irrevocable Gifts: A Valuable Secret

Quite often a client will ask us if there is a way to use an ILIT to own life insurance and still have access to the policy's cash values during retirement. Though many advisors unfamiliar with planning for Doctors would say "No," our estate planning attorney colleagues around the country do this on a regular basis for clients.

Essentially, the only persons who could access the cash values during your life would be the

ILIT beneficiaries. However, if the policy insures your life, then you cannot be the Trustee—or the beneficiary—of the ILIT. Thus, you personally could not have access to the cash values. However, if the policy insures only your life, then your spouse could have access to the cash values if she were a trust beneficiary. Further, if the policy was on your joint lives (often called a "survivorship" or "second-to-die" policy), your children or grandchildren trust beneficiaries could access the cash, or the Trustee could utilize cash values to benefit them. This could include paying college tuition. There are also more advanced combinations of legal entities and insurance policies that combine trusts, irrevocable gifts, LLCs, loans and life insurance policies to allow Doctors to protect assets, manage estate planning challenges and offer access in retirement should the Doctor need it. Advanced strategies like these are outside the scope of this book, but can be included in your comprehensive financial plan.

Irrevocable Trusts for Estate Planning, Estate Tax Planning and Asset Protection

In Chapter #6-8, we covered the asset protection advantages of Irrevocable Trusts and the various design options which should be considered in every Irrevocable Trust. Irrevocable Trusts can also have estate planning and estate tax benefits.

In this section we set out additional design options and suggestions for Irrevocable Trusts for use both in the estate planning arena as well for asset protection. We have also included a brief explanation and review of various Irrevocable Trusts commonly used for estate planning, asset protection and estate tax purposes.

Beneficiary Lifetime Shares in Trust- A Trust Design Suggestion

For years, it has been common in estate planning at the death of a Grantor to either (i) distribute assets outright to a beneficiary (in their own individual name); or (ii) stagger the distribution to a beneficiary based upon certain ages and over a period of years (i.e. make principal distributions at ages 25, and 35, then make the final distribution and close out the trust at age 45). Recently, a number of national trends have developed in the United States that weigh against distributing trust assets outright to individual beneficiaries in their own name. These trends include the drastic increase in the divorce rates, the increased potential for litigation, and the increased size of lawsuit judgments.

Irrevocable Trusts can protect assets from creditors of the beneficiary. Once assets are distributed from the trust to the beneficiary, the beneficiary's creditor can reach them. If instead, the assets remained in trust for the beneficiary's lifetime and the trust is properly designed (key design characteristics include distribution standards and trustee selection) and administered, the beneficiary does not "own" or "control" the trust assets for asset protection purposes. As a result, creditors cannot reach the assets inside the trust.

Case Study: Chris and John

Chris, a successful cosmetic surgeon, dies and establishes at her death an Irrevocable Trust for the benefit of her son, John. The trust has nearly $2,000,000 in assets held for the benefit of John. John worked midnight shifts and after a long shift, John has an accident while returning home, colliding with a school bus. The accident causes many injuries and the court awards judgments in excess of $5,000,000. John is devastated. His auto liability insurance policy only covers him for $1,000,000. Therefore, John's personal assets are exposed in the amount of $4,000,000. Fortunately for John, the inheritance he received from Chris was in trust. While the lawsuit will wipe out any assets that he owns personally, the $2,000,000 in the trust will be completely protected. If John had received his inheritance outright, the inherited insurance proceeds would have become personal assets and been available to his lawsuit creditors. The planning Chris put into place provided valuable protection for her son John that he could not have provided for himself.

The Irrevocable Trust Distribution Rights of a Trust Beneficiary- A Trust Design Option

The distribution design of the Irrevocable Trust established for a beneficiary will determine the level of asset protection a beneficiary enjoys from creditors.

Generally and historically, the typical trust distribution for beneficiaries has been based on "ascertainable standards," an IRS term that uses the words "health, education, maintenance and support." These types of trusts are also called Support Trusts.

The problem with this type of distribution right is that over time the law has evolved to the point where trusts with this "ascertainable standard" distribution may be vulnerable to certain creditor attacks. In other words, the creditor of a beneficiary who has this type of "ascertainable standard" trust distribution may be able to convince a court to force a distribution from the beneficiary's trust share because of these ascertainable standards.

For example, if a beneficiary needed to qualify for certain public or governmental assistance programs (i.e. nursing home care through Medicaid) and the beneficiary had a trust share with ascertainable standards, all of the assets in the Irrevocable Trust share would be accessible to the government agency and would have to be spent before the beneficiary could qualify for government assistance. For general creditors of a beneficiary in Ohio, as opposed to a governmental agency creditor, the protections afforded a trust beneficiary with an ascertainable standards trust share are codified in Ohio Revised Code Section 5805.04. These statutory protections are above average.

On the other hand, the best "distribution asset protection" for a trust beneficiary is afforded by a "wholly discretionary" trust. In other words, there is no ascertainable standard and instead, the distributions are based solely upon the "discretion" of the distribution trustee. With this type of distribution design, creditors of a trust beneficiary cannot force a distribution from, or access in any manner, the beneficiary's trust share. The requirements of a wholly discretionary trust are set forth in the Ohio Revised Code Section 5801.01 (Y).

The wholly discretionary trust is the most protected because it is the most restricted. The beneficiary has no absolute right to any distribution of principal. But in some circumstances, such as Special Needs or Medicaid planning, it is the safest type of protection for the doctor's loved ones.

The Trustee of an Irrevocable Trust Can Be A Beneficiary—A Trust Design Option

The trustee of the Irrevocable Trust has three primary duties: (1) to manage/administer the trust, (2) invest the trust assets and (3) handle the distribution of the trust assets. One trustee can handle all three functions. In many trusts, these three responsibilities are undertaken by a financial services trust company (i.e. a bank) acting as trustee. There are however, many options available for choosing a trustee of the Irrevocable Trust.

One option, if the trust beneficiary is responsible and up to the task, is to permit the trust beneficiary to manage/administer the trust and invest its assets. By doing this, the beneficiary trustee can be actively involved with the Irrevocable Trust created for his/her benefit. However, from an asset protection standpoint, "distribution" of the trust assets must be left to someone other than the trust beneficiary. Typically, this function is left to an "independent trustee" who is not related or subordinate to the beneficiary.

The independent trustee can be an attorney, accountant, financial advisor or a person with exemplary character, excellent business acumen and an understanding of trusts. The "asset protection" reason that the distribution function of the trust must be handled by an independent trustee is that if the beneficiary of the trust can distribute the trust assets to himself or herself, so can his/her creditors. In other words, if the beneficiary has access to the trust assets via the distribution power, his or her creditors can force a distribution from the beneficiary's trust share.

There is also one other related and very powerful trust design option a grantor should consider involving an independent distribution trustee. The Grantor can give the beneficiary of the trust, at a certain age, the right to hire and fire the independent distribution trustee.

Spousal Lifetime Access Trust ("SLATS")—An Irrevocable Trust That Can Provide Multiple Benefits to a Spouse

An Irrevocable Trust strategy that can provide multiple benefits, including asset protection benefits to a spouse and other trust beneficiaries (such as children or grandchildren), is a Spousal Lifetime Access Trust ("SLAT"). The SLAT is a type of Irrevocable Life Insurance Trust ("ILIT").

ILITs are very well established estate planning and asset protection tools (see Lesson 9-4 for further explanation of ILITs). The SLAT works as follows: a Doctor (also called a "grantor"), who would be the insured person in this arrangement, establishes an Irrevocable Life Insurance Trust and names as trust beneficiaries her husband and children. The trust owns the life insurance policy. The premiums for the life insurance are paid by the Doctor from her "separate property" in the form of gifts to the trust, typically on an annual basis.

The unique feature of this type of Irrevocable Life Insurance Trust is that the doctor's spouse can receive distributions of the accumulated cash value of the life insurance during his/her lifetime, hence the name SLAT, which can be tax free. The spouse of the Doctor can in some circumstances be named as a trustee and/or co-trustee, if there is a single life insurance policy in effect. The spouse could handle the investment and administrative trustee matters.

If there is a joint life or survivorship life insurance policy in place, the spouse cannot be a trustee since he is also an insured. An independent trustee or even an independent distribution trustee can also be appointed for increased asset protection purposes. The distribution rights of the spouse or the other beneficiaries can be the same asthose of a "support trust" which are based on health, education, maintenance and support (which, under Ohio law, provides above average asset protection) or they can be based upon a wholly discretionary trust standard (which provides superior asset protection in Ohio and elsewhere). The spousal access rights may also include loans and other withdrawal rights, however, such loans and withdrawals would reduce the insurance policy's death benefit.

If properly structured and designed, the SLAT can also provide that, upon the death of the grantor, the policy's death benefit will be payable to the trust and will be distributed to the spouse and the beneficiaries free of any income or estate tax.

The Family Bank Trust ("FBT")—An Irrevocable Trust Which Avoids Any Estate and Gift Tax

The Family Bank Trust (FBT) is an Irrevocable Trust that utilizes the annual gifting limits between spouses and takes advantage of certain grantor trust income tax strategies. Like most Irrevocable Trusts, it can retain and pass assets to beneficiaries in an asset protected manner.

In order to understand the FBT Trust, one must understand gifting terminology and fundamental gift tax laws. A person who makes a gift of money or property is called a "donor." A person who receives a gift of money or property is called a "donee."

First, spouses can transfer unlimited amounts of property between themselves without incurring any gift tax at the time of the transfer or gift.

Second, as is fairly well known, any person (donor), can make a gift, not to exceed a statutory amount, to another person (donee) each year without any gift tax consequences. For 2009 and 2010, the amount, called the "annual exclusion" amount, is $13,000. The IRS announces each year whether the amount will be adjusted for inflation. A donor can make as many "annual exclusion gifts" as he or she wants as long as it is not to the same donee. Many advisors recommend that doctors make annual exclusion gifts to children and grandchildren, but almost never advise using the annual exclusion for gifts to a spouse.

The FBT trust requires spouses to use their annual exclusion gifts for one another. This trust is designed to prevent its assets from being included in the estate of the donor doctor or the donee spouse and to pass more assets estate tax free to the beneficiaries (typically children) of the doctor and the spouse. If a married couple is (or will be) subject to federal estate tax and does not take advantage of the annual exclusion between themselves, they are effectively wasting $11,700 per year ($13,000 annual exclusion x 2 spouses x 45% federal estate tax rate) plus all the income and growth for as many years as they could have made the exclusion gifts.

The FBT trust works as follows: a Doctor (donor) creates an Irrevocable Trust for the benefit of her spouse (donee) during the spouse's lifetime. This trust is drafted so that any income it generates would be taxed to the donor and not the trust itself. The taxes paid by the doctor on the trust income are economically the same as making an additional annual contribution to the trust. Think of it this way: Because the donor is paying the taxes for the trust, the doctor's least protected (personally owned) assets are being minimized while the most protected (trust owned) assets are being maximized.

Also, the spouse of the Doctor can in some circumstances be named as either a trustee and/or a co-trustee. The spouse could handle the investment and administrative trustee matters. An independent trustee or even an independent distribution trustee can also be appointed for increased asset protection purposes. The distribution rights of the spouse or the other beneficiaries can be structured to provide superior asset protection.

Typically, the Doctor would make an annual gift to the FBT trust in an amount not to exceed $5,000 or 5% of the value of the trust assets whichever is greater, but not to exceed the annual exclusion amount ($13,000) for a given year. However, it is possible to increase the amount of annual contribution by using part of the $1 million lifetime gift exclusion so that $13,000 per year can be gifted from inception.

This type of trust may also be created by the Doctor's spouse for the benefit of the Doctor.

The Advance Inheritance Dynasty Trust—An Irrevocable Trust Which Can Have the Best of "The Asset Protection and Estate Planning Worlds"

The Advance Inheritance Dynasty Trust is an Irrevocable Trust that is:

1. Set up by a third party for the benefit of a doctor—typically the doctor's parent for the doctor's benefit "while" the parent is alive;
2. Funded with assets of the parent during either the lifetime of the parent (i.e. gifts) and/or at the parent's death (from the parents' estates);

3. Designed to remain in effect for perpetuity, in a state that allows perpetual trusts, such as Ohio;
4. Created in such a manner as to avoid estate transfer taxes which can occur from generation to generation (also called generation skipping taxes); and,
5. Designed to achieve maximum asset protection for its beneficiaries from generation to generation.

If structured properly, the Advance Inheritance Trust can achieve all of the planning objectives set forth in paragraphs 1-5 above. As described in Chapters 6-6 and 6-8, an Irrevocable Trust established by a third party for the benefit of a doctor can have the highest level of asset protection (+5). If you know that you will ultimately receive an inheritance from your parents or other family members, the Advance Inheritance Trust is the best way to receive it. Many parents understand that their physician children are particularly vulnerable to creditor claims. As a result, they understand the need to fully protect inheritances by establishing Advance Inheritance Trusts. If the parents' estate planner is not capable of implementing this advanced planning technique, doctors should consider introducing their planning team to their parents.

When appropriate, doctors should advise their parents that because of the unique risks of being a doctor, it would be helpful to you if they would leave your eventual inheritance to you in an Advance Inheritance Trust. Your advisory team can establish the Advance Inheritance Trust for you—your parents simply need to amend their Revocable Trust to name your Advance Inheritance Trust as the beneficiary of your inheritance instead of naming you personally. You can explain that your trust will protect you from creditors (including lawsuits, malpractice and divorce) and future estate taxes.

Case Study: Ophelia

Fred and Ethel have raised Ophelia, a wonderful daughter who has worked extremely hard to become a successful oncologist. Recently, Fred and Ethel have observed the stress that Ophelia has experienced as a result of an increased patient load and decreased income. Ophelia has explained to Fred and Ethel that she has been working so hard on an experimental new cancer treatment that her husband has threatened divorce. Fred and Ethel mentioned all this to their estate planning attorney who recommended they create an Advance Inheritance Trust for Ophelia's benefit.

The trust would be designed to allow Ophelia to serve as her own trustee and manage the assets of the trust. The trust could own any assets Ophelia would need (e.g., marketable securities, residence, vacation home, jewelry, artwork, automobiles, etc.) The trust would name an independent trustee (not Ophelia) to control when the trust makes distributions to Ophelia.

Ophelia's trust is also the perfect vehicle to own Ophelia's interest in her experimental treatment. Assuming that the treatment has little or no value yet, Fred and Ethel could gift sufficient assets to Ophelia's trust so that the trust could buy her interest at its fair market value. It is important that the transaction be structured as an arms length transaction so creditors cannot argue that they were prejudiced by a fraudulent transfer for less than fair market value. If the treatment is successful and the treatment explodes in value, all of the future appreciation is protected from creditors and estate taxes because it is owned by an Irrevocable Trust that is not includable in the taxable estates of either Ophelia or her parents.

Due to the fact that: (1) Ophelia did not create the trust, (2) her assets did not "fund" the trust and (3) most importantly, she does not own the assets (her Irrevocable Dynasty Trust does), the assets in the trust are not subject to any claims of Ophelia's creditors (including Fred and Ethel's disgruntled soon to be ex-son-in-law in a divorce action) and in most instances even the IRS. Yet, she gets to manage and invest the trust's assets—in short, Ophelia has control. So, if she is sued for malpractice and a litigant obtains a successful judgment against her, the litigant cannot attach, levy or execute upon the assets in the Irrevocable Dynasty Trust.

The Diagnosis

As you can see, through the proper use of estate planning and asset planning tools such as Irrevocable Trusts and life insurance, a Doctor not only can shelter, preserve and protect the hard-earned assets and property he or she has spent a lifetime making and accumulating, but a Doctor can also leave a protected legacy for his/her heirs for generations to come

Another way to own life insurance, and other assets, is in either an FLP or LLC. These tools will be discussed in the next chapter.

9-5

FLPs and LLCs as Estate Planning Tools

In Chapter 6-7, we explained how Doctors can use Family Limited Partnerships (FLPs) and Limited Liability Companies (LLCs) to shield assets from risks. In this Chapter, you will learn how FLPs and LLCs—in addition to being excellent asset protectors and income tax reducers—are also superior estate planning tools. In this chapter, we will discuss the estate planning benefits and offer a couple of case studies to help illustrate the power of these tools within a Doctor's estate plan.

Three Estate Planning Benefits

A Family Limited Partnership or Limited Liability Company has at least three major benefits for estate planning. Let us examine each one separately:

- **LLC Assets Avoid Probate and Allow Family Businesses to Continue.** Assets owned by your FLP/LLC do not go through probate. Only your interest in the FLP/LLC will, and even those interests may avoid probate if the interests are titled in the name of your Living Trust. If you structure your LLC so your intended beneficiaries eventually own most of the FLP/LLC shares when you die, these beneficiaries will control the FLP/LLC and its assets before you die. Your beneficiaries can more effectively control the FLP/LLC assets or business while the estate administration process continues its deliberation over distribution of your remaining membership interests. Because probate and trust administration can last several years, this continued control can be crucial for operating a business or real estate interests.
- **FLPs/LLCs allow you to get property out of your estate WITHOUT giving up control.** Because your estate only pays taxes on property you own at death, a common tax-saving strategy is to gift your property away during your lifetime. The property passes to people you wish to inherit your assets at the time of your death and the government gets a smaller share. The main objection you might

have to this type of gifting is that you will have to give up control of the property while you are still alive. That's where the FLP/LLC adds additional value.

If the FLP/LLC owns the asset(s), and you are the FLP general partner or LLC managing member, you get the best of both worlds. You can gift FLP/LLC interests to intended beneficiaries and remove the value of those interests from your estate, yet continue to control the FLP/LLC and all if its assets while you are alive. Let's see how this works by referring to the case study of Stewart's Mutual Funds.

Case Study: Stewart's Mutual Funds

Stewart, a 63-year-old psychotherapist, owned almost $1.1 million in mutual funds. He set up an FLP in 2009 to own the mutual funds, naming himself as the sole general partner. At the outset, he owned 2% of the FLP as general partner and 93% as limited partner, gifting 1% each to his five grandchildren. Since this 1% was worth approximately $13,000, the gifts to each grandchild were tax-free.

Stewart can continue to gift each grandchild $13,000 in FLP interests each year, completely tax-free. If Stewart lives to age 75, he will have given $780,000 worth of FLP interests to his grandchildren ($156,000 each), tax-free. This would equal 71% of the FLP.

This $780,000 will no longer be in his estate and not subject to either federal or Ohio estate tax. Moreover, any future growth of the gifted portion of the FLP will also be out of his estate.

Because Stewart's other assets put him in the 48% state and federal estate tax bracket, his tax savings using the FLP will be $374,400 (48% x $780,000). Because he is the FLP's sole general partner, Stewart retains control over the mutual fund investments while alive and can determine the amount of distributions. In this way, Stewart maintains significant control of his assets for his lifetime, pays less estate tax, and provides more for his grandchildren.

It is critical that the FLP agreement and the gift structuring must be carefully crafted or Stewart's retained control could be grounds for the IRS to rule that his gifted FLP interests must be brought back into his estate for tax purposes.

- **FLPs/LLCs Lower Estate Taxes on Assets They Hold:** You may not want to gift your entire FLP/LLC interests during your lifetime, or you may start such a gifting program too late to "give away" much of your wealth. In either case, you will die owning FLP/LLC interests, which are then subject to the estate tax. The issue thus becomes what valuation the IRS will attach to your remaining FLP/LLC interests. It may not be:

  your % ownership of the FLP/LLC x fair market value of the FLP/LLC assets

You might think that the IRS will determine the value of your remaining interest by simply multiplying the value of all the assets in the FLP by your remaining percentage of ownership of the FLP/LLC, but it may actually be much less because of powerful "discounting" rules that apply to minority interests in closely held entities.

Valuation Discounts With FLPs/LLCs

An important estate tax benefit of the FLP/LLC is that FLP/LLC interests often enjoy discounted values by the IRS. Business appraisers and valuation experts understand, and the IRS has historically been compelled to recognize, that a percentage ownership of an FLP/LLC is generally worth less than the assets it owns. If you own a $100 bill and hold it at death, then the IRS would assign it an estate tax value of $100. However, if you died owning a 20% interest in an LLC with four other family members, all with equal management rights, and the LLC owned $100, the IRS would allow a valuation of your 20% interest at a number well below $20! Let's explain why.

The standard question for appraiser is "What would a willing buyer pay a willing seller, neither one emotionally compelled to buy or sell, with all material facts disclosed." What a buyer is willing to pay a seller is affected by two factors: How marketable is the thing being appraised, and how much less is it worth if someone else controls it?

The IRS would first recognize a *lack of marketability* discount applicable to that interest, because your LLC interest is not really very marketable, reducing its value for estate tax purposes. There is likely not much of a market for your 20% LLC interest when the other LLC members are all family members. Who would want to own part of an LLC worth $100 when the other owners are members of one family? What would an outsider pay for such an interest? This discount is available even if you retain all the management rights in the LLC.

Second, because you own less than 50% of the LLC, the IRS will also recognize a *minority ownership* discount to your interest unless you have retained most or all of the management rights. Again, the IRS recognizes that there is very little market interest for shares of an LLC controlled by others.

Both of the aforementioned tax valuation discounts can be maximized by the proper drafting of the FLP/LLC agreement. Any provisions that restrict the transferability of any FLP/LLC interests will weigh toward a higher *lack of marketability* discount. Likewise, clauses that limit the control of minority interest-holders will support greater *minority ownership* discounts. In this way, with proper drafting, FLPs and LLCs can often enjoy valuation discounts of *20% to 45% or more.* This can translate into millions of dollars in estate tax savings for larger estates.

Case Study Revisited: Stewart's Mutual Funds

Assume that when Stewart dies, he still owns 22% of his FLP interests—having gifted

78% to his grandchildren during his lifetime. This 22% partnership interest, as part of his estate, is subject to estate taxes. Assume also that the mutual funds in his FLP have a value of $2 million when Stewart dies. His 22% interest in the FLP is arguably worth $440,000 (22% x $2 million).

For estate tax valuation purposes, however, the IRS may agree that Stewart's FLP interest is worth less than $270,000. The IRS will allow both the *lack of marketability* discount and the *minority ownership* discount. The lack of marketability discount exists because Stewart's five grandchildren own the other FLP interests, so non-family members would not be interested in buying his interest. Also, under the FLP agreement, the FLP interests, prior to sale, must first be offered to the existing family member partners, and thus are not freely transferable. The minority ownership discount may be applied because Stewart owns only 22% of the FLP when he dies, if he has gifted a majority of both general and limited partnership interests. Even in this situation, he will retain *de facto* control if he retains close to half of the general partnership interest, in which case only one grandchild need side with him to achieve majority control!

These valuation discounts translate into an estate tax savings of about $130,000 ($270,000 x 48%). More important, he retains significant control over his funds while he is alive.

The Diagnosis

The FLP and LLC are tremendous planning tools. Earlier in the book, you learned how they can help Doctors reduce income taxes and protect valuable assets from lawsuits. In this Chapter, you learned how they can afford you valuation gift Leverage and valuation discounts. After speaking to thousands of Doctors in our careers, it is hard for us to imagine how any Doctor's plan could be complete without at least one FLP or LLC. In many cases, multiple LLCs are used. If you review Lessons #6 and #7, you will see the other benefits these tools offer.

Because of imminent potential legislative changes in Washington D. C., we encourage our readers to visit our website at www.forohiodoctors.com to keep track of any potential new laws and changes in this area of the law.

9-6

Avoiding the 70% Tax Trap of Pensions and IRAs

In Chapter 7-7, we highlighted the fact that there is one type of asset that can generate a tax of 70% or more—your tax-qualified retirement plan. This results from a combination of income and estate taxes being applied to retirement plan balances at death. By leaving less than 30% of your retirement plan assets to your heirs, it will be very hard to transfer a high level of affluence to future generations.

One of the "common sense" lessons you will hear repeated in the financial media is that you should contribute as much as you can to your qualified retirement plans (pensions, profit-sharing plans, IRAs, 401(k) plans, etc.). The conventional wisdom is that because you get an income tax deduction and tax-deferred growth, these plans are a huge tax win for the taxpayer. Generally speaking, this isn't bad advice, and we have devoted an entire Chapter (7-2) to this topic.

However, for the most successful Doctors, this "conventional wisdom" requires careful examination. Retirement plans are a potentially dangerous tax trap for three reasons:

1. Although it is likely that Average Americans will be in a lower tax bracket during retirement than during their working years, it is likely that Doctors will ultimately pay income taxes at the same or higher rates.

2. You may not need most (or all) of the funds in retirement.

3. Perhaps most damaging, any funds left in these plans at death will be decimated by taxes. Quite literally, these plans act as "traps," capturing huge sums of money that can be eaten up at tax rates of 70% to 80% before your heirs get to enjoy any of it.

If you can accumulate more in your pension, profit-sharing plan, IRA, or other qualified plan than you will need during retirement (because you have other assets, receive an inheritance or die early), this chapter is a crucial one for your overall estate planning. In this chapter we will discuss how both unaware and very aware taxpayers can get caught in this tax trap as a result of circumstances both in and out of their control. This is what makes this trap so dangerous. Let's examine the three dangerous traps of retirement plans.

Trap #1: You May Pay Tax At The Same—Or Higher—Tax Rates

A common misconception among Doctors and their families is that when they retire, they will be in a lower income tax bracket. Though this may be true for some, there are myriad reasons why this may not be true for you.

One reason is that you may become accustomed to a certain quality of life that you won't wish to "scale back" when you retire. You didn't work hard in your career and as a parent so you could live on tomato soup and grilled cheese sandwiches. In fact, many retirees will increase their expenses and do the things they didn't have time to do when they were working 50, 60 or 70 hours per week. The thing most Doctors will do is travel. Nonetheless, even if you do scale back your quality of life, you may have to pay MORE in living and entertainment expenses because of inflation.

For example, just 15 years ago we paid $3 to $5 to the movies, and a gallon of gas cost well under $1. Last week, we paid $12 per ticket to see a movie and the same gallon of gas cost more than $2.50.

Not only might your lifestyle, which you can control, increase your expenses (and taxes) in retirement but your plan itself might also contribute to increased taxes. The Internal Revenue Service has rules requiring what are called Required Minimum Distributions (RMDs) from retirement plan assets. This means you MUST start taking money out of your retirement plans after the age of 70½, whether you need the money or not. Of course, when you take those distributions, you must pay income tax on every dollar.

These RMDs can be quite high—bringing a higher tax burden with them as well. Typically, you invest your funds inside the retirement plan and those assets grow on a tax-deferred basis. This means you get greater accumulation than in a taxable account. A larger accumulation forces even higher RMDs, which can affect your tax bracket in retirement as well.

You may have other income producing assets like rental real estate, other businesses, limited partnerships, dividend-paying stocks, bonds and money market accounts. Each of these income-producing assets adds to your income, and further increases your income tax bracket.

Given the amount of invested assets inside and outside of retirement plans, and the continued long-term growth of the securities markets, many Doctors will enjoy retirement incomes that keep them in the same tax bracket as when they were working. For example, we have a client named Frank, a 50-year old dermatologist with $500,000 in his profit-sharing plan. By the time he is in his late sixties and begins his planned retirement, assuming 9%-10% annual growth, the plan funds will likely grow to $3 million. If Frank withdraws only the interest from the plan from then on, without using any principal or other sources of income (like Social Security), Frank and his wife will likely remain in the top tax bracket for the rest of their lives.

What this means is that, for the majority of Doctors, the value of the tax deduction and deferral are not as great as "conventional wisdom" would espouse. Clients like this have no tax arbitrage—that is, they simply get the deduction at one tax rate and then pay the tax in the future at the same rate. In fact, the plan may actually cause "reverse arbitrage" if future income tax rates in place when you take distributions exceed the rates in place when you deducted the original contribution, and the current federal budget deficit makes higher tax rates seem almost certain. Recalling the chart we shared earlier with you in the Lesson on taxes, you will remember that tax rates now are the 2nd lowest in the history of the U.S. income tax. Thus, a "reverse arbitrage" is not unlikely. A *Wall Street Journal* columnist reviewed this comparison a few years ago, concluding that for many taxpayers qualified plans were a "fool's game" (April 15, 1999).

Trap #2: You May Not Need The Funds In Retirement

The second dangerous trap of retirement plans is that some people may not need the funds while they are in retirement. Because the amounts contributed to retirement plans are relatively small for high income Doctors, most will accumulate significant non-plan assets over their careers. If plan contributions are capped at $45,000 or less (in most cases), what happens to the rest of the after-tax earnings? Over a career, they end up in non-retirement plan brokerage accounts, ownership interests in closely-held businesses, rental real estate, precious metals or any number of other investments.

Given the compounded interest on your investments in the securities and real estate markets over 10-30 years, these non-plan investments can throw off significant income in retirement—so much so that the retirement plan assets are hardly needed. Though this is a problem we should all hope to have, it is a common problem and needs to be analyzed and understood.

We see this problem with many of our Doctor clients, including, by way of example, our client Charlie, a 58 year-old surgeon. Charlie contributed $20,000 to his pension for each of the last 25 years. Meanwhile, he and wife Margie have also amassed $1.2 million in other investment accounts. By the time Charlie retires, and he plans to do so at age 65, he should have enough in his brokerage accounts for a very comfortable retirement.

Charlie & Margie Won't Need Pension Funds to Retire

Clients:	**Charlie & Margie**
Ages:	Charlie 58; Margie 57
Average Pension Contribution:	$20.000 for 25 years
Non-Pension Investing:	$20,000 for 20 years
Present Pension Balance:	$2.2 million
Outside Investments:	$1.2 million
Planned Retirement Age:	65
Forecasted Pension Balance, Age 65:	$4.4 million (10% gross/year)
Forecasted Outside Investments, Age 65:	$2.3 million (8% post-tax/ year)
Post-Tax Earnings, Outside Investments, Age 65:	$184,000/year ($15,000+/mo.)
Post-Tax Amount Needed For Retirement:	$10,000 post-tax per month

As you can see from the above list, Charlie, who earned about $275,000 per year over the first 25 years of his practice, did not even maximize his pension contributions over that time ($30,000 per year was allowed). Instead, he chose to control some of his investments himself (about $20,000 per year) in a separate investment account. By the time he retires at age 65, Charlie will clearly have enough to fund his retirement (he and Margie need about $10,000 per month post-tax) just from his non-pension plan investments.

To be extremely conservative, let's advise Charlie and Margie to keep another $1.4 million of the pension funds secured for emergencies. That still leaves $3 million of the pension at age 65 that will continue to grow. Charlie and Margie think that this $3 million, plus most of this growth, will benefit their children and grandchildren as designated in their Will and Trust. As you'll see below, they are really benefiting the IRS and state tax agencies because over 70% of the funds will be eaten by taxes if they don't change their plan!

Trap #3: Most Remaining Funds Go To Taxes

The third trap of retirement plans is that any funds in the plan will be decimated by taxes if they are not used by the taxpayer and spouse during their lifetimes. Most Doctors are surprised that the vast majority of these funds end up with state and federal tax agencies. They are shocked to learn that after paying taxes for a lifetime of work, their "tax qualified" plan would be taxed at rates between 70% and 80%! Upon hearing these facts, most clients are shocked, appalled and want to learn how to do something about it. Let's take a look at how these taxes are levied and what you can do. The first thing you must learn is what "IRD" means.

Basics Of IRD

IRD means "income in respect of a decedent" (a deceased person). IRD is income which would have been taxable to the decedent had the decedent lived long enough to receive it. Whoever receives these items of IRD must report them as taxable income and pay any resulting income taxes in the year in which the items are actually received—generally, the year of death (spouses are entitled to defer IRD until payments are actually withdrawn).

The IRD is treated as ordinary income and is subject to income tax in addition to any federal estate taxes and state estate or inheritance taxes. Because federal and state income taxes (including those characterized as IRD) can reach up to 45% in many states (Ohio among them), and estate tax is assessed between 45% and 55% (we will assume 46.5% here), assuming no increase in Ohio's state estate tax. When you combine both taxes, you can see how quickly the combined tax rate escalates. Although the rules provide for a partial income tax deduction for estate taxes paid, the total tax on assets characterized as IRD assets can be over 70%.

What types of assets qualify for the dreaded IRD treatment? Income earned by a decedent but not yet paid, like bonuses or commissions, qualify as IRD. Once they are paid to the estate, they'll be hit with income taxes and estate taxes under the IRD rules. The most important assets hit by IRD? Retirement plans, such as pensions, 401(k)s and IRAs (to the extent contributions were originally tax deductible) and tax deferred annuities.

To see how IRD eats up a Retirement Plan, let's consider the case study of Jim.

Case Study: Jim

Jim is a widowed professor of medicine whose other assets exceed the current estate tax exemption. His IRA is fully taxable as it was funded entirely with tax-deductible contributions. (The same illustration could be made for a married couple but the estate tax wouldn't be due until the second spouse dies if he/she were the plan beneficiary due to the unlimited marital deduction).

Assuming Jim's fully-taxable IRA has a value of $1,000,000 at his death, Jim's estate (or heirs) would first pay $460,000 in estate taxes upon Jim's death, and then pay another $251,212 in state and federal income taxes (i.e., 45% of the remaining amount after giving a deduction for federal estate taxes paid). Thus, only $283,788 is left out of the IRA for Jim's beneficiaries—less than 29%! Over 70% of the funds—built over a lifetime of working and paying income taxes—were taken by the IRD tax system. Let's see how that happened (assuming Jim lived in Ohio) rather than a state with only a "sponge" estate tax prior to the state enacting its own estate tax):

Jim's IRA: IRD Eats Up Over 75% in Ohio!!

IRA Value—IRD Item			**$1,000,000**
Less:			
Federal Estate Taxes (46.5%)	($465,000)		
Ohio Estate Taxes (7%)	($70,000)		
Total Estate Taxes		($535,000)	
Balance in Estate			$465,000
Income in Respect to a Decedent	$1,000,000		
IRD Deduction	$465,000		
Taxable IRD	$535,000		
Income Tax (45%)		($240,750)	
Amount for Beneficiaries		$224,250	
Total Taxes			**$775,750** (77.6%)

NOTE: In this example, we used a 46.5% total tax rate and assumed that the Ohio estate tax remains 7%. If you are in a State other than Ohio, feel free to contact us to determine what the tax rate would be for you.

How to Avoid the Tax Trap

Judge Learned Hand observed that "Anyone may so arrange his affairs that his taxes shall be as low as possible; he is not bound to choose that pattern that will best pay the Treasury; there is not even a patriotic duty to increase one's taxes." For this reason, we all look for ways to reduce our taxes. So what can you do about the pension situation? The answer to that question depends on where you are in your retirement plan funding.

For all Average Americans and some Doctors, it still makes sense to maximize participation in qualified retirement plans, as they are excellent (+5) asset protection tools. In fact, this may be 100% true for your plan at this point. It may also make sense for you to fund some type of "after tax pension" as well.

The analysis depends on an accurate financial analysis of what your plan balance is and what you will need to spend in retirement. If, after such a financial analysis, it looks like you now have more in your retirement plans than you will need in retirement, you should consider ending participation as soon as possible. Ideally, you want to amass just enough in retirement plans to cover retirement expenses and a "safety buffer."

What if you have already built up a large balance in a pension or IRA—and now realize that you won't need some or all of the funds in retirement—like our example of Charlie and Margie earlier? Unless you want 70% or more of these funds to go to State of Ohio and federal taxes, you must do something... and the earlier you act, the better chance you have of avoiding this trap.

Essentially, you have three potential strategies for attempting to reduce the heavy tax burden on qualified plans:

- Stretch IRAs
- Liquidate and Leverage strategy
- Pension Insurance Purchase strategy

Strategy Option #1: Stretch IRAs

Recently, Stretch IRAs have been discussed as a viable tax-reduction option. Stretch IRAs lengthen the time over which distributions must be taken from retirement plans or rollover IRAs. They also allow you to leave the IRA to your heirs, who can then stretch out the distributions over their lifetimes and pay income taxes as they receive the funds. The common belief underlying this strategy is that "tax-deferred growth" is always a great idea. However, when you crunch the numbers, you will realize that the Stretch IRA is generally a bad idea for anyone who will have an estate tax liability and it may be only a minor benefit to everyone else. There are at least three reasons why the Stretch IRAs is not beneficial:

1. Stretch IRAs completely ignore the estate tax problem

2. Stretch IRAs may create additional unnecessary taxes for your heirs
3. Statistically, most children spend, rather than stretch, inherited IRAs.

Let's briefly consider the first two problems.

Stretch IRAs Ignore The Estate Tax Problem

The Stretch IRA gives your heirs the benefit of deferring their withdrawals and deferring their *income tax liabilities*. It ignores estate taxes entirely. The IRS doesn't care whether the children or grandchildren actually receive the money on which your estate pays estate tax. The total value of the IRA will still be included in the estate at the time of your death. This will force your heirs to pay estate taxes right away. To illustrate this point, let's look at the case study of Jeff.

Case Study: Jeff Leaves A Business And A Stretch IRA

Jeff listened to his advisor, who told him to utilize a Stretch IRA to avoid the 70% IRD problem at death. When Jeff passed away, his three children received his family restaurant and a Stretch IRA worth $800,000. The total estate tax bill was $700,000. His children didn't want to sell the restaurant, so they took the $700,000 out of the stretch IRA to pay the estate tax bill. The kids should be happy because they now have the business and an additional $100,000, right?

Wrong! The kids now owe income taxes on the $700,000 withdrawal (income taxes are never waived or avoided with a Stretch IRA). Their average state and federal income tax rates were 40%. Therefore, they owed $280,000 in income taxes because of their $700,000 withdrawal the year before. They used the last $100,000 from the IRA and took out a $180,000 loan against the business to pay the $280,000 tax bill. Then, they owed income taxes on the $100,000 withdrawal—another $40,000 to the IRS—and they owed another $15,000 of interest on the loan. This put them in the hole on another $55,000. Eventually the children had to sell the business to pay off their debts. Jeff's plan failed because he received bad advice from his financial advisor.

Stretch IRAs Could Cost Your Heirs More Taxes

The stretch IRA may generate more taxes to your heirs for three reasons:

1. **Your heirs may be in the same or higher tax bracket than you are by the time you die.** If you die in your seventies, eighties or nineties, your heirs will be in their prime earning years and will likely have another income to put them in that higher marginal tax bracket. You may be deferring 27% taxable income in lieu of 35% taxable income (or higher, if tax rates rise) later.

2. **All withdrawals will be taxed as ordinary income when withdrawn from the plan by you or by your heirs.** The long-term capital gains rate of 15% doesn't apply to IRAs. If you'd taken the funds from the plan and paid the taxes earlier, you would have had the opportunity to invest in long-term investments, and you or your heirs could possibly realize 15% tax on your gains—or no taxes at all if you received a step-up in basis at your death!
3. **You have no flexibility for intergenerational planning.** You can only invest in securities inside a Stretch IRA. You cannot buy life insurance. If you left the Stretch IRA to your children and they didn't need it and wanted to leave it for their children, they would have to let the income-taxable IRA appreciate. It would continue to be income and estate taxable until their children receive the money. If you paid the taxes and left the children after-tax dollars, the children could have invested in tax-free life insurance or a tax-free 529 plan for your grandchildren.

In our opinion the Stretch IRA can be shortsighted ... penny-wise and pound-foolish. Of course, if you or your spouse is completely uninsurable, if your IRA is your only asset and if your estate definitely will not be worth over $1 million when you pass away, the Stretch IRA may make sense for you. If you don't meet all those conditions, you should seriously consider another alternative.

Strategy Option #2: Liquidate & Leverage

The "Liquidate and Leverage" ("L&L") strategy is much superior to the Stretch IRA. In fact, you can think of this strategy as allowing you to Leverage your IRA, 401(k) or pension, five to twenty-five times!

Assume that you and your spouse are 60 years old and have $1 million in your qualified plan. We will also assume that your financial advisory team analyzed your financial situation and found that you could support your quality of life in retirement (and allow for a substantial safety-net) by allocating your after tax investments and $400,000 of your qualified plan funds to this cause. This means that you won't need $600,000 of the funds, or the interest on those funds, in your retirement plan to support your retirement. In this case, more than 70 cents of every dollar in your plan will go to the government if you don't take action. Below, we will discuss a strategy that is very popular with high net worth clients and practically absent from most Doctors' financial plans. A technique known as Liquidate and Leverage can maximize lifetime income from a pension, minimize total taxes, Leverage the gift tax exclusions and maximize the total estate to junior generations.

The L&L Method: One Time Gift

The L&L strategy will ensure that your heirs not only get the full $600,000, but also an additional $2.9 million as well. Best of all, they will receive the $3.5 million tax-free! The L&L steps are as follows:

1. Take $600,000 out of the plan and pay the $240,000 in income taxes (assuming a tax rate of 40%). As we learned from Jim's case, this liquidation eliminates IRD and saves at least 6% of the $600,000, or $36,000.

2. Use a portion of your estate tax exemption amount and gift the remaining $360,000 to a properly drafted Irrevocable Life Insurance Trust (ILIT).

3. The ILIT then purchases a second-to-die life insurance policy on you and your spouse. Depending on your age, health, net worth and other factors, that policy might be worth from $1.5 million to $3.5 million.

4. When you die, the insurance company pays a death benefit of up to $3.5 million, free of *both* income tax and estate tax, to the ILIT.

If you consider that the $600,000 in your plan would have been worth less than $80,000 to your children and grandchildren (if you lived to age 80 and the funds grew at 8%), the L&L strategy left your heirs more than four times that amount—over $2.7 million more to your heirs after-taxes!

8% growth for 20 years = 4.66
4.66 x $600,000 = $2,796,000
After 72% tax, your heirs receive approximately $783,000
Wouldn't you rather leave your heirs $3.5 million than $783,000?

Alternative L&L Method: Guaranteed Income/Annual Gifts

Many Doctors don't like paying for insurance in one lump sum. Others already have life insurance policies that require annual premiums. Still others aren't sure how much of their retirement plans they need. They only know how much they need each month to pay their bills. For these people, the guaranteed income/annual gifts method of L&L is ideal. The guaranteed income/annual gifts method is a combination of three techniques. First, the retirement plan assets are used to purchase a life annuity. A life annuity will pay a monthly, quarterly or annual payment to the annuitant (you or your parents if you chose to purchase a life annuity on your parents) for as long as you live. This way, you never run out of money. Second, the annuitant will gift the after-tax proceeds from the life annuity to an ILIT for the benefit of the second or third generation. Third, the trust will purchase a life insurance policy on the annuitants (usually you and your spouse—or your parents in that application). To illustrate this point, let's consider the case study of Marian.

Case Study: Marian's Guaranteed Income Allows Gifting

Marian, a 78-year old woman, has $800,000 in retirement plan assets. By purchasing a life annuity with the $800,000, she receives a guaranteed monthly income of $8,600.

After-taxes, Marian still has $5,400 per month. Because she has some income from her municipal bonds—which are outside her retirement plan—and additional income from Social Security—she only needs $2,000 of the retirement plan income to pay her family's bills and to fund the college savings plans she created for her grandchildren. This leaves Marian with $3,400 per month of excess income. She gives this $3,400 per month to an ILIT, which pays for a $1 million life insurance policy that is guaranteed to Marian's 115th birthday!

By using the steps, Marian took $800,000 of potentially 70% taxable money and turned it into guaranteed supplemental income for her and a $1 million inheritance for her son and grandchildren.

Strategy Option #3: Pension Insurance Purchase

The IRS and ERISA allow for certain types of retirement plans to purchase life insurance within the plan with pretax dollars. Typically, we use profit-sharing plans here because the rules are most generous for these types of plans. Thus, for clients with roll-over IRAs, they will have to roll the IRA back into a properly-drafted profit-sharing plan (PSP) before being able to take advantage of this strategy.

From this point forward, let's consider that you have a retirement plan that you don't expect to completely empty before you die. What can you do? You can purchase life insurance on yourself inside your retirement plan. When you die, the insurance company will pay a death benefit to your retirement plan.

While some Doctors will argue that life insurance is not a good investment in their plan—consider three factors: (1) The most efficient investment for your heirs may not be the same as the most efficient investment for yourself, because of estate tax and IRD; (2) as noted elsewhere in the book, the policies can reflect almost any underlying investment you want—tied to a money manager you select (PPLI), mutual funds you choose (variable policy) or even a market index (S&P 500); and (3) you MUST consider the tax consequences of the investment. Here, when considering IRD, life insurance will almost always outperform mutual funds.

Mutual Funds vs. Life Insurance—Another Surprise Upset Winner

Let's assume that you could invest $500,000 into mutual funds inside your retirement plan. After 20 years, assuming a 7% return on your mutual funds, you would have approximately $2,000,000 in your retirement plan. If you died at that point, your spouse would have access to the funds—but would have to pay income taxes on any withdrawals. If you assume a combined State of Ohio and federal income tax rate of 40%, the $2,000,000 pension is worth $1,200,000 to your spouse. Then, if your children wanted the funds, there might be estate taxes to pay.

If you invested the same $500,000 into a $1.8 million life insurance policy, you might think you would be at a disadvantage versus investing in the mutual funds. You would be wrong! At the end of 20 years, after paying for mortality costs and administrative expense of the life insurance policy, your policy would have $600,000 of cash value at the time of your passing. When the $1,800,000 death benefit paid to the pension, only $600,000 of the benefit was income taxable to the spouse. $240,000 was due to the IRS and State of Ohio and the remaining $1,560,000 went to the spouse tax-free! That is 30% more money to the survivor from the life insurance policy (as compared to mutual funds). The same estate tax rates would apply, but 30% more money escaped the pension...and the taxes associated with it. This is not an aggressive strategy any more than buying a home partially because the mortgage interest is tax-deductible. It is a benefit that is clearly spelled out in the Internal Revenue Code. It is simple, but very few people take advantage of it.

The Diagnosis

Retirement plans certainly have their appropriate place in planning for Doctors and their employees. Chapter 7-2 explains many of these. However, if you have a sizeable pension balance, you should be concerned that your heirs may unnecessarily have to pay the 70% combined income and estate tax on IRD. What you can do is work with advisory team members who are familiar with pension law, life insurance and estate taxes and ask them to help you with your planning.

There is one other significant threat to your retirement assets. Unlike IRD, this threat raises its ugly head while you are still alive. It is the increasing cost of long-term care. This is addressed in the next chapter.

9-7

Protection From Rising Medical Costs

It may seem like medical costs are a lifetime issue and estate planning is a death issue, but medical costs can be the greatest threat to the assets you want to pass to your loved ones.

Doctors should be familiar with the soaring costs of medical procedures and nursing home care and how they may wipe out retirement funds AND decimate an inheritance for a future generation. This is why we have chosen to include a chapter on long-term care in the estate planning section. Doctors need to realize the folly of relying on government to provide for their medical coverage and their comfortable retirement. Doctors need to recognize the role that Long Term Care Insurance ("LTCI") must play in their financial and estate plan.

Long Term Care is considered a type of health insurance because it pays for a variety of health costs that may or may not be covered by Social Security or Medicare. The details of Long Term Care Insurance and our recommendations on what to look for in an LTCI contract are covered in Chapter 4-3. Chapter 7-4 offers a discussion of the income tax benefits of LTCI planning. The purpose of this brief chapter is to explain why LTCI is an important part of any estate plan. By reading *For Ohio Doctors*, you will gain a full understanding of how LTCI will help you and your family in many areas—including protecting an inheritance from rising medical costs.

If you met with your advisors to discuss your estate plan under EGTRRA, you probably didn't count on having to pay $100-$300 per day for nursing home or in-home care. You also probably didn't calculate medical expense inflation rates of 5%-10% per year that could make a very mediocre $100/day nursing home in year 2010 dollars cost over $650 per day in 2030. If you need long-term care for just one year, it could use up $237,250 of funds that you had hoped would go to your spouse, children, grandchildren, or other beneficiaries.

Do You Need LTCI?

According to the Center for Long Term Care Financing, Americans face approximately a one-in-ten chance of spending at least five or more years in a nursing home after age 65. 48.6% of people age 65 and older may spend time in a nursing home, because there is an almost 50% chance that one spouse of a 65 year old couple will live to 95. More startling is that 71.8% of people over age 65 may use some form of *home-health care*! Do you think the developments in medicine will help or hurt longevity and increase or decrease the need for long-term health care?

The longer people live (as a result of medical advancements) the greater the likelihood that people will eventually need some significant medical assistance on a long term basis. We may find treatments for cancer or osteoporosis, but that just increases the likelihood of eventually having Alzheimer's or some other debilitating disease that forces us to require significant, and very costly, care.

The table below lists some costs, by city, for nursing home care as compiled by the MetLife Assisted Living Market Survey 2007:

The Average Annual Cost of Nursing Home Care

City	Cost	City	Cost
Anchorage, AK	$186,150	Omaha, NE	$73,000
Phoenix, AZ	$71,905	Las Vegas, NV	$73,000
Los Angeles, CA	$78,475	New York, NY	$128,480
San Diego, CA	$86,870	Cleveland, OH	$74,825
San Francisco, CA	$135,415	Portland, OR	$78,110
Stamford, CT	$135,780	Philadelphia, PA	$85,045
Miami, FL	$77,015	Providence, RI	$84,315
Honolulu, HI	$98,915	Nashville, TN	$70,810
Boise, ID	$73,000	Dallas, TX	$60,955
Chicago, IL	$57,305	Houston, TX	$61,685
Boston, MA	$108,405	Alexandria, VA	$94,900
Baltimore, MD	$78,840	Rutland, VT	$86,140
Detroit, MI	$60,955	Seattle, WA	$93,805
St. Paul, MN	$76,650	Milwaukee, WI	$85,410
St. Louis, MO	$57,305		

Source: Met Life Website

Nursing home care costs in most cities in the table above fall between $5,000 and $8,000 per month. Some are as inexpensive as $4,000 per month and some can be over $10,000 per month. Is there any reason to believe that nursing home care will become less expensive? Are you wiling to risk losing this much of your estate to nursing home costs or would you like to plan ahead?

The important point to take from this chapter is that you will most likely eventually pay for long-term care coverage. The question is: "Will it be paid for in advance or will it be paid for from my intended inheritance or retirement funds?"

You may wonder, "Doesn't the State of Ohio or Medicare pay these expenses?" The answer is "Yes... *and* No." Medicaid in Ohio will not pay for a senior's long-term nursing care until that individual has depleted all but $1,500 of his or her net worth. That means that if a retirement plan or any investments are titled in an individual's name, or have been titled in the individual's name in the last 60 months, the State of Ohio will require those assets to be sold to pay for medical costs. In addition, income may disqualify you from receiving any benefit. And if your income is low enough to qualify for Medicaid, the State of Ohio will then take all but $40 per month of your income to help pay them for your long-term care coverage.

It isn't hard to see how this could deplete someone's assets immediately. You are likely willing to buy insurance, create a Living Trust and consider other estate tax planning strategies. But the depletion of an estate by long-term care expense affects all estates, whether or not they are large enough to be affected by estate taxes. Ignoring long-term care planning could be a potentially devastating mistake. Let's plan not to make that mistake.

If you intend to leave an inheritance, you may wish to purchase long-term care insurance now, while you have the money. You can purchase an LTCI policy in one year, over 10 years, over 20 years or make payments every year for the rest of your life. You also have options to have all of your premiums go to your heirs at death even if you collect on the policy during your life. In fact, there are policies on the market today which combine a universal life insurance guaranteed death benefit for your heirs with a guaranteed daily benefit for long-term care costs. This can be an ideal tool to achieve two planning goals with the same dollars.

Do Pride and Dignity Matter To You?

One of the most difficult emotional challenges for any family involves caring for older relatives who are not able to take care of themselves. We know many of you have already seen your parents deal with this with your grandparents and many of you have already dealt with this concern with your own parents and in-laws. By purchasing long-term care insurance, you are shifting the financial risk to someone outside your family—the insurance company.

When someone else is paying the bills for home health coverage, there is never a financial reason to send a relative to a nursing home. Further, the insurance could pay for in-home care for the rest of your life. This way, the family avoids horrible fights and you won't ever be put into a nursing home or have to ask your children or grandchildren for financial assistance to stay out of a nursing home. For many Doctors, this is reason enough to purchase long-term care insurance.

The Diagnosis

Rising medical costs can be a significant cost for any retiree. If planning is not implemented in advance, these costs can wipe out retirement funds and any inheritance that would have otherwise gone to your heirs. This devastating financial situation can also force you (or other relatives) into a nursing home—or into the homes of loved ones—unnecessarily. By purchasing LTCI, you are making sure that soaring medical costs don't deplete your retirement assets, take away the head start you wanted to leave your children or grandchildren or destroy the legacy you wanted to leave behind. LTCI can also support you so you never have to be "put" into a nursing home. For these reasons, LTCI should be an important part of the multi-disciplinary financial plan for every Doctor.

Of course, if you aren't interested in leaving an inheritance to your heirs, you need not sit back and let medical costs and taxes take your money. You can implement charitable planning that will leave your estate to a deserving cause and give you tax benefits while you are alive. This is the focus of the next Chapter.

9-8

Charitable Estate Planning

Doctors spend their entire careers contributing to others. Many Doctors continue their altruistic ways later in life and want to give back to the world that provided them with their success. What many Doctors don't know is how to take this charitable intent and use it to create as much benefit to their family while benefiting a charity at the same time. In this chapter, we will briefly examine only one tool often used in charitable estate planning—the Charitable Remainder Trust (CRT). Because charitable planning is such a vast topic, we can only hope to give you a tiny hint of the types of planning we implement for our clients.

> **"To give away money is an easy matter and in any man's power, but to decide to whom to give it, and how large and when, and for what purpose and how, is neither in every man's power nor an easy matter"—*Aristotle***

Rather than ramble on about a series of planning options, we think it best to be succinct and show the power of charitable planning through the story of Steve and Martha.

Steve is a 56-year old orthopedic surgeon and his wife Martha, age 48, is an OB/GYN. They have two boys in college. As a result of prudent investing, good luck and great investments in some start-up businesses, Steve is considering early retirement so he can travel and enjoy his hobbies of flying and sailing.

In addition to his significant retirement plan account, Steve has $3 million in essentially zero basis stock in his friend's company (that he helped finance in return for stock) that recently went public. He is in line with qualified stock options to acquire an additional $5 million over the next three years. Faced with planning for the disposition of an estate of $10 million (almost all of it in an undiversified portfolio), Steve and Martha decided that they'd like part of their financial plan to include a plan to eliminate estate taxes, if possible. In short, they're willing to give to charity those assets that would otherwise default to the IRS in the form of estate and capital gains taxes.

As a part of this strategy, they will also make aggressive gifts of stock to their two sons and other family heirs over the next few years, through family limited partnerships. By freezing estate growth and squeezing the value of the assets, we hope to be able to eliminate all unnecessary estate taxes. Additionally, our plan will provide an excellent retirement income stream through the use of a CRT.

Examine the following carefully as we compare selling a highly appreciated asset, paying taxes and living off the interest versus contributing the asset to a CRT, selling the asset and living off the annuity from the CRT. We will refer to this chart throughout the Chapter to illustrate a number of points.

Steve and Martha Use a CRT to Benefit Charity & Their Family

	Sell	CRT
Net fair market value (FMV)	$3,000,000	$3,000,000
Taxable gain on sale	$3,000,000	$0
Capital gains tax (20%) at federal level	$600,000	
Net amount invested	$2,400,000	$3,000,000
Annual return of reinvested portfolio	10%	10%
Reinvested for 10% annual income produces annual retirement income of	$240,000	
Trust payout of 5% (averaged with 10% returns over Trust term of 40 years)		$452,999
Annual average after-tax income (at 39% tax and 20% capital gains rate for CRT payout)	$146,400	$321,622
Years—projected joint life expectancy	40	40
Taxes saved with $616,290 deduction at 39%		$240,358
Tax savings and cash flow over 40 years	$5,856,000	$13,105,233
Total increase in cash flow	$5,856,000	$13,105,233
Total value of asset in estate in 40 years	$2,400,000	$0
Estate taxes on this asset at 48%	$1,152,000	
Net value to family	$1,080,000	
Total insurance expense—wealth replacement	$0	($530,000)
Insurance benefit in wealth replacement trust	$0	$3,000,000
CRT remainder value to family charity	$0	$20,415,967

What is happening here? The stock that Steve owns is publicly traded, so its value is readily ascertained and is easily transferable to the Family Charitable Trust. This CRT will take the highly appreciated stock and sell it without being taxed on its sale. It will then reposition the proceeds into a more balanced portfolio of equities designed for both growth and security.

The CRT, with Steve as co-Trustee, will buy and hold stocks and mutual fund shares so that most of the portfolio will continue to appreciate while Steve and Martha, as income beneficiaries, receive quarterly payments of 5% of the Trust's value every year. They've made the decision that leaving each son with a $5 million inheritance is part of their family's financial goals, so with some stock and life insurance held in an ILIT, the two boys will be well protected for the future.

Everything else in their estate will either be spent during retirement or left to their favorite charity when they pass away. After examining the numbers, Steve and Martha felt that it made great sense to re-exert control over their social capital (i.e. the part of their estate that would eventually pass to the government) and follow through with their plan. Because Steve felt a need to sell in order to diversify his unbalanced portfolio, the only comparison to be made was between: (1) selling, paying tax, and reinvesting the net proceeds; and (2) contributing the stock and reinvesting inside the CRT. We have made such a comparison in the "Sell" and "CRT" columns.

You can see that the benefit to their family of the CRT is significant. Steve and Martha will enjoy $118,000 in additional annual retirement income in the CRT scenario ($264,000 post-tax versus $146,000 post-tax). Over their joint life expectancy, this difference will amount to more than $5 million!

Furthermore, because of the use of life insurance in an ILIT (also known as a "wealth replacement Trust"), their kids will get more out of that asset than in the "sale" scenario ($3 million of insurance proceeds income and estate tax-free vs. a $2.4 million asset netting $1.08 million to the family after estate taxes).

By combining a charitable remainder trust with a wealth replacement trust for their heirs, Steve and Martha were able to enjoy a greater retirement income than they had anticipated and leave a substantial legacy to their children (of which they have to pay no estate taxes). As if that were not enough, they were able to leave more than $21 million to charity. This is quite an accomplishment, yet is feasible with the right financial planning and advisors.

The Diagnosis

Although you may not have the wealth of a famous American family like the Rockefellers or Kennedys, you may still be able to benefit from charitable planning. Once you have protected your family wealth from lawsuits, taxes and estate taxes, you have put your family in a better position.

Now, the most important thing to do is to analyze your situation with the help of your advisory team. Work with your team of advisors to see if a charitable planning tool may help you. The last Lesson of the book—Take the Prescribed Medicine—will help you outline the necessary steps for you to start addressing your issues and realizing the benefits that can be achieved from implementing the strategies in *For Ohio Doctors*.

LESSON 10

Take the Prescribed Medicine

Everyone wants to be rich, but only a very small minority of Doctors will become Super-Affluent (defined as having a net worth of $10+ million). Why is this? There are countless ways to fail, but only one way to achieve financial success—that is to efficiently leverage your assets, effort, and time while avoiding financial catastrophes. In this book, we have sought to provide the financial secrets Doctors need to know so they can work less and build more in this very difficult time of increased risk and reduced reimbursements. *For Ohio Doctors* shares the steps to success, explains how to work with advisors, and points out how to address most financial planning needs. Despite this guidance, most readers still won't follow them. Do not be one of them!

Every year, thousands of Doctors spend hard-earned money and valuable time attending our seminars, hoping to learn important financial and legal lessons. Over 90% of the response forms we have received from attendees acknowledge that the information is valuable and that the attendees plan to take immediate action to improve their financial situation. However, when we check in with attendees months, or years, later, we find out that fewer than 10% actually make a serious improvement.

We'll assume that you will be a member of the 10% who will actually take the necessary actions to reach your financial goals. Since you want to achieve desired levels of wealth and we want to help you do so, we would like to show you what you have to do to start the process and successfully continue it throughout your life. If you follow these steps, you can be sure to build your fortune and protect your assets. The steps are:

Step 1—Accept That You Have A Problem You Can't Handle Alone

Step 2—Hire The Right Team

Step 3—Pay Advisors To Help You Develop The Plan

Step 4—Implement The Plan

Step 5—Monitor The Plan

Step 6—Review The Plan (At Least) Annually

Step 7—Question Advisors And Planning Decisions

Step 8—Be Willing To Make Changes To The Plan Or The Advisory Team

There is an old saying, "*Plan to Succeed or Prepare to Fail.*" We can't stress this strongly enough. In the "good old days" when there were fewer Doctors, less bureaucracy, and lower taxes, it was possible to "succeed" with much less attention to the issues we have raised in this volume. Those days are long gone, and you must prepare to fail if you do not plan to succeed. If you follow these eight steps, you will be on your way to building a fortune and protecting assets just like the Savvy Affluent do.

Step #1: Accept That You Have A Problem You Can't Handle Alone

Through years of experience, we have come to understand the unique intelligence, drive, and abilities of Doctors. Clearly, every Doctor has the capacity to do what any of us do, but as the sage once said, "*There is enough time to do anything, but not enough time to do everything.*"

In this book, and in our work with Doctors, we deal with the following areas:

- Accounting
- Asset protection
- Benefits planning
- Business structuring
- Buy-out planning
- Estate planning
- Insurance planning
- Investments
- Tax planning
- And others

This should not need emphasis after the initial lessons on leverage, but we will reiterate here: *You cannot continue to be an expert in your career and become an expert in all the areas of business, finance, and law where you need assistance.* To expect to do all of this alone is akin to expecting a pediatrician to become in expert in other fields of medicine as a patient ages and develops new medical concerns. Understanding and acknowledging the futility of such an attempt leads to Step #2.

Step #2: Hire The Right Team

Once you realize that you need help with your financial planning, you have to find the professionals who have the expertise and experience to help you. Don't let the brevity of the description of this step fool you. This is a very important step in your quest for financial success. The choice of members for your team of advisors is as important to your long-term financial success as the choice of a spouse is to your emotional and familial security. Some might say the advisory team is even more important because many financial mistakes are irreversible.

There is more to choosing advisors than merely identifying expertise. In his book *All I Really Need to Know I Learned in Kindergarten*, author Robert Fulgrum discusses the importance of working with others who "play nice in the sandbox." Smart, experienced advisors have egos, but they need to learn to park them at the door when working on an interdisciplinary team with Doctor clients and other smart, experienced advisors. We once had a very smart, wealthy business client whose wife objected when we recommended that they allow us to bring in an expert from 4 states away to help on a specific esoteric element of their plan. "We don't even know anyone in Arkansas," she objected. "Annie," the businessman said, "it doesn't matter whether we know him or not; what is important is that our advisors know and trust one another."

Not only do you need a good team, but the team needs a "quarterback" through whom all communications flow to you. Whenever there is a "quarterback controversy" in football, coaches usually say something like "competition for the starting quarterback position is good for the team." We would argue that competition among your advisors for control of the team is not good, and among good advisors, it should not matter who is quarterbacking, as long as your goals are being properly defined and met, and a your plan is being properly developed and implemented.

Step #3: Pay Advisors To Help You Develop The Plan

As in medicine, there are credentialed specialties and specialists in business, finance, and law. Professionally, Doctors are accustomed to referring patients to specialists. It doesn't make sense for Doctors to embrace specialization in medicine but ignore specialization in other fields, yet that is often what happens when it comes to managing business, financial, and legal matters.

A scalpel in the hands of a physician is a tool that can save a life. The same scalpel in the hands of a mugger can take a life. How you choose and utilize advisors can be the difference between life and death for your financial stability. Once you have the right team of advisors to help you, you have to make sure you utilize their skills and talents properly. The best way to get the most out of your relationship with your advisors is to pay them to give you their unbiased analysis and recommendations.

Even if your advisors also provide other services or can be paid from the sale of products, they can still be valuable members of your team. By offering to pay them what their time is worth to work with you, they will be able to give you honest advice without an ulterior motive to sell you anything. Doctors should pay advisors to create a plan and then pay these advisors to meet as a group at least once each year to review the plan and provide additional recommendations.

Step #4: Implement The Plan

When Doctors write a prescription or arrange post-procedure therapy, they expect patients to take their meds and/or attend PT sessions. Doctors know the best results are obtained when patients follow "doctor's orders."

Implementing the financial plan may seem like a silly step, but you would be surprised how many people pay for plans to be created only to put the plan on the shelf and let it collect dust. Like an X-ray, MRI, or any diagnostic medical analysis, the financial plan is a document that analyzes the present state of affairs. Like a Doctor's diagnosis and treatment plan, the financial plan also serves as a series of recommendations and action items. It seems foolish to go through the cost and effort of creating a comprehensive plan, only to ignore the analysis and recommendations of the specialists who were paid to create the plan. Yet, we see this lack of implementation from numerous clients each year.

Another common mistake in implementing the financial plan is something we call "the unanimous position dilemma." Some clients won't implement a piece of the plan until they get 100% agreement from every member of the team. Other clients need more—including approval from family, friends, the guy at the health club, the butcher, and whoever else will listen. To get the right plan, Doctors must hire the right team to work together for them. If there is a disagreement within the team on a certain plan element, the best advisors will educate themselves as much as possible and evaluate the merits of each proposal, helping clients avoid the role of "referee." The client may choose to move forward on that element or not, but Doctors need not ask non-expert friends and family for their input, especially when these people are in completely different financial situations. Also, Doctors should not let disagreement among team members on one action item prevent them from implementing other items.

We once proposed a very complex plan for a $50 million developer client. One element of the plan was a sale by our client of a valuable piece of land to another successful—albeit quite old—developer. While they were signing the sale documents, our client told the other developer, "My advisor has suggested we do something called an Alaska Dynasty Trust. What do you think?" The aging developer said, "Sounds risky to me. I wouldn't do it." Our client respected us enough to get a third opinion, and hired a major law firm to review and opine, They reported (for a multiple 5 figure fee) that it was a "state of the art" plan, and they saw no reason why the client should not implement it.

Typically, there will be at least 5 to 10 action items within the financial plan, so the odds are that there will be some element on which all the advisors are not experts. A stalemate on one item should not be allowed to stop all action on other elements of the plan.

Step #5: Monitor The Plan

Given the pace of change in the 21st century, nothing—including a business, financial, and estate plan, remains fixed for very long, so it stands to reason that any plan must be monitored on a regular basis and modified or tweaked as situations and circumstances change.

Step #5 could also be called "*Communication and Monitoring of the Plan.*" Just as the client's active involvement is important in the initial plan creation and implementation, so too is it for the plan monitoring. The crucial role here for the client is communication, especially with whichever advisor is the "quarterback" of the planning team (typically the person or firm who drafted the final plan).

The advisors on your team can't help you monitor your plan if they don't know what everyone else is doing and if they aren't all seeing the same information. Doctors also need to realize that they are too busy to keep everyone abreast of each nuance of the plan. If advisors have to track down data from you or from the other advisors, there is going to be a significant cost for all of the duplication of effort, and a risk that something significant will fall through the cracks. That is another reason it is essential to have a "quarterback" advisor.

To monitor your plan successfully, you need a system and a "quarterback" to make sure that system is working correctly. The "quarterback" is essential to making sure that every member of the team is on the same page.

Technology Can Help

Modern software products can be helpful. Two years ago, in fact, a new client of ours showed us an online tool that tracked all investments daily, kept secure online-accessible scanned copies of every legal document and insurance policy statement, and had tools for the advisors to use to run scenarios for the client under different circumstances and leave them online for every advisor to see. It was such an impressive tool that we went out and bought a license to use it ourselves. Every client of ours who has used this service always has the same reply after it has been in place for a few months—"How did we ever manage without this?" We call this the "ATM" or "cell phone" response!

Step #6: Annual Plan Review Meeting

Doctors rely on peer review as an important element of the practice of medicine. This same philosophy can, and should, apply to financial planning for physicians. Doctors need to have at least one full-day meeting or multiple day retreat with their advisors each year. During these meetings the advisors will review the plan. The reason for the meetings is to force the advisors to be in the same room where they don't have the distractions of their offices. By paying the advisors to be there for you, they will focus solely on your needs and concerns and have time to brainstorm with you on future planning. This is a benefit you would never get from any number of conference calls.

Although you may not be able to attend multi-day wellness retreats in Hawaii or fly fishing retreats in Wyoming, as many of our clients do, you can certainly afford a 3-4 hour meeting with all of your advisors each year. This meeting should be distraction free and should be guided by an agenda developed in advance by the "quarterback" advisor and you.

Step #7: Question Advisors And Planning Suggestions

Doctors should understand that they can trust their advisors and still ask questions about the existing and suggested planning. Most advisors who work well with affluent clients respect the intelligence of their clients and want their input. Surprisingly, this is not true of all advisors. We prefer working with clients who take the time to understand as much of the planning as possible. You should also encourage your other advisors to question the other members of the group. You don't want a fight over every issue, but you do want your team to discuss pros and cons of every possible alternative in an effort to find the best solutions for you. This is especially important on elements of the plan where there are significant arguments on both sides of a proposed action step.

To review the planning process that Jason, Chris and David's firm has created, please visit www.ojmgroup.com.

Step #8: Be Willing To Make Changes To The Plan Or To The Advisory Team

Over time, everything changes: Laws, rules, regulations, family circumstances, your health, medical science, business marketplace, and more. Often these changes can be very significant. These changing circumstances may dictate significant changes to the plan and its implementation. Of course, if there is an open line of communication between the client and "quarterback" advisor and the team of advisors who participate in periodic plan reviews, these changes will not take anyone by surprise. Nonetheless, it is important to be flexible enough to re-examine the plan assumptions when there are significant changes like a divorce, the closing of a practice, or others and be open to making changes to the implementation strategy as well.

As for the advisors on your team, they are not lifetime appointees. They can lose focus, develop a contentious relationship with other team members, change their business model, etc. Some advisors become sufficiently prosperous that they simply stop learning. Earlier in the book, we emphasized the importance of getting second opinions. This is particularly important when you have been with certain advisors for a long time and haven't looked for additional input from outside experts. We also explained why the "if it ain't broke, don't fix it" mentality can sabotage your planning and be very costly to you and your family.

Sometimes, your team requires advisors with different fields of expertise. Other times the interaction of a group is hurt by certain persons or personalities. In these instances, it may be best for you to ask an advisor to leave the team. Actually, since it is your money, you can think of it as "firing" the advisor because you don't need the advisor to agree with your decision. Just because someone has worked with you for a while is not a sufficient reason to keep that advisor on your team if you are not getting good advice or if you might be better served by a new advisor whose expertise or personality may be a better fit under your new circumstances.

Next Steps

We admit to making the planning process seem pretty easy in the last few pages. Practically speaking, there will always be roadblocks. The biggest one you will face is "Time." There will never seem to be enough hours in the day to do what you want to do and there will always be other things that appear to need to be done right away. The only way that you will ever overcome this roadblock will be to make the planning process a priority for you, your family, your business partners, and your advisors. Once you make your planning a priority, you can start to approach the steps to implement the proper planning.

Of course, planning for your long term, sustained financial success requires a significant effort and commitment of your time. This process will cost you money. This process will not be without a certain amount of frustration and aggravation. This is normal, because it is hard to change ingrained habits, and you are trying to change the way you have behaved for years. It can be a challenge, but the most important Lesson to help you achieve your desired level of wealth is to understand that anything worth having is worth the effort required to have it.

Once you find the right team, get it up and running and work through the initial bugs in developing your team process, your financial life will get easier every year. This is another little "secret" that has helped many Doctors build and maintain their wealth and protect their assets through multiple generations.

The Final Diagnosis—Words of Encouragement

Changing your philosophy and planning process to incorporate the lessons in *For Ohio Doctors* may seem overwhelming. There are many different steps to be taken within each of the ten Lessons. On top of that, this book includes only a partial list of the potential strategies that you could utilize to achieve your desired level of wealth. Practically speaking, no one advisor can handle the challenge of planning alone. A team of advisors is required, and you must assemble a team capable of creating a plan that meets all your goals.

Once you hire the team, you must make the time and devote the effort to work through the steps in this chapter. If it seems like a lot to do, you should understand that every wealthy family began as an average family until one person saw greater opportunities to leverage the family's wealth. If you dedicate yourself to the process in this Lesson, you can be that person for your family.

We wish you the success and affluence you desire. If you are having a tough time getting started or need a little help bringing your plan to the next level, please feel free to contact OJM via email at odell@ojmgroup.com or mandell@ojmgroup.com or via phone at 1-877-656-4362.

We always enjoy hearing from our readers and we would be honored to help you achieve your goal of working less and building more wealth so you can achieve your ultimate goal of leading a more enjoyable life. Once we acquire a basic understanding of your situation, we will set up a meeting with one of the authors whose office is most convenient to you.

Appendices

FREE CONSULTATION

Would you like to learn from the Ohio-licensed Authors how to:

- Protect Family and Practice Assets from Lawsuits?
- Legally Reduce Taxes?
- Work Less and Build More Wealth?
- Consolidate Your Financial Affairs?
- Get a Second Opinion on Your Existing Planning?
- Finally Complete Your Estate Plan?

To schedule your FREE consultation with the co-authors to help you address these important concerns,

Asset Protection	Estate Planning
Business Planning	Retirement Planning
Insurance Planning	Investment Analysis
Exit Strategies	Fee-Based Planning

visit www.forohiodoctors.com, Call 1-877-656-4362 or complete the fax request form on the next page.

SCHEDULE FREE CONSULT

The authors have helped over 1,200 Doctors in 45 states with their asset protection, practice structure, retirement, insurance, investment, tax and estate planning concerns.

If you would like to schedule a free consult with one of the authors, please complete this form and fax it to our offices.

Please provide your email address, as we will be sending you a short form to complete before your consultation. This will help us more efficiently address your concerns while on the call.

Name: ______________________________

Specialty: ______________________________

Address: ______________________________

____

City/State/Zip: ______________________________

Phone: ______________________________

Email: ______________________________

Calls are done Monday through Friday between 8am and 7pm Eastern.
Please provide your suggested times for your call.

1st choice: date: __ __ / __ __ time (eastern time): __ __ : __ __

2nd choice: date: __ __ / __ __ time (eastern time): __ __ : __ __

3rd choice: date: __ __ / __ __ time (eastern time): __ __ : __ __

4th choice: date: __ __ / __ __ time (eastern time): __ __ : __ __

Primary concerns: ______________________________

____

____

FAX to (866) 913-4911

DISCOUNTED BOOKS & CDs

For Ohio Doctors: Shedding Light on Asset Protection, Tax and Estate Planning teaches doctors the important lessons they never learned in medical school, residency or fellowship. Doctors will learn how to efficiently leverage their time, money and effort so they can get more out of a medical practice. More specifically, doctors learn how to protect their personal and practice assets from lawsuits, state-specific taxes and bad investments in addition to learning the secrets to building wealth and avoiding catastrophic financial disasters so they get the most out of their practice and leave the most for their heirs. ***For Ohio Doctors*** is a MUST HAVE for any Ohio doctor wishing to achieve financial success.

Risk Management for the Practicing Physician is nationally accredited for 4 hours of Category I continuing medical education (CME) credits in risk management. Co-written by a practicing physician, an attorney and a financial advisor, this monograph includes chapters on: providing care in today's malpractice environment, liability and the doctor-patient relationship, managing diagnosis-related liability, minimizing risks of miscommunication, managing high risk communication areas, managing the dangers of drug therapy, non-medical liability risks for the practicing physician, and liability in the new health care system.

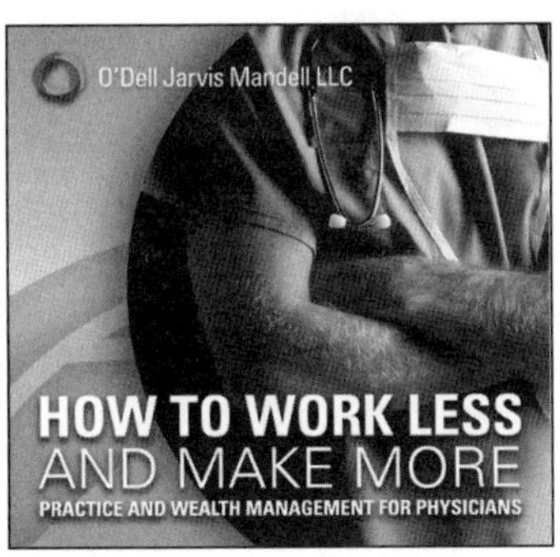

How to Work Less and Make More is an audio program by attorney and financial consultant David B. Mandell that shows doctors how to leverage their assets, effort and time to build greater wealth and protect valuable personal and practice assets as part of a comprehensive legal and financial planning process.

Order Form is on the Back of this Page!

Discounted Book Order Form

Book	Qty	Special Price	Total
For Ohio Doctors: Shedding Light on Asset Protection, Tax and Estate Planning (regularly $99.95)		$50	
Risk Management for the Practicing Physician (*4 Hours of Category I CME Credit—regularly $59.95*)		$30	
Wealth Secrets of the Affluent (regularly $39.95)		$20	
How to Work Less and Make More Audio CD (regularly $10)		FREE	
		Shipping & Handling $5 per item	
		Tax 8.25% in Texas	
		Tax 6.00% in Florida	
		Total	

Credit Card: ___ ___ ___ ___ ___ ___ ___ ___ ___ ___ ___ ___ ___ ___ ___ ___

Exp Date: ___ ___ / ___ ___

Name: ________________________________

Phone: (________) ________ - ____________

Address: ________________________________

Address: ________________________________

City/State/ZIP ________________________________

Auth Signature: ________________________________

FAX TO: (866) 913-4911

WEALTH SECRETS OF THE AFFLUENT

For Your Friends Who Aren't Doctors: The First Book Specifically Written for Affluent Americans

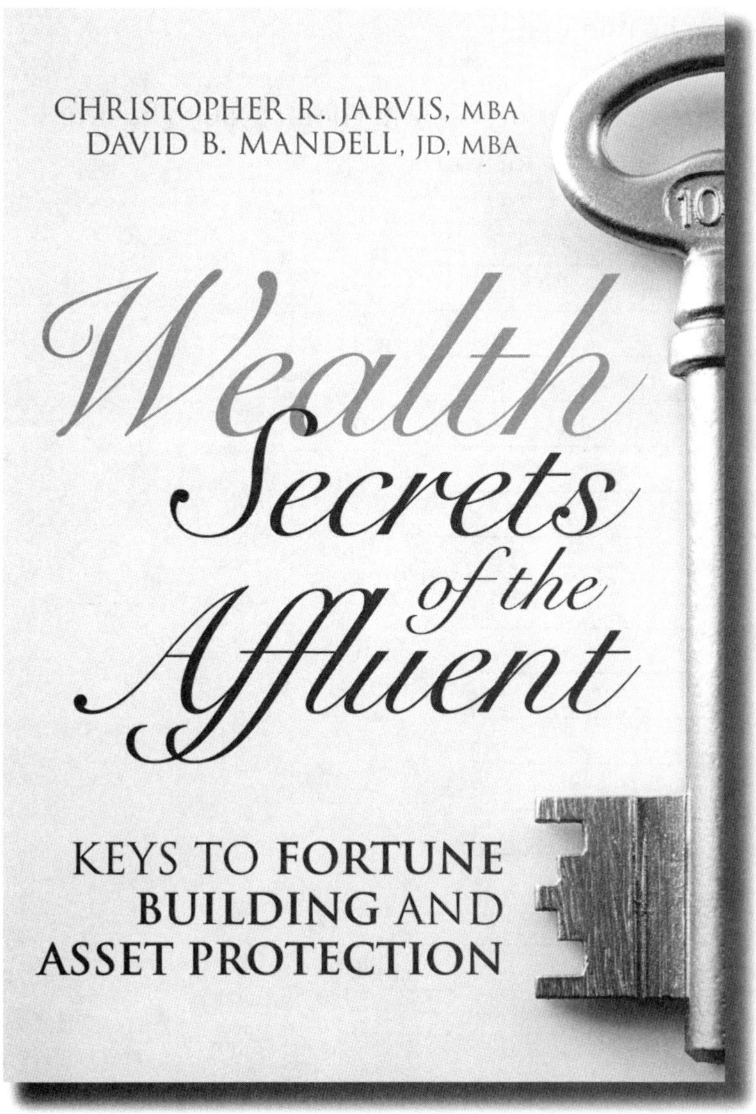

Most financial resources are designed for the average American. As a result, over 20 million affluent families and millions of hard working Americans who strive to be wealthy are confused by what they read in the popular press. *Wealth Secrets of the Affluent* is the first book designed to help affluent families and their advisors take practical steps to build and preserve wealth.

This unique guide touches upon vital topics for wealth-building, including which under-used financial vehicles are integral parts of affluent family planning; why the Nobel Prize-winning asset allocation model used by most firms will fail for affluent clients; and how readers can rate and judge their advisors. Filled with in-depth insights and expert advice, *Wealth Secrets of the Affluent* allows readers to make more informed financial decisions for building and preserving their various assets.

Order online at www.guardpub.com or in person at bookstores nationwide

SCHEDULE A **CME** SEMINAR

Guardian Publishing's education experts have delivered seminars on asset protection, tax and estate planning that range from one to four hours for over 200 medical groups, associations, hospitals and organizations.

Guardian can provide the Category I CME enduring material *Risk Management for the Practicing Physician* to attendees, to provide a CME component. In some instances, seminars can be created to generate revenue for an association. In other situations, seminars can be arranged for only the costs of travel and materials. With many speakers in California, these costs can be minimal.

Please complete the form and someone from our offices will contact you to go over the logistics of arranging this important seminar for you.

Name: ______________________________
Specialty: ______________________________
Address: ______________________________
____
City/State/Zip: ______________________________
Phone: ______________________________
Email: ______________________________

___ Association (name: ____________________)
___ Society (name: ____________________)
___ Group (name: ____________________)
___ Hospital (name: ____________________)
___ Organization (name: ____________________)
___ Other (name: ____________________)

Tentative Date of Presentation: ____________________
Location of Presentation: ____________________
Approximate Number of Attendees: ____________________

FAX to (866) 913-4911

REQUEST AUTHORS' ARTICLES FOR YOUR PUBLICATION

The authors of Guardian Publishing have written eight books for physicians and have written articles for over 100 periodicals, newsletters and websites. The authors have also appeared on hundreds of radio shows and on Bloomberg and Fox television.

Guardian can provide the content to educational publications at no cost, provided the articles include by-lines that instruct readers how to reach the authors if they have questions or require some consulting assistance.

If you are interested in publishing articles by the authors on asset protection, practice management, retirement, insurance, tax and estate planning, please complete this page and fax it back to (866) 913-4911 and someone will get back to you within 2 to 3 business days.

Name: ______________________________

Specialty: ______________________________

Address: ______________________________

____

City/State/Zip: ______________________________

Phone: ______________________________

Email: ______________________________

I am interested in (check all that apply):

___ Articles (magazine: ____________________)

___ Book Review (title: ________________________)

___ Interview (media: ______________________)

Target Audience: __________________________________

FAX to (866) 913-4911